# Lecture Notes in Computer Science

Edited by G. Goos, J. Hartmanis, and J. van Lee

T0250579

# Springer

*Berlin*
*Heidelberg*
*New York*
*Barcelona*
*Hong Kong*
*London*
*Milan*
*Paris*
*Tokyo*

Domenico Ursino

# Extraction and Exploitation of Intensional Knowledge from Heterogeneous Information Sources

## Semi-Automatic Approaches and Tools

 Springer

Series Editors

Gerhard Goos, Karlsruhe University, Germany
Juris Hartmanis, Cornell University, NY, USA
Jan van Leeuwen, Utrecht University, The Netherlands

Author

Domenico Ursino
Università degli Studi di Reggio Calabria
DIMET - Dipartimento di Informatica, Matematica, Elettronica e Trasporti
Via Graziella, Località Feo di Vito, 89100 Reggio Calabria, Italy
E-mail: ursino@ing.unirc.it

Cataloging-in-Publication Data applied for

Die Deutsche Bibliothek - CIP-Einheitsaufnahme

Ursino, Domenico: Extraction and exploitation of intensional knowledge from heterogeneous
information sources : semi-automatic approaches and tools / Domenico Ursino.
- Berlin ; Heidelberg ; New York ; Barcelona ; Hong Kong ; London ; Milan ;
Paris ; Tokyo : Springer, 2002
   (Lecture notes in computer science ; Vol. 2282)
   ISBN 3-540-43347-3

CR Subject Classification (1998): H.2, I.2, H.3

ISSN 0302-9743
ISBN 3-540-43347-3 Springer-Verlag Berlin Heidelberg New York

Springer-Verlag Berlin Heidelberg New York
a member of BertelsmannSpringer Science+Business Media GmbH

http://www.springer.de

© Springer-Verlag Berlin Heidelberg 2002
Printed in Germany

Typesetting: Camera-ready by author, data conversion by Steingräber Satztechnik GmbH, Heidelberg
Printed on acid-free paper      SPIN 10846288      06/3142      5 4 3 2 1 0

*Thank you, my God,*
*for having been my companion*
*in every step of this adventure*

*To my parents Giovanni and Maria,*
*who trusted and supported me*
*in every activity of my life*

*To my brothers Pietro and Raffaello*
*and to my aunt Elisabetta,*
*who shared with me both happy*
*and unhappy moments in these years*

# Foreword

The problem of integrating multiple information sources into a unified data store is currently one of the most important challenges in data management. Within the field of source integration, the problem of automatically generating an integrated description of the data sources is surely one of the most relevant. The significance of the issue can be best understood if one considers the huge number of information sources that an organization has to integrate. Indeed, it is even impossible to try to do all the work by hand. Like other important issues in data management, the problem of integrating multiple data sources into a unique global system has several facets, each of which represents, "per se", an interesting research problem, and comprises, for instance, that of recognizing, at the intensional level, similarities and dissimilarities among scheme objects, that of resolving representation mismatches among schemes, and that of deciding how to obtain an integrated data store out of a set of input sources and of a semantic description of their contents. The research and application relevance of such issues has attracted wide interest in the database community in recent years. And, as a consequence, several techniques have been presented in the literature attacking one side or another of this complex and multifarious problem. However, all the results presented in the past were somehow specific to some of the aspects underlying the general problem of data source integration and no comprehensive approach had ever actually been proposed. The thesis of Domenico Ursino presents a general semi-automatic approach for the construction and the management of Cooperative Information Systems, i.e. Information Systems resulting from the integration of several information sources. From a set of input database schemes describing the information content of multiple sources, the techniques developed in the thesis yield a structured, integrated, and consistent description of the information content, represented in a suitable Data Repository. The thesis also demonstrates how to use the repository for several tasks of data management based on the integrated representation. The proposed techniques are very interesting from several points of view. They are based on a controlled use of many fundamental fields of Computer Science, such as Mining and Learning, Knowledge Representation, Databases, etc. The approach presented in the thesis has been implemented in the prototype system "Database Intensional Knowledge Extractor" (DIKE), which has been experimented in several interesting application domains. Besides its specific technical merits, which the reader will be able to appreciate by proceeding with reading this thesis, Domenico Ursino's approach to data source integration has the characteristics of including a uniform set of techniques for data integration, thus being the first comprehensive approach to attack this problem. For this reason we believe that Domenico Ursino's PhD thesis is an excellent piece of work. It provides a complete description of the state of the art of the field, clearly describes the novel approach, and nicely illustrates the applications. In this sense, it is a unique attempt to deal with all the issues concerning the automatic derivation of semantic properties from multiple sources, and the corresponding construction of the integrated data scheme. The approach is methodologically and scientifically correct, as testified by the numerous papers already published by the author and his colleagues in several prestigious conference proceedings and journals and we think that the thesis will be very useful both for researchers investigating in the area of data integration, and for practitioners working in the field of cooperative information systems. In our role as his PhD thesis advisors, we had the privilege of being able to follow the entire development of the body of research that brought Domenico Ursino to obtain the excellent results that this thesis describes. And here, by writing this brief preface, we have the privilege to testify the quality and the continuity of Domenico's commitment to scientific research, against all odds, during these years, that allowed him to fulfill the objective we had, together with him, fixed beforehand, when all this work started.

January 2002             Prof. Luigi Palopoli,
                         Università "Mediterranea" di Reggio Calabria

                         Prof. Domenico Saccà,
                         Università della Calabria

# Preface

This book is my PhD thesis and presents the research work I did at the Dipartimento di Elettronica, Informatica e Sistemistica, Università degli Studi della Calabria, Cosenza, from 1996 to 1999, under the supervision of Luigi Palopoli and Domenico Saccà.

My research is based on the observation that, in the last decade, the development of new technologies for data acquisition and data storing has produced an enormous growth of information available electronically. A corresponding increase in the number of models and languages used to represent and manipulate data has taken place. These two factors have induced an increasing difficulty in handling data through traditional approaches. In particular, the exploitation of pre-existing and autonomous data resources (often based on very diverse models and systems) is nowadays recognized as a key issue in the area of data management. Cooperative Information Systems (CIS) and Data Warehouses (DW) have thus been designed as the necessary solutions providing friendly and flexible access to heterogeneous information sources, yet maintaining their operational autonomy.

In order to obtain an appropriate design of both CIS and DW, the schemes of involved databases are analyzed to identify similitudes, potential replications, or inconsistencies among data. In such system re-engineering problems, the design emphasis is on the integration of pre-existing information components, where a key problem is that of deriving relations holding among objects in pre-existing schemes [6]. Then, methodologies are needed to extract properties from schemes. Most interesting, in this context, are interscheme properties, that relate objects belonging to different schemes. Indeed, an appropriate exploitation of interscheme properties is crucial for a correct synthesis of global structured dictionaries, which we will refer to as data repositories. However, in reasoning about the intensional semantics of pre-existing databases, many useful properties are not explicitly encoded in database schemes, and so they cannot be immediately exploited.

Some papers (e.g., [32, 65, 126]) put into evidence the need for the adoption of formal languages to describe and manipulate intensional knowledge about data. In particular, [32] proposes a logic formalism largely based on Description Logics to express interscheme properties in CIS and DW.

When the number or the size of database schemes involved in the integration process is large and/or when the set of information resources changes quite frequently over time, manual design of CIS and DW can be very expensive and difficult. Therefore, the construction of semi-automatic integration tools appears to be necessary.

In this thesis, we illustrate a general approach to semi-automatically constructing and managing Cooperative Information Systems and Data Warehouses. The input to our method is the set of source database schemes constituting the base of the Cooperative Information Systems and the Data Warehouses. The output is a structured, integrated, and consistent description of information available in the Cooperative Information Systems or in the Data Warehouses and their properties in the form of a data repository. The data repository is used as the core structure of either the Mediator module of a Cooperative Information System or the reconciled level of a three-level Data Warehouse architecture.

The proposed approach is mainly based on the automatic derivation of properties holding among objects belonging to different input schemes. It consists of a number of steps: *(i)* the enrichment of scheme descriptions, obtained by the semi-automatic extraction of interscheme properties, i.e., terminological and structural properties between objects belonging to different schemes; *(ii)* the exploitation of derived interscheme properties for obtaining, in a data repository, an integrated and abstracted view of available data; *(iii)* the design of both a mediator-based Cooperative Information System and a three-level Data Warehouse having, as their core, the derived data repository. The techniques we have developed have been implemented in a prototype system called D.I.K.E. (Database Intensional Knowledge Extractor).

It is a pleasure to thank the people who have helped me most during this work. First of all, my gratitude goes to my advisors Luigi Palopoli and Domenico Saccà. I would like to thank Luigi not only for his support in my research activity, but also, more importantly, for being a true friend and a precious source of advice and suggestions. He provided the right environment for me to freely carry out my research and to fulfill my objectives. In particular, I owe Luigi special thanks for his support during all the phases of this thesis' submission to the LNCS series. I would like to thank Domenico for his constant push towards in-depth analysis of problems, that taught me to uncover their inner structure in order to find the way to attack them, which is the very nature of scientific research.

I owe very special thanks to my great friend Giorgio Terracina to whom I must express the whole of my gratitude since he helped me during the research activities and was a co-author of many papers, spending many hours together with me working towards the achievement of the results presented here. He has also been a true friend and provided precious support during some difficult moments of my life.

I would like to express my gratitude to my great friend Giampiero Dattilo, who has provided me with his constant support during many years. He has been a true friend to me, constantly helping me to face small and great difficulties of everyday life, even when this has meant sacrifices for him.

I wish to thank all the other people who have collaborated with me during my years of research, particularly Angela Bonifati, Larid Guga, Elisa Iezzi, Massimo La Camera, Fabio Lamberti, Francesco Locane, Alessandro Longo, Alfredo Pellicanò, Tiziana Pugliese, Salvatore Rotundo, Gregorio Sorrentino, Biagio Tramontana, Pasquale Viola.

I would like to thank all the people of the "Dipartimento di Elettronica, Informatica e Sistemistica", in particular the database group who have always been ready to talk about issues related to the thesis, particularly, Stefano Basta, Mario Cannataro, Mario Ettorre, Domenico Famularo, Sergio Flesca, Gianluigi Folino, Sergio Greco, Giovambattista Ianni, Nicola Leone, Elio Masciari, Clara Pizzuti, Luigi Pontieri, Pasquale Rullo, Francesco Scarcello, Giandomenico Spezzano, Domenico Talia, Ester Zumpano.

For about a year now, I have been working with the "Dipartimento di Informatica, Matematica, Elettronica e Trasporti" - Università Mediterranea di Reggio Calabria, and I would like to thank my new colleagues Francesco Buccafurri, Gianluca Lax, Domenico Rosaci, and Giuseppe Maria Luigi Sarnè for helping me in reviewing the last version of this manuscript.

I would like to thank Salvatore Capria, Giovanni Costabile, and Francesco De Marte for their help on several occasions.

I wish to thank Marco Cadoli for being the first to suggest that I submit my PhD thesis to LNCS.

Finally, I would like to gratefully acknowledge the support of the Italian Information System Authority for Public Administration (AIPA). They kindly provided the schemes of the Italian Central Governmental Office databases and the technical support to go with them.

January 2002                                   Domenico Ursino

# Table of Contents

# Part II. Construction of a Cooperative Information System and of a Data Warehouse

## Part III. System Description and Experimentations

## Part IV. Final Issues

# List of Figures

# List of Tables

# 1. Introduction

*This chapter is devoted to introduce the motivations and the general characteristics of our approach to semi-automatic synthesis of Cooperative Information Systems and Data Warehouses from sets of pre-existing heterogeneous databases and to highlight the novelty of our contribution to the field of Information Systems. The plan of the chapter is as follows: in the first section we illustrate the motivations which led to the definition of the proposed approach; the second section aims at illustrating the general characteristics of the proposed methodology. Related works are presented in the third section, whereas the contributions of our approach, as well as its novelties w.r.t. known methodologies, are described in the fourth section. Finally, the last section gives an overview of the thesis organization.*

## 1.1 Motivations

In the last years, an enormous increase of data available in electronic form has been witnessed, as well as a corresponding proliferation of query languages, data models and systems for data management. Nowadays, heterogeneous data management systems often coexist within the same operational environment. Traditional approaches to data management do not seem to guarantee, in these cases, the needed level of access transparency to stored data while preserving the autonomy of local databases. This situation contributed to push the development of new approaches which led to the design of Cooperative Information Systems (CIS) [42, 65, 120, 126] and Data Warehouses (DW) [34, 125]. CIS and DW indeed allow for users to query pre-existing autonomous data sources in a way that guarantees model, language and location transparency.

A main problem to be solved in designing such access systems relies in *scheme integration*, i.e., the activity by which different input database schemes are merged into a unique global structure describing the whole information set available for the query purposes. For very large systems, however, scheme integration alone typically ends up with producing a too complex global scheme, that may, in fact, fail to supply a satisfactory and convenient description of available data. In these cases, scheme integration steps must be completed by executing some *scheme abstraction* steps [6]. Carrying out

D. Ursino: Extr. and Expl. of Intensional Knowledge ..., LNCS 2282, pp. 1–22, 2002.

scheme abstraction amounts to clustering objects belonging to a scheme into homogeneous subsets and producing an abstracted scheme obtained by substituting each subset $S$ with one single object representing $S$.

In order for scheme integration and abstraction to be correctly carried out, the designer has to clearly understand the semantics of involved database schemes. In such system re-engineering problems, the design emphasis is on the integration of pre-existing information components, where a key problem is that of deriving relations holding among objects in pre-existing schemes [6]. Therefore, methodologies are needed to extract properties from schemes. The most interesting of these are *interscheme properties* that relate objects belonging to different schemes [6, 7, 9, 10, 21, 29, 30, 31, 32, 37, 45, 64, 68, 77, 110, 114].

In the literature, several "manual" methods for deriving interscheme properties have been proposed. An important characteristic featured by the best of these methods is being based on semantics, i.e., not only on the analysis of objets' structure, consisting of objects attributes, but also on the analysis of objects' contexts, of object semantic relevance [37] and of objects' inter-relations within schemes [30]. In fact, methods analyzing also objects' semantics have been shown to produce better results than methods solely based on analysing objects' structures [37]. As such, the best manual methods allow to obtain good quality global descriptions. A major limit of manual methods relies, however, in the difficulty of carrying out them to large applications since, in such contexts, it is needed to face integration problems often involving hundreds of scheme objects.

To face large integration/abstraction problems, a number of semi-automatic methods has been also proposed. Semi-automatic approaches are indeed much less resource consuming than manual ones, so that a try-and-check methodology for fine tuning of the derivation process can be effectively adopted. In addition, interscheme properties obtained as the result of running the semi-automatic derivation process can be more simply updated and maintained (which becomes a crucial characteristic if the set of the involved database schemes may change "frequently" over time).

In the past, semi-automatic methods were based on considering only structural similarities among objects belonging to different schemes [77, 112]. However, *"purely structural considerations do not suffice to determine the semantic similarities of classes"* [37]. Therefore, more recently, techniques for deriving interscheme properties taking into account also scheme semantics have been proposed [21, 30, 37, 45, 114]; these new algorithms, however, still require a significant intervention of the human experts.

As for further features, some papers (e.g., [27, 32, 65]) put into evidence the need for the adoption of formal languages to describe and manipulate intensional knowledge about data. In particular, [32] proposes a logic formalism largely based on Description Logics to express interscheme properties. [27] exploits an extension of the formalism of [32] with added expressiveness for representing and manipulating intra- and inter- scheme knowledge in the context of data warehousing applications. [120] discusses mediators for obtaining and filtering information from heterogeneous pre-existing data resources in integrated information systems; mediator capabilities are obtained using logic-based formalisms. For instance, the Information Manifold system uses a special language obtained by adding some Datalog-like rules to Description Logics [65].

## 1.2 Problem Statement and Approach Description

### 1.2.1 General Characteristics

The considerations outlined above have been the premises for the development of our approach. Indeed the proposed methodology considers a set of database schemes and produces a structured, integrated and consistent description of information available in the involved databases and their properties in the form of a data repository [6]. The data repository is used as the core structure of either the mediator module of a Cooperative Information System or the reconciled data level scheme of a Data Warehouse.

The method we propose consists of several steps: *(i)* the enrichment of scheme description, obtained by semi-automatically extracting intensional knowledge from schemes; *(ii)* the exploitation of derived interscheme properties for obtaining, in a semi-automatic fashion, an integrated and abstracted representation of available data, encoded in a data repository; *(iii)* the exploitation of the repository (and of the properties therein encoded), derived in previous steps, to support the designer in realizing either a mediator-based Cooperative Information System or a Data Warehouse over available data.

The availability of some initial background knowledge about scheme object names, in the form of so called "lexical synonymies", is assumed. Lexical synonymies are stored in a *Lexical Synonymy Property Dictionary LSPD* as triplets of the form $[A, B, f]$, where $A$ and $B$ are object names and $f \in [0, 1]$ denotes the corresponding plausibility. The construction of the $LSPD$ is carried out into two steps:

– stating lexical synonymies either by using a standard thesaurus (such as Wordnet) or by enquiring with experts of the domain;
– setting plausibility coefficients; since standard thesauri do not provide plausibilities for synonymies, in this step the support of domain experts is mandatory.

In order to obtain a high objectivity, groups of human experts can be asked to supply plausibility coefficients and mean values are assumed. In particular, human experts are required to specify plausibilities choosing among five possible values, namely H, MH, M, ML, L, to denote a High, Medium

High, Medium, Medium Low and a Low plausibility, resp. These specifications correspond to values $1.0, 0.8, 0.6, 0.4$ and $0.2$, resp., of the corresponding plausibility coefficients.

In real application settings, however, there exists the possibility for errors to occur in plausibility values provided by experts for lexical similarities, although we are entitled to assume that possible errors do not involve most coefficients. By conducting a sensitivity analysis based on varying the values specified for lexical similarities, we have shown that, under the above mentioned condition, the results yielded by our techniques are not significantly influenced by ill-specified plausibility coefficients occurring in the $LSPD$ (see, below, Section 2.7).

From now on, we are assuming that all involved data source schemes are defined in terms of entity/relationship (E/R) diagrams [36].

Given an E/R scheme $S$ and an object $O$ in $S$, the *type* of $O$ tells if $O$ is an entity, a relationship or an attribute in $S$.

In the following subsections, we illustrate in more detail the three main steps composing our approach.

### 1.2.2 Derivation of Interscheme Properties

Interscheme properties can be classified as intensional and extensional. *Intensional* properties are relative to schemes and to the meaning of objects in the schemes; vice versa, *extensional properties* are relative to database instances.

Main interscheme properties fall into one of three categories, namely:

- *Terminological Properties*; these can be classified in their turn as:
  - *Nominal Properties*; this last can be further classified as:
    - *Synonymies* [28, 95, 91, 97, 87, 90, 21, 30, 37, 45, 64, 68, 77, 110, 114]: a synonymy between two objects $O_1$ and $O_2$ tells that $O_1$ and $O_2$ have the same type and the same meaning. Synonymies can be stored as triplets of the form $\langle O_1, O_2, f_{O_1O_2} \rangle$, where $O_1$ and $O_2$ are the involved objects.
    - *Homonymies* [28, 95, 91, 97, 87, 90, 21, 30, 37, 64, 68, 77, 110, 114]: an homonymy between two objects $O_1$ and $O_2$ tells that $O_1$ and $O_2$ have the same type and the same name but different meanings. Homonymies can be stored as triplets of the form $(O_1, O_2, f_{O_1O_2})$, where $O_1$ and $O_2$ are the involved objects.
    - *Hyponymies/Hypernymies* [88, 30, 45]: given two entities $E_1$ and $E_2$, $E_1$ is a hyponym of $E_2$ (which is, in its turn, the hypernym of $E_1$) if $E_1$ has a more specific meaning than $E_2$. As an example, the entity *PhD Student* is a hyponym of the entity *Student*. If $E_1$ and $E_2$ belong to the same scheme (resp., to different schemes) we say that $E_1$ is the intrascheme (resp., the interscheme) hyponym of $E_2$ and that $E_2$ is an intrascheme (resp., an interscheme) hypernym of $E_1$. Hyponymies

can be stored as tuples of the form $\lceil E_1, E_2, f_{E_1 E_2} \rceil$, where $E_1$ and $E_2$ are the involved entities.

- *Overlappings* [88]: given two entities $E_1$ and $E_2$ an overlapping exists between them if there exist non-empty sets of attributes { $A_{11}$, $A_{12}$, ..., $A_{1n}$ } of $E_1$ and $\{A_{21}, A_{22}, \ldots, A_{2n}\}$ of $E_2$ such that, for $1 \leq i \leq n$, $A_{1i}$ is a synonym of $A_{2i}$. Overlappings are stored as tuples of the form $\|E_1, E_2, f_{E_1 E_2}\|$, where $E_1$ and $E_2$ are the involved entities.
- *Type Conflicts* [92, 122, 90, 116, 9, 45, 114]: these properties denote similarities between objects having different types. Given two database schemes $S_i$ and $S_j$, the existence of a type conflict between an object $O_1 \in S_i$ and an object $O_2 \in S_j$ tells that $O_1$ and $O_2$ are different representations of the same portion of the reality. Type conflicts are stored as tuples of the form $\langle O_1, O_2, f_{O_1 O_2} \rangle$, where $O_1$ and $O_2$ are the involved objects.

In all previous definitions $f_{O_1 O_2}$ and $f_{E_1 E_2}$ denote fuzzy coefficients (belonging to the real interval $[0, 1]$) expressing the plausibility of the corresponding property.

- *Object Cluster Similarities* [122, 87, 90, 118, 114]: an object cluster is a set of connected objects within a scheme; therefore object cluster similarities denote similitudes between subschemes of different schemes. Object cluster similarities can be represented as tuples of the form $\langle C_1, C_2, f_{C_1 C_2} \rangle$, where $C_1$ and $C_2$ are the involved clusters and $f_{C_1 C_2}$ is a fuzzy coefficient, in the real interval $[0..1]$, expressing the plausibility of the property.
- *Structural Properties*; these are extensional properties and can be classified as:
  - *Inclusions* [95, 91, 97, 30]: an inclusion of the entity set $E_1$ into the entity set $E_2$ indicates that all instances of $E_1$ are also instances of $E_2$; however some instances of $E_2$ could exist which are not instances of $E_1$. It is then clear that inclusions in fact correspond, at the extensional level, to hyponymies. Inclusions can be represented as tuples of the form $\lfloor E_1, E_2, f_{E_1 E_2} \rfloor$; here $E_1$ and $E_2$ are the involved entity sets whereas the semantics of $f_{E_1 E_2}$ is as follows: provided that the inclusion $E_1 \overset{\cdot}{\leq} E_2$ holds, $f_{E_1 E_2}$ represents the plausibility that the converse inclusion ($E_2 \overset{\cdot}{\leq} E_1$) (and, consequently, ($E_2 \overset{\cdot}{=} E_1$)) holds as well. In other words $f_{E_1 E_2}$ represents the proportion of instances of $E_2$ which are also instances of $E_1$.
  - *Assertions between Knowledge Patterns* [16, 17, 96, 19, 27, 32]: roughly speaking, a knowledge pattern denotes a view and an assertion represents a subsumption; therefore these properties denote subsumptions or equivalences holding between views. Knowledge Pattern Assertions can be represented as tuples of the form $\lfloor P_1, P_2, f_{P_1 P_2} \rfloor$, where $P_1$ and $P_2$ are knowledge patterns and $f_{P_1 P_2}$ has the same semantics as the coefficient associated to inclusions.

We are now able to give an overview of our approaches for deriving inter-scheme properties.

*Extraction of Synonymies, Homonymies and Type Conflicts.* Our approach for extracting synonymies, homonymies and type conflicts basically consists in "measuring" the semantic similarity of pairs of objects.

In order to discover a similarity between two objects $O_1$ and $O_2$, we analyze the structure of both the objects and their neighborhoods. Let $O_1'$ and $O_2'$ be two objects belonging to the neighborhood of $O_1$ and $O_2$, resp. Assume that $O_1'$ and $O_2'$ have been detected to be similar. The question is: to what extent the similarity of $O_1'$ and $O_2'$ must be taken into account in evaluating the similarity of $O_1$ and $O_2$? In our approach, this depends on the *distance* of $O_1'$ (resp., $O_2'$) from $O_1$ (resp., $O_2$) within its scheme; the distance between objects within their scheme is defined according to a suitable metrics.

The metrics we define is based on associating to each scheme $S$ a graph $G(S)$, called *Semantic Distance Graph (SD-Graph)*. $G(S)$ includes a node $N_O$ for each entity, attribute and relationship $O$ in $S$. Arcs in $G(S)$ are either *solid arcs* (*S-arcs* for short), or *dashed arcs* (*D-arcs* for short). *S-arcs* denote strong semantic closeness between objects, whereas *D-arcs* indicate looser relationships.

Neighborhoods are defined by introducing the notion of *context*. The *i_th* context of an object $O \in S$, denoted by $cnt(O, i)$, consists of all objects $O_j$ for which, in $G(S)$, the corresponding nodes $N_{O_j}$ are reachable from $N_O$ through a path with exactly $i$ *D-arcs* and any number of *S-arcs*.

The similarity of two objects is computed on the basis of the similarities of their various contexts. The so obtained object similarity is then used to compute similarities of other objects, and so on.

Given two input schemes $S_1$ and $S_2$, our method consists of the following phases: *(i)* deriving similarities between objects of the same type; *(ii)* detecting type conflicts; *(iii)* solving type conflicts. This last operation is done by properly modifying schemes and associated graphs. This requires the set of object similarities to be recomputed. Hence, steps *(i)*, *(ii)* and *(iii)* above are repeatedly applied until to no new type conflict is detected – this iteration is called "external fixpoint". Returned similarities are those computed at the last iteration of the external fixpoint. By applying suitable filtering functions on them, synonymies and homonymies are derived.

*Extraction of Object Cluster Similarities.* The method for deriving object cluster similarities uses the same technique underlying synonymy, homonymy and type conflict derivation. Therefore, in the whole, we propose a unified, semi-automatic approach for deriving synonymies, homonymies, type conflicts and object cluster similarities.

Given a scheme $S$ with $n$ objects, the number of object clusters is exponential in $n$. To avoid the risk of analyzing such a huge number of clusters, we single out only the most *interesting* ones, according to some constraints.

*Extraction of Hyponymies and Overlappings.* Our approach for deriving hyponymies and overlappings is composed by two algorithms. The first one derives *basic* hyponymies and overlappings; these are valid only in a particular scenario and the entity pairs satisfying this scenario are called *candidate pairs*. The second algorithm uses hyponymies derived by the first one and synonymies existing between scheme objects for extracting more general hyponymies; however this last algorithm is not capable of deriving further overlapping properties.

The algorithm for deriving basic hyponymies takes in input a Starting Synonymy Dictionary $SSD$ storing similarities between all possible pairs of entities, relationships and attributes belonging to involved scheme. For each candidate pair $[E_i, E_j]$, the algorithm considers the structures and the contexts of both $E_i$ and $E_j$ for determining if $E_i$ and $E_j$ either are synonym or are completely distinct or are one hyponym of the other or partially overlap.

The second algorithm takes in input synonymies and hyponymies derived previously and determines other hyponymies. It basically consists of the computation of the fixpoint of a particular function $\Psi$ which, at each step, derives new hyponymies. In the implementation of $\Psi$ we take into account that *(i)* if a hyponymy property holds from an entity $E_i$ to an entity $E_j$ and a further hyponymy exists from $E_j$ to $E_k$, then a hyponymy can be derived to hold from $E_i$ to $E_k$; *(ii)* if a hyponymy property holds from $E_j$ to $E_k$ and a synonymy holds between $E_i$ and $E_j$, then a hyponymy can be derived to hold from $E_i$ to $E_k$; *(iii)* if a hyponymy holds from $E_i$ to $E_j$ and a synonymy exists between $E_j$ and $E_k$, then a hyponymy can be derived to hold from $E_i$ to $E_k$.

*Extraction of Inclusions and Assertions Between Knowledge Patterns.* Our approach for deriving structural properties takes in input synonymies and hyponymies derived previously; it can be subdivided into three phases:

- *Phase 1*, in which an Inclusion Dictionary is constructed. The tuples of this dictionary represent inclusions between class instances (i.e., between data).
- *Phase 2*, in which, for each database, the most interesting classes, i.e., those which semantically best characterize it, are determined. This phase is carried out by computing some weights assigned by an algorithm, which exploits the Synonymy Dictionary, provided in input, and the Inclusion Dictionary, constructed during Phase 1. The focusing phase is important since, in general, there exists a virtually infinite number of properties, which could be extracted; therefore it is crucial to single out most relevant objects so that, when complex properties are extracted, only the most significant ones are taken into account.
- *Phase 3*, in which assertions involving interesting classes, as identified in Phase 2, are derived. For reasoning about database intensional properties, we use a particular Description Logic, called $DL_P$ [96, 19], which extends the logics presented in [32].

### 1.2.3 Construction of a Data Repository

A data repository is primarily intended to provide a global view of data owned by an organization using an integrated, comprehensible, accessible and usable structure. Generally speaking, data repositories allow to understand how information is organized in local databases and indicate how databases describe the same information or similar ones, pointing out differences or similarities and correlations among representations, in that being an effective reference for designing new applications which must use data already present in the available database systems [39, 6, 7, 9].

A data repository is constructed by first grouping database schemes into homogeneous clusters. Databases belonging to each cluster are integrated into a global scheme which is abstracted into a higher abstraction level scheme representing the cluster. This process is iterated over (higher level) schemes thus produced, to yield further higher level schemes. The process terminates when a sufficiently abstract scheme set (possibly consisting of one single scheme) is obtained.

Generally, each transformation operated on schemes for the purpose of repository construction (and, therefore, for the purpose of scheme integration and abstraction) can be described by providing either the input and the output or the input and the set of operations performed during the transformation [6, 7]. Note that there are situations where the first representation is preferable, while others where the second one must be preferred. However, it is difficult to obtain the description of performed operations if the former representation is adopted; similarly, it is expensive to derive the output if the latter representation is assumed. In the literature, almost all scheme integration and abstraction approaches describe transformations using input and output schemes.

An important characteristic of our approach consists in describing scheme integrations and abstractions using both input and output schemes and the set of operations which led to output schemes from input ones. This is obtained by exploiting two support information structures: *(i)* a *Set of Mappings*, describing the way an object belonging to output schemes has been obtained from one or more objects belonging to input schemes; *(ii)* a *Set of Views*, allowing to obtain instances of objects of the output schemes from instances at the input scheme level. In our case maintaining both representations is cheap, automatic and does not need a great amount of storing resources.

### 1.2.4 Exploiting the Data Repository for Constructing a CIS or a DW

The Data Repository constructed in the second step is used, in our approach, as the core structure of either a mediator in a new mediator-based architecture of a Cooperative Information System or the reconciled level scheme of a new Data Warehouse architecture.

**CIS Construction.** Our CIS architecture has been explicitly designed with the purpose of supporting very large integrated access systems. In order to achieve appropriate support for accessing many data sources, it uses the data repository in the place of an ordinary "flat" global scheme and, in this way, it lightens the computational burden lying on the mediator modules, by letting the user perform the selection of local data sources of interest in a friendly, guided manner.

Thus, from the user's perspective, querying consists of two distinct phases. In the former one, the user is guided by the system in "navigating" the structured global scheme in order to select a (set of) database(s). In the latter one, the user submits his/her query on the selected data source using either a QBE-like query interface or a query formulation wizard and gets corresponding answers.

**DW Construction.** The Data Warehouse architecture we propose is a three-level architecture. However, for reconciling data, differently from classical three-level architectures, we do not directly integrate operational schemes to construct a flat global scheme. Rather, we first collect subsets of operational schemes into homogeneous clusters and construct a data repository which is used as the core of the reconciled data level.

In data warehouse architectures presented in the literature, metadata, which are fundamental both for the efficient derivation of data and for their appropriate exploitation in decision making, are derived and updated separately from operational, reconciled and derived data; therefore, they are often not properly related to corresponding schemes (e.g., they can be out of date). A data repository does not only collect database schemes but can also store metadata they are related to; therefore, in our approach, metadata are obtained during the derivation of reconciled data; each time the data repository (and, consequently, the reconciled data level) is updated also the corresponding metadata are updated. This marks an advantage of our architecture over the classical three-level one in its capability to maintain the consistency among reconciled data, metadata and derived data.

When the number of involved data sources is large, manual methodologies for data warehouse design are difficult to be applied. This is due to the presence of presumably hundreds of objects (entities, relationships, attributes) belonging to involved database schemes to be analyzed for the data warehouse design purposes. Our approach to the construction of a data warehouse tackles this difficulty in that it is semi-automatic and requires a limited intervention of human experts.

## 1.3 Related Works

In the literature many proposals have been presented to carry out the single tasks associated to each step of the proposed approach; however, to the best of our knowledge, *no comprehensive approach has been proposed for supporting CIS and DW design in a uniform fashion*. Indeed, the approaches to data repository construction (and, therefore, to scheme integration and abstraction) proposed in the literature assume the availability of interscheme properties provided in one form or another. Similarly, the approaches to constructing CIS and DW structures assume the existence of a global scheme catalogue which is supposed to have been provided by human experts.

As for the specific techniques related to the various parts of the proposed approach, in the following sections we are presenting related literature.

### 1.3.1 Interscheme Property Derivation

Algorithms presented in the literature to derive interscheme properties in a semi-automatic fashion usually focus on object *structures* (e.g., with E-R schemes, object attributes), while missing to consider object neighborhoods within schemes. Vice versa, "manual" methodologies to interscheme property extraction have been devised that do take into account, besides object structures, also neighborhoods. These methodologies have been shown to produce better quality results than those obtained solely considering object structures; however they cannot be applied when the number of involved schemes and their sizes are large.

To the best of our knowledge, no approaches have been proposed in the literature which is able to deal with the extraction of all kinds of interscheme properties presented in Section 1.2.2. The problem of obtaining *uniform* techniques for deriving most interscheme properties has been considered only in few works; as an example [21, 37, 68] derive synonymies, homonymies and structural properties; [30] derives both properties of [21, 37, 68] and hyponymies; some papers tackle the problem of uniformly detecting type conflicts and object cluster similarities [114]; finally [45] derives all properties but homonymies, object cluster similarities and structural properties.

In more detail, some methods have been recently proposed for the derivation of *synonymies and homonymies* [21, 30, 37, 45, 64]. An interesting automatic and semantic technique for the construction of a semantic dictionary is described in [30]. Also the method of [21] is both automatic and based on semantics; however the purpose of [21] is to construct the so called *summary scheme*, which is a hierarchical structure used to allow imprecise query processing and, as such, has a quite different purpose than our own techniques.

In the literature there are very few papers which deal with the detection of *type conflicts* (e.g., [9, 114]). [9] proposes a technique to solve type conflicts, but the approach described there supposes type conflicts have been detected manually by DBAs and, therefore, does not propose any approach for detecting them. [114] proposes an automatic method for solving some semantic conflicts arising with scheme integration in a semi-automatic fashion. In this respect, its aim is somehow similar to our own, even if with a more restricted scope.

[110] contributes to the definition of type conflicts by improving the description of types by associating a semantics to each of them in order to explain the terms of application domain and their interrelations; in order to carry out its task, [110] assumes the existence of a shared ontology for schemes into considerations.

Till now, the extraction of object synonymies and homonymies, on the one hand, and type conflicts, on the other hand, has been carried out separately and using different techniques; in addition, as far as we know, the interaction between interscheme property extraction and type conflict resolution has not been analyzed.

The problem of deriving *hyponymies and hypernymies* received less attention than other kinds of interscheme properties; as a matter of fact, to the best of our knowledge, the only two papers describing a methodology for deriving hyponymies are [30, 45]; the corresponding methodologies, however, require a rather significant intervention of human experts.

In particular, [45] presents a technique allowing to derive *all nominal properties* (except for homonymies) *and type conflicts*. It is based on an iterative procedure, consisting of the following main steps:

1. first, a set of "assumed similarities" is constructed;
2. second, the following steps are repeatedly executed, until to the set of "assumption predicates" has been exhausted;
   a) an "assumed similarity" is selected and analyzed and it is decided if it is valid or not;
   b) in the affirmative case, the (name or type) conflict is resolved;
   c) the actions taken for resolving the above mentioned conflict are propagated to the set of "assumed similarities", by adding/removing elements to/from it.

Note that this method does not modify "factual similarities", i.e., "assumed similarities" which have been already validated. Finally it requires a heavy intervention of the DBA since he/she must validate one "assumed similarity" at each step.

In [32] a formalism for representing *assertions between knowledge patterns* based on Description Logics is described, which forms the basis of our $DL_P$ formalism; however, the purpose of [32] is to *represent* interscheme knowledge and not to derive it. A more recent paper [27] further elaborates on this issues and studies a Description Logics and related reasoning schemes to represent and manipulate intra- and inter-scheme knowledge in the context of data warehousing applications.

### 1.3.2 Data Repository Construction

As far as the construction of a data repository is concerned (which requires scheme integration and abstraction), to the best of our knowledge, no techniques have been proposed to carry it out in a semi-automatic fashion. As a matter of fact, some algorithms for semi-automatic scheme integrations have been presented in the literature (e.g., [6, 9, 30, 45, 114, 120]); as far as these approaches are concerned the following considerations can be drawn: *(i)* only the methods proposed in [6, 7] allow to construct a data repository; *(ii)* the only method proposed in the literature for scheme abstraction (see, again, [6, 7]) is manual and, therefore, it is difficult to apply when the scheme to be abstracted has been obtained from the integration of large number of schemes (such as in Central Public Administration contexts).

The purpose of [45] is, in part, similar to our own, as described in Section 1.2.1. Indeed, in both cases, a (semi-automated) integration of input database schemes, that uses a set of semi-automatic derived interscheme properties, is proposed. However [45] presents neither an approach for scheme abstraction nor a methodology for repository construction.

A classic integration method which is based on semantic similarities and dissimilarities between objects belonging to different schemes is described in [9]. Although this paper presents a number of influential ideas, the method is not automatic. On the other hand, the method in [64] can be made automatic, but it is only based on attribute knowledge (so it is syntax-driven) and may therefore produce unsatisfactory results [37].

### 1.3.3 Synthesis of Cooperative Information Systems

The issue of integrating geographically spread, heterogeneous databases has been dealt with since early seventies and has now received a renewed interest because of the recent technological development of networks and of the availability of numerous data sources.

Multidatabase systems can be considered as the first attempt to realize the integration of existing databases [20]. They achieved connection between DBMS by adopting a strong integration approach which implied the need for a complex and sophisticated software support for communication and information exchange.

Federated databases [66, 111, 115, 119, 126] have been proposed more recently to overcome these limits. Federation requires a much looser integration amongst sites so that the autonomy of local databases is mostly preserved. However, traditional federated databases still have an important drawback in that information flow is not really coordinated, thus possibly causing "dispersion" of information. Such a negative characteristic is negligible for relatively small systems, but becomes relevant when the amount of managed information is large.

Mediator-based Cooperative Information Systems [120, 126] seem to over-come also these limits. Indeed, in such systems, a mediator entity supplies the required coordination of information flow among local databases and users. Mediator-based architectures are two-level structures, consisting of a wrap-ping layer and a mediation one. *Wrappers* translate local languages, models and concepts of the data sources into the global language, model and concepts shared by some or all sources [120, 126]. *Mediators* take in input information from one or more components below them, and supply as the output either information for the components above them or for external users of the sys-tem. Data are not necessarily localized at the mediator. Often the mediator stores just views of real data. These views can be queried by components above them (including system users): it is then up to the mediator retrieving data needed for constructing query answers from the actual data sources. A typical mediator-based architecture is shown in Figure 1.1.

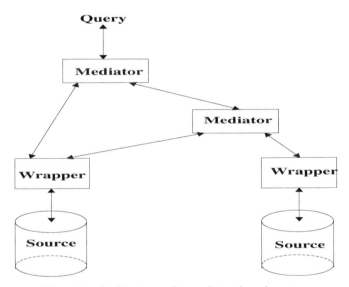

**Fig. 1.1.** Architecture of a mediator-based system

In the last years, some mediator-based systems have been designed and re-alized. For example, the *Information Manifold* [65], developed at the AT&T Laboratories and *TSIMMIS* [42], designed at Stanford University, are ex-amples of the realization of mediator capabilities in integrated information systems. TSIMMIS [42] is based on a *Query Centric* model, i.e., mediated scheme relations are defined as views over the source relations. The mediator describes information contained in the various sources using a global scheme (so there is only one abstraction level); the global scheme is queried by the user in order to access information. In this system data models of the differ-ent local databases are translated into a unique one; the global data model is powerful enough to manage various information representations. Information Manifold [65] is based on a *Source Centric* model, i.e., for the purpose of integration, the source relations are defined as views over mediated scheme relations. Therefore the global scheme is a collection of virtual classes and relations against which the user poses queries.

In both systems the global scheme specifies the mapping between virtual and real relations; in both of them querying takes place at the level of the global scheme and the mediator has the responsibility of constructing subqueries which are dispatched to local wrappers and whose results are collected and merged to form the answer to the user query.

In mediator-based CIS proposed in the literature, the information sources are described in a global flat scheme catalogue. As a consequence, the standard mediator-based architecture can be difficult to realize when the number of involved databases is very large (in the order of hundreds). Indeed, we argue, there are two main problems to be dealt with:

- The adoption of a "flat" global scheme seems not to be adequate to guarantee a reasonably structured and abstract description of available data. Indeed, it can be anticipated that, in situations where hundreds of database schemes are to be integrated, the number and the complexity of relationships holding among involved database objects would be overwhelming. This situation would immediately cause a substantial difficulty for a user to retrieve the information he/she needs.
- The management of querying processes, which could potentially access hundreds of databases for each single user request, may become quite hard a task to be autonomously carried out by the system.

Note, moreover, that CIS construction methods appeared in the literature assume source description to be supplied in full by human experts and propose no approach for deriving them from the structure of involved schemes.

### 1.3.4 Synthesis of Data Warehouses

In the literature, various *conceptual architectures* have been proposed for data warehouses. They can be classified into three groups, depending on the number of levels they are characterized by.

In a *one-level architecture* [55] each piece of data is stored once and only once: a "middleware" level operates as an interface between users and operational databases. Therefore, there is no materialized data warehouse but, rather, it is "simulated" using views (virtual data warehouse). This kind of architecture allows for a rather quick development of a data warehouse with reduced costs.

*Two level architectures* [44, 55, 81, 125] are based on the idea of separating source data from derived ones. In such architectures, the "first" level contains source data whereas derived data are stored in the "second" level. Two-level architectures are the most common ones. They are convenient especially when operational sources are basically homogeneous but have an important disadvantage in that significant data duplication is usually implied.

*Three-level architectures* [84, 53] are obtained by considering that the derivation of data for decision support is performed in two phases: *(i)* the reconciliation of operational data belonging to different sources; *(ii)* the derivation of decision support data from reconciled ones. In this sense, three-level architectures are designed to store operational, reconciled and derived data, resp. The classical three-level architecture of a data warehouse is represented in Figure 1.2. In this model, the first level stores operational data, the second one stores reconciled data, whereas the latter one stores support decision data [53].

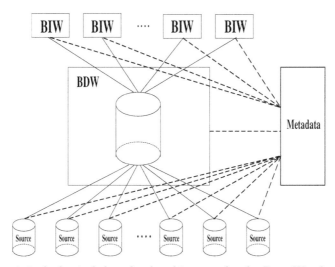

**Fig. 1.2.** A classical three level architecture for the Data Warehouse

However, in spite of its advantages, classical three-level data warehouse architectures show important limitations within application environments (like those typical of Central Public Administrations) comprising lots of complex heterogeneous operational source systems. In such cases, the flat global scheme used within the reconciled level, and obtained by integrating schemes of operational databases, presumably encodes an enormous number and variety of objects, and becomes far too complex to be effectively used. As a result, the derivation of decision support information from this level becomes too complex a task. The application context just described has not a mere speculative relevance, since this is precisely the situation one encounters nowadays in many organizations. We point out that the problem here is due to data source complexity and heterogeneity and not to the data warehouse architecture itself. Analogous difficulties arise also with one- and two-level architectures.

## 1.4 Contribution

As previously pointed out, in the literature several proposals have been presented to carry out the single steps associated to our approach; however, to the best of our knowledge, our approach is the only comprehensive set of techniques which, starting from a set of databases, fully supports the construction of a Cooperative Information System and a Data Warehouse over them in a semi-automatic fashion.

We have seen that the approaches for the construction of a CIS or of a DW proposed in the literature *assume* the existence of a global catalogue which is supposed to have been provided by human experts. In the same way the approaches for constructing a scheme catalogue or a data repository proposed in the literature *assume* the availability of interscheme properties provided in one form or another.

On the contrary, our proposal includes techniques capable of supporting designers from the initial to the final design phases of a CIS or DW. In this respect, it is worth pointing out that the only input required by our system is the set of schemes of involved databases plus a dictionary storing lexical synonymy properties. Moreover, with our approach, two quite different system structures (i.e., those of a CIS and a DW) can be obtained from a unique base structure, i.e., the data repository.

In order to verify the effectiveness of our techniques in dealing with real integration problems, we have carried out many experiments on the set of Italian Central Governmental Office databases, and we have compared the obtained outputs with those produced manually by Italian Information System Authority for Public Administration (AIPA) obtaining encouraging results.

As for the techniques realizing the various steps of our approach, we are highlighting their novelty in the next four subsections. Finally, in the last one, we focus upon experiments we have conducted.

### 1.4.1 Interscheme Property Derivation

Our approach to interscheme property derivation comprises techniques by which most kinds of properties holding among database objects can be obtained. In particular our techniques are able to infer synonymies, homonymies, hyponymies, overlappings, type conflicts, object cluster similarities and knowledge pattern assertions. As such, our approach represents, to the best of our knowledge, the first example of a significantly comprehensive set of support techniques devoted to the reconstruction of database scheme semantics.

All the techniques we devised, except for those concerning the derivation of complex pattern assertions, are based on graph analysis techniques. In that, our techniques share a common methodological core which allows us to obtain a semantically homogeneous characterization of all the scheme properties we derive.

Property derivation thus uses some graphs we formally define from database schemes. A semantic metrics defined on such graphs allows us to consider the relative influence of properties holding between objects belonging to different schemes. In particular, so doing, our techniques establish similarity and dissimilarity properties between scheme objects by taking into account both objects' local semantics (e.g., corresponding to attribute specifications if the analyzed object is an entity) and objects' neighborhoods, including all other objects semantically connected to the analyzed one by means of paths through other scheme objects. As proved in [37], analyzing object neighborhoods guarantees a higher property derivation quality than that achievable by limiting ourselves to object local semantics.

In addition, type conflict detection technique we present allows to directly proceed to restructuring schemes where the type conflict has been detected thus obtaining their automatic normalization.

We shall show that the whole set of graph-based techniques features good computational characteristics, all of them being polynomial in the number of involved scheme objects.

All the properties our techniques derive are encoded in a formal language. This fact allowed us to define a further set of techniques by which knowledge pattern assertions, denoting subsumption and equivalence relations between scheme views, can be derived. In this case the derivation is based on a set of inference rules defined within a Description Logic-based language called $DL_P$, that we introduce for reasoning about interscheme knowledge.

A common characteristic of all the derivation techniques we define is that they reason about and construct properties with which a coefficient measuring the plausibility of the property is associated. This gives us the flexibility needed to properly manage the uncertainty often characterizing interscheme knowledge, allowing us to obtain reliable results, as proved by the experiments we have conducted with a prototype system that implements the techniques, on many real case examples.

Moreover, being defined in a formal way, extracted interscheme properties can be conveniently exploited within further methods we define for the semi-automatic synthesis of CIS and DW, which we comment upon in the following subsections.

As a final important remark we note that the capability of our techniques of handling in a substantially uniform fashion a large number of interscheme property kinds allowed us to obtain a good understanding of their effectiveness in treating real application problems.

## 1.4.2 Data Repository Construction

To the best of our knowledge, our methods to constructing in a semi-automatic fashion a structured description of data sources involved in the integration process are new in the literature. Indeed, we provide an almost automatic technique capable of using interscheme properties constructed in previous steps for synthesizing the data repository by applying in a suitable and non trivial fashion clustering, integration and abstraction steps over handled schemes.

The techniques render the repository immediately available to play the role of reference semantic structure for the realization of applications on involved databases.

From both the designers' and users' points of view the data repository we obtain allows to look at available information at various abstraction levels and gives also the possibility to operate intensional roll-ups and drill-downs by which users and designers are able to immediately understand correspondences among objects of schemes belonging to different abstraction levels. This latter capability is mirrored in the availability of mapping and view descriptions allowing for the prompt synthesis of suitable access paths to extensional data responding to user requests.

Moreover the set of constructed mappings also plays the role of a structured log that may be useful for the designing purposes.

### 1.4.3 Synthesis of a Cooperative Information System

The techniques we define below for constructing a CIS based on the data repository were conceived with the idea of obtaining an architecture supporting integrated access to a large number of information sources. In this respect the data repository plays two fundamental roles. First it provides the structured view of accessible data which would not be provided if a classical flat global scheme would have been adopted. Second, the data repository encodes, in its various abstraction levels, a semantic-oriented reconstruction of accessible data and, as such, it can be conveniently used by a navigation system allowing (even the non expert) user to select the subset of information sources relevant to his/her information need.

This latter characteristic allows us to produce "light" mediation modules since part of the mediation task is carried out (within a friendly framework) by the user. Note that this is particularly relevant exactly in the case of very large integrated access problems like the ones we are focusing upon in this thesis.

### 1.4.4 Synthesis of a Data Warehouse

As far as the synthesis of a Data Warehouse is concerned, we propose a three level architecture which differs from any other proposed in the literature since the reconciled data level is constructed around a data repository instead of a "flat" scheme; in this way we obtain a DW architecture as represented in Figure 1.3.

In order to pinpoint the differences between classical three level architectures and the one we are proposing here, the following observations can be drawn:

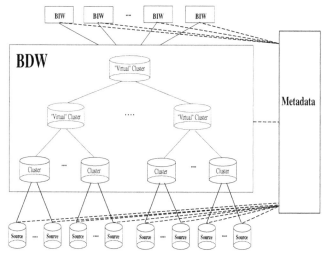

**Fig. 1.3.** Our proposal of three level architecture for DW

- a classical three-level architecture is a particular case of the one proposed
  here;
- the architecture we propose here is naturally conducive to an incremental
  data warehouse construction;
- the design of data marts is presumably simpler than with classical architectures;
- the proposed architecture automatically maintains the consistency among
  reconciled data, metadata and derived data.
- reconciled data are (virtually) represented at various abstraction levels
  within the core data repository; however maintaining several abstraction
  levels do not cause significant problems.

It follows from these observations that, by paying a limited price in terms of
required space and computation time, we obtain an architecture that retains
all worths of classical three-level architectures but overcomes some of their
limitations in the presence of a large number of data sources. Note, by the
way, that in such application contexts, problems analogous to those described
for classical three-level architectures characterize also one- and two- level
architectures.

### 1.4.5 Experiments

Our approach has been validated against several real example cases which
have been exploited also for tuning up optimal values of weights and thresholds we use in our algorithms. In particular we have exploited the Italian
Central Governmental Office (ICGO) databases as our main benchmark for
tuning and validation.

The reason why we decided to carry out the experimentation on this application case is twofold. First, the database schemes we analyzed are complex enough to represent a good benchmark for verifying the effective applicability of our techniques to real application frameworks. Second, this application case is also important "per se" as demonstrated by the relevant resources devoted in various statal organizations to projects aimed at integrating central governmental information sources.

ICGO databases have been studied and classified by the "Italian Information System Authority for Public Administration" (AIPA); this activity brought to the identification, classification and representation of about 300 main databases owned by various central offices [7]. The presence of such large number of databases has induced the need for a reorganization of information by exploiting integrated and structural models in such a way that the involved information become comprehensible and can be exploited more easily.

In addition, some of the ICGO databases (e.g., those owned by central administration offices) have a relevant size, and are based on a variety of data models and systems, and almost no integration form whatsoever existed among them.

All these observations led to the necessity of constructing a data repository for ICGO databases. The ICGO data repository has the tree structure shown in Figure 1.4. In order to obtain it, the pre-existing databases have been grouped into 30 clusters; each cluster encloses semantically homogeneous databases. Upper levels of the tree have been obtained by carrying out integration-abstraction steps on schemes of lower levels. Each node within the tree structure represents a portion of the integrated system of the ICGO at a certain abstraction level.

Initially, we have carried out a tuning phase for setting correct values of coefficients for weights and thresholds. This was done by selecting a small subset of ICGO databases and by running our algorithms on it several times, using different values for coefficients. Final coefficient values have been then validated over several further database schemes, and proved to be well tuned except for some minor adjustments.

A sensitivity analysis has been carried out to verify that (relatively small) variations of the values of weights and thresholds did not cause significant changes on results returned by our algorithms. Results of this analysis showed that our techniques feature a good stability against variations of coefficients.

Then, our algorithms have been executed on significant portions of ICGO databases and the resulting outputs have been compared with the interscheme properties and the repository produced manually by AIPA. This analysis confirmed the appropriateness of our approach in dealing with the extraction of interscheme properties from a great number of complex heterogeneous databases (see Chapter 10 for details about experiments).

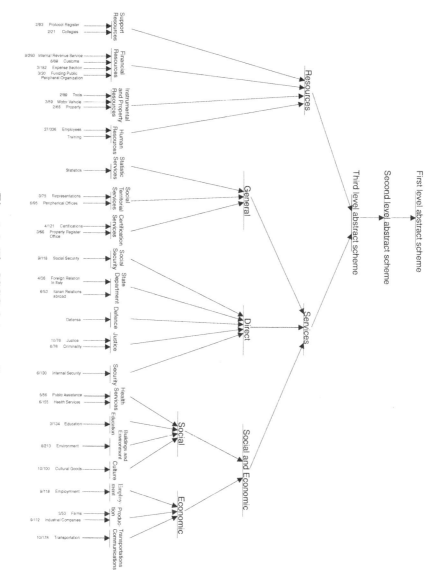

**Fig. 1.4.** The ICGO data repository

## 1.5 Plan of the Thesis

This thesis describes all the phases of the proposed approach, as well as some experiments we have conducted on the ICGO databases for validating the various algorithms implementing these phases.

In particular, the thesis is subdivided into four parts. The first part is devoted to describe the extraction of interscheme properties. More in detail, Chapter 2 describes the extraction of synonymies, homonymies and type conflicts, whereas the extraction of object cluster similarities can be found in Chapter 3. The derivation of hyponymies and overlappings is the subject of Chapter 4 whereas Chapter 5 describes the extraction of assertions between knowledge patterns.

The second part of this thesis is devoted to describing the construction of a Cooperative Information System and of a Data Warehouse. In particular Chapter 6 describes the construction of the Data Repository. The construction of a Cooperative Information System is the argument of Chapter 7. Finally, Chapter 8 presents the construction of a Data Warehouse.

The third part of the thesis is devoted to the description of the system DIKE which implements the proposed approach and to the illustration of experimentation carried out on the set of ICGO databases. In particular, the system DIKE is described in Chapter 9, whereas the various databases used for experiments, as well as the experiments on the derivation of synonymies, homonymies and type conflicts, are described in Chapter 10. Chapter 11 describes experiments about the extraction of hyponymies. Experiments on the derivation of assertions between knwoledge patterns are presented in Chapter 12. Chapter 13 describes experiments about the construction of a data repository. Finally, Chapter 14 illustrates the CIS for ICGO databases we have constructed by applying our techniques.

The fourth part presents some final issues. In particular, in Chapter 15 we have a look at future developments of our research whereas in Chapter 16 we draw our conclusions. The bibliography and an appendix illustrating the E/R model and the theory for type conflict resolution close both this part and the thesis.

Part I

Property Extraction

This part aims at illustrating the approaches for deriving interscheme properties. In particular Chapter 2 describes the extraction of type conflicts, whose derivation and resolution allow to obtain normalized schemes, and the derivation of synonymies and homonymies, which are at the basis of the extraction of the other kinds of properties. The derivation of object cluster similarities, i.e., of similitudes between subschemes, is described in Chapter 3 whereas the derivation of hyponymies is illustrated in Chapter 4. Finally, Chapter 5 presents the extraction of assertions between knowledge patterns which allows to derive complex relations existing among objects belonging to different schemes.

# 2. Extraction of Synonymies, Homonymies, and Type Conflicts

*This chapter is devoted to the illustration of algorithms for extracting synonymies, homonymies and type conflicts. The plan of the chapter is as follows: first we introduce SD-Graphs, graph-based structures which can be associated to database schemes; then we define a metrics associated to SD-Graphs which allows us to measure the semantic distance existing between objects, which is central to support the derivation of interscheme properties. After that the metrics has been introduced we present a framework managing both the derivation of synonymies, homonymies and type conflicts as well as the resolution of these latter ones. Then, we illustrate a complete example showing the behaviour of the presented algorithms. The last two sections of this chapter are devoted to the computation of the complexity of the presented algorithms and to the illustration of a sensitivity analysis carried out on them. In particular, as far as the complexity is concerned, we show that the presented algorithms are polynomial in the size of input schemes. As for the sensitivity analysis, we prove that the quality of the results obtained by the algorithms is not affected by possible (little) errors occurring either in the basic information provided by human experts or in thresholds and weights.*

*The material presented in this chapter is taken from [92, 122, 87, 90, 117, 118].*

## 2.1 General Characteristics of the Approach

Intuitively, our approach basically consists in "measuring" the semantic similarity of pairs of objects whereby synonymies, homonymies and type conflicts are obtained. Our method yields in output two dictionaries, namely a *Synonymy Dictionary SD* and an *Homonymy Dictionary HD*.

Entries in the Synonymy Dictionary (resp., in the Homonymy Dictionary) are represented as triplets $\langle A, B, f \rangle$ (resp., $(A, B, f)$), where $A$ and $B$ are the involved objects and $f$ is a plausibility coefficient in the real interval [0,1], measuring the degree of confidence on the actual existence of the property between the two objects stated in the dictionary.

In order to discover a similarity between two objects $O_1$ and $O_2$, we analyze the structure of both the objects and their neighborhoods. Let $O_1'$ and $O_2'$ be two objects belonging to the neighborhood of $O_1$ and $O_2$, resp.

D. Ursino: Extr. and Expl. of Intensional Knowledge ..., LNCS 2282, pp. 27–62, 2002.
© Springer-Verlag Berlin Heidelberg 2002

Assume that $O'_1$ and $O'_2$ have been detected to be similar. The question is: to what extent the similarity of $O'_1$ and $O'_2$ must be taken into account in evaluating the similarity of $O_1$ and $O_2$? In our approach, this depends on the *distance* of $O'_1$ (resp., $O'_2$) from $O_1$ (resp., $O_2$) within its scheme; the distance between objects within their scheme is defined according to a suitable metrics.

The metrics we define is based on associating to each scheme $S$ a graph $G(S)$, called *Semantic Distance Graph (SD-Graph)*. $G(S)$ includes a node $N_O$ for each entity, attribute and relationship $O$ in $S$. Arcs in $G(S)$ are either *solid arcs* (*S-arcs* for short), or *dashed arcs* (*D-arcs* for short). *S-arcs* denote strong semantic closeness between objects, whereas *D-arcs* indicate looser relationships.

Neighborhoods are defined by introducing the notion of *context*. The $i$-$th$ context of an object $O \in S$, denoted by $cnt(O, i)$, consists of all objects $O_j$ for which, in $G(S)$, the corresponding nodes $N_{O_j}$ are reachable from $N_O$ through a path with exactly $i$ *D-arcs* and any number of *S-arcs*. For each $i$, $i \geq 0$, a weight $p(i)$ is associated to the $i$-$th$ context of $O$, where $p$ is a monotone decreasing function, so that "farthest" contexts have "lightest" weights.

The similarity of two objects is computed on the basis of the similarities of their various contexts. The so obtained object similarity is then used to compute similarities of other objects, and so on.

Our techniques assume the availability of some initial background knowledge about scheme object names, in the form of so called "lexical synonymies", stored in a *Lexical Synonymy Property Dictionary LSPD*. The *LSPD* is constructed as explained in Section 1.2.1.

Let us now turn to presenting the technique in more details. Roughly speaking, given two input schemes $S_1$ and $S_2$, our method for detecting interscheme properties of objects of $S_1$ and $S_2$ consists in:

1. deriving similarities between objects of the same type;
2. detecting type conflicts;
3. solving type conflicts.

Solving type conflicts is done by properly modifying schemes and associated graphs. This requires the set of object similarities to be recomputed. Hence, steps 1., 2. and 3. above are repeatedly applied until to no new type conflict is detected – this iteration is called "external fixpoint". Returned similarities are those computed at the last iteration of the external fixpoint. By applying suitable filtering functions on them, synonymies and homonymies are derived.

Each of steps 1. and 2. are implemented through an "internal" fixpoint, which starts with task (a) below, and then iterates on tasks (b-e) until to all object contexts are analyzed:

(a) Constructing a base set of similarity properties. In the case of similarities between objects of the same type (step 1. above), this set includes rough properties derived from lexical similarities. For type conflicts (step 2.

above), it consists of the set of similarities between objects of the same type derived in the previous step.

(b) Visiting, at each iteration $i$, for each pair of objects $O_1 \in S_1$ and $O_2 \in S_2$, $cnt(O_1, i)$ and $cnt(O_2, i)$, lying at distance $i$ from $O_1$ and $O_2$ within $G(S_1)$ and $G(S_2)$, resp.

(c) Computing the similarity degrees between $cnt(O_1, i)$ and $cnt(O_2, i)$ as a weighted mean of two values obtained running a maximum weight matching algorithm on two bipartite weighted graphs, the first defined from attributes and the latter from entities of the two contexts; arc weights are defined from similarity properties computed so far.

(d) Refining the similarity coefficient of $O_1$ and $O_2$ computed up to step $(i-1)$ using the similarity degree of the $i\_th$ contexts of $O_1$ and $O_2$, computed in step (c), weighted through a monotone decreasing succession $\{p(i)\}$.

(e) Discarding from the set of properties derived in the previous step, type conflicts having a plausibility under a certain threshold, since these are assumed not to hold.

Our techniques rely on the definition of some threshold and weight coefficients. These have been obtained experimentally (see, below, Section 2.3.1). In order to verify the stability of our methods w.r.t. variation of these coefficients' values, we conducted further sensitivity analyses, which are described in Section 2.7.

It is worth pointing out that all methods we are presenting here have been implemented in the system DIKE described in Chapter 9. In addition experiments with ICGO database schemes have been conducted; the results of these experiments are illustrated in Chapter 10.

## 2.2 Definition of the Graph-Based Metrics

In this section we formally introduce the *SD-Graph* $G(S)$ associated to a database scheme $S$ and the related metrics.

The set of all objects in $S$ is denoted by $Obj(S)$ and includes entities $Ent(S)$, relationships $Rel(S)$ and attributes $Att(S)$ of the scheme $S$.

Consider an entity $x \in Ent(S)$; we denote by $Att(x)$ the set of its attributes and by $Rel(x)$ the set of relationships which $x$ participates into. For $x, y \in Ent(S)$, we write $y \preceq x$ if $y$ *is-a* $x$. Next, consider a relationship $y \in Rel(S)$; the set of its attributes is denoted by $Att(y)$ whereas $Ent(y)$ represents the set of entities participating into $y$.

The *SD-Graph* $G(S)$ associated to $S$ is a digraph with two kinds of arcs, called *S-arcs* (solid arcs) and *D-arcs* (dashed arcs), respectively. In more detail:

$$G(S) = (N(S), A(S)) = ((Ent(S) \cup Att(S) \cup Rel(S)), (SA(S) \cup DA(S)))$$

The set of S-arcs, $SA(S)$, is:

$$SA(S) = SA_1(S) \cup SA_2(S) \cup SA_3(S) \cup SA_4(S)$$

where:

- $SA_1(S) = \{(x, y) \mid x \in (Ent(S) \cup Rel(S)), \ y \in Att(x)\}$, i.e., there is an $S$-arc from an entity or a relationship to each of its attributes;
- $SA_2(S) = \{(x, y) \mid x \in Rel(S), \ y \in Ent(x)\}$, i.e., there is an $S$-arc from a relationship to each of the entities participating therein;
- $SA_3(S) = \{(x, y) \mid y \in Ent(S), \ x \in Att(y), \ x \ key \ for \ y \ \}$, i.e., there is an $S$-arc from a key attribute to the entity it belongs to;
- $SA_4(S) = \{(x, y) \mid x, y \in Ent(S), \ y \preceq x \ \}$, i.e., there is an $S$-arc from a parent entity of an *is-a* relationship to the corresponding child one.

The set of D-arcs $DA(S)$ is equal to

$$DA(S) = DA_1(S) \cup DA_2(S) \cup DA_3(S)$$

where:

- $DA_1(S) = \{(x, y) \mid y \in (Ent(S) \cup Rel(S)), \ x \in Att(y) \ and \ x \ is \ not \ a \ key$ for y$\}$, i.e., there is a $D$-arc from a non-key attribute to its entity or relationship;
- $DA_2(S) = \{(x, y) \mid x \in Ent(S), \ y \in Rel(x)\}$, i.e., there is a $D$-arc from an entity to the relationships it participates into;
- $DA_3(S) = \{(x, y) \mid x, y \in Ent(S), \ x \preceq y\}$, i.e., there is a $D$-arc from a child entity of an *is-a* relationship to the corresponding parent one.

The rationale underlying these definitions is as follows: *S-arcs* denote a strong closeness between two objects; an *S-arc* from $O_i$ to $O_j$ indicates that $O_j$ is significant both for completely defining and for distinguishing the concept represented mainly by $O_i$. Yet a *D-arc* from $O_i$ to $O_j$ indicates that $O_j$ is related to $O_i$, in the $E/R$ representation of the scheme $S$, but it provides a minor contribution (w.r.t. the case of an *S-arc*) both in defining and in distinguishing the concept represented by $O_i$.

We are now in the position of establishing our metrics for measuring a "semantic distance" between two objects $O$ and $O'$ within a scheme $S$. To this end, we look at the paths in $G(S)$ connecting $O$ to $O'$: intuitively, the greater is the minimum number of *D-arcs* needed for reaching $O'$ from $O$, the greater is the semantic distance between $O$ and $O'$. This intuition is formalized next by introducing the notions of *D-path$_n$*, *S-path*, *D-shortest path* and *context*.

**Definition 2.2.1.** A *D-path$_n$* is a path in $G(S)$ with exactly $n$ *D-arcs*, and any number of *S-arcs*. A *D-path$_0$* is also called an *S-path*.    □

**Definition 2.2.2.** Given two nodes $x$ and $y$ in $G(S)$, the *D-shortest path* between $x$ and $y$, denoted by $\langle x, y \rangle$, is that having a minimal number of *D-arcs*; if more than one path exists with the same minimum number of *D-arcs*, the *D-shortest path* is that with the minimum number of *S-arcs*; in case of further ties, one of the identified paths is chosen on a random basis.    □

**Definition 2.2.3.** Define the $i\_th$ *context* of an object $x$ as:

$$cnt(x,i) = \{y \mid y \in N(S), y \neq x, \langle x,y \rangle \text{ is a } D\text{-}path_i \text{ in } G(S)\}, \qquad i \geq 0 \qquad \square$$

Thus, $cnt(x,i)$ (the $i\_th$ context of an object $x$) includes all objects that can be reached from $x$ through a *D-shortest path* including $i$ *D-arcs* and any number of *S-arcs*.

**Definition 2.2.4.** For $i \geq 0$, define:

$$A\_cnt(x,i) = Att(S) \cap cnt(x,i);$$

$$E\_cnt(x,i) = \begin{cases} Ent(S) \cap cnt(x,0) & \text{if } i = 0 \\ Ent(S) \cap \bigcup_{0 \leq j \leq i} (cnt(x,j)) & \text{if } i > 0 \quad \text{and} \\ & E\_cnt(x,i-1) \neq Ent(S) \\ \emptyset & \text{otherwise} \end{cases}$$

$\square$

From now on, we shall assume that any *SD-Graph* is connected, that is, every two nodes are reachable in the undirected version of the graph. This assumption is not an actual restriction since any reasonable database scheme corresponds to a connected *SD-Graph*. The following result will be useful in the sequel of the chapter.

**Proposition 2.2.1.** *Let $x \in Obj(S)$. Then, for each $i > 0$, $E\_cnt(x,i-1) \neq Ent(S)$ implies that $E\_cnt(x,i-1) \subset E\_cnt(x,i)$.*
*Proof.* Immediate from definitions and from the assumption about graph connectivity.
$\square$

An example will help in illustrating presented concepts.

*Example 2.2.1.* Consider the schemes $S_1$ and $S_2$ shown in Figures 2.1(a) and 2.1(b), resp. (the example is taken from [114]). They represent two possible views of marriages. $S_1$ is centered around the concept of person, and a marriage is seen as a relationship between two persons. $S_2$ deals with marriage as a legal act and, therefore, it considers the marriage as an entity; it also looks at persons as entities in such a way that exactly two persons are related by each marriage occurrence. Figures 2.1(c) and 2.1(d) show $G(S_1)$ and $G(S_2)$, respectively.

The list of (non-empty) contexts of $G(S_1)$ and $G(S_2)$ follows:
$cnt(RMarriage, 0) = \{Date, Person, Name, BirthDate\}$
$cnt(EMarriage, 0) = \{Date, Location, Contract\}$
$cnt(EMarriage, 1) = \{M, Person, E\#, Name\}$
$A\_cnt(RMarriage, 0) = \{Date, Name, BirthDate\}$
$A\_cnt(EMarriage, 0) = \{Date, Location, Contract\}$
$A\_cnt(EMarriage, 1) = \{E\#, Name\}$
$E\_cnt(RMarriage, 0) = \{Person\}$
$E\_cnt(EMarriage, 1) = \{Person\}$

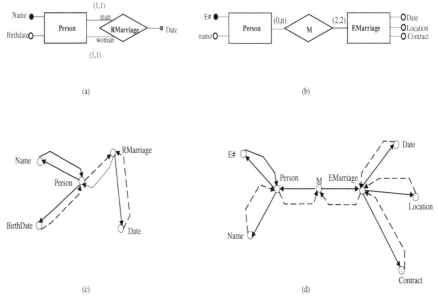

**Fig. 2.1.** (a-b) two possible representations of the marriage concept (c-d) the corresponding $SD$-$Graphs$

## 2.3 External Fixpoint

Our technique for deriving similarities between objects uses the metrics defined above and is defined as a fixpoint computation over the $SD$-$Graphs$. This "external" fixpoint consists in performing, at each step, a number of operations, two of which are defined, in their turn, as further, "internal" fixpoint computations.

This section is devoted to present the general structure of the external fixpoint computation, the functions applied as part of the external fixpoint computation except for the two functions denoting the internal fixpoint computations. These latter ones are illustrated in Section 2.4.

### 2.3.1 Overview

The external fixpoint has schemes $S_1$, $S_2$ and the dictionary of lexical synonymy properties $LSPD$ as the inputs and yields in output a set $T$ of similarities between objects of the same type belonging to $S_1$ and $S_2$.

Recall that the $LSPD$ stores triplets of the form $[A, B, f]$, where $A$ and $B$ are object names and $f$ is a plausibility coefficient (see Section 1.2.1 above for details about the way the $LSPD$ is obtained).

The algorithm works by first computing basic interscheme properties. These are "rough" properties taking into account only similarities between the attributes of involved objects; their role is to form the initial property set needed to derive "actual" properties. The second step of the algorithm consists in deriving similarities of objects of the same type belonging to different schemes. Third, type conflicts are detected by exploiting synonymies computed in the previous step. Schemes and associated graphs are therefore modified to remove detected type conflicts; this modification produces changes in the type and contexts of various scheme objects. As a consequence, new similarities may be induced and, at the same time, some of the properties previously derived to hold could be no longer valid. Therefore the whole derivation process must be iterated. Summarizing, at each iteration, the algorithm executes four main steps:

1. computes basic interscheme properties;
2. derives synonymies;
3. detects type conflicts;
4. modifies the *SD-Graphs* for solving type conflicts.

Steps are iterated until, during one step, no new significant type conflict is detected. The iteration is implemented through the so called external fixpoint.

In order to single out valid synonymies and homonymies from the set of derived similarities, and type conflicts, filter functions are applied that select only properties having a plausibility coefficient greater than a given threshold, for synonymies and type conflicts, and lesser than another given threshold, for homonymies. Thresholds are dynamically obtained as functions of computed plausibilities and of some given coefficients.

In general, all the functions we define use thresholds and weight coefficients. Their values were set and tuned empirically, by conducting a series of experiments. In particular, as already pointed out, we have used the database schemes of the Italian Central Governmental Offices (ICGO) as our main benchmark for tuning and validation (see Section 1.4.5). Values set for threshold coefficients and weights are shown in Table 2.1.

**Table 2.1.** Values of thresholds and weights

| *Coefficients* | *Values* | | *Coefficients* | *Values* |
|---|---|---|---|---|
| $w_n$ | 0.80 | | $w_d$ | 0.15 |
| $w_k$ | 0.05 | | $w_b$ | 1.00 |
| $w_s$ | 1.00 | | $w_{tc}$ | 1.00 |
| $w_{oc}$ | 1.00 | | $w_\zeta(0)$ | 1.00 |
| $w_\zeta(i) \quad \forall i > 0$ | 0.40 | | $w'_\zeta(i) \quad \forall i \geq 0$ | 0.50 |
| $\varphi_{syn}$ | 0.70 | | $\varphi_{hom}$ | 0.33 |
| $\varphi_{tc}$ | 0.66 | | $\varphi_{oc}$ | 0.70 |
| $\varphi_m$ | 0.55 | | $th_\eta$ | 0.25 |
| $th_m^{syn}$ | 0.50 | | $th_M^{hom}$ | 0.35 |
| $th_m^{tc}$ | 0.50 | | $th_m^{oc}$ | 0.50 |

### 2.3.2 Technical Details

In this section, we illustrate details about the structure of the external fix-point computation, and of its steps 1 and 4. Functions implementing core steps 2 and 3 will be described in the following Section 2.4. Computation is described in the form of function applications, which are generally detailed starting from the outmost ones and proceeding innermost.

Let $S_1$ and $S_2$ be the two input schemes under consideration. In order to simplify the presentation of the functions that realize our method, both in this and in the following sections, without loss of generality, we shall assume that:

1. for each triplet $[A, B, f]$ belonging to the $LSPD$, the triplet $[B, A, f]$ belongs to the $LSPD$ as well;
2. in what follows, $G_1$ (resp., $G_2$) is always used as a shorthand for $G(S_1)$ (resp., $G(S_2)$);
3. the two input schemes $S_1$ and $S_2$ as well as the $LSPD$ are implicit parameters for the functions defined below; so, for instance, we shall write $\eta()$ in the place of $\eta(LSPD, S_1, S_2)$.

Synonymies among objects of $S_1$ and $S_2$ are obtained by applying a filtering function $\sigma_{syn}$ to the similarity property set returned by the external fixpoint computation $\Psi^\infty()$; derived synonymies are stored in the *Synonymy Dictionary SD*. Analogously, the function $\sigma_{hom}$ filters homonymies that are thus stored in the *Homonymy Dictionary HD*. Formally:

$$SD = \sigma_{syn}(\Psi^\infty())$$
$$HD = \sigma_{hom}(\Psi^\infty())$$

The function $\sigma_{syn}$ is defined as follows:

$$\sigma_{syn}(T) = \{\langle E_1, E_2, f\rangle \mid \langle E_1, E_2, f\rangle \in T, E_1 \in Ent(S_1),$$
$$E_2 \in Ent(S_2), f > th_{syn}(T)\} \cup$$
$$\{\langle R_1, R_2, f\rangle \mid \langle R_1, R_2, f\rangle \in T, R_1 \in Rel(S_1),$$
$$R_2 \in Rel(S_2), f > th'_{syn}(T)\}$$

Here, the threshold $th_{syn}(T)$ is obtained as:

$$th_{syn}(T) = max((f^{syn}_{min} + f^{syn}_{max}) \times \varphi_{syn}, th^{syn}_m)$$

where *(i)* $f^{syn}_{min}$ (resp., $f^{syn}_{max}$) represents the minimum (resp., the maximum) value of the plausibility factors associated to the tuples of $T$ representing entity similarities; *(ii)* $\varphi_{syn}$, belonging to the real interval $[0, 1]$, is a tuning coefficient; *(iii)* $th^{syn}_m$ is a minimum acceptable value for plausibility synonymy coefficients. Values for $\varphi_{syn}$ and $th^{syn}_m$, which we have derived experimentally, can be found in Table 2.1. The function $th'_{syn}(T)$ is obtained analogously.

The function $\sigma_{hom}$ behaves in a similar way, singling out significant homonymies:

$$\sigma_{hom}(T) = \{(O_1, O_2, 1 - f) \mid \langle O_1, O_2, f \rangle \in T, O_1 \in Ent(S_1),$$
$$O_2 \in Ent(S_2), f < th_{hom}(T)\}$$

Here,

$$th_{hom}(T) = min((f_{min}^{hom} + f_{max}^{hom}) \times \varphi_{hom}, th_M^{hom})$$

where the meaning of $f_{min}^{hom}$, $f_{max}^{hom}$, $\varphi_{hom}$ is as above, whereas $th_M^{hom}$ is a maximum acceptable value for similarity coefficients, which the corresponding homonymy coefficients are derived from.

$\Psi^\infty$ returns the set $T$ of derived similarities as triplets $\langle A, B, f \rangle$, where $A$ is an object of $S_1$, $B$ is an object of $S_2$, and $f$ is the associated plausibility coefficient. The external fixpoint computation is defined as follows:

$$\begin{cases} \Psi^0() = \emptyset \\ \Psi^i() = \Psi(\Psi^{i-1}()) \qquad\qquad for\ i > 0 \end{cases}$$

At the generic iteration, the computation proceeds by *(i)* constructing basic interscheme properties which form the starting set of properties for the derivation of similarities, *(ii)* deriving synonymies, *(iii)* detecting type conflicts, *(iv)* modifying schemes and associated graphs to remove detected type conflicts. The function $\Psi$, implementing a single iteration of the fixpoint computation is, therefore, as follows (the parameter $T$ denotes a set of triplets and is ignored since, at each iteration of the external fixpoint, the derivation of interscheme properties starts "from scratch", but on modified schemes and graphs):

$$\Psi(T) = \mu(\xi(\rho(\eta())))$$

where:

- Function $\eta$ computes the set of basic interscheme properties;
- Function $\rho$ derives similarities between objects of the same type;
- Function $\xi$ detects type conflicts;
- Function $\mu$ modifies graphs for removing type conflicts.

In the rest of this section we describe functions $\eta$ and $\mu$. Functions $\xi$ and $\rho$ will be illustrated in Section 2.4.

**The Function $\eta$ for Computing Basic Interscheme Properties.** The function $\eta$ computes basic interscheme properties. As already pointed out, these are support properties needed to derive "actual" similarity properties of scheme objects. $\eta$ returns an initial set of type conflicts, synonymies between attributes, synonymies between entities and synonymies between relationships. In fact, $\eta$ consists in applying one specific function for each of these kinds of properties. Since the order of application here does not matter, we have:

$$\eta() = \eta_{TC}() \cup \eta_A() \cup \eta_E() \cup \eta_R()$$

Next, we describe functions $\eta_{TC}$, $\eta_A$, $\eta_E$ and $\eta_R$.

*Function $\eta_{TC}$.*. This function returns basic type conflicts $\langle O_i, O_j, f \rangle$ such that $O_i$ and $O_j$ belong to different schemes and have different types and the factor $f$ is computed as follows: if the *LSPD* stores a tuple mentioning $O_i$ and $O_j$ and $f'$ is the associated factor, then $f$ is set to $f'$; otherwise $f$ is set to 0. Let $Name(O)$ denote the name of the object $O$. We have:

$$\eta_{TC}() = \{\langle O_1, O_2, f' \rangle \mid (\langle Name(O_1), Name(O_2), f' \rangle \in LSPD),$$
$$O_1 \in S_1,\ O_2 \in S_2,\ O_1\ and\ O_2\ of\ different\ types\} \cup$$
$$\{\langle O_1, O_2, 0 \rangle \mid (\not\exists f)(\langle Name(O_1), Name(O_2), f \rangle \in LSPD),$$
$$O_1 \in S_1,\ O_2 \in S_2,\ O_1\ and\ O_2\ of\ different\ types\}$$

*Function $\eta_{A}$.*. This function returns the set of basic attribute synonymies including triplets of the form $\langle A_i, A_j, f \rangle$, where $A_i$ and $A_j$ are attributes belonging to different input schemes. In order to compute the factor $f$, we proceed as follows. First we check whether a tuple involving $Name(A_i)$ and $Name(A_j)$ occurs in the *LSPD*. If this is not the case, then $f$ is set to 0. Otherwise, let $\langle Name(A_1), Name(A_2), f' \rangle \in LSPD$; then $f$ is obtained from $f'$ by taking into account four characteristics of the involved attributes, namely:

1. attribute names;
2. attribute domains;
3. attribute *key characterization*, that indicates if an attribute is a primary key (denoted PK), is a candidate key (denoted CK) or is not a key (denoted NK);
4. attribute *semantic relevance*, i.e., how much the attribute characterizes the semantics of the object which it belongs to [97, 37]; for instance an attribute *BirthPlace* is more characterizing than an attribute *Identifier* in distinguishing the entity *Student* from the entity *Course*.

Thus, $\eta_A$ is obtained by composing two functions: $\eta_A^{II}$, accounting for attribute semantic relevance, and $\eta_A^{I}$, accounting for other characterizations referred to above:

$$\eta_A() = \eta_A^{II}(\eta_A^{I}())$$

where:

- $\eta_A^{I}() = \{\langle A_1, A_2, \sigma_\eta(\gamma(A_1, A_2, f)) \rangle \mid \langle Name(A_1), Name(A_2), f \rangle \in LSPD,$
$$A_1 \in Att(S_1), A_2 \in Att(S_2)\} \cup$$
$$\{\langle A_1, A_2, 0 \rangle \mid (\not\exists f)(\langle Name(A_1), Name(A_2), f \rangle \in LSPD),$$
$$A_1 \in Att(S_1), A_2 \in Att(S_2)\}$$
- $\eta_A^{II}(T) = \{\langle A_1, A_2, f \times C(A_1, A_2) \rangle \mid \langle A_1, A_2, f \rangle \in T\}$

The formulae above use functions $\sigma_\eta$, $\gamma$ and $C$ defined next:

- $\sigma_\eta(g) = \begin{cases} g & if\ g > th_\eta \\ 0 & otherwise \end{cases}$

– $\gamma$ accounts for attribute name, domain and key characterization, by returning the following weighted mean:

$$\gamma(A_1, A_2, f) = w_n \times f + w_d \times D(A_1, A_2) + w_k \times K(A_1, A_2)$$

where $w_n$, $w_d$ and $w_k$ are weighting factors, and

$$D(A_1, A_2) = \begin{cases} 1 \text{ if the domains of } A_1 \text{ and } A_2 \text{ are the same, i.e.,} \\ \quad \text{they are, for example, both integers or both chars} \\ \quad \text{or both reals} \\ 0.5 \text{ if the domains of } A_1 \text{ and } A_2 \text{ are compatible; by} \\ \quad \text{default, chars are compatible with strings and} \\ \quad \text{integers with reals. Further compatibilities can} \\ \quad \text{be defined by human experts} \\ 0 \text{ if the domains of } A_1 \text{ and } A_2 \text{ are different and} \\ \quad \text{incompatible} \end{cases}$$

$$K(A_1, A_2) = \begin{cases} 1 \text{ if } A_1 \text{ and } A_2 \text{ are both PK or both CK or both NK} \\ 0.5 \text{ if one of them is PK and the other is CK or if one} \\ \quad \text{is CK and the other is NK} \\ 0 \text{ if one of them is PK and the other is NK} \end{cases}$$

– $C$ accounts for attribute semantic relevance [97, 37], by returning the following values:

$$C(A_1, A_2) = \begin{cases} 1 \text{ if both attributes are NK} \\ 0.9 \text{ if an attribute is CK and the other is NK} \\ 0.8 \text{ if both attributes are CK or if one is PK and the} \\ \quad \text{other is NK} \\ 0.6 \text{ if an attribute is PK and the other is CK} \\ 0.4 \text{ if both attributes are PK} \end{cases}$$

Values of coefficients and weights used above are shown in Table 2.1.

*Function $\eta_{\mathbf{E}}$..* This function returns basic entity synonymies by composing the three functions $\nu$, $\theta$ and $\eta_A$, as follows:

$$\eta_E() = \nu(\theta(\eta_A(), w_b), w_b)$$

Functions $\theta$ and $\nu$ are as detailed next:

– *Function $\theta$.* This function takes in input a set $AS$ of attribute synonymies and computes the plausibility for two generic entities to be synonyms, taking into account only the corresponding attributes. Given two entities $E_1$ and $E_2$ and the set $AS$, we define, from their attributes, a weighted bipartite graph $G_{E_1 E_2} = (Att(E_1) \cup Att(E_2), Ed)$, where $(A_1, A_2, f) \in Ed$ if $\langle A_1, A_2, f \rangle \in AS$, $A_1 \in Att(E_1)$ and $A_2 \in Att(E_2)$. The plausibility coefficient computed for the pair $(E_1, E_2)$ is obtained from the objective function associated with the maximum weight matching computed over $G_{E_1 E_2}$ as follows:

$$\theta(AS, w_b) = \{\langle E_1, E_2, \delta(\mu_s(AS, Att(E_1), Att(E_2)), Att(E_1), Att(E_2), w_b)\rangle \\ \mid E_1 \in Ent(S_1), E_2 \in Ent(S_2)\}$$

where:

- $\mu_s(ST, OS_1, OS_2)$ takes in input *(i)* a set of synonymy triplets $ST$, *(ii)* two sets of objects $OS_1$ and $OS_2$, and returns a weight matrix $F$ such that it has a row for each object belonging to $OS_1$, a column for each object belonging to $OS_2$ and $F_{O_1 O_2} = f$ if $\langle O_1, O_2, f\rangle \in ST$, 0 otherwise;
- $\delta(F, P, Q, w)$ returns a factor obtained from computing the objective function of a maximum weight matching, as explained next. The input here are: *(i)* two sets of objects $P = \{p_1, \ldots, p_n\}$ and $Q = \{q_1, \ldots, q_m\}$, *(ii)* a weight matrix $F$ on $P$ and $Q$ such that, for each $p_i \in P$ and $q_j \in Q$, $0.0 \le f_{ij} \le 1.0$, where $f_{ij} = F_{p_i q_j}$ and *(iii)* a coefficient $w$. The output is a value in the real interval $[0, 1]$. Let $BG = (P \cup Q, A)$ be a bipartite weighted graph, where $A$ is the set of weighted edges $\{(p_i, q_j, f_{ij}) \mid f_{ij} > 0\}$. The maximum weight matching for $BG$ is a set $A' \subseteq A$ of edges such that for each node $x \in P \cup Q$ there is at most one edge of $A'$ incident onto $x$ and $\phi(A') = \sum_{(p_i, q_j, f_{ij}) \in A'} f_{ij}$ is maximum (for algorithms solving maximum weight matching, see [41]). Now, if $A' = \emptyset$, then $\delta(F, P, Q, w)$ returns 0, otherwise, let $\overline{\phi}(A') = \frac{\phi(A')}{|A'|}$; the value returned by $\delta(F, P, Q, w)$ is:

$$\delta(F, P, Q, w) = \left(1 - \tfrac{1}{2}w \times \frac{abs(|P| - |Q|) + 2 \times (min(|P|, |Q|) - |A'|)}{|P| + |Q|}\right) \times \overline{\phi}(A')$$

In this formula the ratio denotes the percentage of unrelated objects of the bipartite graph w.r.t. the entire set $P \cup Q$. More details about the objective function associated to the maximum weight matching can be found in [41].

- *Function $\nu$.* In order to take into account semantic relevance of attributes, plausibility coefficients have been multiplied by $C(A_i, A_j)$. This causes values of coefficients to be underestimated; the normalization implemented in the function $\nu$ is devoted to balance this underestimation.
The function $\nu$ carries out the coefficient normalization, as follows:

$$\nu(US, w) = \{\langle O_1, O_2, f \times \alpha(US, w)\rangle \mid \langle O_1, O_2, f\rangle \in US\}$$

where $\alpha(US, w) = \frac{\alpha^I(\alpha_O(US), w)}{\alpha_M(US)}$, and

- $\alpha_M$ selects the maximum of the plausibility coefficients associated to triplets in $US$;
- $\alpha_O$ selects one pair $(E_i, E_j)$ of entities having this maximum plausibility coefficient;
- $\alpha^I$ computes the plausibility associated to the similarity of $E_i$ and $E_j$ without taking into account the semantic relevance of attributes; to do this the function $\eta^I_A$ is applied; $\alpha^I$ is as follows:

$$\alpha^I((E_i, E_j), w) = \delta(\mu_s(\eta^I_A(), Att(E_i), Att(E_j)), Att(E_i), Att(E_j), w)$$

Thus, intuitively, the normalization multiplier is obtained as the ratio $\frac{\hat{f}}{M}$, where $M$ is the maximum plausibility coefficient associated to entity synonymies and $\hat{f}$ is the plausibility of the similarity of an entity pair associated with $M$, without considering attribute semantic relevance.

*Function $\eta_\mathbf{R}$..* This function returns basic relationship synonymies as follows:

$$\eta_R() = \nu_R(\theta_R(\eta_A(), w_b), w_b)$$

where $\nu_R$ and $\theta_R$ are the analogous, for relationships, of functions $\nu$ and $\theta$ defined above.

**Modifying Graphs.** The function $\mu$ singles significant type conflicts out of the set of computed similarities and modifies input schemes $S_1$ and $S_2$ and associated graphs $G_1$ and $G_2$ for removing them. $\mu$ is defined as follows:

$$\mu(T) = \mu_G(\sigma(T))$$

Functions $\sigma$ and $\mu_G$ are described next.

*Function $\sigma$..* This function selects from $T$ some of the triplets representing type conflicts. A triplet $\langle O_i, O_j, f \rangle$ is selected if the following conditions hold:

1. $O_i$ and $O_j$ have different types;
2. $f$ is greater than the threshold $th_{tc}$; the formula for defining this threshold is analogous to that used for computing $th_{syn}$ and $th'_{syn}$ (see, above, the beginning of Section 2.3.2);
3. both $O_i$ and $O_j$ and the objects belonging to $cnt(O_i, 0)$ and $cnt(O_j, 0)$ are not involved in any synonymy with a plausibility greater than $th_{syn}$;
4. $f$ is the largest plausibility coefficient among those relative to triplets involving either $O_i$ or $O_j$.

Condition 3 above is justified by the following reasoning: the plausibility factor associated to the similarity of $O_i$ and $O_j$ significantly depends upon the similarity of their contexts 0; now assume that $O_j$ is a synonym of some object $O' \in cnt(O_i, 0)$ with high plausibility; in this case, a type conflict would be detected to hold for $O_i$ and $O_j$ just because of the (already derived) high similarity of $O'$ and $O_j$, which is not reasonable.

*Function $\mu_\mathbf{G}$..* This function takes in input a set of triplets including, in general:

- conflicts of entities and relationships,
- conflicts of entity attributes and entities,
- conflicts of relationship attributes and entities,
- conflicts of entity attributes and relationships,
- conflicts of relationship attributes and relationships,

and modifies schemes $S_1$ and $S_2$ and graphs $G_1$ and $G_2$ to remove them. $\mu_G$ is, in fact, defined as a composition of the functions $\mu_{ER}$, $\mu_{EAE}$, $\mu_{RAE}$, $\mu_{EAR}$ and $\mu_{RAR}$, each of which is intended to handle one of the conflicts listed above:

$$\mu_G(T) = \mu_{RAR}(\mu_{EAR}(\mu_{RAE}(\mu_{EAE}(\mu_{ER}(T))))).$$

Note that, when a type conflict is solved, one of the involved objects, say $O'$, must assume the same type of the other, say $O''$; this is done by modifying $O'$ into $O'_M$, in such a way that $O'_M$ has the same type of $O''$. High similarity holding for $O'$ and $O''$, and previously represented by the solved type conflict, determines a high similarity between $O'_M$ and $O''$, which must induce a synonymy between them. Since the similarity depends mainly on the context 0 of the two objects, a way to transfer the similarity between $O'$ and $O''$ into a similarity between $O'_M$ and $O''$ consists in adding a "hidden" attribute to both objects. The hidden attribute contributes neither to define object semantics nor to modify attribute relevance, but has the only purpose to "store" the similarity information previously encoded in the solved type conflicts. For this reason, each hidden attribute has a type apart, no value, and is not a key. Let $f$ be the plausibility factor associated to the (solved) type conflict between $O'$ and $O''$. Then, a synonymy property for the hidden attributes of $O'_M$ and $O''$, associated with the same plausibility factor $f$, is added to the current set of similarity properties. For the sake of simplicity, the following transformations will be illustrated referring to binary relationships. Their generalizations to n-ary relationships is straightforward.

Next, we define functions $\mu_{EAE}$, $\mu_{ER}$, $\mu_{RAE}$, $\mu_{EAR}$ and $\mu_{RAR}$.

– *Function $\mu_{EAE}$*. This function solves conflicts between an entity attribute and an entity. It is implemented by adapting the technique of [9] to our context. We are now able to illustrate how $\mu_{EAE}$ works. The transformations to be carried out on the *SD-Graph* which the *entity* involved in the type conflict belongs to, are depicted in Figure 2.2(b) and thus consist in adding to the graph a node $E\_H$ representing the hidden attribute, a solid arc $(E, E_H)$ and a dashed arc $(E_H, E)$ (see, in Figure 2.2(a), the corresponding modification of the E/R diagram).

Figure 2.3 illustrates the transformations to be executed on the other graph, the one which the *entity attribute* involved in the type conflict belongs to. Here the node $A$, denoting the attribute involved in the conflict, and the corresponding arcs are removed from the graph, and four new nodes are added, representing: *(i)* the entity $A$, substituting the attribute $A$, *(ii)* its key attribute $A_I$, *(iii)* the relationship $R$ linking $A$ to the entity $E$, which the old attribute $A$ belonged to, and, finally, *(iv)* the hidden attribute $A\_H$ associated to $A$. Added solid arcs link $R$ with $E$, $R$ with $A$, $A$ with $A_I$ and vice versa, and $A$ with $A\_H$. Added dashed arcs link $E$ with $R$, $A$ with $R$ and $A\_H$ with $A$.

Obviously, an input graph could have to be modified either because one of its entity attributes or because one of its entities is involved in a type conflict; the function $\mu_{EAE}$ must carry out transformations corresponding to both cases.

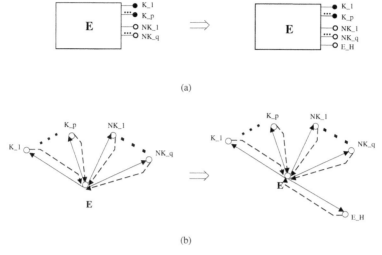

(a)

(b)

**Fig. 2.2.** Solving a conflict involving an entity

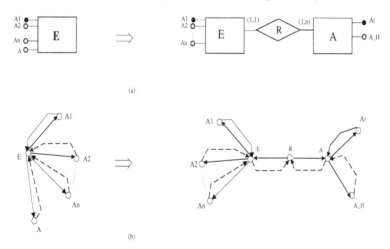

(a)

(b)

**Fig. 2.3.** Solving an entity-entity attribute conflict - the entity attribute graph

– *Function* $\mu_{ER}$. The function $\mu_{ER}$ solves conflicts involving a relationship and an entity. The modifications to be carried out in the graph which the entity involved in the conflict belongs to are the same as those illustrated above in Figure 2.2(b).

Modifications of the E/R diagram, which the relationship involved in the type conflict belongs to, are shown in Figure 2.4; the corresponding modifications of the associated *SD-Graph* are illustrated in Figure 2.5. In detail, the node $R$ denoting the relationship and related solid and dashed arcs are removed. Then, nodes $R$, $R_1$ and $R_2$ are added to the corresponding *SD-Graph*, as well as $p$ nodes $K1\_1, \ldots, K1\_p$, representing the key attributes inherited by $R$ from $E_1$, and $r$ nodes $K2\_1, \ldots, K2\_r$, representing the key attributes inherited by $R$ from $E_2$. A further node $R\_H$ is also added to represent the hidden attribute. $R$ inherits all the arcs of the original relationship $R$. Further arcs are added for linking $R_1$ to $E_1$ and $R$, $R_2$ to $R$ and $E_2$, $R$ to $R\_H$ and $R$ to nodes $K1\_1, \ldots, K1\_p, K2\_1, \ldots, K2\_r$.

Also in this case, the same *SD-Graph* may need to be modified in both ways. In this case, entities involved in type conflicts are taken care of first, and then relationships are dealt with.

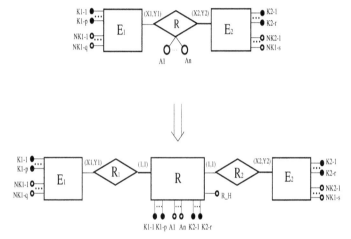

**Fig. 2.4.** Modifying a relationship involved in a type conflict: E/R model

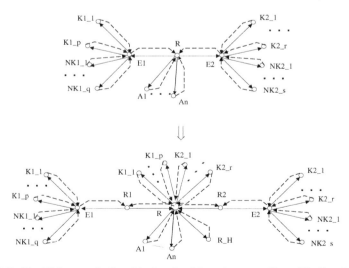

**Fig. 2.5.** Modifying a relationship involved in a type conflict: *SD-Graph* model

– *Function $\mu_{RAE}$*. This function solves conflicts between a relationship attribute and an entity [9]. In particular, first it transforms the relationship into an entity with the same technique used within $\mu_{ER}$ (except that no hidden attribute $R\_H$ is added to $R$); so doing, the original conflict is turned into a conflict between an entity attribute and an entity; consequently the function $\mu_{EAE}$ is applied to solve the conflict. Transformations carried out by $\mu_{RAE}$ on the *SD-Graph* of the attribute involved in the conflict to be solved are illustrated in Figure 2.6.

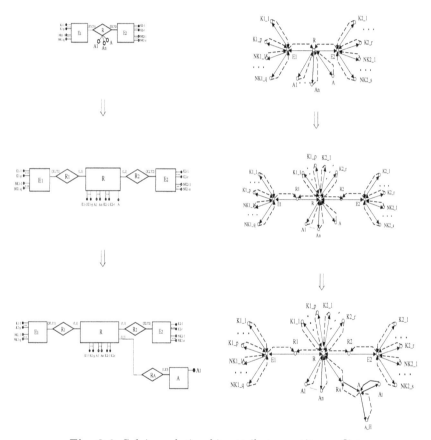

**Fig. 2.6.** Solving relationship attribute - entity conflict

– *Functions $\mu_{EAR}$ and $\mu_{RAR}$*. The function $\mu_{EAR}$ (resp., $\mu_{RAR}$) solves conflicts between an entity attribute (resp., a relationship attribute) and a relationship. The strategy implemented here consists in first transforming the involved relationship into an entity (see Figures 2.4 and 2.5) in the same way as done within the function $\mu_{ER}$ (except that no hidden attribute $R\_H$ is added to $R$); this reduces the original conflict to a conflict between an

entity attribute (resp., relationship attribute) and an entity, which is solved
in turn by applying the function $\mu_{EAE}$ (resp., $\mu_{RAE}$) discussed above. Note
that, in this case, hidden attributes are added to the entity which the relationship involved in the type conflict is transformed into and to the entity
which the attribute involved in the conflict is transformed into.

## 2.4 Internal Fixpoints

In this section we illustrate the core steps of interscheme property derivation,
encoded in the functions $\xi$, that returns type conflicts, and $\rho$, that returns
synonymies. Before giving technical details, we provide a brief overview of
the method.

### 2.4.1 Overview

Our technique for detecting synonymies (resp., type conflicts) works by considering each pair of objects $O_1$ and $O_2$ having the same type (resp., different
types) and belonging to $S_1$ and $S_2$ and computes the associated similarity
degree factor $f$; if $f$ is high, i.e., above a certain threshold, a synonymy (resp.,
a type conflict) between $O_1$ and $O_2$ is derived.

At the heart of our method for detecting synonymy (resp., type conflict)
triplets $\langle O_1, O_2, f \rangle$, there is the internal fixpoint computation $\Gamma_{syn}^{\infty}$ (resp.,
$\Gamma_{tc}^{\infty}$) over *SD-Graphs* $G_1$ and $G_2$. The fixpoint starts with a given base set
of triplets provided by the function $\eta$ described in Section 2.3.2 (resp., by
the function $\rho$), and representing basic interscheme properties (resp., synonymies).

At the generic step $i$ of the computation, the $i\_th$ contexts of each pair of
objects $O_1 \in S_1$ and $O_2 \in S_2$ with the same type (resp., with different types)
are analyzed and their similarity coefficient is established using a maximum
weight matching algorithm. This is used to refine the coefficient $f'$ associated
with the synonymy (resp., type conflict) between $O_1$ and $O_2$ up to step $i-1$.
The established similarity between $cnt(O_1, i)$ and $cnt(O_2, i)$ refines $f'$ in a way
that is inversely proportional to $i$. Indeed, the decreasing succession $\{p(i)\}$ of
factors is introduced to "weigh" the similarity factor obtained for $cnt(O_1, i)$
and $cnt(O_2, i)$ against the value of $i$. As usual, the semantic relevance of
attributes in distinguishing the objects which they belong to is considered.

### 2.4.2 Technical Details

The following preliminary definitions are needed. Let $T$ be a set of triplets
$\langle O_i, O_j, f \rangle$, where $O_i$ and $O_j$ are scheme objects and $f \in [0, 1]$. We define the
following subsets of $T$:

**Definition 2.4.1.**

1. $E\_Syn(T) = \{\langle\ E_1,\ E_2,\ f\rangle \in T \mid\ E_1 \in Ent(S_1), E_2 \in Ent(S_2)\}$, the set of entity synonymies in $T$;
2. $A\_Syn(T) = \{\langle\ A_1,\ A_2,\ f\rangle \in T \mid\ A_1 \in Att(S_1), A_2 \in Att(S_2)\}$, the set of attribute synonymies in $T$;
3. $R\_Syn(T) = \{\langle\ R_1,\ R_2,\ f\rangle \in T \mid\ R_1 \in Rel(S_1), R_2 \in Rel(S_2)\}$, the set of relationship synonymies in $T$;
4. $Syn(T) = E\_Syn(T) \cup A\_Syn(T) \cup R\_Syn(T)$, the set of all synonymies in $T$;
5. $Conf(T) = T - Syn(T)$, the set of type conflicts in $T$.

$\square$

**Derivation of Synonymies.** Recall that, in the following function definitions, we are assuming schemes $S_1$ and $S_2$ as well as the $LSPD$ as implicit parameters.

Synonymies are returned by the function $\rho$ which takes in input the set of triplets yielded by the function $\eta()$ defined in Section 2.3.2.

Remember that, within the fixpoint function $\Psi$, the function $\rho$ is called as follows:

$$\rho(\eta()) = \rho(\eta_{TC}() \cup \eta_A() \cup \eta_E() \cup \eta_R())$$

Although the task solved by $\rho$ consists in computing synonymies relative to any object type, it refines only entity and relationship plausibility coefficients; indeed attribute synonymies are to be considered as a support for the computation of other synonymies. The evaluation of $\rho$ consists of two steps: the first one, implemented by the fixpoint computation $\Gamma_{syn}^\infty$, returns underestimated synonymies, taking into account the semantic relevance of attributes; the second one, realized by the function $\nu_{syn}$, normalizes these underestimated values:

$$\rho(T) = Conf(T) \cup A\_Syn(T)\ \cup\ \nu_{syn}(E\_Syn(\Gamma_{syn}^\infty(T)), w_s)\ \cup\ \nu_{syn}(R\_Syn(\Gamma_{syn}^\infty(T)), w_s)$$

*Function $\Gamma_{syn}^\infty$..* $\Gamma_{syn}^\infty$ takes a triplet set $T$ as its input and returns it modified by adding new similarity triplets. The fixpoint computation $\Gamma_{syn}^\infty$ is defined as follows:

$$\begin{cases} \Gamma_{syn}^0(T) = T \\ \Gamma_{syn}^i(T) = \Gamma_{syn}(\Gamma_{syn}^{i-1}(T), i-1) & \text{for } i > 0 \end{cases}$$

Now, for any scheme $S$, let $K(S)$ be the minimum integer such that $K(S) > 0$ and $(\forall x \in S)(E\_cnt(x, K(S)) = \emptyset)$. By Proposition 2.2.1, $K(S) \leq |Ent(S)| + 1$. Therefore we have:

**Proposition 2.4.1.** $\Gamma_{syn}^\infty(T) = \Gamma_{syn}^{\overline{K}}(T)$, *where* $\overline{K} = max(K(S_1), K(S_2))$.
*Proof.* Immediate.

$\square$

The base functor $\Gamma_{syn}$ of the fixpoint computation $\Gamma^{\infty}_{syn}$, takes a set of triplets and an integer as its inputs and returns a set of triplets, as follows:

$$\Gamma_{syn}(T, i) = A\_Syn(T) \cup \{\langle O_1, O_2, \beta_p(T, i, f, O_1, O_2, w_s)\rangle \mid$$
$$\langle O_1, O_2, f \rangle \in (E\_Syn(T) \cup R\_Syn(T))\}$$

The function $\beta_p$ returns the refined value of the plausibility coefficient for $O_1$ and $O_2$ and is defined as follows:

$$\beta_p(T, i, f, O_1, O_2, w_s) = \begin{cases} p(i) \times \zeta(T, O_1, O_2, i, w_s) + [1 - p(i)] \times f \\ \quad\quad\quad if\ \zeta(T, O_1, O_2, i, w_s) \neq 0 \\ \\ f \quad\quad\quad\quad\quad\quad\quad\quad\quad otherwise \end{cases}$$

where $\{p(i)\}$ is the succession of factors used to take into account distances between objects and their contexts and $\zeta(T, O_1, O_2, i, w_s)$ measures the similarity between the $i\_th$ context of $O_1$ and the $i\_th$ context of $O_2$. As already stated, the succession $\{p(i)\}$ is monotone decreasing since farther objects influence the similarity of $O_1$ and $O_2$ less than closer objects. Some interesting forms for $\{p(i)\}$ are the inverse polynomial ($p(i) = \frac{1}{(i+1)^k}$, $k \geq 1$) and the inverse exponential ($p(i) = \frac{1}{2^i}$).

Function $\zeta(T, O_1, O_2, i, w_s)$ returns a weighted mean of the similarities of $A\_cnt(O_1, i)$ and $A\_cnt(O_2, i)$ and the similarity of $E\_cnt(O_1, i)$ and $E\_cnt(O_2, i)$. The similarity factor of $A\_cnt(O_1, i)$ and $A\_cnt(O_2, i)$ and that of $E\_cnt(O_1, i)$ and $E\_cnt(O_2, i)$ result from a maximum weight matching and are obtained by calling functions $\delta$ and $\mu_S$ described in Section 2.3.2. Therefore $\zeta$ is defined as follows:

$$\zeta(T, O_1, O_2, i, w_s) = w_\zeta(i) \times \delta(\mu_s(A\_Syn(T), A\_cnt(O_1, i), A\_cnt(O_2, i)),$$
$$A\_cnt(O_1, i), A\_cnt(O_2, i), w_s) +$$
$$(1 - w_\zeta(i)) \times \delta(\mu_s(E\_Syn(T), E\_cnt(O_1, i), E\_cnt(O_2, i)),$$
$$E\_cnt(O_1, i), E\_cnt(O_2, i), w_s)$$

where weights $w_\zeta(i)$ are as defined in Table 2.1.

*Function $\nu_{syn}$.*. The function $\nu_{syn}$ performs a normalization of synonymy coefficients by multiplying input plausibilities by a factor returned by a function $\alpha_{syn}$. Both $\nu_{syn}$ and $\alpha_{syn}$ are analogous to the corresponding functions $\nu$ and $\alpha$ presented in Section 2.3.2, that is:

$$\nu_{syn}(US, w_s) = \{\langle O_1, O_2, f \times \alpha_{syn}(US, w_s)\rangle \mid \langle O_1, O_2, f \rangle \in US\},$$

where:

- $\alpha_{syn}(US, w_s) = \frac{\alpha^I_{syn}(\alpha_O(US), w_s)}{\alpha_M(US)}$, and
- $\alpha_M$ and $\alpha_O$ are described in Section 2.3.2;
- the function $\alpha^I_{syn}$ returns the plausibility coefficient, associated to the synonymy of the object pair yielded by $\alpha_O$, without taking into account the semantic relevance of attributes, as follows:

$$\alpha_{syn}^I((O_1, O_2), w_s) = \sigma_t(\Gamma_{syn}^\infty(\eta_{TC}() \cup \eta_A^I() \cup \eta_E() \cup \eta_R()), O_1, O_2),$$

where $\sigma_t(T, O_1, O_2) = g$ such that $\langle O_1, O_2, g \rangle \in T$.

**Derivation of Type Conflicts.** Type conflicts, returned by the function $\xi$, are derived by a technique that is similar to that used for synonymies. We recall that, within the fixpoint function $\Psi$, the function $\xi$ is called as follows:

$$\xi(\rho(\eta())) = \xi(\rho(\eta_{TC}() \cup \eta_A() \cup \eta_E() \cup \eta_R()))$$

As for $\rho$, computing $\xi$ consists of two steps: the first one computes type conflicts taking into account the semantic relevance of attributes; this produces an underestimation of the associated factors; the second step normalizes these values:

$$\xi(T) = Syn(T) \cup \nu_{tc}(Conf(\Gamma_{tc}^\infty(T)), w_{tc})$$

*Function $\Gamma_{tc}^\infty$..* The fixpoint computation $\Gamma_{tc}^\infty$ is defined as follows:

$$\begin{cases} \Gamma_{tc}^0(T) = T \\ \Gamma_{tc}^i(T) = \Gamma_{tc}(\Gamma_{tc}^{i-1}(T), i-1) & \text{for } i > 0 \end{cases}$$

Also in this case, by Proposition 2.2.1, $\Gamma_{tc}^\infty(T) = \Gamma_{tc}^{\overline{K}}(T)$, where $\overline{K} = max(K(S_1), K(S_2))$ (see above). The base function $\Gamma_{tc}$ is defined as follows:

$$\Gamma_{tc}(T, i) = Syn(T) \cup \{\langle O_1, O_2, \beta_p(T, i, f, O_1, O_2, w_{tc}) \rangle \mid \\ \langle O_1, O_2, f \rangle \in Conf(T)\}$$

where the function $\beta_p$ is as defined in the previous section.

*Function $\nu_{tc}$..* As for the other analogous functions $\nu$ and $\nu_{syn}$, function $\nu_{tc}$ performs a normalization of plausibility coefficients:

$$\nu_{tc}(US, w_{tc}) = \{\langle O_1, O_2, f \times \alpha_{tc}(US, w_{tc}) \rangle \mid \langle O_1, O_2, f \rangle \in US\}$$

where:

- $\alpha_{tc}(US, w_{tc}) = \frac{\alpha_{tc}^I(\alpha_O(US), w_{tc})}{\alpha_M(US)}$, and
- $\alpha_{tc}^I((O_1, O_2), w_{tc}) =$
$$\sigma_t(\Gamma_{tc}^\infty(\eta_{TC}() \cup \eta_A^I() \cup E\_Syn(\rho(\eta())) \cup R\_Syn(\rho(\eta()))), O_1, O_2)$$

where functions $\alpha_O$ and $\alpha_M$ are defined in Section 2.3.2, whereas $\sigma_t$ has been defined above.

## 2.5  A Complete Example

Consider schemes in Figure 2.7 and in Figure 2.9. *SD-Graphs* associated to them are represented in Figure 2.8 and in Figure 2.10, resp.
    Suppose the following *LSPD* is given:

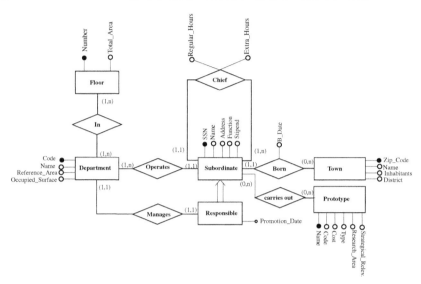

**Fig. 2.7.** Scheme PD: the Production Department Database

$[Number,\ Identifier,\ 0.8]$ $[Number,\ Code,\ 0.85]$
$[District,\ Birthplace,\ 0.45]$ $[Reference\_Area,\ Reference\_Section,\ 0.8]$
$[Code,\ Identifier,\ 0.9]$ $[Zip\_Code,\ Code,\ 0.55]$
$[SSN,\ Code,\ 0.8]$ $[Function,\ Qualification,\ 0.6]$
$[Residence,\ District,\ 0.3]$ $[Regular\_Hours,\ Number\_Of\_Hours,\ 0.8]$
$[Birthdate,\ B\_Date,\ 0.9]$ $[Name,\ Identifier,\ 0.7]$
$[Birthplace,\ Zip\_Code,\ 0.6]$ $[Zip\_Code,\ Identifier,\ 0.55]$
$[SSN,\ Identifier,\ 0.8]$ $[Strategical\_Relevance,\ Priority,\ 0.7]$
$[Stipend,\ Salary,\ 0.9]$ $[Cost,\ Price,\ 0.8]$
$[Address,\ Residence,\ 0.9]$ $[Extra\_Hours,\ Number\_Of\_Hours,\ 0.3]$
$[SSN,\ Number,\ 0.75]$ $[Town,\ Birthplace,\ 0.8]$
$[Type,\ Format,\ 0.55]$ $[Cost,\ Economic\_Value,\ 0.7]$

$$SD = \sigma_{syn}(\Psi^{\infty}())$$
$$HD = \sigma_{hom}(\Psi^{\infty}())$$

First, the fixpoint $\Psi^{\infty}$ must be computed. Therefore, basic interscheme properties are obtained by evaluating $\eta()$. $Col_1$ of Table 2.2 illustrates the resulting set of basic synonymies (hereafter called Basic Synonymy Set, or BSS) for all entities and some attributes, and type conflicts.

The computation proceeds by applying the function $\rho$ that derives synonymies. In order to clarify the behaviour of $\rho$, let us focus on entities *Subordinate* and *Employee*. The function $\rho$ uses object contexts; in particular the contexts of considered objects are:

$$A\_cnt(Subordinate, 0) = \{SSN, Name, Address, Function, Stipend,$$
$$Promotion\_Date\}$$

$E\_cnt(Subordinate, 0) = \{Responsible\}$

$A\_cnt(Subordinate, 1) = \{Code_{[Department]}{}^{1}, Name_{[Department]},$
$Reference\_Area, Occupied\_Surface,$
$Regular\_Hours, Extra\_Hours, B\_Date,$
$Name_{[Town]}, Zip\_Code, Inhabitants, District,$
$Code_{[Prototype]}, Name_{[Prototype]}, Cost, Type,$
$Research\_Area, Strategical\_Relevance\}$

$E\_cnt(Subordinate, 1) = \{Department, Responsible, Town, Prototype\}$

$A\_cnt(Subordinate, 2) = \{Number, Total\_Area\}$

$E\_cnt(Subordinate, 2) = \{Floor, Department, Responsible, Town,$
$Prototype\}$

$A\_cnt(Employee, 0) = \{Code, Birthdate, Name, Birthplace, Residence,$
$Salary, Qualification, Type\}$

$E\_cnt(Employee, 0) = \{Engineer\}$

$A\_cnt(Employee, 1) = \{Code, Name, Reference\_Section,$
$Number\_Of\_Hours\}$

$E\_cnt(Employee, 1) = \{Division, Engineer\}$

$A\_cnt(Employee, 2) = \{Identifier, Name_{[Product]}, Colour, Unit, Cost,$
$Format, Number, Name_{[Project]}, Economic\_Value,$
$Priority\}$

$E\_cnt(Employee, 2) = \{Product, Division, Engineer, Project\}$

$A\_cnt(Employee, 3) = \{Identifier, Duration\}$

$E\_cnt(Employee, 3) = \{Product, Warranty, Division, Engineer, Project\}$

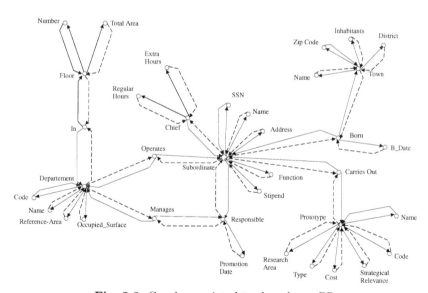

**Fig. 2.8.** Graph associated to the scheme PD

---

[1] Here and in the following, when two attributes having the same name are present in the same context, we indicate them using the formalism $A_{[E]}$, where $A$ is the attribute and $E$ is the entity which it belongs to.

The evaluation of $\rho$ proceeds by activating the fixpoint computation $\Gamma_{syn}^{\infty}(BSS)$; in particular:

$$\Gamma_{syn}^{0}(BSS) = BSS$$
$$\Gamma_{syn}^{1}(BSS) = \Gamma_{syn}(\Gamma_{syn}^{0}(BSS), 0) = \Gamma_{syn}(BSS, 0)$$

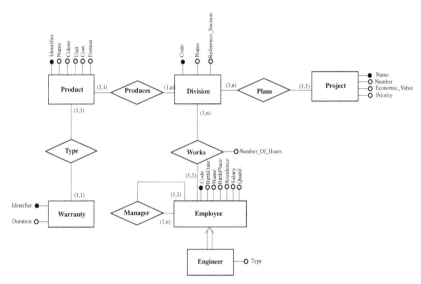

**Fig. 2.9.** Scheme AD: the Administration Department Database

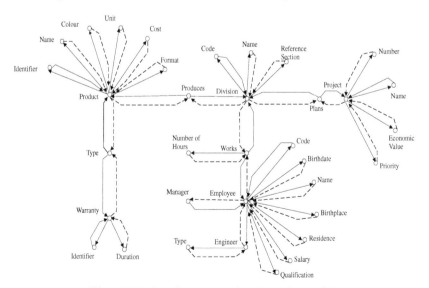

**Fig. 2.10.** Graph associated to the scheme AD

The *Synonymy Dictionary SD* and the *Homonymy Dictionary HD* associated to *PD* and *AD* are obtained as:

As far as the two considered objects are concerned, the computed value of associated plausibility coefficient is:

$$f = p(0) \times \zeta(BSS, Subordinate, Employee, 0, 1) + [1 - p(0)] \times f'$$

Here and in the following, we will adopt the quadratic decreasing function for $p(i)$, that is $p(i) = \frac{1}{(i+1)^2}$. Thus, if we set *A_Sub_0=A_cnt(Subordinate,0)*, *A_Emp_0=A_cnt(Employee,0)*, *E_Sub_0=E_cnt(Subordinate,0)* and *E_Emp_0=E_cnt(Employee,0)*, we obtain:

$$f = \zeta(BSS, Subordinate, Employee, 0, 1) =$$
$$w_\zeta(0) \times \delta(\mu_s(A\_Syn(BSS), A\_Sub\_0, A\_Emp\_0), A\_Sub\_0, A\_Emp\_0, 1) +$$
$$(1 - w_\zeta(0)) \times \delta(\mu_s(E\_Syn(BSS), E\_Sub\_0, E\_Emp\_0), E\_Sub\_0, E\_Emp\_0, 1)$$

Recalling that $w_\zeta(0) = 1$ and $w_\zeta(i) = 0.4$, for $i > 0$, the application of the maximum weight matching returns:

$$f = \delta(\mu_s(A\_Syn(BSS), A\_Sub\_0, A\_Emp\_0), A\_Sub\_0, A\_Emp\_0, 1)$$
$$A' = \{(SSN, Code, 0.28), (Name, Name, 0.8),$$
$$(Address, Residence, 0.92), (Stipend, Salary, 0.92),$$
$$(Function, Qualification, 0.68)\}$$

Therefore, $\overline{\phi}(A') = \frac{\phi(A')}{|A'|} = 0.72$; since the value returned by $\delta$ is $\left(1 - \frac{1}{2} \times \frac{2 + 2 \times (6 - 5)}{6 + 8}\right) \times 0.72 = 0.62$ we obtain $f = 0.62$.

Consider now $\Gamma_{syn}^2(BSS) = \Gamma_{syn}(\Gamma_{syn}^1(BSS), 1)$. As far as considered objects are concerned, we have:

$$f = p(1) \times \zeta(\Gamma_{syn}^1(BSS), Subordinate, Employee, 1, 1) + [1 - p(1)] \times f'$$

Therefore, if we set *A_Sub_1=A_cnt(Subordinate,1)*, *A_Emp_1=A_cnt(Employee,1)*, *E_Sub_1=E_cnt(Subordinate,1)* and *E_Emp_1=E_cnt(Employee,1)*, we obtain:

$$\zeta(\Gamma_{syn}^1(BSS), Subordinate, Employee, 1, 1) =$$
$$w_\zeta(1) \times \delta(\mu_s(A\_Syn(\Gamma_{syn}^1(BSS)), A\_Sub\_1, A\_Emp\_1),$$
$$A\_Sub\_1, A\_Emp\_1, 1) +$$
$$(1 - w_\zeta(1)) \times \delta(\mu_s(E\_Syn(\Gamma_{syn}^1(BSS)), E\_Sub\_1, E\_Emp\_1),$$
$$E\_Sub\_1, E\_Emp\_1, 1)$$

For $\delta(\mu_s(A\_Syn(\Gamma_{syn}^1(BSS)), A\_Sub\_1, A\_Emp\_1), A\_Sub\_1, A\_Emp\_1, 1)$, we obtain:

$$A' = \{(Name, Name, 0.8), (Reference\_Area, Reference\_Section, 0.84),$$
$$(Regular\_Hours, Number\_Of\_Hours, 0.84), (Code, Code, 0.59)\}$$

and, therefore, $\overline{\phi}(A') = \frac{\phi(A')}{|A'|} = 0.76$; hence, the value returned by $\delta$ is

$\left(1 - \frac{1}{2} \times \frac{13+2\times(4-4)}{17+4}\right) \times 0.76 = 0.52$.

For $\delta(\mu_s(E\_Syn(\Gamma^1_{syn}(BSS)), E\_Sub\_1, E\_Emp\_1), E\_Sub\_1, E\_Emp\_1, 1)$, we obtain:

$$A' = \{(Department, Division, 0.68), (Prototype, Engineer, 0.28)\}$$

and, therefore, $\overline{\phi}(A') = \frac{\phi(A')}{|A'|} = 0.48$; hence, the value returned by $\delta$ is

$\left(1 - \frac{1}{2} \times \frac{2+2\times(2-2)}{4+2}\right) \times 0.48 = 0.40$.

We can therefore compute $\zeta(\Gamma^1_{syn}(BSS), Subordinate, Employee, 1, 1)$, and obtain $\zeta(\Gamma^1_{syn}(BSS), Subordinate, Employee, 1, 1) = 0.4 \times 0.52 + (1 - 0.4) \times 0.40 = 0.45$, and, therefore, $f = 0.25 \times 0.45 + (1 - 0.25) \times 0.62 = 0.58$. $\Gamma^3_{syn}(BSS) = \Gamma_{syn}(\Gamma^2_{syn}(BSS), 2)$ is computed analogously. For the considered pair of objects, we obtain

$$f = p(2) \times \zeta(\Gamma^2_{syn}(BSS), Subordinate, Employee, 2, 1) + [1 - p(2)] \times f' =$$
$$0.11 \times 0.23 + (1 - 0.11) \times 0.58 = 0.54.$$

Similarly, the value of $f$ for $\Gamma^4_{syn}(BSS)$ is $f = 0.06 \times 0.20 + (1 - 0.06) \times 0.54 = 0.52$.

Plausibility values associated to all other entity pairs are computed analogously. These are shown in $Col_2$ of Table 2.2. From these, by applying the function $\nu_{syn}$, normalized synonymy coefficients are finally obtained, which are shown in $Col_3$ of Table 2.2. The computation of relationship synonymies is carried out analogously.

After that synonymies have been returned by the function $\rho$, the function $\xi$ is applied for deriving type conflicts. The function $\xi$ works in a way that is similar to $\rho$; in particular, it computes the fixpoint $\Gamma^\infty_{tc}(ESS)$, where $ESS$ is the set of synonymies returned by $\rho$:

$\Gamma^0_{tc}(ESS) = ESS$
$\Gamma^1_{tc}(ESS) = \Gamma_{tc}(\Gamma^0_{tc}(ESS), 0) = \Gamma_{tc}(ESS, 0)$

As before, for the sake of space, we limit our attention to one pair of objects, namely, the entity $Town$ and the attribute $Birthplace$. The $A\_cnts$ and $E\_cnts$ for $Town$ and $Birthplace$ are the following:

$A\_cnt(Town, 0) = \{Name, Zip\_Code, Inhabitants, District\}$
$E\_cnt(Town, 0) = \{\}$
$A\_cnt(Town, 1) = \{SSN, Name, Address, Function, Stipend,$
$\qquad Promotion\_Date, B\_Date\}$
$E\_cnt(Town, 1) = \{Subordinate, Responsible\}$
$A\_cnt(Town, 2) = \{Code_{[Department]}, Name_{[Department]}, Reference\_Area,$
$\qquad Occupied\_Surface, Regular\_Hours, Extra\_Hours,$
$\qquad Code_{[Prototype]}, Name_{[Prototype]}, Cost, Type,$
$\qquad Research\_Area, Strategical\_Relevance\}$
$E\_cnt(Town, 2) = \{Department, Subordinate, Responsible, Prototype\}$
$A\_cnt(Town, 3) = \{Number, Total\_Area\}$
$E\_cnt(Town, 3) = \{Floor, Department, Subordinate, Responsible,$
$\qquad Prototype\}$

$A\_cnt(Birthplace, 0) = \{\}$
$E\_cnt(Birthplace, 0) = \{\}$
$A\_cnt(Birthplace, 1) = \{Code, Birthdate, Name, Residence, Salary,$
$\qquad\qquad\qquad\qquad Qualification, Type\}$
$E\_cnt(Birthplace, 1) = \{Employee, Engineer\}$
$A\_cnt(Birthplace, 2) = \{Code, Name, Reference\_Section,$
$\qquad\qquad\qquad\qquad Number\_Of\_Hours\}$
$E\_cnt(Birthplace, 2) = \{Division, Employee, Engineer\}$
$A\_cnt(Birthplace, 3) = \{Identifier, Name_{[Product]}, Colour, Unit, Cost,$
$\qquad\qquad\qquad\qquad Format, Number, Name_{[Project]}, Economic\_Value,$
$\qquad\qquad\qquad\qquad Priority\}$
$E\_cnt(Birthplace, 3) = \{Product, Division, Employee, Engineer, Project\}$
$A\_cnt(Birthplace, 4) = \{Identifier, Duration\}$
$E\_cnt(Birthplace, 4) = \{Product, Warranty, Division, Employee, Engineer,$
$\qquad\qquad\qquad\qquad Project\}$

As for $\Gamma_{tc}^1(ESS)$, the value of the plausibility coefficient associated to the type conflict corresponding to the pair of objects under consideration is:

$$f = p(0) \times \zeta(ESS, Town, Birthplace, 0, 1) + [1 - p(0)] \times f'$$

Since $A\_cnt(Birthplace, 0)$ is empty, $\zeta(ESS, Town, Birthplace, 0, 1) = 0$ and the value of $f'$ is assigned to $f$ (remember that, for type conflict detection, $f'$ is initialized to the corresponding values of $ESS$); therefore, in this case, $f = 0.8$.

Consider now $\Gamma_{tc}^2(ESS)$. Applying the same procedure as described for $\Gamma_{syn}^2(BSS)$, to the pair $(Town, Birthplace)$, we obtain the value:

$$f = 0.25 \times 0.49 + (1 - 0.25) \times 0.8 = 0.72.$$

In the same way, within $\Gamma_{tc}^3(ESS)$, $\Gamma_{tc}^4(ESS)$ and $\Gamma_{tc}^5(ESS)$, we obtain the following refined coefficients for $Town$ and $Birthplace$:

$$f = 0.11 \times 0.43 + (1 - 0.11) \times 0.72 = 0.69;$$
$$f = 0.06 \times 0.30 + (1 - 0.06) \times 0.69 = 0.67;$$
$$f = 0.04 \times 0.25 + (1 - 0.04) \times 0.67 = 0.65.$$

The final normalization phase returns the triplet $\langle Town, Birthplace, 0.66 \rangle$. This and other derived type conflicts are shown in $Col_4$ of Table 2.2; the filtering phase returns $\langle Town, Birthplace, 0.66 \rangle$ as the only significant type conflict.

To complete the computation of $\Psi^1$, the function $\mu$, which modifies schemes and associated graphs for removing derived type conflicts is applied. Resulting modified $SD$-$Graphs$ are shown in Figures 2.11 and 2.12.

Since, in the last application of $\Psi$, one type conflict has been detected, a new iteration is required. Thus, $\Psi^2$ is computed. New basic synonymies, returned by the function $\eta$, and new refined synonymies, returned by the function $\rho$, are shown in $Col_5$ and $Col_6$ of Table 2.2. The application of function $\xi$ does not detect any new significant type conflict, and the computation of $\Psi^2$ terminates. Since no new type conflicts have been detected in the last step, the overall computation terminates.

**Table 2.2.** Interscheme properties for objects belonging to $PD$ and $AD$

| First Object | Second Object | $Col_1$ | $Col_2$ | $Col_3$ | $Col_4$ | $Col_5$ | $Col_6$ |
|---|---|---|---|---|---|---|---|
| Floor | Product | 0.08 | 0.19 | 0.26 | - | 0.08 | 0.27 |
| Floor | Warranty | 0.16 | 0.20 | 0.28 | - | 0.16 | 0.27 |
| Floor | Division | 0.16 | 0.15 | 0.20 | - | 0.16 | 0.20 |
| Floor | Employee | 0.09 | 0.18 | 0.24 | - | 0.10 | 0.22 |
| Floor | Birthplace | - | - | - | - | 0.00 | 0.15 |
| Floor | Engineer | 0.00 | 0.13 | 0.17 | - | 0.00 | 0.17 |
| Floor | Project | 0.16 | 0.27 | 0.37 | - | 0.16 | 0.37 |
| Department | Product | 0.26 | 0.24 | 0.33 | - | 0.26 | 0.32 |
| Department | Warranty | 0.17 | 0.16 | 0.21 | - | 0.17 | 0.21 |
| Department | Division | 0.68 | 0.47 | 0.63 | - | 0.68 | 0.65 |
| Department | Employee | 0.26 | 0.20 | 0.27 | - | 0.28 | 0.28 |
| Department | Birthplace | - | - | - | - | 0.00 | 0.17 |
| Department | Engineer | 0.00 | 0.13 | 0.18 | - | 0.00 | 0.20 |
| Department | Project | 0.34 | 0.27 | 0.30 | - | 0.34 | 0.36 |
| Subordinate | Product | 0.24 | 0.21 | 0.28 | - | 0.24 | 0.28 |
| Subordinate | Warranty | 0.15 | 0.15 | 0.21 | - | 0.15 | 0.21 |
| Subordinate | Division | 0.31 | 0.27 | 0.35 | - | 0.31 | 0.35 |
| Subordinate | Employee | 0.70 | 0.52 | 0.70 | - | 0.77 | 0.75 |
| Subordinate | Birthplace | - | - | - | - | 0.00 | 0.12 |
| Subordinate | Engineer | 0.00 | 0.08 | 0.11 | - | 0.00 | 0.12 |
| Subordinate | Project | 0.28 | 0.22 | 0.30 | - | 0.28 | 0.29 |
| Responsible | Product | 0.00 | 0.14 | 0.19 | - | 0.00 | 0.20 |
| Responsible | Warranty | 0.00 | 0.08 | 0.11 | - | 0.00 | 0.12 |
| Responsible | Division | 0.00 | 0.10 | 0.14 | - | 0.00 | 0.16 |
| Responsible | Employee | 0.00 | 0.12 | 0.16 | - | 0.00 | 0.15 |
| Responsible | Birthplace | - | - | - | - | 0.00 | 0.19 |
| Responsible | Engineer | 0.00 | 0.16 | 0.21 | - | 0.00 | 0.23 |
| Responsible | Project | 0.00 | 0.14 | 0.19 | - | 0.00 | 0.20 |
| Town | Product | 0.23 | 0.22 | 0.30 | - | 0.21 | 0.28 |
| Town | Warranty | 0.17 | 0.18 | 0.24 | - | 0.15 | 0.23 |
| Town | Division | 0.35 | 0.29 | 0.38 | - | 0.31 | 0.35 |
| Town | Employee | 0.34 | 0.26 | 0.27 | - | 0.22 | 0.26 |
| Town | Birthplace | - | - | - | - | 0.66 | 0.66 |
| Town | Engineer | 0.00 | 0.18 | 0.24 | - | 0.00 | 0.24 |
| Town | Project | 0.31 | 0.27 | 0.37 | - | 0.27 | 0.34 |
| Prototype | Product | 0.49 | 0.35 | 0.49 | - | 0.49 | 0.47 |
| Prototype | Warranty | 0.13 | 0.15 | 0.20 | - | 0.13 | 0.21 |
| Prototype | Division | 0.30 | 0.25 | 0.34 | - | 0.30 | 0.35 |
| Prototype | Employee | 0.33 | 0.32 | 0.44 | - | 0.36 | 0.45 |
| Prototype | Birthplace | - | - | - | - | 0.00 | 0.20 |
| Prototype | Engineer | 0.28 | 0.31 | 0.44 | - | 0.28 | 0.45 |
| Prototype | Project | 0.61 | 0.43 | 0.57 | - | 0.61 | 0.57 |
| Town | Birthplace | 0.80 | - | - | 0.66 | - | - |
| Town | Residence | 0.00 | - | - | 0.16 | - | - |
| Town | Salary | 0.00 | - | - | 0.16 | - | - |
| Town | Qualification | 0.00 | - | - | 0.16 | - | - |
| Town | Type | 0.00 | - | - | 0.08 | - | - |
| Stipend | Salary | 0.92 | - | - | - | - | - |
| Name | Name | 0.80 | - | - | - | - | - |
| Reference_Area | Reference_Section | 0.84 | - | - | - | - | - |
| Regular_Hours | Number_Of_Hours | 0.84 | - | - | - | - | - |
| Code | Code | 0.59 | - | - | - | - | - |
| Number | Number | 0.40 | - | - | - | - | - |

## 2.6 Complexity Issues

In this section we discuss the complexity of the algorithms presented above. In particular, we show that all of them terminate in a number of steps which is polynomial in the number of input scheme objects.

In the following we denote by $n_1$ (resp., $n_2$) the number of objects belonging to the scheme $S_1$ (resp., $S_2$) and by $n$ the maximum of $n_1$ and $n_2$.

Object similarities are obtained by executing the following steps: *(i)* constructing *SD-Graphs*; *(ii)* constructing contexts; *(iii)* deriving basic interscheme properties; *(iv)* deriving synonymies; *(v)* detecting type conflicts; *(vi)* modifying graphs to solve type conflicts; *(vii)* filtering valid synonymies and homonymies. Observe that steps *(ii)*, *(iii)*, *(iv)*, *(v)* and *(vi)* are executed

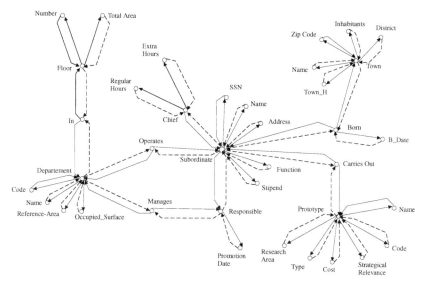

**Fig. 2.11.** Modified PD *SD-Graph*

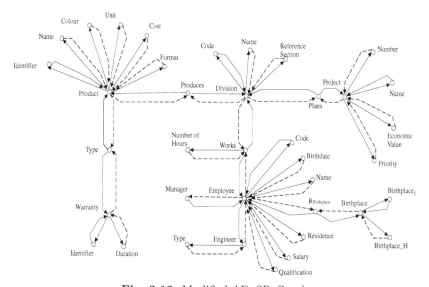

**Fig. 2.12.** Modified AD *SD-Graph*

several times. We analyze the complexity of steps *(i)* - *(vii)* along with the number of iteration over steps *(ii)* - *(vi)* needed to reach the fixpoint.

**Proposition 2.6.1.** *The worst case time complexity of constructing* SD-Graphs *is* $O(n^2)$.

*Proof.* Straightforward.                                                                              □

**Proposition 2.6.2.** *The worst case time complexity of constructing contexts is $O(n^3)$.*

*Proof.* The construction of contexts of all objects of a scheme $S$ corresponds to computing all minimum paths. Hence the result.                    □

**Proposition 2.6.3.** *The worst case time complexity of deriving basic interscheme properties is $O(n^5)$.*

*Proof.* The possible basic interscheme properties are:

- *synonymies between attributes*: the number of pairs of objects to be considered is $|Att(S_1)| \times |Att(S_2)|$; since the size of the $LSPD$ is independent of both $n_1$ and $n_2$, for each pair, the computation of the similarity coefficient is executed in constant time, hence the computation is $O(n^2)$.
- *synonymies between entities (resp., relationships)*: the number of pairs to be considered is $|Ent(S_1)| \times |Ent(S_2)|$ (resp., $|Rel(S_1)| \times |Rel(S_2)|$), for each of these pairs, a maximum weight matching algorithm is executed, having a complexity $O((max(|Att(S_1)|, |Att(S_2)|))^3)$. Therefore the total complexity for deriving synonymies between entities and relationships is $O(n^5)$.
- *type conflicts*: in this case, the number of pairs is $|Ent(S_1)| \times |Rel(S_2)| + |Ent(S_1)| \times |Att(S_2)| + |Rel(S_1)| \times |Ent(S_2)| + |Rel(S_1)| \times |Att(S_2)| + |Att(S_1)| \times |Ent(S_2)| + |Att(S_1)| \times |Rel(S_2)|$; since the size of the $LSPD$ is independent of both $n_1$ and $n_2$, for each pair a constant-time computation is required; therefore this task is $O(n^2)$.

The total resulting complexity is therefore $O(n^5)$.                    □

**Proposition 2.6.4.** *The worst case time complexity of computing $\Gamma_{syn}^{\infty}$ is $O(n^6)$.*

*Proof.*

- By Proposition 2.4.1 $\Gamma_{syn}^{\infty}(T) = \Gamma_{syn}^{\overline{K}}(T)$, where $\overline{K} = max(K(S_1), K(S_2))$. By Proposition 2.2.1, $\overline{K} \leq max(|Ent(S_1)|, |Ent(S_2)|) + 1$; therefore $O(n)$ is an upper bound of the total number of iterations.
- During each iteration, $\Gamma_{syn}$ computes similarities between entities or relationships; the number of potential similarities into consideration is $|Ent(S_1)| \times |Ent(S_2)| + |Rel(S_1)| \times |Rel(S_2)|$ and, consequently, is upper bounded by $O(n^2)$.
- The computation of each similarity requires the application of a maximum weight matching, whose complexity is $O(n^3)$.

The total complexity is, hence, $O(n^6)$.                    □

**Proposition 2.6.5.** *The worst case time complexity of computing $\Gamma_{tc}^{\infty}$ is $O(n^6)$.*

*Proof.* The proof is analogous to that of Proposition 2.6.4.    □

**Proposition 2.6.6.** *The worst case time complexity of modifying* SD-Graphs *to solve type conflicts is* $O(n)$.

*Proof.* Each object can induce at most one transformation to be applied; therefore the maximum number of transformations is $O(n)$. Each transformation requires to carry out a constant number of modifications. Therefore the total number of modifications is $O(n)$.    □

**Proposition 2.6.7.** *The maximum number of iterations required by the external fixpoint to terminate is* $O(n^2)$.

*Proof.* Consider the following preliminary observations:

- *Observation 1.* The new relationships and hidden attributes, introduced by the type conflict resolution, are support objects, without a semantic on their own. Moreover, their names are artificial and, as such, do not occur in the *LSPD*. Therefore, they cannot be detected to be similar to any object of the "other" input scheme. Consequently, relationships and hidden attributes introduced during the resolution of a type conflict cannot be involved in further type conflicts.
- *Observation 2.* A key attribute $A_I$, introduced, during the resolution of the type conflict between an entity attribute $A$ and an entity, in the scheme which $A$ belongs to, is the only attribute of the new entity $A$; therefore, by the definition of function $\sigma$, point 3 (see Section 2.3.2), $A_I$ shall not be involved in further type conflicts.

We are now able to determine the maximum number of iterations required by the external fixpoint to terminate. Consider a scheme $S$. The resolution of type conflicts tends to transform involved objects into entities and support objects. Support objects cannot be involved in further type conflicts, due to Observations 1 and 2; obtained entities could be involved in further type conflicts but, if this would happen, no object different from entities and support objects would be further created in the corresponding scheme whereas, in the other scheme, an object different from an entity is transformed into entities and support objects.

We have the worst case when all possible type conflicts occur in schemes and, during one iteration, only one type conflict is detected and solved. Hence, in the worst case, the number of iterations for the external fixpoint to converge coincides with the number of possible type conflicts of the two schemes. Now, consider the following facts:

- If an entity $E$ of a scheme is involved in a type conflict, the corresponding scheme transformations cause a hidden attribute to be added to the entity. The hidden attribute cannot be involved in a further type conflict (see Observation 1); on the contrary a type conflict could involve again the entity. Note that, each time an entity is involved in a type conflict, an object of the other scheme is transformed into an entity; consequently the maximum number of type conflicts possibly generated by an entity depends on the number of objects different from entities or support objects that either exist or are generated in the other scheme. Note that this is also the maximum number of type conflicts possibly generated by the set of entities of a scheme.

– If an entity attribute is involved in a type conflict, its resolution implies that it is transformed into an entity; objects generated by its resolution are: a key attribute, a hidden attribute, a support relationship (all these objects cannot be involved in a further type conflict – see Observations 1 and 2) and an entity (this could be involved in a type conflict but, if this happens, some object of the other scheme is transformed into an entity). In the worst case all attributes are entity attributes and are involved in a type conflict; therefore the total number of possible steps for transforming all entity attributes into entities or support objects is $|Att(S)|$.

– If a relationship or a relationship attribute is involved in a type conflict, its resolution implies that the relationship is transformed into an entity; objects generated by its resolution are: *(i)* a new entity, *(ii)* two support relationships, *(iii)* a hidden attribute (if the conflict is between an entity and a relationship) and *(iv)* an attribute for each attribute belonging to the foreign key of the relationship. Among these new objects, only new attributes obtained from the foreign key could cause new type conflicts; this transformation can create, in the worst case, $|Att(S)|$ new entity attributes for each relationship; consequently the maximum number of newly generated attributes is $|Att(S)| \times |Rel(S)|$ and, in the worst case, each of them is involved in a further type conflict. Therefore the total number of possible steps for transforming all relationships into entities or into support objects are $|Att(S)| \times |Rel(S)| + |Rel(S)|$.

Summarizing, the number of iterations of the external fixpoint depends on the number of type conflicts; this last depends on the number of steps necessary to transform attributes and relationships of each scheme into entities and support objects. It follows from the reasoning above that, in the worst case, this number is $O(n^2)$.

□

**Proposition 2.6.8.** *The worst case time complexity of filtering significant derived properties is $O(n^2)$.*

*Proof.* The filtering phase requires just a linear scan of the results yielded by $\Psi^\infty$; their size is $O(n^2)$.                                      □

Overall, for obtaining similarities between objects, we have:

**Theorem 2.6.1.** *The worst case time complexity of the overall algorithm for computing interscheme properties of objects is* $O(n^8)$.

*Proof.* At the beginning, *SD-Graphs* are constructed $(O(n^2))$; within one iteration of the external fixpoint we construct contexts $(O(n^3))$, compute synonymies $(O(n^6))$, type conflicts $(O(n^6))$, modify graphs for solving type conflicts $(O(n))$. Therefore the complexity of each iteration of the external fixpoint is $O(n^6)$. The maximum number of iterations is $O(n^2)$. The total complexity is, therefore, $O(n^8)$.

$\square$

## 2.7 Sensitivity Analysis

In order to verify the stability of our approach against errors potentially occurring in *LSPD* coefficients and in weight values, we have carried out some sensitivity analyses. In particular, we have verified the changes induced in the results returned by our techniques as a consequence of modifying *(i)* the plausibility coefficients associated to properties stored in the *LSPD*, *(ii)* weight $w_s$, *(iii)* weights $w_\zeta(i)$, *(iv)* weights $w_n$, $w_d$ and $w_k$. The results of these analyses are reported next.

### 2.7.1 Changes in the LSPD

In carrying out this analysis we have considered various cases depending on the number and on the consistence of errors of *LSPD* coefficients. For each case we have measured some quality parameters, namely, *maximum increment*, *mean variation* and *maximum decrement* in returned plausibility coefficients, *changes of synonymy threshold values*, *differences in the set of recognized synonymies* (recall that, in our framework, synonymy threshold values are calculated and that all coefficients belongs to the real interval $[0, 1]$).

We have considered a percentage of wrong coefficient entries equal to *(i)* 10%, *(ii)*, 20%, *(iii)* 30%, *(iv)* 40%, *(v)* 50% of the total. For each of these cases we have considered six situations:

(a) All wrong entries are underestimated of one unit (e.g., the exact estimate would be *Medium* and the set value is *MediumLow*);
(b) All wrong entries are overestimated of one unit;
(c) All wrong entries are underestimated of two units;
(d) All wrong entries are overestimated of two units;
(e) Half of the wrong entries are underestimated of one unit and half of them are overestimated of one unit;
(f) Half of the wrong entries are underestimated of two units and half of them are overestimated of two units.

Furthermore, we have also considered the following further cases:

(g) Ten percent of wrong entries are underestimated of one unit, ten percent of them are underestimated of two units and ten percent of them are underestimated of three units.

(h) Ten percent of wrong entries are overestimated of one unit, ten percent of them are overestimated of two units and ten percent of them are overestimated of three units.

(i) Thirty percent of wrong entries are underestimated of three units.

(j) Thirty percent of wrong entries are overestimated of three units.

Table 2.3 (resp., 2.4, 2.5, 2.6 and 2.7) shows results for case *(i)* (resp., *(ii)*, *(iii)*, *(iv)* and *(v)*).

Table 2.8 shows results obtained for the last four cases.

**Table 2.3.** Values of quality parameters for case *(i)*

|  | (a) | (b) | (c) | (d) | (e) | (f) |
|---|---|---|---|---|---|---|
| *Maximum Increment* | 0.000 | 0.000 | 0.000 | 0.056 | 0.000 | 0.000 |
| *Mean Variation* | 0.000 | -0.008 | 0.000 | -0.009 | -0.001 | -0.009 |
| *Maximum Decrement* | 0.000 | 0.006 | 0.000 | 0.012 | 0.000 | 0.006 |
| *Similarity Threshold Change* | 0.000 | -0.009 | 0.000 | -0.013 | -0.001 | -0.011 |
| *Differences of Recognized Synonymies* | none | none | none | none | none | none |

**Table 2.4.** Values of quality parameters for case *(ii)*

|  | (a) | (b) | (c) | (d) | (e) | (f) |
|---|---|---|---|---|---|---|
| *Maximum Increment* | 0.000 | 0.000 | 0.000 | 0.000 | 0.000 | 0.063 |
| *Mean Variation* | 0.000 | -0.007 | -0.001 | -0.011 | -0.008 | 0.000 |
| *Maximum Decrement* | 0.000 | 0.006 | 0.001 | 0.011 | 0.006 | 0.008 |
| *Similarity Threshold Change* | -0.001 | -0.008 | -0.002 | -0.006 | -0.009 | -0.002 |
| *Differences of Recognized Synonymies* | none | none | none | none | none | none |

**Table 2.5.** Values of quality parameters for case *(iii)*

|  | (a) | (b) | (c) | (d) | (e) | (f) |
|---|---|---|---|---|---|---|
| *Maximum Increment* | 0.000 | 0.040 | 0.000 | 0.053 | 0.045 | 0.051 |
| *Mean Variation* | -0.014 | -0.005 | -0.019 | -0.016 | 0.001 | -0.023 |
| *Maximum Decrement* | 0.009 | 0.007 | 0.012 | 0.019 | 0.010 | 0.023 |
| *Similarity Threshold Change* | -0.028 | -0.017 | -0.042 | -0.010 | -0.002 | -0.040 |
| *Differences of Recognized Synonymies* | none | none | none | none | none | none |

**Table 2.6.** Values of quality parameters for case *(iv)*

|  | (a) | (b) | (c) | (d) | (e) | (f) |
|---|---|---|---|---|---|---|
| *Maximum Increment* | 0.000 | 0.037 | 0.000 | 0.056 | 0.000 | 0.000 |
| *Mean Variation* | -0.001 | -0.014 | 0.000 | -0.011 | -0.007 | -0.011 |
| *Maximum Decrement* | 0.000 | 0.019 | 0.000 | 0.010 | 0.006 | 0.010 |
| *Similarity Threshold Change* | -0.001 | -0.014 | 0.000 | -0.002 | -0.007 | 0.009 |
| *Differences of Recognized Synonymies* | none | none | none | none | none | none |

**Table 2.7.** Values of quality parameters for case *(v)*

|  | (a) | (b) | (c) | (d) | (e) | (f) |
|---|---|---|---|---|---|---|
| *Maximum Increment* | 0.000 | 0.037 | 0.000 | 0.053 | 0.045 | 0.000 |
| *Mean Variation* | -0.004 | 0.001 | -0.009 | -0.014 | 0.001 | -0.020 |
| *Maximum Decrement* | 0.003 | 0.008 | 0.005 | 0.016 | 0.010 | 0.013 |
| *Similarity Threshold Change* | -0.014 | -0.006 | -0.029 | -0.008 | -0.002 | -0.043 |
| *Differences of Recognized Synonymies* | none | none | none | none | none | none |

**Table 2.8.** Values of quality parameters for tests *(g)*, *(h)*,*(i)* and *(j)*

|  | (g) | (h) | (i) | (j) |
|---|---|---|---|---|
| *Maximum Increment* | 0.000 | 0.058 | 0.000 | 0.080 |
| *Mean Variation* | -0.020 | -0.007 | -0.024 | -0.005 |
| *Maximum Decrement* | 0.013 | 0.010 | 0.015 | 0.008 |
| *Similarity Threshold Change* | -0.043 | -0.008 | -0.057 | 0.014 |
| *Differences of Recognized Synonymies* | none | none | none | none |

### 2.7.2 Changes in the Weights $w_s(i)$

In this case, we have measured quality parameters discussed above by varying $w_s$ in the following way: (recall that the set value of $w_s$ is 1.0) *(k)* $w_s = 0.8$, *(l)* $w_s = 0.85$, *(m)* $w_s = 0.9$, *(n)* $w_s = 0.95$, *(o)* $w_s = 1.05$, *(p)* $w_s = 1.10$, *(q)* $w_s = 1.15$, *(r)* $w_s = 1.20$. Tables 2.9 and 2.9 show results obtained from testing these cases.

**Table 2.9.** Values of quality parameters for tests *(k)*, *(l)*,*(m)* and *(n)*

|  | (k) | (l) | (m) | (n) |
|---|---|---|---|---|
| *Maximum Increment* | 0.009 | 0.007 | 0.005 | 0.002 |
| *Mean Variation* | 0.013 | 0.009 | 0.006 | 0.003 |
| *Maximum Decrement* | 0.000 | 0.000 | 0.000 | 0.000 |
| *Similarity Threshold Change* | 0.006 | 0.005 | 0.003 | 0.002 |
| *Differences of Recognized Synonymies* | none | none | none | none |

**Table 2.10.** Values of quality parameters for tests *(o)*, *(p)*,*(q)* and *(r)*

|  | (o) | (p) | (q) | (r) |
|---|---|---|---|---|
| *Maximum Increment* | 0.000 | 0.000 | 0.000 | 0.000 |
| *Mean Variation* | -0.003 | -0.006 | -0.009 | -0.013 |
| *Maximum Decrement* | 0.002 | 0.005 | 0.007 | 0.009 |
| *Similarity Threshold Change* | -0.002 | -0.003 | -0.005 | -0.006 |
| *Differences of Recognized Synonymies* | none | none | none | none |

### 2.7.3 Changes in the Weight $w_\zeta$

Here we have considered quality parameters when values of $w_\zeta(i)$, $i > 0$, change of at most $\pm 25\%$ from its set value (which is 0.4). Values taken into consideration are: *(s)* 0.3, *(t)* 0.35, *(u)* 0.45 and *(v)* 0.5. Table 2.11 shows results obtained from this set of experiments.

**Table 2.11.** Values of quality parameters for changes of weights $w_\zeta(i)$, $i > 0$

|  | (s) | (t) | (u) | (v) |
|---|---|---|---|---|
| *Maximum Increment* | 0.007 | 0.004 | 0.000 | 0.000 |
| *Mean Variation* | 0.002 | 0.001 | -0.001 | -0.002 |
| *Maximum Decrement* | 0.000 | 0.000 | 0.005 | 0.011 |
| *Similarity Threshold Change* | 0.010 | 0.005 | -0.005 | -0.010 |
| *Differences of Recognized Synonymies* | none | none | none | none |

### 2.7.4 Changes in the Weights $w_n$, $w_d$ and $w_k$

In this set of tests we have considered quality parameters when weights $w_n$, $w_d$ and $w_k$ change from their set values ($w_n = 0.8$, $w_d = 0.15$, $w_k = 0.05$) as follows:

(x)  $w_n = 0.7$, $w_d = 0.2$ and $w_k = 0.1$;
(y)  $w_n = 0.75$, $w_d = 0.18$ and $w_k = 0.07$;
(w)  $w_n = 0.85$, $w_d = 0.11$ and $w_k = 0.04$;
(z)  $w_n = 0.9$, $w_d = 0.07$ and $w_k = 0.03$.

Table 2.12 presents the values of quality parameters we have obtained with these experiments.

**Table 2.12.** Values of quality parameters for changes of weights $w_n$, $w_d$ and $w_k$

|  | (x) | (y) | (w) | (z) |
|---|---|---|---|---|
| *Maximum Increment* | 0.000 | 0.000 | 0.000 | 0.000 |
| *Mean Variation* | 0.000 | 0.000 | 0.000 | 0.000 |
| *Maximum Decrement* | 0.000 | 0.000 | 0.000 | 0.000 |
| *Similarity Threshold Change* | 0.001 | 0.000 | 0.000 | -0.001 |
| *Differences of Recognized Synonymies* | none | none | none | none |

### 2.7.5 Result Summary

We note that our techniques show a good stability w.r.t. the errors of DBAs in providing $LSPD$ entries, as well as w.r.t. variation of weights. Even if errors are made when the $LSPD$ is constructed or when weights are tuned, the changes in the obtained plausibility values yielded by algorithms are generally quite small. In addition, note that, even if changes in obtained plausibility values are significant (i.e., greater than 0.05), recognized synonymies do not necessarily change, since our thresholds are computed as functions of plausibility coefficients. However, we stress that if errors in the construction of the $LSPD$ or in tuning weights would be significantly larger than those discussed above, the changes in the results would be significant and differences would therefore be determined also in the set of recognized synonymies.

# 3. Extraction of Object Cluster Similarities

*In this chapter we illustrate our approach for extracting object cluster similarities. More in particular, the plan of the chapter is as follows: in the first section we illustrate the general characteristics of the approach; in particular we show that it is analogous to that used for deriving synonymies, homonymies and type conflicts. The second section illustrates the approach in all details. After it has been deeply illustrated, in the third section, we provide a complete example showing how it works. In the last section of the chapter we compute the complexity of the presented algorithms and we prove that they are polynomial w.r.t. the number of objects belonging to the involved schemes.*

*The material presented in this chapter is taken from [92, 122, 87, 90, 117, 118].*

## 3.1 General Characteristics of the Approach

In the previous chapter we have illustrated a technique for detecting type conflicts i.e., situations where the same concept is represented in two different ways in schemes. However there are situations where a certain portion of the reality is represented as two different *sets of connected objects* (hereafter called *object clusters*) within two input schemes. So, an object cluster similarity denotes a similitude between two subschemes included into two schemes.

In this chapter we present methods whereby such subscheme similarities can be detected. These methods use the same techniques underlying synonymy, homonymy and type conflict derivation. Therefore, in the whole, we propose a unified semi-automatic approach for deriving synonymies, homonymies, type conflicts and object cluster similarities. To the best of our knowledge, in the literature, there is no other uniform approach for deriving all these kinds of interscheme properties.

Given a scheme $S$ with $n$ objects, the number of object clusters is exponential in $n$. To avoid the risk of analysing such a huge number of clusters, we single out only the most *interesting* ones, according to the following constraints:

D. Ursino: Extr. and Expl. of Intensional Knowledge ..., LNCS 2282, pp. 63–69, 2002.
© Springer-Verlag Berlin Heidelberg 2002

– We consider only clusters corresponding, in the *SD-Graph* $G(S)$, to linear paths or to the union of two non disjoint linear paths and, for any pair of nodes, we only consider the *D-shortest path* between them. Let $PS_1$ and $PS_2$ be the set of such paths in $S_1$ and $S_2$, resp. Let $\overline{SP} = \{(P_1, P_2) \mid P_1 \in PS_1, P_2 \in PS_2\}$.

– We discard from $\overline{SP}$ those pairs of paths $(P_1, P_2)$ such that $P_1$ (resp., $P_2$) contains an entity $E$ which has no attribute having a significant similarity with attributes of the objects of $P_2$ (resp., $P_1$).

Analogously to what we have done for deriving object similarities, in order to compute the similarity between object clusters, we introduce the concept of cluster context and define a fixpoint computation $\Gamma_{oc}^{\infty}$ over *SD-Graphs* $G_1$ and $G_2$ in a way that is similar to the definition of $\Gamma_{syn}^{\infty}$ and $\Gamma_{tc}^{\infty}$ illustrated in the previous sections. Also in this case, semantic relevance of attributes to objects is taken into account. Recall that, in the following definitions, we are assuming schemes $S_1$, $S_2$ and the *LSPD* as implicit parameters of functions.

## 3.2 Derivation of Object Cluster Similarities

The following definition introduces the concept of object cluster.

**Definition 3.2.1.** Let $S$ be an E-R scheme and let $G(S)$ be the associated *SD-Graph*. An *object cluster* of $S$ can be a basic object cluster of $S$ or a derived object cluster of $S$. A *basic object cluster* is a subscheme of $S$ corresponding to a linear path in $G(S)$. A *derived object cluster* of $S$ is a subscheme of $S$ corresponding to a derived path in $G(S)$, that is, the union of two non-disjoint linear paths of $G(S)$.                                                                □

**Definition 3.2.2.** The *context* of an object cluster $C$ is defined as follows:

$$\begin{cases} oc\_cnt(C, 0) = \{y \mid (\exists x \in C)(y \in cnt(x, 0))\} \\ oc\_cnt(C, i) = \{y \mid ((\exists x \in C)(y \in cnt(x, i)) \land \\ \qquad\qquad \land ((\forall j)(0 \le j < i)(y \notin oc\_cnt(C, j))))\} \; for \; i > 0 \end{cases}$$

□

**Definition 3.2.3.** Given an object cluster $C$ belonging to the scheme $S$, for $i \ge 0$, define:

$$A\_oc\_cnt(C, i) = Att(S) \cap oc\_cnt(C, i);$$

$$E\_oc\_cnt(C, i) = \begin{cases} Ent(S) \cap oc\_cnt(C, 0) & for \; i = 0 \\ Ent(S) \cap \bigcup_{0 \le j \le i} (oc\_cnt(C, j)) \\ \qquad for \; i > 0 \; and E\_oc\_cnt(C, i-1) \ne Ent(S) \\ \emptyset & otherwise \end{cases}$$

□

Assuming, as we have done before, that input *SD-Graphs* are connected, we have the following result:

**Proposition 3.2.1.**
*Let $S$ be a scheme. Let $C$ be an object cluster of $S$. Then, for each $i > 0$,
$E\_oc\_cnt(C, i-1) \neq Ent(S)$ implies that $E\_oc\_cnt(C, i-1) \subset E\_oc\_cnt(C, i)$.*
*Proof.* Immediate.                                                                    $\square$

Among all the pairs of object clusters belonging to the two input schemes, we select a subset thereof, including cluster pairs that are interesting for the similarity analysis purposes. This subset is constructed by computing $\gamma_P(\gamma_C(S_1), \gamma_C(S_2))$. Functions $\gamma_P$ and $\gamma_C$ are as follows:

- *Function $\gamma_P$.* This function takes in input two sets of object clusters $CS_1$ and $CS_2$ and returns a set of *promising* pairs of object clusters; these are pairs $(C_1, C_2)$ such that $C_1 \in CS_1$, $C_2 \in CS_2$ and each entity of $C_1$ (resp., $C_2$) has at least one attribute $A$ such that for at least one attribute $A'$ of $A\_oc\_cnt(C_2, 0)$ (resp., $A\_oc\_cnt(C_1, 0)$), the similarity coefficient of $A$ and $A'$ is greater than the threshold $th_\eta$ defined in Table 2.1. More formally:

$$\gamma_P(CS_1, CS_2) = \{(C_1, C_2) \mid C_1 \in CS_1, C_2 \in CS_2,$$
$$((\forall E_1 \in Ent(C_1))(\forall A_i \in Att(E_1))(\exists A_j \in A\_oc\_cnt(C_2, 0))$$
$$(\langle A_i, A_j, f \rangle \in \eta_A(), f > th_\eta)) \wedge$$
$$((\forall E_2 \in Ent(C_2))(\forall A_j \in Att(E_2))(\exists A_i \in A\_oc\_cnt(C_1, 0))$$
$$(\langle A_i, A_j, f \rangle \in \eta_A(), f > th_\eta))\}$$

- *Function $\gamma_C$.* This function takes in input a scheme $S$ and returns a subset of its object clusters as follows:

$$\gamma_C(S) = \{BC_1 \cup BC_2 \mid BC_1, BC_2 \in \{\langle E_l, E_m \rangle \mid E_l, E_m \in S\},$$
$$BC_1, BC_2 \text{ not disjoint}\}$$

Recall that $\langle E_l, E_m \rangle$ denotes the *D-shortest path* between $E_l$ and $E_m$ (see Definition 2.2.2). Thus $\gamma_C$ returns the set of unions of two basic object clusters. Note that, since $BC_1$ and $BC_2$ may coincide, $\gamma_C(S)$ also returns basic object clusters.

The set of object cluster similarities $OCSD$ of schemes $S_1$ and $S_2$ is obtained as follows:

$$OCSD = \sigma_{oc}(\nu_{oc}(\Gamma_{oc}^\infty(\tau_{oc}(\gamma_P(\gamma_C(S_1), \gamma_C(S_2))), E\_Syn(SD) \cup \eta_A()), w_{oc}))$$

Here:

1. $\sigma_{oc}(T) = \{\langle C_1, C_2, f \rangle \mid \langle C_1, C_2, f \rangle \in T, f > th_{oc}(T)\}$, where $th_{oc}(T) = max(f_{max}^{oc} \times \varphi_{oc}, th_m^{oc})$, and *(i)* $f_{max}^{oc}$ denotes the maximum plausibility factor associated to tuples of $T$; *(ii)* $\varphi_{oc}$ is a coefficient, belonging to the real interval $[0, 1]$, used to tune up the threshold value; *(iii)* $th_m^{oc}$ is the minimum acceptable value for the plausibility coefficients associated to an object cluster similarity; values for $\varphi_{oc}$ and $th_m^{oc}$ are shown in Table 2.1;

2. $\tau_{oc}(OCP) = \{\langle C_1, C_2, 0 \rangle \mid (C_1, C_2) \in OCP\}$, that is, this function takes pairs of object clusters as the input and, for each of them, constructs a corresponding triplet; the plausibility value is initially set to 0, and is later modified by $\Gamma_{oc}^{\infty}$;

3. $\Gamma_{oc}^{\infty}$ denotes the fixpoint computation for the object cluster similarity derivation, and is defined as follows:

$$\begin{cases} \Gamma_{oc}^0(T, BS) = T \\ \Gamma_{oc}^i(T, BS) = \Gamma_{oc}(\Gamma_{oc}^{i-1}(T, BS), BS, i - 1) \qquad for\ i > 0 \end{cases}$$

As for other fixpoint computations defined in Section 2.4.2, we have the following :

**Proposition 3.2.2.** $\Gamma_{oc}^{\infty}(T, BS) = \Gamma_{oc}^{\overline{K}}(T, BS)$, *where* $\overline{K} = max(K(S_1), K(S_2))$.
*Proof.* Immediate. □

The base functor $\Gamma_{oc}$ takes in input *(i)* a set of triplets denoting object cluster similarities, *(ii)* a set of triplets denoting entity and attribute synonymies (used as a support during the computation of object cluster similarities) and *(iii)* a non-negative integer. It returns a set of modified object cluster similarity triplets, as follows:

$$\Gamma_{oc}(T, BS, i) = \left\{ \langle C_1, C_2, \beta_p^{oc}(BS, i, f, C_1, C_2, w_{oc}) \rangle \mid \langle C_1, C_2, f \rangle \in T \right\}, where$$
$$\beta_p^{oc}(BS, i, f, C_1, C_2, w_{oc}) =$$
$$\begin{cases} p(i) \times \zeta_{oc}(BS, C_1, C_2, i, w_{oc}) + [1 - p(i)] \times f \\ \qquad\qquad if\ \zeta_{oc}(BS, C_1, C_2, i, w_{oc}) \neq 0 \\ f \qquad\qquad otherwise \end{cases}$$
$$\zeta_{oc}(BS, C_1, C_2, i, w_{oc}) =$$
$$w_{\zeta}'(i) \times \delta(\mu_s(A\_Syn(BS), A\_oc\_cnt(C_1, i), A\_oc\_cnt(C_2, i)),$$
$$A\_oc\_cnt(C_1, i), A\_oc\_cnt(C_2, i), w_{oc}) +$$
$$(1 - w_{\zeta}'(i)) \times \delta(\mu_s(E\_Syn(BS), E\_oc\_cnt(C_1, i), E\_oc\_cnt(C_2, i)),$$
$$E\_oc\_cnt(C_1, i), E\_oc\_cnt(C_2, i), w_{oc})$$

Functions $\mu_s$ and $\delta$ have been already described in Section 2.3.2. Function $\nu_{oc}$ behaves similarly to functions $\nu$, $\nu_{syn}$ and $\nu_{tc}$ illustrated in Sections 2.3.2 and 2.4.2. Finally, weights $w_{\zeta}'(i)$ are as defined in Table 2.1.

## 3.3 A Complete Example

Consider schemes in Figure 2.7 and in Figure 2.9. *SD-Graphs* associated to them are represented in Figure 2.8 and in Figure 2.10, resp. Suppose that the $SD$ and the $HD$ associated to these schemes and derived in Chapter 2 are given. The Object Cluster Similarity Dictionary $OCSD$, associated to $PD$ and $AD$, is obtained by computing:

$$OCSD = \sigma_{oc}(\nu_{oc}(\Gamma_{oc}^{\infty}(\tau_{oc}(\gamma_P(\gamma_C(PD), \gamma_C(AD))), E\_Syn(SD) \cup \eta_A()), w_{oc}))$$

In order to simplify the presentation below, we shall refer to $\tau_{oc}(\gamma_P(\gamma_C(PD), \gamma_C(AD)))$ as $CPS$ and to $E\_Syn(SD) \cup \eta_A()$ as $BS$.

The first step of the computation consists in selecting promising cluster pairs by applying the function $\gamma_P$. Then, a fixpoint computation starts for determining the similarity degree of promising cluster pairs. In order to clarify the behaviour of $\Gamma_{oc}^{\infty}$, let us focus on clusters $Cl_1 = <Subordinate - Operates - Department>$ and $Cl_2 = <Employee - Works - Division>$.

$\Gamma_{oc}^0(CPS, BS) = CPS$; as far as $Cl_1$ and $Cl_2$ are concerned, $\Gamma_{oc}^0$ returns $\langle Cl_1, Cl_2, 0\rangle$. $\Gamma_{oc}^1(CPS, BS) = \Gamma_{oc}(\Gamma_{oc}^0(CPS, BS), BS, 0)$; as for $Cl_1$ and $Cl_2$, the value of associated plausibility coefficient is:

$$f = p(0) \times \zeta_{oc}(BS, Cl_1, Cl_2, 0, 1) + [1 - p(0)] \times f'.$$

Here we choose $p(i) = \frac{1}{(i+1)^3}$. Thus, if we set, $A\_Cl_1\_0 = A\_oc\_cnt(Cl_1, 0)$, $A\_Cl_2\_0 = A\_oc\_cnt(Cl_2, 0)$, $E\_Cl_1\_0 = E\_oc\_cnt(Cl_1, 0)$, $E\_Cl_2\_0 = E\_oc\_cnt(Cl_2, 0)$, we obtain:

$f = \zeta_{oc}(BS, Cl_1, Cl_2, 0, 1) =$
$\qquad w'_\zeta(0) \times \delta(\mu_S(A\_Syn(BS), A\_Cl_1\_0, A\_Cl_2\_0), A\_Cl_1\_0, A\_Cl_2\_0, 1) +$
$\qquad (1 - w'_\zeta(0)) \times \delta(\mu_S(E\_Syn(BS), E\_Cl_1\_0, E\_Cl_2\_0), E\_Cl_1\_0, E\_Cl_2\_0, 1).$

Recalling that $w'_\zeta(i) = 0.5$, for $i \geq 0$, we obtain:

$f = \zeta_{oc}(BS, Cl_1, Cl_2, 0, 1) =$
$\qquad 0.5 \times \delta(\mu_S(A\_Syn(BS), A\_Cl_1\_0, A\_Cl_2\_0), A\_Cl_1\_0, A\_Cl_2\_0, 1) +$
$\qquad 0.5 \times \delta(\mu_S(E\_Syn(BS), E\_Cl_1\_0, E\_Cl_2\_0), E\_Cl_1\_0, E\_Cl_2\_0, 1) =$
$\qquad 0.5 \times 0.56 + 0.5 \times 0.50 = 0.53.$

$\Gamma_{oc}^2(CPS, BS) = \Gamma_{oc}(\Gamma_{oc}^1(CPS, BS), BS, 1)$; as far as $Cl_1$ and $Cl_2$ are concerned, the value of the associated plausibility coefficient is $f = 0.125 \times 0.43 + (1 - 0.125) \times 0.53 = 0.52$.

This is the plausibility coefficient obtained at the fixpoint and the tuple $\langle Cl_1, Cl_2, 0.52\rangle$ is returned by $\Gamma_{oc}^{\infty}$. The function $\nu_{oc}$ performs the normalization phase; as for $Cl_1$ and $Cl_2$, after its application, we obtain $\langle Cl_1, Cl_2, 0.65\rangle$. The overall list of significant derived object cluster similarities is shown in Table 3.1.

## 3.4 Complexity Issues

In this section we discuss the complexity of the algorithm presented above. In particular, we show that it terminates in a number of steps which is polynomial in the number of input scheme objects.

If we denote by $n_1$ (resp., $n_2$) the number of objects belonging to the scheme $S_1$ (resp., $S_2$) and by $n$ the maximum of $n_1$ and $n_2$, we can enunciate the following result:

**Theorem 3.4.1.** *The worst case time complexity of deriving object cluster similarities is $O(n^{12})$.*

**Table 3.1.** Object Cluster Similarities relative to $PD$ and $AD$

| First Cluster | Second Cluster | Value |
|---|---|---|
| Town ↔ Born ↔ Subordinate ↔ Operates ↔ Department | Birthplace ↔ R_Birthplace ↔ Employee ↔ Works ↔ Division | 0.71 |
| Town ↔ Born ↔ Subordinate | Birthplace ↔ R_Birthplace ↔ Employee | 0.69 |
| Town ↔ Born ↔ Subordinate ↔ Operates ↔ Department | Project ↔ Plans ↔ Division ↔ Works ↔ Employee ↔ R_Birthplace ↔ Birthplace | 0.66 |
| Subordinate↔ Operates ↔ Department ↔ Prototype↔ Carries_Out ↔ Born ↔ Town | Birthplace↔R_Birthplace↔ Employee ↔ Works ↔ Division ↔ Project ↔ Plans ↔ Engineer | 0.66 |
| Town ↔ Born ↔ Subordinate ↔ Operates ↔ Department | Birthplace ↔ R_Birthplace ↔ Employee ↔ Works ↔ Division ↔ Produces ↔ Product | 0.66 |
| Subordinate ↔ Operates ↔ Department ↔ Prototype ↔ Carries_Out ↔ Born ↔ Town | Project ↔ Plans ↔ Division ↔ Works ↔ Employee ↔ R_Birthplace ↔ Birthplace | 0.66 |
| Subordinate ↔ Operates ↔ Department | Employee ↔ Works ↔ Division | 0.65 |

*Proof.*

- By Propositions 3.2.1 and 3.2.2 required iterations of $\Gamma_{oc}^{\infty}$ are $O(n)$.
- During each iteration, $\Gamma_{oc}^{\infty}$ computes similarities between object clusters. In the scheme $S_1$ it is possible to construct $O(n_1^2)$ basic object clusters and $O(n_1^4)$ derived object clusters; the total number of object clusters associated to $S_1$ is, therefore, $O(n_1^4)$. In the scheme $S_2$, the number of object clusters is $O(n_2^4)$. Hence, the number of similarities to be taken into account is $O(n^8)$.
- For deriving the similarity coefficient of each pair of object clusters a maximum weight matching algorithm, having a complexity of $O(n^3)$, is applied.
- For filtering significant object cluster similarities, a linear scan of the derived object cluster similarities is carried out. This costs $O(n^8)$.

The total complexity is therefore $O(n^{12})$.

□

It is worth pointing out that the actual number of cluster pairs taken into consideration in the computation of object cluster similarities is generally much lesser than the theoretical one. This observation is justified by the following considerations:

– unions of object clusters are taken into consideration only if involved clusters are not disjoint;
– the union of different pairs of basic object clusters can lead to the same
derived object cluster;
– the similarity associated to a pair of object clusters is computed only if it
is a *promising pair* (see function $\gamma_P$ in Section 3.2).

# 4. Extraction of Hyponymies and Overlappings

*This chapter is devoted to illustrate the algorithms for deriving the last two kinds of nominal properties we manage, i.e., hyponymies and overlappings. In particular in the first section we state the problem and present two algorithms for deriving these kinds of properties. The second section describes in full details the first algorithm by (i) presenting the general characteristics of the approach, (ii) illustrating technical details, (iii) describing how thresholds and factors have been tuned and, finally, (iv) presenting a complete example. The third section describes the second algorithm for deriving hyponymies and provides an example showing how it works.*

*The material presented in this chapter is taken from [95, 97, 88].*

## 4.1 Introduction

In Section 1.2.2 we have seen that:

- Given two entities $E_1$ and $E_2$, $E_1$ is a *hyponym* of $E_2$ (which is, in its turn, the hypernym of $E_1$) if $E_1$ has a more specific meaning than $E_2$. As an example, the entity *PhD_Student* is a hyponym of the entity *Student*. If $E_1$ and $E_2$ belong to the same scheme (resp., to different schemes) we say that $E_1$ is an intrascheme (resp., an interscheme) hyponym of $E_2$ and that $E_2$ is the intrascheme (resp., the interscheme) hypernym of $E_1$.
- Given two entities $E_1$ and $E_2$ an overlapping exists between them if there exist non-empty sets of attributes $\{A_{11}, A_{12}, \ldots, A_{1n}\}$ of $E_1$ and $\{A_{21}, A_{22}, \ldots, A_{2n}\}$ of $E_2$ such that, for $1 \leq i \leq n$, $A_{1i}$ is a synonym of $A_{2i}$.

Deriving hyponymies and overlappings is important in order for the (relative) semantics of input database schemes to be correctly reconstructed [97, 85, 21, 30]. For instance, [97, 30] show how reliable scheme object similarities can be obtained, once a set of hyponymy properties is available. In addition [97, 85, 83, 9, 30, 45] show how scheme integration can benefit of synonymies, distinctnesses, hyponymies and overlappings. The following example should serve to better clarify this last point.

Consider the schemes $S_e$ (Figure 4.1) representing an estate agency database, and $S_b$ (Figure 4.2), relative to a building agency (in the figures, *is-*

D. Ursino: Extr. and Expl. of Intensional Knowledge ..., LNCS 2282, pp. 71–85, 2002.

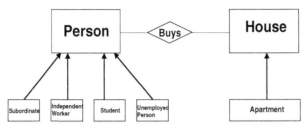

**Fig. 4.1.** Scheme $S_e$

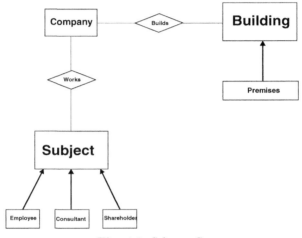

**Fig. 4.2.** Scheme $S_b$

a relationships[1] are represented by bold arrows and attributes are not shown for simplicity).

The application of a synonymy algorithm, such as that presented in Chapter 2 leads to the following results:

– *Person* of $S_e$ is synonym of *Subject* of $S_b$;
– *House* of $S_e$ is synonym of *Building* of $S_b$.

The techniques presented in the rest of this section allow to obtain the following further set of properties:

– Concerning the intrascheme hyponyms of *Person* in $S_e$ and *Subject* in $S_b$, the following relationships are derived:
  – *Subordinate* of $S_e$ and *Employee* of $S_b$ are synonyms;
  – *Consultant* of $S_b$ is a hyponym of *Independent Worker* of $S_e$;
  – all other intrascheme hyponyms of *Person* in $S_e$ and *Subject* in $S_b$ are distinct.

---

[1] In the E/R model an intrascheme hyponymy is represented by an *is-a* relationship from the hyponym to the hypernym.

- For intrascheme hyponyms relative to *House* of $S_e$ and *Building* of $S_b$ the following relationship is obtained:
  - *Apartment* of $S_e$ and *Premises* of $S_b$ partially overlap.

Therefore, in a global scheme integrating $S_e$ and $S_b$, the following decisions can be taken:

- there is a unique entity *Person* standing for *Person* of $S_e$ and *Subject* of $S_b$;
- there is a unique entity *Building* standing for *House* of $S_e$ and *Building* of $S_b$;
- there is a unique entity *Employee* standing for *Subordinate* of $S_e$ and *Employee* of $S_b$;
- entities *Consultant* and *Independent Worker* are both present; there is an *is-a* relationship from *Independent Worker* to *Subject* and an *is-a* relationship from *Consultant* to *Independent Worker*;
- attributes causing *Apartment* of $S_e$ and *Premises* of $S_b$ to overlap are merged and assigned to the entity *Building* substituting, in the integrated scheme, *House* of $S_e$ and *Building* of $S_b$; both *Apartment* and *Premises* are kept in the integrated scheme as specialized entities of *Building*, but without their overlapping attributes;
- all other specialized entities are present in the integrated scheme; there is no relationship between them.

The integrated scheme is as depicted in Figure 4.3.

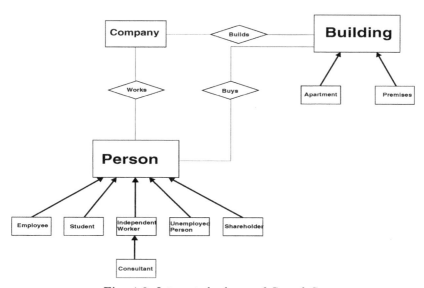

**Fig. 4.3.** Integrated scheme of $S_e$ and $S_b$

This example clearly illustrates how, for integration purposes, the availability of interscheme hyponymies and partial overlappings is as important as for the other properties which received much more attention in the literature.

In this chapter we shall describe two algorithms for deriving hyponyms and overlappings. The first one derives basic hyponymies and overlappings which are valid in a particular scenario. The second one uses hyponymies derived by the first algorithm and synonymies existing between scheme objects (derived using either the algorithms presented in Chapter 2 or any other approach proposed in the literature for deriving this kind of properties) for extracting more general hyponymies; however this last algorithm is not capable of deriving further overlapping properties.

## 4.2 Deriving Basic Hyponymies and Overlappings

Basic hyponymies and overlappings are those which can be derived in the following scenario. Consider a scheme $S_1$ and suppose that, here, $E_i$ is an intrascheme hyponym of $E_i'$. In addition, consider a scheme $S_2$ and suppose that it contains $E_j$ that is an intrascheme hyponym of $E_j'$. Finally, assume that $E_i'$ and $E_j'$ are synonyms. If all these conditions hold, $[E_i, E_j]$ is called a *candidate pair*. Now the question is: *Which relationship holds between $E_i$ and $E_j$?*

There are four kinds of relationships that may hold between candidate pairs $[E_i, E_j]$ and, consequently, four different decisions can be taken about the representation of $E_i$ and $E_j$ in the global scheme obtained from integrating schemes $S_1$ and $S_2$ (note that $E_i'$ and $E_j'$ will be represented, in the global scheme $S_{12}$, by a unique entity $E_{ij}'$). The four relationships possibly holding between $E_i$ and $E_j$ and the corresponding decisions are the following:

- $E_i$ *and* $E_j$ *are synonyms*: in this case the global scheme $S_{12}$ contains a unique entity representing both $E_i$ and $E_j$; this is a specialized entity of $E_{ij}'$.
- $E_i$ *and* $E_j$ *are distinct*: in this case both $E_i$ and $E_j$ are present in $S_{12}$; both of them are specialized entities of $E_{ij}'$ and no relationships hold between them.
- $E_i$ *is a hyponym of* $E_j$: in this case the global scheme contains both of them; $E_j$ is a specialized entity of $E_{ij}'$ and $E_i$ is a specialized entity of $E_j$. The opposite case (i.e., $E_j$ is a hyponym of $E_i$) leads to an analogous situation.
- *There are non-empty sets of attributes* $\{A_{i1}, A_{i2}, \ldots, A_{in}\}$ *of* $E_i$ *and* $\{A_{j1}, A_{j2}, \ldots, A_{jn}\}$ *of* $E_j$ *such that, for* $1 \leq k \leq n$, $A_{ik}$ *is a synonym of* $A_{jk}$ (we call the set of these attributes *overlapping attributes*). In this case the global scheme contains two entities $E_i''$ and $E_j''$, obtained from $E_i$ and $E_j$ by eliminating the overlapping attributes. Both $E_i''$ and $E_j''$ are specialized entities of $E_{ij}'$ and no relationship holds between them. Moreover, for each

$k$, an attribute $A_k$ is added to $E'_{ij}$ to represent both overlapping attributes $A_{ik}$ and $A_{jk}$ ($1 \leq k \leq n$).

The algorithms presented in this section identify which of the situation above holds for any given candidate pair.

### 4.2.1 General Characteristics of the Approach

The inputs to our approach are two schemes $S_1$ and $S_2$, and a *Starting Synonymy Dictionary* ($SSD$) storing similarities between all possible pairs of entities, relationships and attributes belonging to $S_1$ and $S_2$. The $SSD$ must be structured as a set of triplets $\langle O_i, O_j, f \rangle$, where $O_i$ and $O_j$ are objects of the same type belonging to different schemes and $f$ is a coefficient, in the real interval $[0, 1]$, denoting the plausibility of the property. This dictionary can be obtained from $S_1$ and $S_2$ by applying either the algorithms for deriving synonymies presented in Chapter 2 or any other approach for deriving synonymies presented in the literature.

Intuitively, for each candidate pair $[E_i, E_j]$, the algorithm implementing our technique carries out the following steps:

1. It verifies if $E_i$ and $E_j$ are themselves synonyms by checking for the existence of a tuple $\langle E_i, E_j, f \rangle$ in the $SSD$ such that $f$ is greater than a certain threshold. In the affirmative case, $E_i$ and $E_j$ are to be considered synonyms and the algorithm terminates; otherwise the second step is executed.

2. The algorithm takes into account attributes of $E_i$ and $E_j$ for computing a similarity degree $\overline{f}$ associated to them. If $\overline{f}$ is under a given threshold, $E_i$ and $E_j$ are to be considered distinct and the algorithm terminates; otherwise the third step is executed.

3. The algorithm verifies if $E_i$ is a hyponym of $E_j$ or vice versa. To this end, $E'_i$ (the intrascheme hypernym of $E_i$) and $E'_j$ (the intrascheme hypernym of $E_j$) are also considered. In particular, the algorithm constructs the set $AS_i$, containing the attributes of both $E_i$ and $E'_i$, and the set $AS_j$, including the attributes of both $E_j$ and $E'_j$; then, if all attributes of $AS_j$ are similar to the attributes of $AS_i$, but there is at least an attribute of $AS_i$ which is not similar to any attribute of $AS_j$, we conclude that $E_i$ is a hyponym of $E_j$. An analogous check verifies if $E_j$ is a hyponym of $E_i$. If $E_i$ is a hyponym of $E_j$, or vice versa, the algorithm terminates, otherwise the fourth step is executed.

4. The fourth step computes a further similarity degree for $E_i$ and $E_j$, taking together into consideration not only attributes of $E_i$ and $E_j$ but also attributes of $E'_i$ and $E'_j$; indeed attributes of $E'_i$ (resp., of $E'_j$) are to be considered also attributes of $E_i$ because $E_i$ (resp., $E_j$) is a hyponym of $E'_i$ (resp., $E'_j$) and a hyponym inherits all the attributes of its hypernym. If the resulting similarity degree is greater than a certain threshold, the

algorithm concludes that $E_i$ and $E_j$ partially overlap; otherwise $E_i$ and $E_j$ are to be considered distinct.

In order to decide which property holds between entities $E_i$ and $E_j$, a maximum weight matching algorithm is executed on some suitable bipartite graphs (for the definition of these graphs see, below, Section 4.2.2).

The output of our technique consists of dictionaries storing the relationships existing between intrascheme hyponyms. More specifically, the four dictionaries are:

- a *Dictionary of Synonymies between Intrascheme Hyponyms* (*IHSD*), including tuples of the form $\langle E_i, E_j, f_{E_i E_j} \rangle$ denoting that $E_i$ and $E_j$ are synonyms;
- a *Dictionary of Distinctnesses between Intrascheme Hyponyms* (*IHDD*), including tuples of the form $\langle\langle E_i, E_j, f_{E_i E_j} \rangle\rangle$ denoting that $E_i$ and $E_j$ are distinct;
- a *Dictionary of Hyponymies between Intrascheme Hyponyms* (*IHHD*), including tuples of the form $\lceil E_i, E_j, f_{E_i E_j} \rceil$ denoting that $E_i$ is a hyponym of $E_j$;
- a *Dictionary of Overlappings between Intrascheme Hyponyms* (*IHOD*), including tuples of the form $\| E_i, E_j, f_{E_i E_j} \|$ denoting that $E_i$ and $E_j$ partially overlap.

In all these properties $f_{E_i E_j}$ is a fuzzy coefficient, in the real interval $[0, 1]$, denoting the plausibility of the property.

### 4.2.2 Technical Details

Our technique takes two schemes $S_1$ and $S_2$ and a Starting Synonymy Dictionary (*SSD*) as the input and yields in output the four dictionaries *IHSD*, *IHDD*, *IHHD* and *IHOD*. In the following we will describe into details how each of these dictionaries is constructed.

*Constructing the Synonymy Dictionary.* First consider the following preliminary definitions:

- For any value $th \in [0, 1]$, let $SSD_{th} = \{\langle O_i, O_j, f \rangle \in SSD \mid f > th\}$.
- *CandS* denotes the set of candidate pairs of $S_1$ and $S_2$, i.e., the set of pairs $[E_i, E_j]$ such that *(i)* $E_i$ is an intrascheme hyponym of $E_i'$ in $S_1$, *(ii)* $E_j$ is an intrascheme hyponym of $E_j'$ in $S_2$ and *(iii)* the triplet $\langle E_i', E_j', f \rangle$ belongs to $SSD_{th_s}$.

Then the Dictionary of Synonymies between Intrascheme Hyponyms can be represented as follows:

$$IHSD = \{\langle E_i, E_j, f_{E_i E_j} \rangle \mid ([E_i, E_j] \in CandS) \wedge (\langle E_i, E_j, f_{E_i E_j} \rangle \in SSD_{th_s})\}$$

In plain words, $IHSD$ contains pairs of intrascheme hyponyms stored, in their turn, as synonyms in the $SSD$ and having a "high" plausibility coefficient; value of $th_s$, as well as values of other thresholds and weights introduced below, have been empirically tuned. All details of the tuning activity can be found in Section 4.2.3.

*Constructing the Hyponymy Dictionary.* In order to define the $IHHD$, we need the following preliminary definitions:

- $CandH$ denotes the set of candidate hyponym pairs and can be obtained as follows:

$$CandH = \{[E_i, E_j] \mid ([E_i, E_j] \in CandS) \wedge (\langle E_i, E_j, f \rangle \notin IHSD)\}$$

- Let $OS_1$ and $OS_2$ be two sets of objects and $TS$ be a generic set of triplets $\langle O_i, O_j, f \rangle$ such that $O_i \in OS_1$ and $O_j \in OS_2$. Then $\mu_{\langle TS, OS_1, OS_2 \rangle}$ denotes a matrix with a row (resp., column) for each object $O_i$ in $OS_1$ (resp., $O_j$ in $OS_2$) and $\mu_{\langle TS, OS_1, OS_2 \rangle}[O_i, O_j] = f$ if $\langle O_i, O_j, f \rangle \in TS$, $\mu_{\langle TS, OS_1, OS_2 \rangle}[O_i, O_j] = 0$ otherwise.
- The function $\delta(F, P, Q, \omega_v)$, already defined in Section 2.3.2, returns a factor obtained from computing the objective function of a maximum weight matching, as explained next. The input here are: *(i)* two sets of objects $P = \{p_1, \ldots, p_n\}$ and $Q = \{q_1, \ldots, q_m\}$, *(ii)* a weight matrix $F$ on $P$ and $Q$ such that, for each $p_i \in P$ and $q_j \in Q$, $0.0 \le f_{ij} \le 1.0$, and *(iii)* a coefficient $\omega_v$. The output is a value in the real interval $[0, 1]$. If $P = \emptyset$ or $Q = \emptyset$, then $\delta(F, P, Q, \omega_v)$ returns 0. Otherwise, let $BG = (P \cup Q, A)$ be a bipartite weighted graph, where $A$ is the set of weighted edges $\{(p_i, q_j, f_{ij}) \mid f_{ij} > 0\}$; the maximum weight matching for $BG$ is a set $A' \subseteq A$ of edges such that for each node $x \in P \cup Q$ there is at most one edge of $A'$ incident onto $x$ and $\phi(A') = \left( \sum_{(p_i, q_j, f_{ij}) \in A'} f_{ij} \right)$ is maximum (for algorithms solving maximum weight matching, see [41]). Now, let $\overline{\phi}(A') = \frac{\phi(A')}{|A'|}$. The value returned by $\delta(F, P, Q, \omega_v)$ is:

$$\delta(F, P, Q, \omega_v) = \left( 1 - \tfrac{1}{2}\omega_v \times \tfrac{abs(|P|-|Q|) + 2 \times (min(|P|, |Q|) - |A'|)}{|P|+|Q|} \right) \times \overline{\phi}(A')$$

In the formula above, the ratio denotes the fraction of objects unrelated in the constructed matching w.r.t. the total ones.
- The function $\delta'(F, P, Q)$ is analogous to the function $\delta(F, P, Q, \omega_v)$ but it computes the objective function of the corresponding maximum weight matching without taking into account the presence of arcs which do not participate into the matching. In particular, if we consider the definitions of $BG$, $A'$ and $\phi(A')$ introduced for $\delta$, the function $\delta'$ is defined as:

$$\delta'(F, P, Q) = \frac{\phi(A')}{|A'|}$$

- $Att(E)$ denotes the set of attributes of the entity $E$, whereas $AttH(E)$ denotes $Att(E)$ plus the set of attributes of $E$'s intrascheme hypernym.

- The set $\sigma_{\langle E_i, E_j \rangle}$ includes all triplets $\langle A_1, A_2, f \rangle$ in $SSD_{th_\alpha}$ such that $A_1 \in Att(E_i)$ and $A_2 \in Att(E_j)$; $th_\alpha$ is a threshold value in the real interval $[0, 1]$.
- The value $\delta_\sigma(E_i, E_j)$ is computed by determining the objective function associated to the maximum weight matching of a bipartite graph whose nodes are the attributes of $E_i$ and $E_j$ and whose edges have a weight equal to the synonymy coefficient existing between the corresponding attributes. In the computation of the objective function, the number of attributes which do not participate to the matching is taken into account:

$$\delta_\sigma(E_i, E_j) = \delta(\mu_{\langle \sigma_{\langle E_i, E_j \rangle}, Att(E_i), Att(E_j) \rangle}, Att(E_i), Att(E_j), \omega_v)$$

- The value $\delta'_\sigma(E_i, E_j)$ is analogous to $\delta_\sigma(E_i, E_j)$ except that, in the computation of the result, it considers only the attributes participating to the matching. More formally we have:

$$\delta'_\sigma(E_i, E_j) = \delta'(\mu_{\langle \sigma_{\langle E_i, E_j \rangle}, Att(E_i), Att(E_j) \rangle}, Att(E_i), Att(E_j))$$

- *PotH*, the set of potential interscheme hyponyms of $S_1$ and $S_2$, is defined as the set of pairs $[E_i, E_j]$ being candidate hyponym pairs and having a value of $\delta_\sigma(E_i, E_j)$ greater than a certain threshold. More formally *PotH* can be expressed as:

$$PotH = \{[E_i, E_j] \in CandH \mid \delta_\sigma(E_i, E_j) > th_l\}$$

where $th_l$ is a threshold value in the real interval $[0, 1]$.
- Let $AS$ and $AS'$ be two sets of attributes and $TS$ a set of triplets of the form $\langle A, A', f \rangle$, where $A$ and $A'$ are attributes and $f$ is a plausibility coefficient. Then $AS \subseteq_{TS} AS'$ if $(\forall A \in AS)(\exists A' \in AS')(\langle A, A', f \rangle \in TS)$. $AS \subset_{TS} AS'$ if $(AS \subseteq_{TS} AS')$ and $(AS' \not\subseteq_{TS} AS)$.

We are now in the condition of defining $IHHD$, as follows:

$$\begin{aligned} IHHD = \{&\lceil E_i, E_j, \delta'_\sigma(E_i, E_j) \rceil \mid \\ &((([E_i, E_j] \in PotH) \wedge (AttH(E_j) \subset_{SSD_{th_\alpha}} AttH(E_i)) \vee \\ &(([E_j, E_i] \in PotH) \wedge (AttH(E_i) \subset_{SSD_{th_\alpha}} AttH(E_j)))\} \end{aligned}$$

The rationale underlying this definition is the following. Given an intrascheme hyponym $E$, all attributes of $E$'s intrascheme hypernym are also attributes of $E$. $E_i$ is an interscheme hyponym of $E_j$ if all attributes of $E_j$ and of $E_j$'s intrascheme hypernym are similar to attributes of $E_i$ or of $E_i$'s intrascheme hypernym but at least one attribute of $E_i$ or of $E_i$'s intrascheme hypernym is not similar to any attribute of $E_j$ or of $E_j$'s intrascheme hypernym.

*Constructing the Overlapping Dictionary.* Also in this case, we need to introduce some preliminary concepts:

- *NHD* denotes the set of candidate pairs $[E_i, E_j]$ such that $E_i$ and $E_j$ are neither synonyms nor hyponyms. It is defined as follows:

$$NHD = \{[E_i, E_j] \mid ([E_i, E_j] \in PotH) \wedge (\lceil E_i, E_j, f \rceil \notin IHHD\}$$

- The set $\nu_{\langle E_i, E_j \rangle}$ includes triplets of the form $\langle A_1, A_2, f' \rangle$, where $A_1 \in AttH(E_i)$, $A_2 \in AttH(E_j)$ and either $(A_1 \in Att(E_i))$ or $(A_2 \in Att(E_j))$, and $f'$ is a coefficient derived from the (sufficiently high) synonymy coefficient associated to $[A_1, A_2]$ in the $SSD$. Formally:

$$\nu_{\langle E_i, E_j \rangle} = \left\{ \begin{array}{l} \langle A_1, A_2, f' \rangle \mid A_1 \in AttH(E_i), A_2 \in AttH(E_j), \\ (A_1 \in Att(E_i) \vee A_2 \in Att(E_j)), \langle A_1, A_2, f \rangle \in SSD_{th_\alpha}, \\ f' = \left\{ \begin{array}{ll} f & \text{if } A_1 \in Att(E_i) \wedge A_2 \in Att(E_j) \\ c_\nu \times f & \text{otherwise} \end{array} \right. \end{array} \right\}$$

Since synonymies involving an attribute belonging to an intrascheme hypernym provide a minor contribution to the final decision than those where both involved attributes belong to intrascheme hyponyms, the factor $c_\nu$ $(0 \le c_\nu \le 1)$ is used to normalize the corresponding coefficient.

- The value $\delta_\nu(E_i, E_j)$ is computed by determining the objective function associated to the maximum weight matching of a bipartite graph constructed from the attributes of $E_i$ and $E_i$'s hypernym, on the one hand, and of $E_j$ and $E_j$'s hypernym on the other hand. More formally we have:

$$\delta_\nu(E_i, E_j) = \delta(\mu_{\langle \nu_{\langle E_i, E_j \rangle}, AttH(E_i), AttH(E_j) \rangle}, AttH(E_i), AttH(E_j), \omega_v)$$

Therefore each pair of matching nodes represents a pair of synonym attributes; the set of attributes associated to pairs of matching nodes constitutes the *overlapping attributes*.

We are finally in the condition to define $IHOD$, as follows:

$$IHOD = \{ \| E_i, E_j, \delta_\nu(E_i, E_j) \| ) \mid$$
$$([E_i, E_j] \in NHD) \wedge (\delta_\nu(E_i, E_j) > th_d) \}$$

where $th_d$ is a suitable threshold value in the real interval $[0, 1]$.

*Constructing the Distinctness Dictionary.* The dictionary $IHDD$ is defined as follows:

$$IHDD = \{ \langle \langle E_i, E_j, 1 - f_{E_i E_j} \rangle \rangle \mid (\langle E_i, E_j, f_{E_i E_j} \rangle \in SSD) \wedge$$
$$((([E_i, E_j] \in CandH) \wedge ([E_i, E_j] \notin PotH)) \vee$$
$$((([E_i, E_j] \in NHD) \wedge (\| E_i, E_j, g \| \notin IHOD)))\}$$

Intuitively, $IHDD$ contains all candidate pairs $[E_i, E_j]$ such that $E_i$ is to be considered distinct from $E_j$. Since there are two kinds of entity diversities, the set $IHDD$ consists of two subsets:

- entity pairs $[E_i, E_j]$ such that they are yielded as candidate entity pairs by $CandH$ but they are completely distinct, i.e., their attributes are so different that the function $\delta_\sigma$ returns a value under a certain (low) threshold.
- entity pairs $[E_i, E_j]$ such that they are not completely different (as those contained in the first subset) but their overall similarity, computed taking into consideration also the attributes of their intrascheme hypernyms, is low enough that they can be considered neither synonym, nor hyponym, nor partially overlapping.

### 4.2.3 Tuning Thresholds and Factors

Our technique exploits some thresholds and weighting factors. In order to set and tune them we have carried out some experiments taking into account some sets of databases, which differ in various characteristics such as dimension, heterogeneity, application domain and so on. The most important of these consists of the set of the ICGO databases.

Final values for thresholds and weights thus obtained, which are shown in Table 4.1, have been validated by applying our algorithm to several ICGO databases and results obtained by our methodology have been compared with those produced manually by the "Italian Information System Authority for Public Administration" (AIPA). The application of the techniques proposed here to three databases of the ICGO is illustrated in Chapter 11.

**Table 4.1.** Values of thresholds and factors

| Threshold or factor | Value |
|:---:|:---:|
| $th_l$ | 0.25 |
| $th_d$ | 0.33 |
| $th_s$ | 0.52 |
| $th_\alpha$ | 0.55 |
| $th_\varphi$ | 0.6 |
| $c_\nu$ | 0.7 |
| $\omega_v$ | 2 |

### 4.2.4 A Complete Example

As the running example, we shall use scheme $S_e$ and scheme $S_b$, shown in Figures 4.1 and 4.2, resp. In particular we shall consider the fragments reported in Figures 4.4(a) and 4.4(b), resp. The first fragment includes entities *Apartment* and *House* such that *Apartment* is an intrascheme hyponym of *House*. The other one includes entities *Premises* and *Building*, such that *Premises* is an intrascheme hyponym of *Building*.

The $SSD$ is obtained by applying any algorithm proposed in the literature for determining synonymies between $S_e$ and $S_b$. In particular, by applying the algorithm described in Chapter 2, the following tuples are derived to constitute the $SSD$:

$\langle Street,\ Address,\ 0.88\rangle$      $\langle Code,\ Identifier,\ 0.88\rangle$

$\langle Engineer,\ Designer,\ 0.8\rangle$      $\langle House,\ Building,\ 0.74\rangle$

$\langle Street\ Number,\ Street\ Number,\ 1\rangle$      $\langle Year,\ Building\ Year,\ 0.8\rangle$

$\langle Size,\ Size,\ 1\rangle$      $\langle Value,\ Value,\ 1\rangle$

$\langle Owner,\ Owner,\ 1\rangle$      $\langle Tenant,\ Tenant,\ 1\rangle$

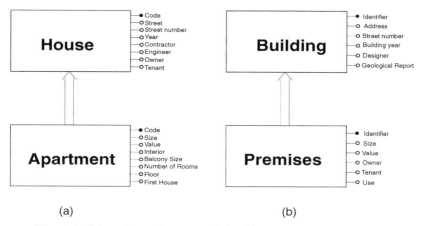

**Fig. 4.4.** (a) a scheme fragment of $S_e$, (b) a scheme fragment of $S_b$

Note, in particular, that the $SSD$ records the fact that *House* of $S_e$ is synonym with *Building* of $S_b$.

For our schemes shown in Figures 4.4(a) and 4.4(b), we obtain that:

$$CandS = \{[Apartment, Premises]\}$$

However, no tuple of the form $\langle Apartment, Premises, f \rangle$ belongs to $SSD$. Therefore the algorithm sets $IHSD = \emptyset$. Let us now verify if $\lceil Apartment, Premises, f \rceil$ (or $\lceil Premises, Apartment, g \rceil$) belongs to $IHHD$. We have that $CandH = \{[Apartment, Premises]\}$; we must then check if $[Apartment, Premises] \in PotH$. To this end, we must verify if $\delta_\sigma(Apartment, Premises) > th_l$; $th_l$ has been fixed to 0.25 (see Table 4.1). Note that $\sigma_{\langle Apartment, Premises \rangle} = \{\langle Code, Identifier, 0.88 \rangle, \langle Size, Size, 1 \rangle, \langle Value, Value, 1 \rangle\}$. Then:

$$\mu_{\langle \sigma_{\langle Apartment, Premises \rangle}, Att(Apartment), Att(Premises) \rangle} = \begin{pmatrix} 0.88 & 0 & 0 & 0 & 0 & 0 \\ 0 & 1 & 0 & 0 & 0 & 0 \\ 0 & 0 & 1 & 0 & 0 & 0 \\ 0 & 0 & 0 & 0 & 0 & 0 \\ 0 & 0 & 0 & 0 & 0 & 0 \\ 0 & 0 & 0 & 0 & 0 & 0 \\ 0 & 0 & 0 & 0 & 0 & 0 \\ 0 & 0 & 0 & 0 & 0 & 0 \end{pmatrix}$$

Therefore, we have:

$\frac{\overline{\phi}(A')}{|A'|} = \frac{0.88+1+1}{3} = 0.96$, and

$\delta_\sigma(Apartment, Premises) = \left(1 - \frac{1}{2} \times 2 \times \frac{2+2\times3}{14}\right) \times 0.96 = \frac{6}{14} \times 0.96 = 0.41$.

Since $\delta_\sigma(Apartment, Premises) > th_l$, $PotH = \{[Apartment, Premises]\}$.

Now, since *Apartment* has at least one attribute which is not similar to any attribute of *Premises* or *Building* and *Premises* has at least one attribute which is not similar to any attribute of *Apartment* or *House*, $IHHD = \emptyset$.

Next, we want to check if $\|Apartment, Premises, f\| \in IHOD$. We begin by verifying if $[Apartment, Premises]$ belongs to $NHD$. By the definition of $NHD$ we obtain $NHD = \{[Apartment, Premises]\}$.

Now $\delta_\nu(Apartment, Premises)$ must be computed and compared with $th_d$ (whose value has been experimentally set to $0.33$ – see Table 4.1). If it is greater than $th_d$, we shall conclude that $Apartment$ and $Premises$ partially overlap. $AttH(Apartment)$ (resp. $AttH(Premises)$) includes all the attributes belonging to $Apartment$ (resp., $Premises$) and to $Houses$ (resp., $Building$). Thus, we have:

$$\nu_{\langle Apartment, Premises \rangle} =$$
$$\{\langle Code, Identifier, 0.88 \rangle, \langle Size, Size, 1 \rangle, \langle Value, Value, 1 \rangle\} \cup$$
$$\{\langle Code, Identifier, 0.7 \times 0.88 \rangle\} \cup$$
$$\{\langle Code, Identifier, 0.7 \times 0.88 \rangle, \langle Owner, Owner, 0.7 \times 1 \rangle,$$
$$\langle Tenant, Tenant, 0.7 \times 1 \rangle\}$$
$$A' = \{\langle Code, Identifier, 0.88 \rangle, \langle Size, Size, 1 \rangle, \langle Value, Value, 1 \rangle,$$
$$\langle Owner, Owner, 0.7 \rangle, \langle Tenant, Tenant, 0.7 \rangle\}$$
$$\frac{\overline{\phi}(A')}{|A'|} = \frac{0.88 + 1 + 1 + 0.7 + 0.7}{5} = 0.86.$$

Thus, $\delta_\nu(Apartment, Premises) = 0.49 > th_d$. We therefore conclude that $\|Apartment, Premises, 0.49\|$ belong to $IHOD$; the overlapping attributes of $Apartment$ are $Code$, $Size$, $Value$, $Owner$, $Tenant$[2] whereas those of $Premises$ are $Identifier$, $Size$, $Value$, $Owner$, $Tenant$.

Observe that $\|Apartment, Premises, 0.49\| \in IHOD$ implies that neither $\langle Apartment, Premises, f \rangle$ belongs to $IHSD$ nor $\lceil Apartment, Premises, g \rceil$ is a tuple of $IHHD$ nor $\langle\langle Apartment, Premises, h \rangle\rangle$ belongs to $IHDD$. In fact, we have already verified the first two of these conditions. The third one can be easily checked by noting that $[Apartment, Premises]$ belongs to $CandH$, $PotH$ and $NHD$ and that $\|Apartment, Premises, 0.49\|$ belongs to $IHOD$.

## 4.3 Extracting Further Hyponymies

### 4.3.1 Description of the Approach

In this section we illustrate an algorithm that derives further hyponymies. The inputs to the algorithm are a set $S$ of schemes, a Synonymy Dictionary $SSD$ (derived using either the techniques presented in Chapter 2 or any other technique proposed in the literature) and a Hyponymy Dictionary $IHHD$, possibly derived by the algorithm presented in the previous section. The algorithm returns an enriched Hyponymy Dictionary.

In particular the Hyponymy Dictionary is constructed by a function $\gamma$:

$$IHHD = \gamma(\langle S, SSD, IHHD \rangle)$$

---

[2] Remember that attributes of $House$ are also attributes of $Apartment$.

The function $\gamma$ basically executes a fixpoint computation using a base function $\Psi$:

$$\gamma(\langle S, SSD, IHHD \rangle) = \pi_2 \left( \Psi^\infty \left( \langle SSD, \zeta(S, IHHD) \rangle \right) \right)$$

where $\pi$ is the usual projection operator.

The function $\zeta(S, IHHD)$ takes in input a set of schemes $S$ and a Hyponymy Dictionary $IHHD$, storing basic hyponymies holding between objects belonging to the schemes of $S$. The function enriches the $IHHD$ by adding a tuple for each intrascheme hyponymy holding in $S$; each added tuple has a plausibility coefficient equal to 1.

The fixpoint associated to the function $\Psi$ is defined as follows:

$$\begin{cases} \Psi^0(\langle SSD, HD \rangle) = \langle SSD, HD \rangle \\ \Psi^i(\langle SSD, HD \rangle) = \Psi(\Psi^{i-1}(\langle SSD, HD \rangle)) \quad \text{for } i > 0 \end{cases}$$

The functor $\Psi$ takes in input a Synonymy Dictionary and a Hyponymy Dictionary and enriches the latter one by deriving new hyponymy properties. It yields in output the Synonymy Dictionary, as it was received in input, and the Hyponymy Dictionary enriched with the new derived properties.

In order to comprehend the behaviour of $\Psi$ we observe that new properties can be obtained in one of the following cases:

– A hyponymy property holds from an entity $E_i$ to an entity $E_j$ and a further hyponymy exists from $E_j$ to $E_k$, in which case a hyponymy can be derived to hold from $E_i$ to $E_k$;
– A hyponymy property holds from $E_j$ to $E_k$ and a synonymy holds between $E_i$ and $E_j$, in which case a hyponymy can be derived to hold from $E_i$ to $E_k$;
– A hyponymy holds from $E_i$ to $E_j$ and a synonymy exists between $E_j$ and $E_k$, in which case a hyponymy can be derived to hold from $E_i$ to $E_k$.

It is worth pointing out that some hyponymies could be detected which have a low plausibility. Consequently, a filtering function is necessary for discarding those properties whose plausibility coefficient is under a certain threshold.

All observations above lead to the following formalization of the functor $\Psi$:

$$\Psi(\langle SSD, HD \rangle) = \langle SSD, HD \cup \xi_1(\langle SSD, HD \rangle) \cup \\ \xi_2(\langle SSD, HD \rangle) \cup \xi_3(\langle SSD, HD \rangle) \rangle$$

The function $\xi_1$ (resp., $\xi_2$ and $\xi_3$) manages the first (resp., the second and the third) case described above. It can be encoded as follows:

$$\xi_1(\langle SSD, HD \rangle) = \varphi(\theta_1(\langle SSD, HD \rangle))$$
$$\theta_1(\langle SSD, HD \rangle) = \{ \lceil E_i, E_k, \tau(f_{E_i E_j}, f_{E_j E_k}) \rceil \mid (\lceil E_i, E_k, f \rceil \notin HD) \wedge \\ (\lceil E_i, E_j, f_{E_i E_j} \rceil \in HD) \wedge (\lceil E_j, E_k, f_{E_j E_k} \rceil \in HD) \}$$

In the function above, for computing the coefficient associated to the new derived hyponymy, we use a fuzzy operator $\tau(\alpha, \beta)$. In particular the operator $\tau(\alpha, \beta)$ is a t-norm [37]. We recall that t-norms are dyadic functions from $[0, 1] \times [0, 1]$ to $[0, 1]$ that are monotonic, commutative and associative and have been used to define fuzzy set intersection. We shall restrict ourselves to the following t-norms:

$$\tau_1(\alpha, \beta) = max(0, \alpha + \beta - 1) \qquad\qquad exclusive$$
$$\tau_2(\alpha, \beta) = \alpha \times \beta \qquad\qquad independent$$
$$\tau_3(\alpha, \beta) = min(\alpha, \beta) \qquad\qquad inclusive$$

It can easily be shown that $\tau_1(\alpha, \beta) \leq \tau_2(\alpha, \beta) \leq \tau_3(\alpha, \beta)$ holds for $0 \leq \alpha, \beta \leq 1$, and so $\tau_1$ is the most "pessimistic" t-norm whereas $\tau_3$ is the most "optimistic" one. From experiments (see Section 4.2.3) we have determined that the most appropriate t-norm to be applied in the function $\theta_1$ (as well as in functions $\theta_2$ and $\theta_3$) is $\tau_2(\alpha, \beta)$.

The function $\varphi$ takes in input a set of triplets denoting hyponymies and discards the weakest ones. In more detail $\varphi$ discards all properties having a plausibility coefficient under a certain threshold. The function $\varphi$ can be encoded as follows:

$$\varphi(T) = \{\lceil E_i, E_j, f_{E_i E_j} \rceil \mid (\lceil E_i, E_j, f_{E_i E_j} \rceil \in T) \wedge (f_{E_i E_j} > th_\varphi)\}$$

Here $th_\varphi$ is a suitable threshold derived experimentally (see Section 4.2.3 for all details about these experiments).

Functions $\xi_2$ and $\xi_3$ manage the second and the third situation above and can be encoded as follows:

$$\xi_2(\langle SSD, HD \rangle) = \varphi(\theta_2(\langle SSD, HD \rangle))$$
$$\theta_2(\langle SSD, HD \rangle) = \{\lceil E_i, E_k, \tau(f_{E_i E_j}, f_{E_j E_k}) \rceil \mid (\lceil E_i, E_k, f \rceil \notin HD) \wedge$$
$$(\langle E_i, E_j, f_{E_i E_j} \rangle \in SSD) \wedge (\lceil E_j, E_k, f_{E_j E_k} \rceil \in$$
$$HD)\}$$
$$\xi_3(\langle SSD, HD \rangle) = \varphi(\theta_3(\langle SSD, HD \rangle))$$
$$\theta_3(\langle SSD, HD \rangle) = \{\lceil E_i, E_k, \tau(f_{E_i E_j}, f_{E_j E_k}) \rceil \mid (\lceil E_i, E_k, f \rceil \notin HD) \wedge$$
$$(\lceil E_i, E_j, f_{E_i E_j} \rceil \in HD) \wedge (\langle E_j, E_k, f_{E_j E_k} \rangle \in SSD)\}$$

It should be clear, from the definition of $\theta_1$, $\theta_2$ and $\theta_3$, that the derivation of a hyponymy at the step $i$ of the fixpoint could lead to the possibility of deriving new hyponymies at the step $i + 1$. Therefore the fixpoint terminates when, during one iteration, no new hyponymies are found. The number of steps of the fixpoint is polynomial in the number of scheme objects since the computation of the fixpoint is equivalent to the transitive closure of a suitable graph.

### 4.3.2 An Example

Consider schemes $S_e$ and $S_b$ shown in Figures 4.1 and 4.2. Suppose that *(i)* an entity *Manager* exists in a third scheme; *(ii)* the triplet

$\lceil Manager, Subordinate, 0.9 \rceil$ belongs to $IHHD$; *(iii)* the triplet $\langle Subordinate, Employee, 0.8 \rangle$ belongs to $SSD$. Let us consider how the function $\gamma$ works for enriching $IHHD$. Remember that:

$$IHHD = \gamma(\langle S, SSD, IHHD \rangle)$$
$$\gamma(\langle S, SSD, IHHD \rangle) = \pi_2(\Psi^{\infty}(\langle SSD, \zeta(S, IHHD) \rangle))$$
$$HD = \zeta(S, IHHD) = IHHD \cup \{ \text{ A tuple for each intrascheme}$$
$$\text{hyponymy relative to schemes into consideration } \}$$

Then, in order to obtain the result provided by $\gamma$, we must compute the fixpoint of $\Psi$. As for this computation, we obtain:

$$\Psi^0(\langle SSD, HD \rangle) = \langle SSD, HD \rangle$$
$$\Psi^1(\langle SSD, HD \rangle) = \Psi(\Psi^0(\langle SSD, HD \rangle)) = \Psi(\langle SSD, HD \rangle)$$

Suppose that the only interesting properties for the functor $\Psi$ are those indicated in *(ii)* and in *(iii)*. In this case we have:

$$\Psi(\langle SSD, HD \rangle) = \langle SSD, HD \cup \xi_1(\langle SSD, HD \rangle) \cup \xi_2(\langle SSD, HD \rangle)$$
$$\cup \, \xi_3(\langle SSD, HD \rangle) \rangle$$

$$\xi_1(\langle SSD, HD \rangle) = \emptyset$$
$$\xi_2(\langle SSD, HD \rangle) = \emptyset$$
$$\xi_3(\langle SSD, HD \rangle) = \varphi(\theta_3(\langle SSD, HD \rangle))$$

Since we have set $\tau(\alpha, \beta) = \tau_2(\alpha, \beta)$, the result of the function $\theta_3$ is:

$$\theta_3(\langle SSD, HD \rangle) = \{\lceil Manager, Employee, 0.72 \rceil\}$$

Since the plausibility coefficient associated to the triplet is greater than $th_{\varphi}$, the function $\varphi$ selects it as interesting. As a consequence we have:

$$\xi_3(\langle SSD, HD \rangle) = \{\lceil Manager, Employee, 0.72 \rceil\}$$
$$\Psi^1(\langle SSD, HD \rangle) = \Psi(\langle SSD, HD \rangle) =$$
$$\langle SSD, HD \cup \{\lceil Manager, Employee, 0.72 \rceil\} \rangle$$

This is also the final value obtained by computing the fixpoint of $\Psi$. Therefore the enriched $IHHD$, provided in output by the function $\gamma$, contains all tuples of the $IHHD$ taken in input, plus a tuple for each intrascheme hyponymy relative to schemes into consideration plus the tuple $\lceil Manager, Employee, 0.72 \rceil$.

# 5. Extraction of Assertions
# between Knowledge Patterns

*This chapter describes the extraction of assertions between knowledge patterns which allows the derivation of complex relations, holding among sets of objects, identified by particular view expressions defined on input schemes. The plan of the chapter is as follows: first we provide a general description of the approach. Then we introduce the language $DL_P$, which constitutes the formal framework for deriving and representing assertions. After that, we illustrate our approach as mainly consisting of three phases, each of which is described in a section of the chapter: the first phase is a pre-processing phase constructing some basic inclusion properties which are exploited in the following phases; the second phase singles out the most promising objects upon which assertions will be derived; finally, the third phase is devoted to the extraction of the assertions. After describing these three phases, we illustrate an example which clarifies the behaviour of the present technique and, in the last section, we discuss possible application domains which can benefit of the availability of assertions between knowledge patterns.*

*The material presented in this chapter has been derived from [16, 17, 18, 96, 19].*

## 5.1 General Characteristics of the Approach

The problem of understanding the intensional semantics of databases is an essential task for dealing with data management and utilization in the most appropriate way. In fact, the need for more generalized exploitation of intensional knowledge for describing data intensive applications, especially over multiple source data systems, is nowadays recognized. Recent papers point out such needs by discussing various aspects of using knowledge about database schemes in various application contexts, including accessing integrated and cooperative data resource systems [1, 32, 65, 120], query optimization and view maintenance [35], structuring of data warehouses and data constraints [27, 47].

Some of these papers put into evidence the need for the adoption of formal languages to describe and manipulate intensional knowledge about data. [32] proposes a logic formalism largely based on Description Logics (DLs) to express interscheme properties in cooperative database systems. [27] exploits an

D. Ursino: Extr. and Expl. of Intensional Knowledge ..., LNCS 2282, pp. 87–108, 2002.
© Springer-Verlag Berlin Heidelberg 2002

extension of the formalism of [32] with added expressiveness for representing and manipulating intra- and inter- scheme knowledge in the context of data warehousing applications. [120] discusses mediators for obtaining and filtering information from heterogeneous pre-existing data resources in integrated information systems; mediator capabilities are obtained using logic-based formalisms. For instance, the Information Manifold uses a particular Description Logic with Datalog-like rules [65].

A difficulty that is encountered while reasoning about intensional semantics of pre-existing databases is that, most often, the only available intensional knowledge consists of properties explicitly encoded in database schemes whereas many other useful properties are implicit, hidden within scheme structures and, as such, cannot be directly exploited.

In order to represent and manipulate intensional knowledge, we use a logic language, called $DL_P$, which is obtained by extending the language presented in [32] along two directions: first, besides expressing structural properties of object classes, most notably, class inclusions, our formalism allows also to express synonymies and homonymies between class names; second, each logic assertion is associated with a real number between 0 and 1, used to measure assertions' strength, in a way that will be explained shortly.

The presented approach does not make any particular assumption about manipulated database schemes, except that they are formalized using this same $DL_P$ formalism [96, 19] (even if, for the sake of readability, we will use the E/R model to represent them). We note that this is not a real limitation, since there exist translations from virtually all data models to $DL_P$ [32].

The adoption of a formalism derived from Description Logics is motivated by two main reasons. First, Description Logics are well suited for representing complex semantic properties of domains into consideration, and indeed we focus on complex semantic properties of database schemes. Second, DLs feature a precise formal inference system, which we take advantage of as the basis for deriving scheme properties.

Our technique takes in input a list of database schemes $S = S_1, \ldots, S_n$, a Synonymy Dictionary $SD$, storing synonymies between objects belonging to $S_1, \ldots, S_n$, and a Hyponymy Dictionary $HD$, storing intrascheme and interscheme hyponymies between objects belonging to $S_1, \ldots, S_n$. The Synonymy Dictionary can be obtained by applying the techniques presented in Chapter 2 whereas the Hyponymy Dictionary could be constructed by adopting the approach presented in Chapter 4; however other approaches proposed in the literature for deriving synonymies and hyponymies could be adopted.

The approach yields in output a Dictionary of Assertions between Knowledge Patterns $KPAD$. The structure and the semantics of the tuples stored in this dictionary are explained in Section 5.2.3.

The approach can be subdivided into three phases:

- *Phase 1*, in which an Inclusion Dictionary is constructed. The tuples of this dictionary represent inclusions between class instances (i.e., between real data). Each tuple has the form $\lfloor A, B, f_{AB} \rfloor$, where $A$ is the included class of objects, $B$ is the including class of objects and $f_{AB}$ indicates the percentage of objects of $B$ which are also objects of $A$ (the semantics of this coefficient is described in all details in Section 1.2.2).

– *Phase 2*, in which, for each database, the most interesting classes, i.e., those which semantically best characterize it, are determined. This phase is carried out by computing some weights assigned by an algorithm, which exploits the Synonymy Dictionary, provided in input, and the Inclusion Dictionary, constructed during Phase 1. The focusing phase is important since, in general, there exists a virtually infinite number of properties, which could be extracted; therefore it is crucial to single out most relevant objects so that, when complex properties are extracted, only the most significant ones are taken into account.

– *Phase 3*, in which assertions involving interesting classes, as identified in Phase 2, are derived.

## 5.2 The Language $DL_P$

For reasoning about database intensional properties, we use a particular Description Logic, called $DL_P$ [96, 19], which extends the logics presented in [32]. We implicitly assume that our input database schemes are represented in $DL_P$. This is not an actual limitation, since translations exist from all data models to $DL_P$ [32]. However, for the sake of the presentation, in the following discussion, we shall refer to Entity Relationship database schemes.

### 5.2.1 Preliminary Definitions

In our model the universe of discourse is partitioned into an *instance level* and a *class level*. Basic elements of the instance level are *objects*; these are atomic elements and are represented through a unique symbol identifying each of them. Generally objects are grouped into *classes*; objects of a class $C$ form the set of *instances* of $C$.

Associations between objects are expressed grouping them into *tuples*. The number of objects composing a tuple is called the *arity* of the tuple.

The class level, specified using a scheme, consists of a group of class symbols, called *alphabet*, and by some specifications about how classes are related to each other. More precisely, an alphabet is a list of symbols that represent entities, relationships, roles, attributes, values and domains.

An *entity* is an abstraction of a class of objects; objects constitute instances of the class. Properties of an entity are determined by its attributes and by relationships with other entities.

As previously mentioned, a *relationship* is a class of object tuples of the same arity; this is also the arity of the relationship. Tuples form the set of instances of the relationship.

A *role* represents a component of a relationship; therefore the number of roles of a relationship is equal to its arity. Each class participating in a relationship is associated with a role of the relationship and is called *filler* of this role. For example the relationship **Teaches** has two roles: **Teacher** and **Student**. Each tuple of the relationship has one component for each role of the corresponding relationship.

A *domain* is a set of values. Examples of domains are integers, strings, dates, reals etc. An *attribute* is a named relationship linking an entity or a relationship with a domain.

### 5.2.2 Syntax

**Syntax of the Language of [30].** The language is based on an alphabet $B$ of symbols including class names, the special symbols $\top$, $\bot$, $\sqcap$, $\sqcup$, $\exists$, $\forall$, plus usual parentheses.

A *class expression* is either an entity expression or a relationship expression.

An *entity expression* over the alphabet $B$ is constructed according to the following syntax:

$$
\begin{aligned}
C, F \longrightarrow{} & E| \\
& C \sqcup F| \\
& C \sqcap F| \\
& \neg C| \\
& \forall R[U].T_1 : C_1, ..., T_n : C_n| \\
& \exists R[U].T_1 : C_1, ..., T_n : C_n| \\
& \forall A.D| \\
& \exists A.D
\end{aligned}
$$

where $E$, $R$, $T_1$, ..., $T_n$, $U$, $A$, and $D$ indicate symbols of the alphabet $B$. In particular, $E$ is an entity name, $R$ is a relationship name, $T_1$, ..., $T_n$, $U$ are role names, $A$ is an attribute name and $D$ is a domain. Finally $C$ and $F$ indicate entity expressions.

A *relationship expression* is an expression of the form $R[U_1, U_2, \ldots, U_n]$ where $n$ is a nonnegative number, $R$ is a relationship symbol over the alphabet $B$ and $Rol(R) = \{U_1, U_2, \ldots, U_n\}$. Let $R$ be a relationship, $U \in Rol(R)$ and $r$ a tuple in $R$. Then $r[U]$ denotes the filler of the role $U$ in $r$.

Knowledge about scheme properties is expressed in such a logic in the form of assertions. An *assertion* is either a statement of the form $L_1 \leq L_2$ or a statement of the form $L_1 \doteq L_2$, where $L_1$ and $L_2$ are class expressions of the same type.

**Additional Syntactic Features Defined in $DL_P$.** $DL_P$ extends the language above by allowing three kinds of triplets:

- $\lfloor L_1, L_2, W_{L_1 L_2} \rfloor$, where $L_1$ and $L_2$ are class expressions of the same type and $W_{L_1 L_2}$ is a coefficient in the real interval $[0, 1]$;

- $\langle L_1, L_2, V_{L_1 L_2}\rangle$, where $L_1$ and $L_2$ are class expressions of the same type and $V_{L_1 L_2}$ is a coefficient in the real interval $[0, 1]$;
- $(L_1, L_2, Z_{L_1 L_2})$, where $L_1$ and $L_2$ are class expressions of the same type and $Z_{L_1 L_2}$ is a coefficient in the real interval $[0, 1]$.

### 5.2.3 Semantics

**Semantics of the Language of [30].** Language semantics is based on interpretations. An *interpretation* $I = (\Delta^I, .^I)$ consists of: (1) a non empty set $\Delta^I$, called *universe of I*, which comprises all domain objects, (2) a mapping $.^I$, called *interpretation function* of $I$. For each $I$, the interpretation function of $I$ assigns to each entity expression a subset of $\Delta^I$, according to the following rules:

$$\top^I = \Delta^I$$
$$\bot^I = \emptyset$$
$$(C \sqcap F)^I = C^I \cap F^I$$
$$(C \sqcup F)^I = C^I \cup F^I$$
$$(\neg C)^I = \{a \in \Delta^I \mid a \notin C^I\}$$
$$(\forall R[U].T_1 : C_1, ..., T_n : C_n)^I = $$
$$\{a \mid \forall r \in R^I.(r[U] = a) \Rightarrow (r[T_1] \in C_1^I \wedge ... \wedge r[T_n] \in C_n^I)\}$$
$$(\exists R[U].T_1 : C_1, ..., T_n : C_n)^I = $$
$$\{a \mid \exists r \in R^I.(r[U] = a) \wedge (r[T_1] \in C_1^I \wedge ... \wedge r[T_n] \in C_n^I)\}$$
$$(\forall A.D)^I = \{a \mid \forall (a, b) \in A^I.b \in D^I\}$$
$$(\exists A.D)^I = \{a \mid \exists (a, b) \in A^I.b \in D^I\}$$

The interpretation function of $I$ assigns a set of labeled tuples to each relationship expression as:

$$(R[U_1, U_2, \ldots, U_n])^I = R^I$$

where, if $R$ is a relationship with roles $\{U_1, U_2, \ldots, U_n\}$, $R^I$ is a set of labeled tuples of the form $\langle U_1 : u_1, \ldots, U_m : u_m\rangle$ and $u_1, \ldots, u_m \in \Delta^I$.

The semantics of the *assertion* $L_1 \leq L_2$ is given as follows:

- If $L_1$ and $L_2$ are entity expressions, the assertion is satisfied by an interpretation $I$ if $L_1^I \subseteq L_2^I$.
- If $L_1 = R_1[U_1, \ldots, U_n]$ and $L_2 = R_2[T_1, \ldots, T_m]$ are relationship expressions, then the assertion is satisfied in $m = n$ and for each tuple $\langle U_1 : d_1, \ldots, U_n : d_n\rangle$ in $R_1^I$, the tuple $\langle T_1 : d_1, \ldots, T_n : d_n\rangle$ is in $R_2^I$.

An assertion $L_1 \doteq L_2$ is satisfied if both $(L_1 \leq L_2)$ and $(L_2 \leq L_1)$ are satisfied.

An interpretation $I$ is called a *model* of a set of assertions $\Sigma$ if each assertion in $\Sigma$ is satisfied by $I$.

*Example 5.2.1.* Referring to a schema concerning the information about the organization of a conference, the two assertions:

$$((\exists\texttt{WrittenBy}[\texttt{Writer}]) \stackrel{.}{\leq} \texttt{Author})$$
$$((\exists\texttt{WrittenBy}[\texttt{Publication}]) \stackrel{.}{\leq} \texttt{Paper})$$

can be used to specify that the relationship `WrittenBy` is typed with the entity `Author`, in the role `Writer`, and with the entity `Paper` in the role `Publication`. Similarly, the assertion:

$$\texttt{ItalianPaper} \stackrel{.}{=} \texttt{Paper} \sqcap \forall\texttt{WrittenBy}[\texttt{Publication}].\texttt{Author} : \texttt{Italian}$$

can be used to define Italian papers as those papers whose authors are all Italian.

### Additional Semantic Features Defined in $DL_P$.

- Each triplet $\lfloor L_1, L_2, W_{L_1 L_2} \rfloor$ is associated to an inclusion assertion $L_1 \stackrel{.}{\leq} L_2$. Its semantics is as follows: provided that the inclusion $L_1 \stackrel{.}{\leq} L_2$ holds, $W_{L_1 L_2}$ represents the plausibility that the converse inclusion $(L_2 \stackrel{.}{\leq} L_1)$ (and, consequently, $(L_2 \stackrel{.}{=} L_1)$) holds as well. In other words $W_{L_1 L_2}$ represents the proportion of instances of $L_2$ which are also instances of $L_1$ (see Section 1.2.2).
- Each triplet $\langle L_1, L_2, V_{L_1 L_2} \rangle$ is associated to a synonymy property holding among class names. Its semantics is as follows: $\langle L_1, L_2, V_{L_1 L_2} \rangle$ indicates that a synonymy is believed to exist between the class name $L_1$ and the class name $L_2$; $V_{L_1 L_2}$ is a fuzzy coefficient, in the real interval $[0, 1]$, which expresses the plausibility of the assertion (see Section 1.2.2). Note that this property makes sense only if $L_1$ and $L_2$ are class expressions denoting classes belonging to different input database schemes.
- The semantics of $(L_1, L_2, Z_{L_1 L_2})$ is analogous to $\langle L_1, L_2, V_{L_1 L_2} \rangle$ except that it is associated to homonymy properties holding among class names.

In the following we suppose that triplets of the form $\lfloor L_1, L_2, W_{L_1 L_2} \rfloor$ form the *Dictionary of Assertions between Knowledge Patterns – KPAD*; analogously $\langle L_1, L_2, V_{L_1 L_2} \rangle$ and $(L_1, L_2, Z_{L_1 L_2})$ constitute the *Synonymy Dictionary – SD* and the *Homonymy Dictionary – HD*, resp.

## 5.3 Constructing the Inclusion Dictionary

The algorithm for constructing the Inclusion Dictionary receives a set of databases $D = D_1, \ldots, D_n$, whose schemes are $S_1, \ldots, S_n$, and a Hyponymy Dictionary $HD$ as the input and yields in output an Inclusion Dictionary $ID$.

   In order to comprehend the behaviour of the algorithm, it is worth pointing out that hyponymies are *intensional* properties, i.e., they are relative to schemes and to the meaning of objects in the schemes; vice versa inclusions are *extensional* properties, i.e., they are relative to instances of databases. A hyponymy from $A$ to $B$ indicates that $A$ has a more specific meaning than

$B$; as an example, an entity *PhD Student* is a hyponym of the entity *Student*. An inclusion of $A$ into $B$ indicates that all instances of $A$ are also instances of $B$; however some instances of $B$ could exist which are not instances of $A$. It appears clear from the discussion above that inclusions in fact correspond, at the extensional level, to hyponymies.

We are now able to explain how the algorithm for constructing the *Inclusion Dictionary* works. In particular:

− For each intrascheme hyponymy $\lceil E_i, E_j, 1\rceil \in HD$ it adds an inclusion $\lfloor E_i, E_j, Y_{E_i E_j}\rfloor$ to $ID$; $Y_{E_i E_j} = \frac{|E_i|}{|E_j|}$, where $|E_i|$ (resp., $|E_j|$) denotes the number of tuples of $E_i$ (resp., of $E_j$).
− For each interscheme hyponymy $\lceil E_i, E_k, W_{E_i E_k}\rceil \in HD$, it adds an inclusion $\lfloor E_i, E_k, Y_{E_i E_k}\rfloor$ to $ID$; if $\lceil E_i, E_k, W_{E_i E_k}\rceil$ belongs to $HD$, then one of the following cases holds (see Sections 4.2.2 and 4.3.1):
  − $(\lceil E_i, E_j, W_{E_i E_j}\rceil \in HD) \wedge (\langle E_j, E_k, V_{E_j E_k}\rangle \in SD)$; this is the case for basic hyponymies and hyponymies derived by the function $\xi_3$ described in Section 4.3.1;
  − $(\langle E_i, E_j, V_{E_i E_j}\rangle \in SD) \wedge (\lceil E_j, E_k, W_{E_j E_k}\rceil \in HD)$; this is the case for hyponymies derived by the function $\xi_2$ described in Section 4.3.1;
  − $(\lceil E_i, E_j, W_{E_i E_j}\rceil \in HD) \wedge (\lceil E_j, E_k, W_{E_j E_k}\rceil \in HD)$; this is the case for hyponymies derived by the function $\xi_1$ described in Section 4.3.1.

As far as the first situation is concerned, let $Y_{E_i E_j} = \frac{|E_i|}{|E_j|}$ be the percentage of instances of $E_j$ which are also instances of $E_i$ (obviously all instances of $E_i$ are also instances of $E_j$); analogously, let $X_{E_j E_k}$ be the number of instances of $E_k$ which are also instances of $E_j$; then an instance of $E_k$ can be an instance of $E_i$ only if it is also an instance of $E_j$ and it is among those instances of $E_j$ which are also instances of $E_i$. Therefore:

$$Y_{E_i E_k} = Y_{E_i E_j} \times X_{E_j E_k}$$

If we consider the definition of t-norms, illustrated in Section 4.3.1, we can conclude that:

$$Y_{E_i E_k} = \tau_2(Y_{E_i E_j}, X_{E_j E_k})$$

An analogous reasoning can be carried out for deriving $Y_{E_i E_k}$ in the second and in the third case listed above.

## 5.4 Singling out the Most Interesting Classes

This procedure exploits the information stored in $SD$ and $ID$ for associating an interest weight to entities and relationships of each input scheme. Indeed, in general, there may exists a virtually infinite number of properties which could be extracted; therefore it is crucial to single out the most relevant objects so that only the properties regarding them are extracted. In order to single out interesting entities, an interest weight, denoted by the function $\sigma(\cdot)$, is associated to entities and relationships.

The interest coefficient associated to a relationship $R_i$ is defined as:

$$\sigma_{R_i} = Val(R_i) + \sum_{p=1}^{n} Val(E_p)$$

where the $E_p$'s represent entities directly connected to $R_i$. The interest coefficient associated to an entity $E_i$ is defined as:

$$\sigma_{E_i} = Val(E_i) + \sum_{q=1}^{n} Val(R_q) + \sum_{t=1}^{m} Val(E_t)$$

where the $R_q$'s represent relationships directly connected to $E_i$ and the $E_t$'s represent entities linked to $E_i$ by an *is-a* relationship.

The function $Val(O_j)$ ($O_j$ can be an entity or a relationship) returns a value encoding the "local" interest of the class $O_j$ and is defined as:

$$Val(O_j) = \sum_{k=1}^{l} Max(W_{O_j O_k}, V_{O_j O_k})$$

where $l$ is the number of objects related in the dictionaries to the class $O_j$ by a synonymy property, an inclusion property or both[1]. The underlying assumption here is that the more a class is involved in properties appearing in dictionaries with high factors, the more probable is that this class will be used to extract new interesting properties from schemes.

In order to single out interesting relationships, an interest threshold value relative to relationships is used. The threshold value is defined as:

$$Th_{\sigma_R} = \frac{Min(\sigma_R) + Max(\sigma_R)}{\delta_R}$$

where $Min(\sigma_R)$ and $Max(\sigma_R)$ denote the minimum and the maximum interest coefficient we have computed, and $\delta_R$ is a normalization factor used to tune up the threshold: the smaller its value is, the more selective the threshold will be. All relationships with interest coefficient greater then $Th_{\sigma_R}$ are considered interesting. Interesting entities are singled out in an analogous way.

Our method proceeds by first populating the $KPAD$ with all tuples belonging to $ID$. Note that inclusions are particular assertions where each knowledge pattern (generally consisting of a class expression) is a class name.

Now, let $R_i$ be an interesting relationship. Let $C_1, \ldots, C_n$ be the entities connected to $R_i$ through roles $T_1, \ldots, T_n$, resp. Then, after the insertion of inclusions, our method tentatively populates the $KPAD$ with the triplets:

---

[1] Note that $W_{E_j E_k}$ and $V_{E_j E_k}$ are assumed to be equal to 0 if the corresponding property is not in the dictionary.

$$\lfloor \exists R_i[T_1].T_2 : C_2, ..., T_n : C_n, C_1, W_{Expr_1} \rfloor$$
$$\lfloor \forall R_i[T_1].T_2 : C_2, ..., T_n : C_n, C_1, W'_{Expr_1} \rfloor$$
$$\lfloor \exists R_i[T_2].T_1 : C_1, ..., T_n : C_n, C_2, W_{Expr_2} \rfloor$$
$$\lfloor \forall R_i[T_2].T_1 : C_1, ..., T_n : C_n, C_2, W'_{Expr_2} \rfloor$$

$$\cdots$$

$$\lfloor \exists R_i[T_n].T_1 : C_1, ..., T_{n-1} : C_{n-1}, C_n, W_{Expr_n} \rfloor$$
$$\lfloor \forall R_i[T_n].T_1 : C_1, ..., T_{n-1} : C_{n-1}, C_n, W'_{Expr_n} \rfloor$$

Note that, with our semantics, the plausibility coefficients associated to triplets shown above measure the proportion of instances of $C_j$ that are also instances of

$$\exists R_i[T_j].T_1 : C_1, \ldots, T_{j-1} : C_{j-1}, T_{j+1} : C_{j+1}, \ldots, T_n : C_n,$$

and

$$\forall R_i[T_j].T_1 : C_1, \ldots, T_{j-1} : C_{j-1}, T_{j+1} : C_{j+1}, \ldots, T_n : C_n.$$

Moreover, note that these assertions pertain to objects belonging to a single database $DB$. In order to associate them with proper inclusion coefficients, we proceed by first asking the database expert to state which of these assertions are meaningful and then by submitting a suitable aggregate query on $DB$ to get the coefficient associated to meaningful assertions (note that both the left-hand and the right-hand sides of the assertions above correspond to simple queries). An example of how the coefficient associated to an assertion can be determined by submitting aggregate queries can be found in Section 5.6. The resulting $DL_P$ assertions are stored in the $KPAD$. Note that all assertions derived in this phase are *intrascheme* assertions, i.e., assertions involving objects belonging to the same scheme. The techniques we are presenting below allow us to derive *interscheme* assertions, i.e., assertions involving sets of objects belonging to different schemes.

## 5.5 Discovering Complex Interscheme Properties

In this section, Phase 3 of our method is illustrated. As already mentioned, the general form of $DL_P$ assertions extracted by our method corresponds to formulae $L_1 \le L_2$ (see Section 5.2), to which an inclusion factor $f$ is associated to form a triplet $\lfloor L_1, L_2, f \rfloor$. Here, both $L_1$ and $L_2$ are class expressions. The Inclusion Dictionary contains properties where both $L_1$ and $L_2$ are simple entity symbols. The method we are presenting next derives properties in which $L_1$ and $L_2$ generally are complex entity expressions, and stores them in the $KPAD$. The method works by case analysis: each of the following subsections is devoted to the illustration of one of such inference cases.

### 5.5.1 Expressions Containing ⊓ and ⊔

Here, we consider the case in which $L_1$ is an intersection or a union between two subexpressions. To illustrate, assume the following properties were extracted in the preprocessing phase:

$$\lfloor A, \quad C, \quad W_{AC} \rfloor \quad \lfloor B, \quad C, \quad W_{BC} \rfloor$$

To establish the coefficient associated to the assertions

$$(A \sqcap B) \stackrel{.}{\leq} C \quad (A \sqcup B) \stackrel{.}{\leq} C$$

we reason as follows. First of all, note that there are two extreme situations to be considered:

– $A$ and $B$ are included either ways into one another, in which case the derived coefficients are:

$$W_{(A \sqcap B, C)} = min(W_{AC}, W_{BC}) \quad W_{(A \sqcup B, C)} = max(W_{AC}, W_{BC})$$

– $A$ and $B$ have minimal intersection, i.e., their symmetric difference is as large as possible[2], in which case we derive the following coefficients:

$$W_{(A \sqcap B, C)} = max(0, W_{AC} + W_{BC} - 1)$$
$$W_{(A \sqcup B, C)} = min(1, W_{AC} + W_{BC})$$

To obtain the general coefficient form, we compute the mean value between those extremal ones; thus, derived coefficients will be:

$$W_{(A \sqcap B, C)} = \frac{min(W_{AC}, W_{BC}) + max(0, W_{AC} + W_{BC} - 1)}{2}$$
$$W_{(A \sqcup B, C)} = \frac{max(W_{AC}, W_{BC}) + min(1, W_{AC} + W_{BC})}{2}$$

### 5.5.2 Expressions Containing ∃

Assume that relationship $R$ has been judged interesting, according to weights computed in Phase 2. Assume, moreover, that $R$ is connected to the entity $C_1$ through the role $T_1$ and to the entity $E$ through the role $U$. Finally, suppose that the assertion $\exists R[U].T_1 : C_1 \stackrel{.}{\leq} E$ holds. Then, using the knowledge stored in the dictionaries and analyzing the schemes, we infer some assertions obtained from $\exists R[U].T_1 : C_1 \stackrel{.}{\leq} E$. To this aim, assume that the following property is stored in the $KPAD$:

$$\lfloor \exists R[U].T_1 : C_1, E, W_{C_1 \exists E} \rfloor$$

Our derivation algorithm considers several cases, which are illustrated next.

---

[2] Note that there are situations where $A$ and $B$ "necessarily" intersects, e.g., with $\lfloor A, C, 0.9 \rfloor, \lfloor B, C, 0.9 \rfloor$

- **Case 1: There exists a subset property between an expression E'
  and the entity $C_1$**

  Suppose the assertion $\lfloor E', C_1, W_{E'C_1} \rfloor$ is stored in the $KPAD$, where $E'$
  is a generic $DL_P$ expression. Then, we infer the assertion $\lfloor \exists R[U].T_1 :$
  $E', E, W_{E' \exists E} \rfloor$ where $W_{E' \exists E} = 1 - min\left(1, \left[(1 - W_{C_1 \exists E}) \times \left(\frac{1}{W_{E'C_1}}\right)^\alpha\right]\right)$
  and $\alpha$ is a coefficient, which is used to normalize $W_{E'C_1}$ in the formula.
  The expression used to compute $W_{E' \exists E}$ is justified by the following observations:

  i) $W_{C_1 \exists E}$ indicates the proportion of instances of $E$ that participate in
  the relationship $R$ through tuples whose filler for role $T_1$ is an instance
  of $C_1$.

  ii) $(1 - W_{C_1 \exists E})$ corresponds to the proportion of instances of $E$ that do
  not participate in the relationship $R$ through tuples whose filler for
  role $T_1$ is an instance of $C_1$.

  iii) $min\left(1, \left[(1 - W_{C_1 \exists E}) \times \left(\frac{1}{W_{E'C_1}}\right)^\alpha\right]\right)$ represents the proportion of instances of $E$ that do not participate in the relationship $R$ through
  tuples whose filler for role $T_1$ is an instance of $E'$. Their number is,
  obviously, greater than the instances of point ii) above because $E'$ is
  a subset of $C_1$. Note that $\alpha$ is a coefficient which tunes the variation
  of $W_{E' \exists E}$ w.r.t. the corresponding variation of $W_{E'C_1}$.

  iv) $1 - min\left(1, \left[(1 - W_{C_1 \exists E}) \times \left(\frac{1}{W_{E'C_1}}\right)^\alpha\right]\right)$ represents the proportion of
  instances of $E$ that participate in the relationship $R$ through tuples
  whose filler for role $T_1$ is an instance of $E'$. And this is exactly $W_{E' \exists E}$.

- **Case 2: Entity F includes entity E**

  Suppose that the assertion $\lfloor E, F, W_{EF} \rfloor$ belongs to the $KPAD$. Then,
  the algorithm infers $\lfloor \exists R[U].T_1 : C_1, F, W_{C_1 \exists F} \rfloor$. The associated coefficient
  $W_{C_1 \exists F}$ is, in this case, simply equal to $W_{C_1 \exists E} \times W_{EF}$.

- **Case 3: Entity $C_1$ is included in entity $C_2$**

  Suppose that $\lfloor C_1, C_2, W_{C_1 C_2} \rfloor$ belongs to the $KPAD$. Then, the algorithm
  derives $\lfloor \exists R[U].T_1 : C_2, E, W_{C_2 \exists E} \rfloor$ where
  $W_{C_2 \exists E} = 1 - [(1 - W_{C_1 \exists E}) \times (W_{C_1, C_2})^\alpha]$. The expression used to compute
  $W_{C_2 \exists E}$ is justified by the following observations:

  i) $W_{C_1 \exists E}$ indicates the proportion of instances of $E$ that participate in
  the relationship $R$ through tuples whose filler for role $T_1$ is an instance
  of $C_1$;

  ii) $(1 - W_{C_1 \exists E})$ represents the proportion of instances of the entity $E$ that
  do not participate in the relationship $R$ through tuples whose filler for
  role $T_1$ is an instance of $C_1$;

  iii) $(1 - W_{C_1 \exists E}) \times (W_{C_1 C_2})^\alpha$ corresponds to the proportion of instances of
  $E$ that do not participate in the relationship $R$ through tuples whose
  filler for role $T_1$ is an instance of $C_2$. Since $C_2$ is a superset of $C_1$,
  the number of instances of $C_2$ is greater than the number of instances
  of $C_1$; hence, the number of tuples of $R$ whose filler for role $T_1$ is an

instance of $C_2$ is greater than the number of tuples of $R$ whose filler for role $T_1$ is an instance of $C_1$; consequently the number of instances of $E$ that do not participate in $R$ through tuples whose filler for role $T_1$ is an instance of $C_2$ should be smaller w.r.t. the number of instances of $E$ that do not participate in $R$ through tuples whose filler for role $T_1$ is an instance of $C_1$. Again, here $\alpha$ is a suitable coefficient, which tunes the variation of $W_{C_2 \exists E}$ w.r.t. the corresponding variation of $W_{C_1 C_2}$.

*iv)* finally, $W_{C_2 \exists E}$ is equal to $1 - [(1 - W_{C_1 \exists E}) \times (W_{C_1 C_2})^\alpha]$.

- **Case 4: R has more than one role**

Assume we have already derived the following assertions:

$$\lfloor \exists R[U].T_1 : C_1, E, W_{C_1 \exists E} \rfloor \qquad \lfloor \exists R[U].T_2 : C_2, E, W_{C_2 \exists E} \rfloor$$

where $T_1$ and $T_2$ are roles of the same relationship $R$. Suppose we want to single out the inclusion coefficient associated to the assertion $\lfloor \exists R[U].T_1 : C_1, T_2 : C_2, E, W_{expr} \rfloor$. Note that $DL_P$ expressions such as the one above, where two roles occur in the selection part, are equivalent to intersection expressions, as those treated is Section 5.5.1 and, therefore, we can use the reasoning shown there to set:

$$W_{expr} = \frac{min\big(W_{C_1 \exists E}, W_{C_2 \exists E}\big) + max\big(0, W_{C_1 \exists E} + W_{C_2 \exists E} - 1\big)}{2}$$

### 5.5.3 Expressions Containing $\forall$

Assume that relationship $R$ has been judged interesting, according to weights computed in Phase 2. Assume $R$ is connected to entity $C_1$ through role $T_1$ and to entity $E$ through role $U$. Furthermore, assume that the assertion $\forall R[U].T_1 : C_1 \le E$ holds. Assume, finally, that the $KPAD$ stores the assertion $\lfloor \forall R[U].T_1 : C_1, E, W_{C_1 \forall E} \rfloor$. Again, we proceed by case analysis, as follows.

- **Case 1: There exists a subset property between an expression E' and the entity $C_1$**

Suppose that the property $\lfloor E', C_1, W_{E'C_1} \rfloor$ is stored in the $KPAD$, where $E'$ is a generic $DL_P$ expression. From this, we infer the triplet $\lfloor \forall R[U].T_1 : E', E, W_{E' \forall E} \rfloor$ where $W_{E' \forall E} = W_{C_1 \forall E} \times (W_{E'C_1})^\mu$ and $\mu$ is the average number of fillers of the role $T_1$ in $R$.

As usual the difficult part of the derivation process consists in associating an appropriate coefficient to the assertion. In this case the adopted formula is based on the following observations:

*i)* Consider $\lfloor \forall R[U].T_1 : C_1, E, W_{C_1 \forall E} \rfloor$; the plausibility coefficient corresponds to the proportion of instances of $E$ participating in the relationship $R$ and associated, through role $T_1$, only to instances of $C_1$.

*ii)* Consider $\lfloor \forall R[U].T_1 : E', E, W_{E' \forall E} \rfloor$; the plausibility coefficient denotes the proportion of instances of $E$ participating in the relationship

$R$ and associated, through role $T_1$, only to instances of $E'$. Therefore all instances of $E$ participating in the relationship $R$ and associated, through role $T_1$, to instances of $C_1$ which are not instances of $E'$, are taken into account in *(i)* but are not considered in *ii)*.

*iii)* Say $\mu$ is the average number of fillers of the role $T_1$ in $R$. Consider an instance $e_1$ of $E$ which is filler of $U$ in $R$; suppose that all the corresponding $\mu$ fillers of $T_1$ belong to $C_1$ (therefore $e_1$ contributes to the value of $W_{C_1 \forall E}$); $e_1$ contributes to the value of $W_{E' \forall E}$ only if the $\mu$ fillers of $T_1$ belonging to $C_1$ belong also to $E'$. The probability for this to happen is $(W_{E' C_1})^{\mu}$.

The derived coefficient is then $W_{E' \forall E} = W_{C_1 \forall E} \times (W_{E' C_1})^{\mu}$.

- **Case 2: Entity F includes entity E**
  In this case the corresponding rule for $\exists$ can be applied.
- **Case 3: The expression has two roles**
  In this case the corresponding rule for $\exists$ can be applied.
- **Case 4: E is a complex expression**
  In this case the corresponding rule for $\exists$ can be applied.

### 5.5.4 Computing Complex Expressions

Assume that $E$ is a complex expression (i.e., not an entity symbol) and $A$ and $C$ are simple or complex expressions. Suppose that the following properties have been already derived:

$$\lfloor A, \quad C, \quad W_{AC} \rfloor \quad \lfloor E, \quad C, \quad W_{EC} \rfloor$$

Now, if $W_{AC} < W_{EC}$, the plausibility coefficient corresponding to the expression $\lfloor A, E, W_{AE} \rfloor$ can be evaluated. For determining $W_{AE}$, we again analyze two extreme cases:

- the subsets $A$ and $E$ have minimal intersection, in which case the coefficient $W_{AE}$ is:
$$W_{AE} = \frac{max(0, W_{AC} + W_{EC} - 1)}{max(W_{AC}, W_{EC})}$$

- the two subsets $A$ and $E$ are included into one another in either ways, in which case we infer:
$$W_{AE} = \frac{min(W_{AC}, W_{EC})}{max(W_{AC}, W_{EC})}$$

We proceed as we have done before and take the mean value between the two values above as the value for $W_{AE}$:

$$W_{AE} = \frac{max(0, W_{AC} + W_{EC} - 1) + min(W_{AC}, W_{EC})}{2 \times max(W_{AC}, W_{EC})}$$

### 5.5.5 Negation

In DLs, the negation of a class represents all the instances of the domain which are not instances of that class (see Section 5.2.3). In order to preserve evaluation safety, we shall avoid computing complements w.r.t. the entire domain and, therefore, we shall evaluate negation by intersection with one of the superset classes. Thus, properties for negation of a class can be derived only if an inclusion property concerning that class exists. Assume, then, that the $KPAD$ includes the triplet $\lfloor B, A, W_{BA} \rfloor$. Then, our algorithm infers $\lfloor \neg B, A, (1 - W_{BA}) \rfloor$. Once the coefficient for $\neg B \leq A$ has been derived, $\neg B$ can be handled as any other subset of $A$ for the purpose of deriving other complex properties.

### 5.5.6 Discarding Weak or Repeated Assertions

Once assertions have been derived a validation phase must be carried out for checking for the presence of weak or repeated properties. In order to determine weak assertions a threshold must be dynamically computed and all properties having a coefficient lesser than the threshold must be discarded. If a pair of repeated assertions exists that having the weakest plausibility coefficient must be discarded from the $KPAD$.

## 5.6 A Complete Example

*Example 5.6.1.* Consider the schemes in Figures 5.1 and 5.2, representing the Production (denoted PD) and Administration (denoted AD) Departments of an organization, respectively.

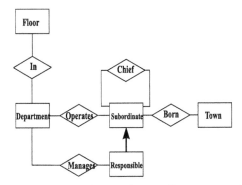

**Fig. 5.1.** Scheme PD: The Production Department database

By applying to these schemes the approach described in Chapter 2, the following Synonymy Dictionary is derived:

$\langle \text{Department}_{[PD]}, \text{Division}_{[AD]}, 0.57 \rangle$    $\langle \text{Town}_{[PD]}, \text{BirthPlace}_{[AD]}, 0.98 \rangle$

$\langle \text{Subordinate}_{[PD]}, \text{Employee}_{[AD]}, 0.74 \rangle$    $\langle \text{Operates}_{[PD]}, \text{Works}_{[AD]}, 0.57 \rangle$

$\langle \text{Born}_{[PD]}, \text{Born}_{[AD]}, 0.97 \rangle$    $\langle \text{Chief}_{[PD]}, \text{Manager}_{[AD]}, 0.73 \rangle$

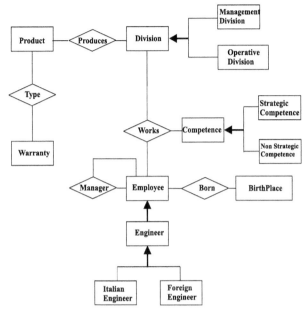

**Fig. 5.2.** Scheme AD: The Administration Department database

The algorithm for constructing an Inclusion Dictionary returns the following $ID$:

$$\lfloor \text{Engineer}_{[AD]}, \text{Subordinate}_{[PD]}, 0.35 \rfloor$$
$$\lfloor \text{Responsible}_{[PD]}, \text{Employee}_{[AD]}, 0.21 \rfloor$$

Interest coefficients associated to entities and relationships of schemes are:

$$
\begin{aligned}
\sigma_{In_{[PD]}} &= Val(\text{Floor}_{[PD]}) + Val(\text{In}_{[PD]}) + \\
&\quad Val(\text{Department}_{[PD]}) &= 0.95 \\
\sigma_{Operates_{[PD]}} &= Val(\text{Department}_{[PD]}) + Val(\text{Operates}_{[PD]}) + \\
&\quad Val(\text{Subordinate}_{[PD]}) &= 3.41 \\
\sigma_{Manages_{[PD]}} &= Val(\text{Department}_{[PD]}) + Val(\text{Manages}_{[PD]}) + \\
&\quad Val(\text{Responsible}_{[PD]}) &= 1.92 \\
\sigma_{Born_{[PD]}} &= Val(\text{Subordinate}_{[PD]}) + Val(\text{Born}_{[PD]}) + \\
&\quad Val(\text{Town}_{[PD]}) &= 3.67 \\
\sigma_{Type_{[AD]}} &= Val(\text{Product}_{[AD]}) + Val(\text{Type}_{[AD]}) + \\
&\quad Val(\text{Warranty}_{[AD]}) &= 0 \\
\sigma_{Produces_{[AD]}} &= Val(\text{Product}_{[AD]}) + Val(\text{Produces}_{[AD]}) + \\
&\quad Val(\text{Division}_{[AD]}) &= 1.95 \\
\sigma_{Works_{[AD]}} &= Val(\text{Employee}_{[AD]}) + Val(\text{Works}_{[AD]}) + \\
&\quad Val(\text{Division}_{[AD]}) + Val(\text{Competence}_{[AD]}) &= 5.61 \\
\sigma_{Born_{[AD]}} &= Val(\text{Employee}_{[AD]}) + Val(\text{Born}_{[AD]}) + \\
&\quad Val(\text{BirthPlace}_{[AD]}) &= 3.87 \\
\sigma_{Floor_{[PD]}} &= Val(\text{Floor}_{[PD]}) + Val(\text{In}_{[PD]}) &= 0 \\
\sigma_{Department_{[PD]}} &= Val(\text{In}_{[PD]}) + Val(\text{Operates}_{[PD]}) + \\
&\quad Val(\text{Department}_{[PD]}) + \\
&\quad Val(\text{Manages}_{[PD]}) &= 1.74
\end{aligned}
$$

$$
\begin{aligned}
\sigma_{Subordinate_{[PD]}} &= Val(\text{Chief}_{[PD]}) + Val(\text{Operates}_{[PD]}) + \\
&\quad Val(\text{Born}_{[PD]}) + \\
&\quad Val(\text{Subordinate}_{[PD]}) + \\
&\quad Val(\text{Responsible}_{[PD]}) &= 5.58 \\
\sigma_{Responsible_{[PD]}} &= Val(\text{Responsible}_{[PD]}) + \\
&\quad Val(\text{Subordinate}_{[PD]}) + \\
&\quad Val(\text{Manages}_{[PD]}) &= 2.64 \\
\sigma_{Town_{[PD]}} &= Val(\text{Born}_{[PD]}) + Val(\text{Town}_{[PD]}) &= 2 \\
\sigma_{Product_{[AD]}} &= Val(\text{Product}_{[AD]}) + \\
&\quad Val(\text{Produces}_{[AD]}) + \\
&\quad Val(\text{Type}_{[AD]}) &= 0 \\
\sigma_{Warranty_{[AD]}} &= Val(\text{Warranty}_{[AD]}) + Val(\text{Type}_{[AD]}) &= 0 \\
\sigma_{Division_{[AD]}} &= Val(\text{Produces}_{[AD]}) + \\
&\quad Val(\text{Division}_{[AD]}) + \\
&\quad Val(\text{Works}_{[AD]}) + \\
&\quad Val(\text{ManagementDivision}_{[AD]}) + \\
&\quad Val(\text{OperativeDivision}_{[AD]}) &= 3.74 \\
\sigma_{Competence_{[AD]}} &= Val(\text{Competence}_{[AD]}) + \\
&\quad Val(\text{Works}_{[AD]}) + \\
&\quad Val(\text{NonStrategicCompetence}_{[AD]}) + \\
&\quad Val(\text{StrategicCompetence}_{[AD]}) &= 2.79 \\
\sigma_{OperativeDivision_{[AD]}} &= Val(\text{Division}_{[AD]}) + \\
&\quad Val(\text{OperativeDivision}_{[AD]}) &= 2.65 \\
\sigma_{ManagementDivision_{[AD]}} &= Val(\text{Division}_{[AD]}) + \\
&\quad Val(\text{ManagementDivision}_{[AD]}) &= 2.25 \\
\sigma_{StrategicCompetence_{[AD]}} &= Val(\text{Competence}_{[AD]}) + \\
&\quad Val(\text{StrategicCompetence}_{[AD]}) &= 1.4 \\
\sigma_{NonStrategicCompetence_{[AD]}} &= Val(\text{Competence}_{[AD]}) + \\
&\quad Val(\text{NonStrategicCompetence}_{[AD]}) &= 1.6 \\
\sigma_{Employee_{[AD]}} &= Val(\text{Employee}_{[AD]}) + \\
&\quad Val(\text{Works}_{[AD]}) + Val(\text{Born}_{[AD]}) + \\
&\quad Val(\text{Engineer}_{[AD]}) + \\
&\quad Val(\text{Manager}_{[AD]}) &= 6.78 \\
\sigma_{Engineer_{[AD]}} &= Val(\text{Employee}_{[AD]}) + \\
&\quad Val(\text{Engineer}_{[AD]}) &= 4.04 \\
\sigma_{BirthPlace_{[AD]}} &= Val(\text{Born}_{[AD]}) + \\
&\quad Val(\text{BirthPlace}_{[AD]}) &= 2 \\
\sigma_{ItalianEngineer_{[AD]}} &= Val(\text{ItalianEngineer}_{[AD]}) + \\
&\quad Val(\text{Engineer}_{[AD]}) &= 3.07 \\
\sigma_{ForeignEngineer_{[AD]}} &= Val(\text{ForeignEngineer}_{[AD]}) + \\
&\quad Val(\text{Engineer}_{[AD]}) &= 2.27
\end{aligned}
$$

The threshold for relationships ($\delta_R$ set to 3) is:

$$
Th_{\sigma_R} = \frac{0 + 5.61}{3} = 1.85
$$

and, thus, the relationships Works$_{[AD]}$, Born$_{[PD]}$, Born$_{[AD]}$, Operates$_{[PD]}$, Produces$_{[AD]}$ and Manages$_{[PD]}$ are considered interesting. The threshold for entities is computed analogously ($\delta_E$ set to 3):

$$
Th_{\sigma_E} = \frac{0 + 6.78}{3} = 2.24
$$

Hence, the entities Employee$_{[AD]}$, Subordinate$_{[PD]}$, Engineer$_{[AD]}$, Division$_{[AD]}$, ItalianEngineer$_{[AD]}$, Competence$_{[AD]}$,

OperativeDivision[AD], ForeignEngineer[AD], ManagementDivision[AD] and Responsible[PD] are singled out as interesting. Two of the assertions tentatively selected to populate the $KPAD$ are:

$$\lfloor \exists \texttt{Born[NL].IN} : \texttt{Employee}_{[AD]}, \texttt{BirthPlace}_{[AD]}, \texttt{W}_{\texttt{Expr1}} \rfloor$$
$$\lfloor \exists \texttt{Born[IN].NL} : \texttt{BirthPlace}_{[AD]}, \texttt{Employee}_{[AD]}, \texttt{W}_{\texttt{Expr2}} \rfloor$$

The former assertion denotes the subset of employees born in at least one birthplace; it does not appear meaningful and will be probably discarded by the DBA. The latter assertion denotes the subset of birthplaces where at least one employee was born and appears semantically meaningful, and, thus, will not be discarded. Therefore, a plausibility factor must be associated to the latter assertion. To this purpose, the following aggregate intrascheme queries can be executed (SQL has been used for simplicity):

```
SELECT COUNT (DISTINCT E.BIRTHPLACE) AS A_ATT
INTO A_REL
FROM EMPLOYEE E
SELECT COUNT (DISTINCT B.BIRTHPLACE_CODE) AS B_ATT
INTO B_REL
FROM BIRTHPLACE B
SELECT A_ATT/B_ATT
FROM A_REL, B_REL
```

The query returns the ratio of the number of birthplaces where at least one employee was born over the total number of birthplaces. The ratio could be assumed as the plausibility factor of the assertion; obviously, the DBA is asked to validate or possibly tune it.

By applying the rules described in Section 5.5.1, the following new properties are derived and inserted in the $KPAD$:

$$\lfloor \texttt{Eingeneer}_{[AD]} \sqcap \texttt{Responsible}_{[PD]}, \ \texttt{Subordinate}_{[PD]}, \ 0.15 \rfloor$$
$$\lfloor \texttt{Eingeneer}_{[AD]} \sqcup \texttt{Responsible}_{[PD]}, \ \texttt{Subordinate}_{[PD]}, \ 0.50 \rfloor$$

Suppose, now, the following assertions have already been inserted in the $KPAD$:

$$\lfloor \exists \texttt{Born}_{[AD]}[\texttt{NL}].\texttt{IN} : \texttt{Employee}_{[AD]}, \texttt{BirthPlace}_{[AD]}, 0.98 \rfloor$$
$$\lfloor \exists \texttt{Manager}_{[AD]}[\texttt{ID}].\texttt{DI} : \texttt{Employee}_{[AD]}, \texttt{Employee}_{[AD]}, 0.3 \rfloor$$
$$\lfloor \exists \texttt{Works}_{[AD]}[\texttt{IL}].\texttt{DL} : \texttt{Division}_{[AD]} \sqcap \texttt{ManagementDiv}_{[AD]}, \texttt{Employee}_{[AD]}, 0.7 \rfloor$$
$$\lfloor \exists \texttt{Works}_{[AD]}[\texttt{IL}].\texttt{LC} : \texttt{Competence}_{[AD]} \sqcap \texttt{StrategicalComp}_{[AD]}, \texttt{Employee}_{[AD]}, 0.5 \rfloor$$
$$\lfloor \exists \texttt{Born}_{[PD]}[\texttt{NL}].\texttt{IN} : \texttt{Subordinate}_{[PD]}, \texttt{Town}_{[PD]}, 0.94 \rfloor$$

then the following assertions can be derived by applying the rules described in Section 5.5.2:

from Case 1:

$$\lfloor \exists \texttt{Born}_{[AD]}[\texttt{NL}].\texttt{IN} : \texttt{Engineer}_{[AD]}, \texttt{BirthPlace}_{[AD]}, 0.92 \rfloor$$

$\lfloor \exists \text{Born}_{[AD]}[\text{NL}].\text{IN} : (\text{Engineer}_{[AD]} \sqcap \text{Responsible}_{[PD]}), \text{BirthPlace}_{[AD]}, 0.56 \rfloor$
$\lfloor \exists \text{Born}_{[AD]}[\text{NL}].\text{IN} : (\text{Engineer}_{[AD]} \sqcup \text{Responsible}_{[PD]}), \text{BirthPlace}_{[AD]}, 0.92 \rfloor$
$\lfloor \exists \text{Born}_{[AD]}[\text{NL}].\text{IN} : (\exists \text{Manager}_{[AD]}[\text{ID}].\text{DI} : \text{Employee}_{[AD]}), \text{BirthPlace}_{[AD]}, 0.78 \rfloor$

from Case 2:

$\lfloor \exists \text{Born}_{[AD]}[\text{NL}].\text{IN} : \text{Engineer}_{[AD]}, \quad \text{Town}_{[PD]}, \quad 0.87 \rfloor$

from Case 3:

$\lfloor \exists \text{Born}_{[AD]}[\text{NL}].\text{IN} : \text{Subordinate}_{[PD]}, \text{BirthPlace}_{[AD]}, 0.99 \rfloor$

from Case 4:

$\lfloor \exists \text{Works}_{[AD]}[\text{IL}].\text{DL} : (\text{Division}_{[AD]} \sqcap \text{ManagDivi}_{[AD]}),$
$\qquad\qquad \text{LC} : (\text{Competence}_{[AD]} \sqcap \text{StratCompe}_{[AD]}), \text{Employee}_{[AD]}, 0.35 \rfloor$

Suppose now that also the following properties have been already stored in the $KPAD$:

$\lfloor \forall \text{Works}_{[AD]}[\text{DL}].\text{IL} : \text{Engineer}_{[AD]}, \text{Division}_{[AD]}, 0.4 \rfloor$
$\lfloor \forall \text{Works}_{[AD]}[\text{DL}].\text{IL} : \text{Subordinate}_{[PD]}, \text{Division}_{[AD]}, 0.5 \rfloor$
$\lfloor \forall \text{Works}_{[AD]}[\text{DL}].\text{IL} : (\text{Engineer}_{[AD]} \sqcap \text{Employee}_{[AD]}), \text{Division}_{[AD]}, 0.4 \rfloor$
$\lfloor \forall \text{Works}_{[AD]}[\text{DL}].\text{LC} : (\text{StrategicCompe}[\text{AD}] \sqcap \text{Competence}_{[AD]}), \text{Division}_{[AD]}, 0.7 \rfloor$
$\lfloor \exists \text{Chief}_{[PD]}[\text{DC}].\text{CD} : \text{Subordinate}_{[PD]}, \text{Subordinate}_{[PD]}, 0.4 \rfloor$

then the following assertions can be inferred and inserted in the $KPAD$ by applying the rules described in Section 5.5.3:

$\lfloor \forall \text{Works}_{[AD]}[\text{DL}].\text{IL} : (\text{Engineer}_{[AD]} \sqcap \text{ItalianEngin}_{[AD]}), \text{Division}_{[AD]}, 0.29 \rfloor$
$\lfloor \forall \text{Works}_{[AD]}[\text{DL}].\text{IL} : (\text{Engineer}_{[AD]} \sqcap \text{ItalianEngin}_{[AD]}), \text{Department}_{[PD]}, 0.28 \rfloor$
$\lfloor \forall \text{Works}_{[AD]}[\text{DL}].\text{LC} : (\text{StrategicCompe}_{[AD]} \sqcap \text{Competence}_{[AD]}),$
$\qquad\qquad\qquad \text{IL} : (\text{Engineer}_{[AD]} \sqcap \text{Employee}_{[AD]}), \text{Division}_{[AD]}, 0.25 \rfloor$
$\lfloor \forall \text{Works}_{[AD]}[\text{DL}].\text{IL} : \exists \text{Chief}_{[PD]}[\text{DC}].\text{CD} : \text{Subordinate}_{[PD]}, \text{Division}_{[AD]}, 0.03 \rfloor$
$\lfloor \forall \text{Works}_{[AD]}[\text{DL}].\text{IL} : (\text{Engineer} \sqcap \text{Employee}_{[AD]}),$
$\qquad\qquad \forall \text{Works}_{[AD]}[\text{DL}].\text{LC} : (\text{StrategicComp}_{[AD]} \sqcap \text{Competence}_{[AD]}), 0.36 \rfloor$

This latter assertion says that the proportion of divisions managing all strategical competences which are also divisions in which all working persons are engineers and employees is 0.36.

Taking into account all properties already derived, the following assertion can be inferred by applying the rules described in Section 5.5.4:

$\lfloor \exists \text{Born}_{[AD]}[\text{NL}].\text{IN} : (\text{Engineer}_{[AD]} \sqcap \text{Responsible}_{[PD]}),$
$\qquad\qquad\qquad \exists \text{Born}_{[AD]}[\text{NL}] : \text{IN} : \text{Subordinate}_{[PD]}, 0.52 \rfloor$

This assertion indicates that the proportion of towns, in which at least one subordinate was born, which are also birthplaces where at least one engineer who is also (project) responsible was born, is 0.52.

## 5.7 Application Domains

$DL_P$ assertions describing intensional knowledge concerning sets of database schemes have many applications, and all of them can profitably exploit assertions between knowledge patterns as those we have presented in this section. Applications include:

- the design of information integration layers, such as mediators, on the top of existing database systems, (see [96, 42, 65, 120, 126]), and, more in general, the development of tools for supporting the integrated access to Cooperative Information Systems [96, 32, 104];
- query optimization [19, 35] and view materialization [96, 35, 50];
- structuring and maintenance of warehouses and constraints [27, 47];
- the design of Web-based Information Systems.

In the following, we describe some examples of applications of complex pattern assertions to query optimization, view maintenance and Web-based Information Systems. The applications in the field of Cooperative Information Systems will be described in Chapter 7.

### 5.7.1 Query Optimization

Complex assertions can be exploited for the query optimization purposes. The key idea here is that queries can be expressed as Description Logics class expressions and that some relationships, again in the form of $DL_P$ assertions, can be found to hold between the class expression denoting a certain query and other ones; these expressions can be exploited for solving some queries in a simpler, optimized way. There are also situations where the result of a query is predictable without executing it. In the following, some example cases are presented to illustrate more precisely these ideas.

**Case 1.** Assume we want to retrieve all the objects belonging to either the class $A$ or the class $B$ or the class $C$, i.e., we want to execute the query:

$$Q = A \sqcup B \sqcup C$$

where classes $A$, $B$ and $C$ denote complex expressions. Suppose, moreover, that the assertion $\lfloor B, C, W_{BC} \rfloor$, has been derived and stored in the $KPAD$. In this case the query $Q$ can be reduced to $A \sqcup C$.

*Example 5.7.1.* Assume the query $Q = \mathtt{Italian} \sqcup \mathtt{Engineer} \sqcup \mathtt{Employee}$ must be executed. Suppose, moreover, that the $KPAD$ stores the assertion $\lfloor \mathtt{Engineer}, \mathtt{Employee}, 0.95 \rfloor$. Then, the previous query can be reduced to the simpler form $Q = \mathtt{Italian} \sqcup \mathtt{Employee}$.

**Case 2.** This case is analogous to the previous one. Consider the following query:

$$Q = A \sqcap B \sqcap C$$

where classes $A$, $B$ and $C$ denote complex expressions. Suppose that an assertion of the form $\lfloor B, C, W_{BC} \rfloor$ has been derived. In this case the previous query can be reduced to $Q = A \sqcap B$.

**Case 3.** The extraction of assertions may allow to remove redundant constraints. As an example suppose the following constraints have been defined for a database:

$$A \stackrel{.}{\leq} B \qquad\qquad\qquad A \stackrel{.}{\leq} C$$

Moreover, suppose that the $KPAD$ stores $\lfloor B, C, W_{BC} \rfloor$. Then the constraint $A \stackrel{.}{\leq} C$ can be removed, since it is redundant.

*Example 5.7.2.* Assume that the following constranints have been stored for a query:

$$\texttt{Engineer} \stackrel{.}{\leq} \texttt{Italian} \qquad\qquad \texttt{Engineer} \stackrel{.}{\leq} \texttt{EuropeanUnionCitizen}$$

If the $KPAD$ stores $\lfloor \texttt{Italian}, \texttt{EuropeanUnionCitizen}, \texttt{f} \rfloor$, the constraint $\texttt{Engineer} \stackrel{.}{\leq} \texttt{EuropeanUnionCitizen}$ is redundant.

**Case 4.** Suppose that the following assertions have been derived:

$$\lfloor \exists R[U].T_1 : C_1, A, W_{Expr1} \rfloor \qquad\qquad \lfloor \exists R[U].T_2 : C_2, B, W_{Expr2} \rfloor$$
$$\lfloor A, C, W_{AC} \rfloor \qquad\qquad\qquad \lfloor B, \neg C, W_{B \neg C} \rfloor$$

in particular the third assertion denotes that $A$ is a subset of $C$ with plausibility $W_{AC}$ whereas the fourth assertion indicates that $B$ is a subset of $\neg C$ with plausibility $W_{B \neg C}$. Suppose the following query must be executed:

$$Q = \exists R[U].T_1 : C_1, T_2 : C_2$$

In this case we can conclude that the result of $Q$ is empty, without any need to actually retrieve data.

*Example 5.7.3.* Suppose the following assertions belong to the $KPAD$:

$$\lfloor \exists \texttt{Works}[\texttt{DL}].\texttt{IL} : \texttt{Engineer}, \texttt{ManagementDivision}, 0.70 \rfloor$$
$$\lfloor \exists \texttt{Works}[\texttt{DL}].\texttt{IS} : \texttt{LowSalary}, \texttt{SecondaryDivision}, 0.80 \rfloor$$

the first one indicates that divisions in which at least one engineer works are a subset of management divisions with plausibility 0.70; the latter one denotes that divisions in which at least one person earns a low salary form a subset of Secondary Divisions with plausibility 0.80.

Suppose that the $KPAD$ also stores:

$\lfloor$ManagementDivision, StrategicalDivision, 0.98$\rfloor$
$\lfloor$SecondaryDivision, ¬StrategicalDivision, 0.95$\rfloor$

Finally, assume that the following query is to be executed:

$$Q = \exists \texttt{Works}[\texttt{DL}].\texttt{IL} : \texttt{Engineer}, \texttt{IS} : \texttt{LowSalary},$$

i.e., we look for divisions where at least an engineer earning a low salary works. Then, we can conclude that the result of the query is the empty set without actually executing it.

**Case 5.** Suppose that the following complex assertion has been derived:

$$\lfloor \exists R[U].T_1 : C_1, \bot, W_{Expr} \rfloor$$

and assume the following query must be executed:

$$Q = \forall R[U].T_1 : C_1$$

By noting that, clearly, the following assertion holds:

$$\lfloor \forall R[U].T_1 : C_1, \exists R[U].T_1 : C_1, 1 \rfloor$$

we can conclude that the empty set is the query answer. This result also holds for any query $Q$ such that an assertion of the form $\lfloor Q, \exists R[U].T_1 : C_1, W_Q \rfloor$ has been derived.

*Example 5.7.4.* Suppose that the assertion

$$\lfloor \exists \texttt{Works}[\texttt{DL}].\texttt{IL} : \texttt{Engineer}, \bot, 0.95 \rfloor$$

has been obtained, indicating that there are no divisions where at least one engineer works. If the query $\forall \texttt{Works}[\texttt{DL}].\texttt{IL} : \texttt{Engineer}$ is to be executed asking for divisions in which the personnel consists of engineers only, the empty set can be immediately yielded as the query result.

### 5.7.2 View Materialization

The availability of assertions between knowledge patterns can be used to decide a criterion guiding view materialization [35, 50]. For deriving a view materialization criterion the following reasoning can be drawn: suppose a complex query $B$, involving a great number of objects, must be executed; the result of its execution can be considered as a virtual view. Suppose, now, that another complex query $A$ must be executed. As usual $A$ and $B$ can be looked at as $DL_P$ class expressions. Suppose that the assertion $\lfloor A, B, W_{AB} \rfloor$ has been derived by our approach. Then, the view $B$ can be conveniently materialized and the query $A$ can be efficiently executed on the materialized view corresponding to $B$.

Obviously we cannot materialize all possible views, therefore the necessity arises of a criterion for determining which views are to be materialized. The problem is difficult because it is hard to figure out which queries are going to be executed in the future. However, we argue that the greater the number of assertions in which a given expression $E$ appears as a superset is, the higher the probability of answering queries exploiting the view corresponding to $E$ is. For a fixed given number of assertions in which $E$ appears, the greater the values of coefficients associated to $E$ are, the most convenient the materialization of views corresponding to $E$ is.

Therefore, we can define a materialization coefficient $M$ for each expression that appears as superset in the $KPAD$, as follows:

$$M(E) = \beta \times N_{Incl} + (1 - \beta) \times \sum_{i=1}^{N_{Incl}} W_{Expr_i}$$

where $N_{Incl}$ is the number of assertions where $E$ appears as the superset, $W_{Expr_i}$ represents the associated coefficients and $\beta$ is a factor used for tuning purposes. After determining the materialization coefficient of each expression, we set a materialization threshold, as follows:

$$Th_M = \rho \times (M_{MAX} + M_{MIN})$$

where $M_{MAX}$ is the greatest materialization coefficient we have computed, whereas $M_{MIN}$ is the smallest one and, as usual, $\rho$ is a tuning-up factor. Then, only views corresponding to expressions whose materialization coefficient is greater than the threshold, will be materialized.

### 5.7.3 Web-Based Information Systems

A further potential application domain of $DL_P$ formulae is advanced searching techniques for retrieving connected information among various web sources. Indeed, we argue that the semi-automatic derivation of assertions between knowledge patterns, such as those presented here, could be of interest for analyzing sources in the Web and for obtaining some form of "integration" among them.

In order to achieve these results the following steps should be carried out:

- extending our techniques for deriving basic synonymy and inclusion properties in such a way that they can operate with models, such as that described in [1, 79], capable to represent Web sources;
- deriving correspondences between models representing Web sources and $DL_P$ in order for them to be properly represented as $DL_P$ formulae;
- applying techniques described here to Web sources represented as $DL_P$ formulae.

These issues will be subject of our future research.

Part II

Construction of a Cooperative Information
System and of a Data Warehouse

This part of the dissertation aims at illustrating how interscheme properties derived by adopting the techniques illustrated in Part I can be exploited for constructing a Cooperative Information System (CIS) or a Data Warehouse (DW). Both the CIS and the DW architecture have a data repository as their core. The plan of the part is, therefore, as follows: Chapter 6 describes how a data repository can be constructed by exploiting the interscheme properties derived in Part I. The construction of a Cooperative Information System having a data repository as its core is described in Chapter 7. Finally Chapter 8 illustrates a three-level architecture of a DW which uses the data repository for storing information relative to the reconciled data level.

# 6. Construction of a Data Repository

*This chapter describes a methodology for the semi-automatic construction of a Data Repository using interscheme properties derived by techniques described in Part I. The plan of the chapter is as follows: in the first section we state the problem and describe the general characteristics of the approach. The second section is devoted to describe an Intensional Information Base used to support the various algorithms presented in the chapter, whereas the general framework for constructing the Data Repository is presented in the third section. The next three sections describe the three most important substeps of the Data Repository construction, i.e., scheme clustering, scheme integration and scheme abstraction. In all these sections we consider the construction of the Data Repository from an intensional point of view. In the final section of this chapter we present the Data Repository construction from an extensional point of view.*

*The material presented in this chapter has been derived from [28, 95, 91, 97, 85, 83].*

## 6.1 Introduction

A Data Repository is primarily intended to provide a global view of data owned by an organization using an integrated, comprehensible, accessible and usable structure. Generally speaking, data repositories allow to understand how information is organized in local databases and indicate how databases describe the same information or similar ones, pointing out differences or similarities and correlations among representations, in that being an effective reference for designing new applications which must use data already present in the available database systems [39, 6, 7, 9].

A Data Repository is constructed by first grouping database schemes into homogeneous clusters. Databases belonging to each cluster are integrated into a global scheme which is abstracted into a higher abstraction level scheme representing the cluster. This process is iterated over (higher level) schemes thus produced, to yield further higher level schemes. The process terminates when a sufficiently abstract scheme set (possibly consisting of one single scheme) is obtained.

D. Ursino: Extr. and Expl. of Intensional Knowledge ..., LNCS 2282, pp. 113–142, 2002.
© Springer-Verlag Berlin Heidelberg 2002

More formally, a repository consists of a hierarchy of clusters. Each cluster represents a group of homogeneous schemes and is, in its turn, represented by a scheme (hereafter called *C-scheme*[1]). The cluster hierarchy consists of several levels so that each cluster belongs to one level; clusters of level $n$ are obtained grouping some C-schemes of level $n - 1$;[2] clusters of level 0 are obtained grouping input database schemes. Therefore each cluster $Cl$ is characterized by: *(i)* its identifier C-id; *(ii)* its C-scheme; *(iii)* the group of identifiers of clusters whose C-schemes originated the C-scheme of $Cl$ (hereafter called O-identifiers) and *(iv)* a level index. Given a cluster $Cl$, we define O-schemes all schemes associated to O-identifiers of $Cl$. Clusters are classified as basic and derived. A *basic cluster* has level 0 and its O-schemes are input database schemes; a *derived cluster* is a cluster obtained grouping C-schemes representing other clusters.

It is clear, from the reasoning above, that the three fundamental operations for obtaining a Data Repository are:

- *scheme clustering*, which takes in input a set of schemes and groups them into semantically homogeneous clusters;
- *scheme integration*, which is devoted to producing a global conceptual scheme from a set of heterogeneous input schemes;
- *scheme abstraction*, which groups objects of a scheme into homogeneous object clusters and represents each cluster, in the abstracted scheme, with only one object.

To guarantee the data access transparency, the construction of the following structures is in order:

1. A global semantic dictionary (or metascheme) storing information about input schemes, the integrated global scheme, relations between input and global schemes, objects belonging to schemes, properties relating various objects etc.
2. A set of mappings storing transformations operated upon input schemes for obtaining the global integrated and abstracted scheme.

The global dictionary and the set of mappings are exploited in designing software layers (e.g., wrappers/mediators) needed to obtain actual access to local data in Cooperative Information Systems (see Chapter 7) or for obtaining data belonging to the reconciled data level in Data Warehouses (see Chapter 8).

Our method for the scheme repository construction is largely *automatic* since human intervention is limited to special cases; the involved algorithms are also *semantic* in that they consider object contexts and semantic relevance

---

[1] As for other schemes, also C-schemes are characterized by unique identifiers.

[2] Actually, in our architecture, clusters of level $n$ can be obtained grouping some C-schemes of any level $l \leq n - 1$ (see below).

and, in addition, they exploit semantic relations holding among scheme objects as encoded in a set of *interscheme properties* (see Section 1.2.2). These are assumed to be given; as a matter of fact they can be extracted from input schemes using the approaches proposed in Part I or any other approach presented in the literature (e.g., [21, 30, 37, 45, 64, 68, 110, 114]).

A further important characteristic of our approach consists in describing scheme integrations and abstractions using both input and output schemes and the set of operations which led to output schemes from input ones (see Section 1.2.3). In our case maintaining both representations is cheap, automatic and does not need a great amount of storing resources, as shown in the following.

The techniques we are presenting here work as follows. All information about schemes and their objects are stored in an Intensional Information Base $IIB$; this is composed by a *Metascheme $IIB.M$* and a set of meta-operators acting on $IIB.M$. Insertions, deletions and modifications of scheme objects and properties among them, which will be often referred to in the following, are realized by meta-operators modifying the content of the metascheme. Besides information traditionally stored in the metascheme, $IIB.M$ stores also a *Set of Mappings* (hereafter denoted by $IIB.M.SoM$) and *a Set of Views* (hereafter called $IIB.M.SoV$). $IIB.M.SoM$ describes the way an object belonging to output schemes has been obtained from one or more objects belonging to input schemes. $IIB.M.SoV$ allows to obtain instances of objects of the output schemes from instances at the input scheme level. Note that views are well-suited to form the basis for constructing software modules to access data stored in local databases (e.g., in the form of mediator/wrapper modules) in the Cooperative Information Systems, or to produce reconciled data in the Data Warehouse. Views are defined using a template language, independent from conceptual and logical scheme models, whose basic operators are parametric procedures that, once instantiated, allow to compute derived data instances from input data instances.

The algorithm for repository construction stores in $IIB.M$ all information about the global scheme, the objects belonging to it and properties relating them; in addition, each operation performed during the repository construction is stored in $IIB.M.SoM$; views corresponding to $IIB.M.SoM$ entries are stored in $IIB.M.SoV$.

Analogously to the approaches for deriving interscheme properties described in Part I, the algorithms presented here have been validated by exploiting Italian Central Governmental Office (ICGO) databases; the results of the application of our algorithms to some of the ICGO databases are illustrated in Chapter 13.

## 6.2 Support Intensional Information Base

The approach for constructing a Data Repository exploits an Intensional Information Base as a support for storing input data, intermediate and final results. The Intensional Information Base includes a *Metascheme* storing metadata, dictionaries and final results, and a group of operators allowing to modify or to query the metascheme (we call these operators *Meta-Operators*). In the following we describe the metascheme first and then the meta-operators. Before doing so, the following definitions must be introduced:

**Definition 6.2.1.** Given an attribute $A$, the *structure* of $A$ is $A$ itself; the *context* of $A$ consists of the entity which $A$ belongs to, and its attributes, except, obviously, $A$ itself.                                                                    $\square$

**Definition 6.2.2.** Given an entity $E$, the *structure* of $E$ consists of the set of its attributes; the *context* of $E$ consists of relationships it takes part into and of all other entities linked by these relationships.                              $\square$

**Definition 6.2.3.** Given a relationship $R$, the *internal structure* of $R$ consists of its attributes; the *structure* of $R$ consists of its internal structure plus the entities involved in $R$ and their attributes; the *foreign keys* of $R$ consist of the primary key attributes of entities belonging to its structure; the *context* of $R$ consists of entities linked (through some other relationship different from $R$) to entities belonging to the structure of $R$.                              $\square$

### 6.2.1 The Metascheme

The Metascheme of the support Intensional Information Base is represented in Figure 6.1.

In the metascheme, the central entity is the entity *Object*. An object is characterized by an identifier and a name; it can be an entity, an attribute or a relationship. An object can be similar to other objects: this similarity is represented by the relationship *Synonymy*; in more detail a synonymy indicates that, within their schemes, two objects have the same name and the same meaning. This relationship owns an attribute *Sinonymy_Coeff*, indicating the strength of the similarity. Once translated in a suitable logic model, this relationship stores the Synonymy Dictionary $SD$. In an analogous way, the metascheme contains the relationship *Homonymy*. Once translated into a suitable logic model, this relationship stores the Homonymy Dictionary $HD$. Details about these two dictionaries can be found below.

An *Entity* can be connected to more than one relationship and this concept is expressed by the relationship *E-R*; for each connection, the minimum and the maximum cardinality and the role owned by the entity in the relationship

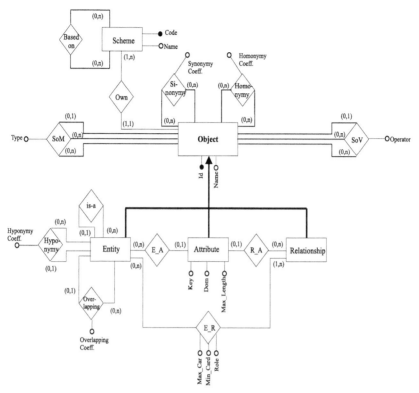

**Fig. 6.1.** The Metascheme of the Support Intensional Information Base

must be specified; an entity can own more than one attribute (relationship *E-A*). An entity $E_1$ can be linked to another entity $E_2$ by an hyponymy; a hyponymy from an object $E_1$ to an object $E_2$, having the same type of $E_1$, indicates that $E_1$ has a more specific meaning than $E_2$. If $E_1$ and $E_2$ belong to the same scheme (resp., to different schemes) we say that $E_1$ is an intrascheme (resp., an interscheme) hyponym of $E_2$ and that $E_2$ is the intrascheme (resp., the interscheme) hypernym of $E_1$. This concept is represented by the relationship *Hyponymy*; this relationship owns an attribute *Hyponymy_Coeff* indicating the plausibility of the property. Once translated in a suitable logic model, this relationship stores the *Hyponymy Dictionary HyD*.

An entity $E_1$ can be connected to another entity $E_2$ because of an overlapping; given two entities $E_1$ and $E_2$ an overlapping exists between them if there exist non-empty sets of attributes $\{A_{11}, A_{12}, \ldots, A_{1n}\}$ of $E_1$ and $\{A_{21}, A_{22}, \ldots, A_{2n}\}$ of $E_2$ such that, for $1 \leq i \leq n$, $A_{1i}$ is a synonym of $A_{2i}$. This concept is represented by the relationship *Overlapping*; this relationship owns an attribute *Overlapping_Coeff* indicating the plausibility of the property. Once translated in a suitable logic model, this relationship stores the *Overlapping Dictionary OD*. Details about the *HyD* and the *OD* are described below.

An entity can be connected to other entities by an *is-a* relationship. Note that, in the E/R model, *is-a* relationships are nothing but intrascheme hyponymies; therefore they could be stored by exploiting the *HyD*. However, we preferred to store this concept in an independent relationship because an *is-a* relationship represent a property of scheme objects and may exist independently from the *HyD* being constructed.

An *Attribute* can be a primary key, a secondary key or a non-key: the attribute *Key* is used for representing this information. The attribute is also characterized by a field *Dom*, representing its domain, and a field *Max_Length*, representing the attribute maximum size. An attribute belongs to an entity or to a relationship; this is encoded in the relationships *E-A* and *R-A*.

The entity *Relationship* is a specialization of the entity *Object*; it can own more than one attribute and can be linked to one or more entities; relationships *R_A* and *E_R* store this information.

An object belongs to a *Scheme*; this is characterized by a code and by a name; a scheme can have one or more objects. A scheme can be based on one or more schemes (this happens when it is obtained by integrating or abstracting other schemes).

The ternary relationship *SoM* is used for storing the Set of Mappings; the attribute *Type* indicates the type of the mapping. Similarly, the ternary relationship *SoV* is used for storing the Set of Views. For each entry, the attribute *Operator* indicates the parametric procedure which the view corresponding to the entry is an instance of. The next three sections are devoted to describe in details the dictionaries, the Set of Mappings and the Set of Views.

**Dictionaries of Interscheme Properties.** As explained above, our algorithms assume that a set of interscheme properties, describing relationships holding among input scheme objects, is given. In the literature different approaches have been proposed for extracting interscheme properties [21, 30, 37, 45, 64, 68, 110, 114]. As for our contribution in this field, we have developed semi-automatic techniques for deriving synonymies, homonymies and type conflicts [92, 122, 87, 90, 117, 118] (see Chapter 2), for deriving object clusters [92, 122, 87, 117, 118, 90] (see Chapter 3), for determining hyponymies [95, 97, 88] (see Chapter 4) and for extracting assertions between knowledge patterns [16, 17, 18, 96, 19] (see Chapter 5).

Here we assume to have available:

- a *Synonymy Dictionary M.SD*, which stores scheme-specific synonymy properties between scheme objects. Each tuple of this dictionary has the form $\langle O_1, O_2, f \rangle$, where $O_1$ and $O_2$ are the involved objects. *SD* can be obtained by adopting the approach described in Chapter 2.
- a *Homonymy Dictionary M.HD*, storing homonymies between scheme objects. Each tuple of this dictionary has the form $(O_1, O_2, f)$, where $O_1$ and

$O_2$ are the involved objects. $HD$ can be obtained by adopting the approach described in Chapter 2.

- a *Hyponymy Dictionary M.HyD*, storing hyponymies between scheme objects. Each tuple of this dictionary has the form $\lceil E_1, E_2, f \rceil$, where $E_1$ and $E_2$ are the involved entities. $HyD$ can be obtained by adopting the techniques described in Section 4.2.2 and 4.3.1.
- an *Overlapping Dictionary M.OD*, which stores overlappings between intrascheme hyponyms (see Chapter 4). Each tuple of this dictionary has the form $\|E_1, E_2, f\|$, where $E_1$ and $E_2$ are the involved entities. $OD$ can be obtained by adopting the approaches described in Section 4.2.2.

In all the definitions above, $f$ denotes a fuzzy coefficient, belonging to the real interval $[0, 1]$, expressing the plausibility of the corresponding property

**The Set of Mappings (M.SoM).** The Set of Mappings $M.SoM$ can be looked at as to store the way a scheme object has been obtained from other objects through integration/abstraction steps; $M.SoM$ entries are used to define views belonging to $M.SoV$. $M.SoM$ includes an entry for each new object obtained along with the application of the integration and abstraction algorithms. Thus, a Set of Mappings can be assumed to consist of a set of tuples, each of which must have one of the following forms:

- $\langle E_p, E_q, E_{pq}, EMerge \rangle$: it indicates that entities $E_p$ and $E_q$ are merged into the entity $E_{pq}$; note that $E_{pq}$ can coincide with either $E_p$ or $E_q$.
- $\langle A_l, A_m, A_{lm}, AMerge \rangle$ and $\langle R_u, R_v, R_{uv}, RMerge \rangle$: they are the analogous, for attributes and relationships, of the tuple $\langle E_p, E_q, E_{pq}, EMerge \rangle$.
- $\langle E_p, E_q, R, IsaCreate \rangle$: it indicates the creation of an *is-a* relationship $R$ from $E_p$ to $E_q$.
- $\langle R', E_q, E_t, IsaModify \rangle$: it indicates that the *is-a* relationship $R'$ changes its hypernym from $E_q$ to $E_t$. It is supposed that an *is-a* relationship $R''$ exists from $E_t$ to $E_q$.
- $\langle R, -, E, CRDelToE \rangle$: it indicates the merging of the cyclic relationship $R$ into the corresponding entity $E$[3].

All these tuples are generated during the integration and the abstraction process.

**The Set of Views (M.SoV).** The Set of Views $M.SoV$ stores a view for each object belonging to schemes obtained by the execution of integration and abstraction steps (and, therefore, a view for each tuple of $M.SoM$). Views allow to obtain instances of a new object from instances of objects it derives from.

Views are defined by a "template" language, independent from conceptual and logic scheme models, whose basic operators are parametric procedures that, once instantiated and translated into procedures valid for the DBMS

---

[3] A cyclic relationship is a relationship $R$ linking an entity $E$ twice.

storing data which they operates upon, compute derived data instances from input data instances. In other words, each view is an instance of one among a set of parametric views expressed using a meta-language and is obtained *(i)* by substituting formal parameters with real objects according to $M.SoM$ entries, *(ii)* by translating the obtained view from the original meta-language, which it was expressed in, to the language of the DBMS storing data which the view operates upon. The task of each view consists of taking in input instances of some objects and returning instances of new objects whose structure has been derived in the previous phases.

The basic parametric views are the following:

- $D\_EMerge(E_p, E_q, E_{pq})$ is associated to merging entities $E_p$ and $E_q$ into the entity $E_{pq}$ and derives instances of $E_{pq}$ from instances of $E_p$ and $E_q$.
- $D\_RMerge(R_u, R_v, R_{uv})$ and $D\_AMerge(A_l, A_m, A_{lm})$ behave similarly to $D\_EMerge(E_p, E_q, E_{pq})$ but for relationships and attributes.
- $D\_IsaCreate(E_p, E_q, R)$ is associated to the creation of an is-a relationship $R$ from $E_p$ to $E_q$ and derives instances of $R$ from instances of $E_p$ and of $E_q$.
- $D\_IsaModify(R', E_q, E_t)$ is associated to the modification of an *is-a* relationship $R'$ such that the corresponding hypernym changes from $E_q$ to $E_t$. It assumes that an *is-a* relationship $R''$ exists from $E_t$ to $E_q$. It derives instances of the "new" $R'$ from instances of the "old" $R'$ and of $R''$.
- $D\_CRDelToE(R, E_p)$ is associated to the merge of the (cyclic) relationship $R$ into the entity $E_p$ it links and derives instances of the "new" $E_p$ from instances of $R$ and of the "old" $E_p$.

### 6.2.2 The Meta-operators

The Meta-Operators associated to the metascheme of the Intensional Information Base can be classified into *Meta-Procedures*, allowing the manipulation of the information stored in the metascheme, and *Meta-Functions*, allowing for querying the information stored in the metascheme.

The Meta-Procedures used in the following are:

- $A\_Add(A, O)$, which takes in input an attribute $A$ and an object $O$ and adds $A$ to $O$.
- $E\_Add(S, E)$, which takes in input a scheme $S$ and an entity $E$ and adds $E$ to $S$.
- $R\_Add(S, R)$, which takes in input a scheme $S$ and a relationship $R$ and adds $R$ to $S$.
- $A\_Delete(A)$, which takes in input an attribute $A$ and deletes $A$ from the scheme $S$ which $A$ belongs to.
- $E\_Delete(E)$, which takes in input an entity $E$ and deletes $E$ from the scheme $S$ which $E$ belongs to.

- $R\_Delete(R)$, which takes in input a relationship $R$ and deletes $R$ from the scheme $S$ which $R$ belongs to.
- $Isa\_Modify(R', E_q, E_t)$, which takes in input an *is-a* relationship $R'$ from an entity $E_p$ to an entity $E_q$ and changes its hypernym from $E_q$ to $E_t$.
- $A\_Characterize(A_l, A_m, A_{lm})$, which takes in input three attributes $A_l$, $A_m$ and $A_{lm}$ and defines the features of $A_{lm}$ (i.e., its name, its domain and its key characterization) from the features of both $A_l$ and $A_m$. More in particular, as for the name of $A_{lm}$, the human expert is asked to choose it between the name of $A_l$ and that of $A_m$. As far as the domain of $A_{lm}$ is concerned, if the domain of $A_l$ and the domain of $A_m$ are included into one another in either ways, the largest one is set as the domain of $A_{lm}$; otherwise (the domains are incomparable) the human intervention is required. As for the key characterization, if (at least) one of the input attributes is not a key one, then $A_{lm}$ will not be a key; otherwise $A_{lm}$ will be a key.
- $E\_Characterize(E_p, E_q, E_{pq})$, which takes in input three entities $E_p$, $E_q$ and $E_{pq}$ and defines the features of $E_{pq}$ (i.e., its name) from those of $E_p$ and $E_q$. If the names of $E_p$ and $E_q$ are different, this procedure needs the support of the human expert for deciding if $E_{pq}$ must inherit either the name of $E_p$ or that of $E_q$.
- $R\_Characterize(R_u, R_v, R_{uv})$, which takes in input three relationships $R_u$, $R_v$ and $R_{uv}$ and defines the features of $R_{uv}$ (i.e., its name) from those of $R_u$ and $R_v$. If the names of $R_u$ and $R_v$ are different, this procedure needs the support of the human expert for deciding if $R_{uv}$ must inherit either the name of $R_u$ or that of $R_v$.
- $E\_Transfer\_Att(E_p, E_q)$, which takes in input two entities $E_p$ and $E_q$ and transfers attributes of $E_p$ so that they become attributes of $E_q$.
- $E\_Transfer\_Rel(E_p, E_q)$, which takes in input two entities $E_p$ and $E_q$ and transforms relationships of $E_p$ so that they become relationships of $E_q$ (also *is-a* relationships are transferred).
- $R\_Transfer\_Att(R_u, R_v)$, which takes in input two relationships $R_u$ and $R_v$ and transfers attributes of $R_u$ so that they become attributes of $R_v$.
- $R\_Transfer\_Ent(R_u, R_v)$, which takes in input two relationships $R_u$ and $R_v$ and modifies the metascheme so that entities linked by $R_u$ are modified to become linked by $R_v$.
- $RE\_Transfer\_Att(R, E)$, which takes in input a relationship $R$ and an entity $E$ and transfers attributes of $R$ to $E$.
- $RE\_Assign\_ForeignKey(R, E)$, which takes in input a relationship $R$ and an entity $E$ and assigns the foreign key attributes of $R$ to $E$.

The Meta-Functions used in the following are listed below:

- $E\_Structure(E) \rightarrow AS$, which takes in input an entity $E$ and returns the set $AS$ of attributes belonging to the structure of $E$.

- $R\_Isa\_Structure(R) \to (E_p, E_q)$, which takes in input a relationship $R$ and yields in output an entity pair $(E_p, E_q)$ such that $E_p$ is an intrascheme hyponym of $E_q$.
- $E\_Isa\_Context(E) \to RS$, which takes in input an entity $E$ and yields in output the set $RS$ of *is-a* relationships belonging to the context of $E$.
- $E\_NonIsa\_Context(E) \to RS$, which takes in input an entity $E$ and yields in output the set $RS$ of non *is-a* relationships belonging to the context of $E$.
- $EE\_Detect\_Isa(E_p, E_q) \to R$, which takes in input two entities $E_p$ and $E_q$ such that an *is-a* relationship $R$ exists from $E_p$ to $E_q$, and yields $R$ in output.
- $EE\_Detect\_NonIsa(E_p, E_q) \to RS$, which takes in input two entities $E_p$ and $E_q$ and returns the set of relationships, different from *is-a*, existing between $E_p$ and $E_q$.
- $E\_Retrieve\_Hyponyms(E) \to ES$, which takes in input an entity $E$ and returns the set $ES$ of its hyponyms.
- $R\_Ent\_Structure(R) \to ES$, which takes in input a relationship $R$ and returns the set $ES$ of entities belonging to the structure of $R$.
- $R\_Int\_Structure(R) \to AS$, which takes in input a relationship $R$ and returns the set $AS$ of attributes belonging to the internal structure of $R$.
- $R\_ForeignKey(R) \to AS$, which takes in input a relationship $R$ and yields in output the set $AS$ of its foreign keys (see above for the definition of foreign key attributes).
- $S\_Cyclic(S) \to CRS$, which takes in input a scheme $S$ and yields in output the set $CRS$ of cyclic relationships of $S$.
- $S\_Rel(S) \to RS$, which takes in input a scheme $S$ and yields in output the set $RS$ of non *is-a* relationships belonging to $S$.
- $S\_Isa(S) \to RS$, which takes in input a scheme $S$ and yields in output the set $RS$ of *is-a* relationships belonging to $S$.
- $Old(O_1) \to O_2$, which takes in input an object $O_1$, obtained by applying some transformation to an object $O_2$ and returns the object $O_2$ itself.
- $Detect\_Scheme(O) \to S$, which takes in input an object $O$ and yields in output the scheme which $O$ belongs to.

## 6.3 Constructing a Data Repository

### 6.3.1 Description of the Approach

The algorithm for constructing a Data Repository takes in input a list of schemes $S_1, \ldots, S_n$ and an Intensional Information Base $IIB$. It yields in output a Data Repository represented as a set of clusters (see Section 6.1); the construction of the Data Repository leads to construct also the $IIB.M.SoM$ and the $IIB.M.SoV$.

More in particular, the algorithm first normalizes schemes by transforming non-binary relationships into binary ones. Normalizations lead to some transformations of scheme objects which are stored in $IIB.M.SoM$ and are used for constructing corresponding views.

The algorithm then groups schemes into clusters; cluster schemes are integrated to obtain a global scheme; this is eventually abstracted for producing the cluster C-scheme which is stored in the repository. Scheme object transformations implied by integration and abstraction steps are stored in $IIB.M.SoM$ too; they will have to be considered for defining corresponding views. Once all clusters of the lowest level have been obtained, interscheme properties holding between objects belonging to them are derived and stored in the dictionaries $IIB.M.SD$, $IIB.M.HD$, $IIB.M.HyD$ and $IIB.M.OD$. After that, C-schemes corresponding to basic clusters are grouped in more abstract clusters and integrated; obtained global schemes are abstracted, in their turn, for producing higher level C-schemes. These steps are iterated until to only one global scheme representing all databases is obtained. When this happens, further abstraction steps can be applied to it. In more detail the algorithm for constructing the Data Repository is as follows:

---

**Algorithm for the construction of a Data Repository**
*Input*: a list $S$ of database schemes and an Intensional Information Base $IIB$
*Output*: a Data Repository $DR$ and the modified Intensional Information Base $IIB$

    **var**
        $SC$: a list of cluster identifiers;
        $SS$: a list of schemes;
        $AbstractYes$: boolean;
        $k, lev : 1..n$;
    **begin**
        $SS := S$;
        $lev := 0$;
        $NBR\_Normalization(IIB, SS, DR)$;
        **repeat**
            $Group\_Clusters(IIB, SS, lev, SC, DR)$;
            **for each** cluster $SC_j \in SC$ **do begin**
                $Integrate\_Schemes(IIB, SS, SC_j, DR)$;
                $Abstract\_Scheme(IIB, SC_j, AbstractYes, DR)$;
            **end**
            $SS := \emptyset$;
            **for** $k := 1$ **to** $|SC|$ **do**
                $SS_k :=$ the C-scheme of the cluster identified by $SC_k$;
            $Extract\_Interscheme\_Properties(SS, IIB)$:
            $lev := lev + 1$;
        **until not** $AbstractYes$
    **end**

---

It is worth pointing out that the algorithm above manages also the situations when a unique scheme has been obtained and it must be further abstracted. In this case the procedure $Group\_Cluster$ simply produces a cluster of an immediately higher level than that received in input; the procedure *Integrate_Schemes* returns the same scheme received in input and the procedure *Abstract_Scheme* further abstracts the scheme; in this case the procedure *Extract_Interscheme_Properties* extracts no new properties.

In the following we describe in details the procedures *Group_Clusters*, *Integrate_Schemes* and *Abstract_Scheme*. We will not describe the procedure
*NBR_Normalization* since it follows the classical rules for transforming every $n - ary$ relationship $(n \geq 3)$ into a set of binary ones [113].

### 6.3.2 Complexity Issues

Here we prove that the algorithm for the construction of the Data Repository converges in a finite number of steps.

**Proposition 6.3.1.** *Let $n_s$ be the number of involved schemes and let $n_o$ be the maximum number of objects belonging to a scheme. Then, in the worst case, the maximum number of iterations required by the algorithms to terminate is $(n_s(n_o + 1) - 1)$.*

*Proof.*

At the generic iteration $i$, the clusters of level $i$ of the Data Repository are constructed. The C-schemes of these clusters could be equal to those of level $i - 1$ or not.

In the first case, both the Data Repository and the dictionaries returned by the $i\_th$ iteration of the algorithm are equal to those returned by the $(i - 1)\_th$ iteration and the algorithm terminates.

In the second case, clusters of level $i$ may be different from those of level $i-1$ because either *(i)* at least two C-schemes of level $i-1$ have been grouped into a cluster of level $i$, or *(ii)* because the C-scheme of at least one cluster of level $i - 1$ has been further abstracted. In the first case the number of clusters has been reduced at least of one unit; in the second case, the number of objects in a C-scheme has been reduced at least of one unit.

In the worst case during each iteration only two schemes are grouped into a cluster and the integration consists of only a scheme juxtaposition without any reduction of the object number; consequently, in order to integrate all schemes, $n_s - 1$ iterations are necessary and the global scheme includes $n_o n_s$ objects. Once the global scheme has been obtained, in the worst case, $(n_o n_s - 1)$ abstraction steps are necessary. Therefore, the total number of iterations for the algorithm to converge is upper bounded by $(n_s - 1) + (n_o n_s - 1) + 1 = n_s(n_o + 1) - 1$. □

## 6.4 Grouping Schemes into Clusters

The procedure *Group_Clusters* takes in input an Intensional Information Base *IIB*, a Data Repository *DR*, a list of schemes *SS*, which are the C-schemes relative to clusters of level $(lev - 1)$ of $DR$, and groups them into a set of homogeneous clusters constituting the clusters of level $lev$ of $DR$; the C-id of the new clusters are put into $SC$.

The algorithm uses a matrix $M_{Cl}$ such that $M_{Cl}[i, j]$ stores a coefficient representing the similarity between schemes $S_i$ and $S_j$. Given two schemes $S_i$ and $S_j$, in order to obtain $M_{Cl}[i, j]$, interscheme properties relative to $S_i$ and $S_j$ are exploited. The general idea is that the greater the percentage of objects involved in significant interscheme properties relative to $S_i$ and $S_j$ is, the higher the similarity degree between $S_i$ and $S_j$ will be. To this purpose, we consider three kinds of interscheme properties, namely, synonymies, hyponymies and overlappings. For each kind of interscheme property, a similarity coefficient for $S_i$ and $S_j$ is obtained by defining a maximum weight matching on a suitable bipartite graph, as explained below. The overall similarity coefficient is computed as a weighted mean of the three partial values, namely, $SynSim$, $HypSim$ and $OvSim$, taking into account synonymies, hyponymies and overlappings holding between objects belonging to schemes $S_i$ and $S_j$. Weights have been experimentally defined.

The grouping of schemes into clusters is obtained by executing any clustering algorithm (e.g., $PAM$ based on the k-medoids method) [56, 60]. The procedure then stores clusters of the new level in the $DR$; in addition it returns their C-id into $SC$. In more detail, the procedure is as follows:

---

**Procedure** $Group\_Clusters$ ($IIB$: an Intensional Information Base; $SS$ a list of schemes; $lev : integer$; **var** $SC$: a list of cluster identifier; **var** $DR$: a Data Repository);
    **const**
        $W_{Syn} = 0.50; W_{Hyp} = 0.20; W_{Ov} = 0.30; \omega_E = 1;$
    **var**
        $SP$: a set of synonymies between entities;
        $HP$: a set of hyponymies between entities;
        $OP$: a set of overlappings between entities;
        $SynSim, HypSim, OvSim : real \in [0, 1];$
        $P, Q$: a set of objects;
        $M_{SP}, M_{HP}, M_{OP}, M_{Cl}$: a matrix of reals $\in [0, 1];$
        $i, j$: integer;
    **begin**
        **for** $i := 1$ **to** $|SS|$ **do**
            **for** $j := 1$ **to** $|SS|$ **do begin**
                $SP := \emptyset; HP := \emptyset; OP := \emptyset;$
                $P := \{ E_p \mid E_p$ is an entity $of\ S_i \};$
                $Q := \{ E_q \mid E_q$ is an entity $of\ S_j \};$
                **for each** pair of entities $E_p \in P$ and $E_q \in Q$ **do begin**
                    $SP := SP \cup \{(E_p, E_q, f_{E_p E_q}) \mid$
                            $\langle E_p, E_q, f_{E_p E_q} \rangle \in IIB.M.SD\};$
                    $IP := IP \cup \{(E_p, E_q, g_{E_p E_q}) \mid$
                            $\lceil E_p, E_q, g_{E_p E_q} \rceil \in IIB.M.HyD\};$
                    $OP := OP \cup \{(E_p, E_q, h_{E_p E_q}) \mid$
                            $\| E_p, E_q, h_{E_p E_q} \| \in IIB.M.OD\};$
            **end**;
            $M_{SP} := Mat(SP, P, Q);$

$$M_{HP} := Mat(HP, P, Q);$$
$$M_{OP} := Mat(OP, P, Q);$$
$$SynSim := Matching(P, Q, M_{SP}, \omega_E);$$
$$HypSim := Matching(P, Q, M_{HP}, \omega_E);$$
$$OvSim := Matching(P, Q, M_{OP}, \omega_E);$$
$$M_{Cl}[i, j] := W_{Syn} \times SynSim + W_{Hyp} \times HypSim +$$
$$W_{Ov} \times OvSim$$

      **end**;
$$Cluster(M_{Cl}, SS, lev, SC, DR)$$
**end**

The function *Mat* implements the function $\mu_s$ introduced in Section 2.3.2. In particular it takes in input two sets of objects $P$ and $Q$ and a set $TS$ of triplets denoting interscheme properties between objects of $P$ and $Q$; it creates a matrix $M$ having a row for each object $O_p \in P$, a column for each object $O_q \in Q$ and $M[O_p, O_q]$ equal to the plausibility value associated in $TS$ to the pair $O_p$ and $O_q$.

The function *Matching* implements the function $\delta$ introduced in Section 2.3.2, that we recall next. It takes in input *(i)* two sets of objects $P = \{p_1, \ldots, p_r\}$ and $Q = \{q_1, \ldots, q_s\}$; *(ii)* a weight matrix $M$ on $P$ and $Q$ such that, for each $p_i \in P$ and $q_j \in Q$, $0.0 \leq M[p_i, q_j] \leq 1.0$; *(iii)* a coefficient $\omega_v$. It computes a factor $v$, in the real interval $[0, 1]$, obtained from calculating a maximum weight matching . If $P = \emptyset$ or $Q = \emptyset$ then *Matching* returns $v = 0$. Otherwise, let $BG = (P \cup Q, A)$ be a bipartite weighted graph, where $A$ is the set of weighted edges $\{(p_i, q_j, f_{ij}) \mid f_{ij} > 0\}$; the maximum weight matching for $BG$ is a set $A' \subseteq A$ of edges such that for each node $x \in P \cup Q$ there is at most one edge of $A'$ incident onto $x$ and $\phi(A') = \sum_{(p_i, q_j, f_{ij}) \in A'} f_{ij}$ is maximum [41]. Now, let $\overline{\phi}(A') = \frac{\phi(A')}{|A'|}$. The value $v$ returned by *Matching* is defined as:

$$v = \left(1 - \frac{1}{2} \times \omega_v \frac{abs(|P| - |Q|) + 2 \times (min(|P|, |Q|) - |A'|)}{|P| + |Q|}\right) \times \overline{\phi}(A')$$

Observe that $\omega_v$ is used to weight the importance of "unrelated" edges.

The procedure *Cluster* takes in input a matrix $M_{Cl}$, a list $SS$ of schemes and an integer $lev$; it groups schemes belonging to $SS$ into a set of clusters which are stored as the clusters of level $lev$ in $DR$. It first constructs, from the similarity matrix $M_{Cl}$, a corresponding dissimilarity matrix $DM_{Cl}$ and calls $PAM$ with $DM_{Cl}$ as the input. The procedure returns the list of new cluster identifiers in $SC$.

## 6.5 Scheme Integration

The procedure *Integrate_Schemes* takes in input a support Intensional Information Base $IIB$, a set of schemes $SS$ representing all schemes of a Data Repository level, a cluster $Cl$ and a Data Repository $DR$; it integrates O-schemes of $Cl$ for obtaining its C-scheme. Clearly, integration is carried out by modifying the metascheme $IIB.M$ for taking into account the transformations performed during the integration step.

At the beginning, the procedure juxtaposes all schemes of $SS$ constituting the O-schemes of $Cl$ to obtain a (temporary redundant and inconsistent) C-scheme of $Cl$. After this, interesting synonym pairs are determined: this task is carried out by *(i)* computing a suitable threshold from the set of synonymy coefficients, *(ii)* selecting the triplets of $IIB.M.SD$ having a synonymy coefficient greater than the threshold. If an entity is involved in more than one selected triplet, the human expert is asked to select one. After interesting synonym pairs have been selected, the algorithm uses the information stored in the dictionaries for determining which of the objects belonging to involved schemes must be assumed to coincide, to be completely distinct, to overlap or to be one hyponym of the other in the global scheme; then it carries out the corresponding transformations. Finally it stores a tracing of performed transformations in $IIB.M.SoM$ and the corresponding Set of Views in $IIB.M.SoV$.

More precisely, for each pair $[E_p, E_q]$ belonging to the set of interesting synonymy pair, $E_p$ and $E_q$ must be considered coincident in the integrated scheme. In this case the hyponyms of $E_p$ and $E_q$ (if any) must be taken into account to determine the interscheme relationships holding between them. In particular an hyponym of $E_p$, say $E_{pi}$, and one of $E_q$, say $E_{qj}$, could overlap, could be distinct, could be one hyponym of the other or could be synonym. After that the interscheme relationship holding between $E_{pi}$ and $E_{qj}$ has been determined, a corresponding transformation must be carried out. Note that if $E_{pi}$ and $E_{qj}$ are synonym, they must be merged in the integrated scheme and their (possible) further hyponyms must be considered in turn for deriving their interscheme relationships; therefore, for each pair $[E_p, E_q]$ belonging to the set of interesting synonym pairs, the process proceeds recursively until to, during one iteration, two synonym entities are found such that no further synonymy relationship exists between their intrascheme hyponyms.

Finally, note that a pair $(E', E'')$ such that $\langle E', E'', f \rangle \in IIB.M.SD$ and $f$ is "high" can be examined for two possible reasons: *(i)* $(E', E'')$ is selected from the set of interesting synonymy pairs, and *(ii)* $E'$ is an intrascheme hyponym of an entity $E_1$, $E''$ is an intrascheme hyponym of an entity $E_2$ and the examination of $(E', E'')$ is required as a step of the examination of $E_1$ and $E_2$. In order to avoid that $(E', E'')$ is considered twice, we maintain a set $Examined$ of examined pairs; note that these pairs are unordered; consequently if a pair $(E_p, E_q)$ belongs to $Examined$, also $(E_q, E_p)$ is intended to belong to $Examined$.

The procedure for scheme integration is defined as follows:

---

**Procedure** *Integrate_Scheme*(**var** $IIB$: a support Intensional Information Base; $SS$: a set of schemes; $Cl$: a cluster; **var** $DR$: a Data Repository);

```
const
    D_th = 0.20^4;
    th_m = 0.55;
var
    Examined: a set of entity pairs;
    E: a set of entities;
    th_t, th_s: real;
    ISS: a set of entity pairs [E', E''];
begin
    Juxtaposition(SS, Cl);
    th_t := D_th × (Max(IIB.M.SD) + SubMax(IIB.M.SD)+
                SubSubMax(IIB.M.SD) + Min(IIB.M.SD)+
                SubMin(IIB.M.SD) + SubSubMin(IIB.M.SD));
    th_s := max(th_m, th_t);
    Examined := ∅;
    Select_Interesting_Syn(IIB.M.SD, th_s, ISS);
    for each [E_p, E_q] ∈ ISS such that (E_p, E_q) ∉ Examined do begin
        Examined := Examined ∪ {(E_p, E_q)};
        E_Merge(Cl.C-scheme, E_p, E_q, E_pq, IIB);
        Handle_Intrascheme_Hyp(Cl.C-scheme, Examined, E_p, E_q, E_pq, IIB)
    end
end
```

Procedures called within the algorithm have the following meaning:

- *Juxtaposition* takes in input a group of schemes $SS$ and a cluster $Cl$; in order to determine the (temporary) C-scheme of $Cl$, it computes the juxtaposition of schemes belonging to $SS$ and constituting the O-schemes of $Cl$.

- *Select_Interesting_Syn* takes in input a dictionary of synonymies $IIB.M.SD$, a threshold $th_s$ and determines a set $ISS$ of interesting pairs of synonyms. In order to construct the $ISS$, the procedure *(i)* selects all triplets $\langle E_p, E_q, f_{E_p E_q} \rangle$ such that $f_{E_p E_q}$ is greater than $th_s$; *(ii)* for each selected triplet, derives a corresponding pair to belong to $ISS$; *(iii)* if one entity belongs to more than one pair, the human expert is asked to choose the pair he considers the most correct.

- *Max* (resp., *SubMax* and *SubSubMax*) and *Min* (resp., *SubMin* and *SubSubMin*) take in input a dictionary $IIB.M.SD$ and return the maximum (resp., the sub-maximum and the sub-sub-maximum) and the minimum (resp., the sub-minimum and the sub-sub-minimum) value of all plausibility coefficients associated to tuples of $IIB.M.SD$. The choice of computing these and no other values has been made empirically by conducting a series of experiments.

- *E_Merge* takes in input a scheme $S$, entities $E_p$, $E_q$ and $E_{pq}$ belonging to $S$ and a support Intensional Information Base $IIB$ and merges $E_p$ and $E_q$ into $E_{pq}$, obtaining a unique entity.

---

[4] These values, as well as values of the other weights and thresholds, have been determined experimentally from the ICGO databases. In Chapter 13 we describe some of these experiments.

– *Handle_Intrascheme_Hyp* takes in input a scheme $S$, the set of examined pairs, three entities $E_p$, $E_q$ and $E_{pq}$ belonging to $S$ such that $E_p$ and $E_q$ have been merged into $E_{pq}$ and a support Intensional Information Base $IIB$. It manages hyponyms of $E_p$ and $E_q$ *(i)* by determining the kind of relationship (synonymy, distinctness, hyponymy, overlapping) existing between each pair $(E_{pi}, E_{qj})$ such that $E_{pi}$ is an intrascheme hyponym of $E_p$ and $E_{qj}$ is an intrascheme hyponym of $E_q$; *(ii)* by modifying $S$ accordingly.

In the following we will describe in details only the procedures *E_Merge* and
*Handle_Intrascheme_Hyp* since procedures *Juxtaposition*, *Max*, *SubMax*, *SubSubMax*, *Min*, *SubMin*, *SubSubMin* and *Select_Interesting_Syn* do not present any particular conceptual difficulty.

### 6.5.1 Merging Entities

The procedure *E_Merge* takes in input a global scheme $GS$, three entities $E_p$, $E_q$ and $E_{pq}$ belonging to $GS$ and the support Intensional Information Base $IIB$. It merges entities $E_p$ and $E_q$ into $E_{pq}$ and updates $IIB.M.SoM$ and $IIB.M.SoV$ accordingly.

In particular, it creates the new entity, transfers attributes and relationships of $E_p$ and $E_q$ to the new entity and deletes $E_p$ and $E_q$. Some synonymy may hold between an attribute of $E_p$ and an attribute of $E_q$; when $E_p$ and $E_q$ are merged into $E_{pq}$ both synonym attributes are inherited by $E_{pq}$. If this happen, each pair $(A_l, A_m)$ of synonym attributes must be merged into a unique attribute. The merging is carried out by *(i)* adding a new attribute to the entity, *(ii)* characterizing it and *(iii)* deleting old attributes. The procedure is as follows:

---

**Procedure** *E_Merge*(**var** $GS$: a global scheme; **var** $E_p$, $E_q$, $E_{pq}$: an entity; **var** $IIB$: a support Intensional Information Base);
**const**
    $th_{us} = 0.75$;
**var**
    $E$: a set of entities;
    $A$: a set of attributes;
**begin**
    $IIB.E\_Add(GS, E_{pq})$;
    $IIB.E\_Characterize(E_p, E_q, E_{pq})$;
    $IIB.E\_Transfer\_Att(E_p, E_{pq})$;
    $IIB.E\_Transfer\_Att(E_q, E_{pq})$;
    $IIB.E\_Transfer\_Rel(E_p, E_{pq})$;
    $IIB.E\_Transfer\_Rel(E_q, E_{pq})$;
    $IIB.E\_Delete(E_p)$;
    $IIB.E\_Delete(E_q)$;
    $IIB.M.SoM := IIB.M.SoM \cup \{\langle E_p, E_q, E_{pq}, EMerge \rangle\}$;
    $IIB.M.SoV := IIB.M.SoV \cup \{D\_EMerge(E_p, E_q, E_{pq})\}$;

**for each** $A_l, A_m \in IIB.E\_Structure(E_{pq})$ **such that**
$\langle A_l, A_m, f \rangle \in IIB.M.SD$ **and** $f > th_{us}$ **do begin**
    $IIB.A\_Add(A_{lm}, E_{pq})$;
    $IIB.A\_Characterize(A_l, A_m, A_{lm})$;
    $IIB.A\_Delete(A_l)$;
    $IIB.A\_Delete(A_m)$;
    $IIB.M.SoM := IIB.M.SoM \cup \{\langle A_l, A_m, A_{lm}, AMerge \rangle\}$;
    $IIB.M.SoV := IIB.M.SoV \cup \{D\_AMerge(A_l, A_m, A_{lm})\}$
**end**
**end**

---

### 6.5.2 Handling Intrascheme Hyponyms

The procedure *Handle_Intrascheme_Hyp* takes in input a global scheme $GS$, the set *Examined* of examined entities, three entities $E_p$, $E_q$ and $E_{pq}$ belonging to $GS$ such that $E_p$ and $E_q$ have been merged into $E_{pq}$ and a support Intensional Information Base $IIB$.

For each pair $\lfloor E_{pi}, E_{qj} \rfloor$ such that $E_{pi}$ (resp., $E_{qj}$) is an intrascheme hyponym of $E_p$ (resp., of $E_q$) and $(E_{pi}, E_{qj})$ does not belong to *Examined*, the procedure *Handle_Intrascheme_Hyp* determines the kind of relationship holding between entities of the pair and carries out the corresponding scheme transformations. Four cases are to be considered:

- $E_{pi}$ *and* $E_{qj}$ *are distinct*: in this case no scheme transformation is carried out;
- $E_{pi}$ *is an hyponym of* $E_{qj}$: in this case an *is-a* relationship is created from $E_{pi}$ to $E_{qj}$ and the pair $(E_{pi}, E_{qj})$ is added to *Examined*; the dual situation leads to analogous transformations;
- *an overlapping exists for* $E_{pi}$ *and* $E_{qj}$: in this case no relationship is created between $E_{pi}$ and $E_{qj}$ but the overlapping attributes are transferred from $E_{pi}$ and $E_{qj}$ to $E_{pq}$ and the pair $(E_{pi}, E_{qj})$ is added to *Examined*;
- $E_{pi}$ *and* $E_{qj}$ *are synonyms*: in this case $E_{pi}$ and $E_{qj}$ are merged and, consequently, the procedure *Handle_Intrascheme_Hyp* must be recursively activated for managing the hyponyms of $E_{pi}$ and $E_{qj}$ in turn; the pair $(E_{pi}, E_{qj})$ is also added to *Examined*.

The procedure is encoded as follows:

---

**Procedure** *Handle_Intrascheme_Hyp*(**var** $GS$: a global scheme;
**var** *Examined*: a set of entity pairs; $E_p, E_q, E_{pq}$: an entity; **var** $IIB$: a support Intensional Information Base);
**var**
    $HS_p, HS_q$: a set of entities;
    $E_{p_i q_j}$: an entity;
**begin**
    $HS_p := IIB.E\_Retrieve\_Hyponyms(E_p)$;
    $HS_q := IIB.E\_Retrieve\_Hyponyms(E_q)$;

**for each** $E_{pi} \in HS_p$ **do**
    **for each** $E_{qj} \in HS_q$ **do**
        **if** $(E_{pi}, E_{qj}) \notin Examined$ **then**
            **if** $\|E_{pi}, E_{qj}, f\| \in IIB.M.OD$ **then begin**
                $Examined := Examined \cup \{(E_{pi}, E_{qj})\};$
                $E\_Overlap(GS, E_{pi}, E_{qj}, E_{pq}, IIB)$
            **end**
            **else if** $\lceil E_{pi}, E_{qj}, f \rceil \in IIB.M.HyD$ **then begin**
                $Examined := Examined \cup \{(E_{pi}, E_{qj})\};$
                $E\_Hyponym(GS, E_{pi}, E_{qj}, E_{pq}, IIB)$
            **end**
            **else if** $\lceil E_{qj}, E_{pi}, f \rceil \in IIB.M.HyD$ **then begin**
                $Examined := Examined \cup \{(E_{pi}, E_{qj})\};$
                $E\_Hyponym(GS, E_{qj}, E_{pi}, E_{pq}, IIB)$
            **end**
            **else if** $\langle E_{pi}, E_{qj}, f \rangle \in IIB.M.SD$ **then begin**
                $Examined := Examined \cup \{(E_{pi}, E_{qj})\};$
                $E\_Merge(GS, E_{pi}, E_{qj}, E_{p_i q_j}, IIB);$
                $Handle\_Intrascheme\_Hyp(GS, Examined, E_{pi}, E_{qj},$
                                        $E_{p_i q_j}, IIB)$
        **end**
**end**

---

Procedures called within the algorithm above have the following behaviour:

- *E_Overlap* takes in input a scheme $GS$, two (hyponym) entities $E_{pi}$ and $E_{qj}$ and an entity $E_{pq}$, and a support Intensional Information Base $IIB$. It determines the overlapping attributes of $E_{pi}$ and $E_{qj}$ and transfers them to $E_{pq}$.
- *E_Hyponym* takes in input a scheme $GS$, two (hyponym) entities $E_p$ and $E_q$ and an entity $E_{pq}$ and a support Intensional Information Base $IIB$. It deletes the *is-a* relationship existing from $E_p$ to $E_{pq}$ and creates an *is-a* relationship from $E_p$ to $E_q$; in addition it merges synonym attributes of $E_p$ and $E_q$ and associates obtained attributes to $E_q$.
- *E_Merge* has been already illustrated above.

In the following sections we describe the procedures *E_Overlap* and *E_Hyponym* in detail.

**Procedure E_Hyponym.** The procedure *E_Hyponym* takes in input a global scheme $GS$, three entities $E_{pi}$, $E_{qj}$ and $E_{pq}$ and a support Intensional Information Base $IIB$. It first deletes the *is-a* relationship existing from $E_{pi}$ to $E_{pq}$ and creates an *is-a* relationship from $E_{pi}$ to $E_{qj}$ (recall that an *is-a* relationship already exists from $E_{qj}$ to $E_{pq}$). Then the procedure verifies if some pair of attributes $A_l \in E_{pi}$ and $A_m \in E_{qj}$ are synonyms and, in the affirmative case, it merges $A_l$ and $A_m$ and assigns the obtained attribute $A_{lm}$ to $E_{qj}$. The procedure is as follows:

---

**Procedure** *E_Hyponym*(**var** $GS$ a global scheme; **var** $E_{pi}$, $E_{qj}$, $E_{pq}$: an entity; **var** $IIB$: a support Intensional Information Base);

**const**
  $th_{us} = 0.75$;
**var**
  $A$: a set of attributes;
  $R_{Isa}, R'$: an *is-a* relationship;
**begin**
  $R' := IIB.EE\_Detect\_Isa(E_{pi}, E_{pq})$;
  $IIB.Isa\_Modify(R', E_{pq}, E_{qj})$;
  $IIB.M.SoM := IIB.M.SoM \cup \{\langle R', E_{pq}, E_{qj}, IsaModify \rangle\}$;
  $IIB.M.SoV := IIB.M.SoV \cup \{D\_IsaModify(R', E_{pq}, E_{qj})\}$;
  **for each** pair $(A_l, A_m)$ **such that** $A_l \in IIB.E\_Structure(E_{pi})$ **and**
  $A_m \in IIB.E\_Structure(E_{qj})$ **and** $\langle A_l, A_m, f \rangle \in IIB.M.SD$ **and**
  $f > th_{us}$ **do begin**
    $IIB.A\_Add(A_{lm}, E_{qj})$;
    $IIB.A\_Characterize(A_l, A_m, A_{lm})$;
    $IIB.A\_Delete(A_l)$;
    $IIB.A\_Delete(A_m)$;
    $IIB.M.SoM := IIB.M.SoM \cup \{\langle A_l, A_m, A_{lm}, AMerge \rangle\}$;
    $IIB.M.SoV := IIB.M.SoV \cup \{D\_AMerge(A_l, A_m, A_{lm})\}$
  **end**
**end**

---

**Procedure E_Overlap.** The procedure *E_Overlap* takes in input *(i)* a global scheme $GS$; *(ii)* two intrascheme hyponyms $E_{pi}$ and $E_{qj}$; *(iii)* the entity $E_{pq}$, which is, in $GS$, the hypernym of $E_{pi}$ and $E_{qj}$, and has been obtained by merging $E_p$ (the hypernym of $E_{pi}$) and $E_q$ (the hypernym of $E_{qj}$); *(iv)* a support Intensional Information Base $IIB$.

The procedure must verify if pairs $(A_l, A_m)$ of synonym attributes exist such that $A_l \in E_{pi}, A_m \in E_{qj}$; if this happens $A_l$ and $A_m$ must be merged into an attribute $A_{lm} \in E_{pq}$. Note that, in the original scheme before integration, also attributes of $E_p$ (resp., $E_q$) had to be considered attributes of $E_{pi}$ (resp., of $E_{qj}$); in the global scheme attributes of $E_p$ and $E_q$ have been inherited by $E_{pq}$. Therefore the possible existence of synonym attributes $(A'_l, A'_m)$ (resp. $(A''_l, A''_m)$) such that $A'_l \in E_{pq}, A'_m \in E_{qj}$ (resp., $A''_l \in E_{pi}, A''_m \in E_{pq}$) must be considered. Note that the attribute $A'_l$ (resp. $A''_m$) of $E_{pq}$ can be inherited only from $E_p$ (resp., from $E_q$); indeed $A'_l$ (resp., $A''_m$) cannot be inherited from $E_q$ (resp., from $E_p$) because, if this would happen, in the original scheme, $E_{qj}$ (resp., $E_{pi}$) and $E_q$ (resp., $E_p$) would have two synonym attributes $A'_l$ and $A'_m$ and this would imply that $E_{qj}$ (resp., $E_{pi}$) would have a pair of synonym attributes.

The procedure is encoded as follows:

---

**Procedure** *E_Overlap*(**var** $GS$: a global scheme; **var** $E_{pi}$, $E_{qj}$, $E_{pq}$: an entity; **var** $IIB$: a support Intensional Information Base);
**const**
  $th_{us} = 0.75$;
**var**
  $A$: a set of attributes;
**begin**
  **for each** $A_l \in IIB.E\_Structure(E_{pi})$, $A_m \in IIB.E\_Structure(E_{qj})$

such that $\langle A_l, A_m, f \rangle \in IIB.M.SD$ **and** $f > th_{us}$ **do begin**
    $IIB.A\_Add(A_{lm}, E_{pq})$;
    $IIB.A\_Characterize(A_l, A_m, A_{lm})$;
    $IIB.A\_Delete(A_l)$;
    $IIB.A\_Delete(A_m)$;
    $IIB.M.SoM := IIB.M.SoM \cup \{\langle A_l, A_m, A_{lm}, AMerge \rangle\}$;
    $IIB.M.SoV := IIB.M.SoV \cup \{D\_AMerge(A_l, A_m, A_{lm})\}$
**end**;
**for each** $A'_l \in IIB.E\_Structure(E_{pq})$, $A'_m \in IIB.E\_Structure(E_{pi})$
such that $\langle A'_l, A'_m, f \rangle \in IIB.M.SD$ **and** $f > th_{us}$ **do begin**
    $IIB.A\_Add(A'_{lm}, E_{pq})$;
    $IIB.A\_Characterize(A'_l, A'_m, A'_{lm})$;
    $IIB.A\_Delete(A'_l)$;
    $IIB.A\_Delete(A'_m)$;
    $IIB.M.SoM := IIB.M.SoM \cup \{\langle A'_l, A'_m, A'_{lm}, AMerge \rangle\}$;
    $IIB.M.SoV := IIB.M.SoV \cup \{D\_AMerge(A'_l, A'_m, A'_{lm})\}$
**end**;
**for each** $A''_l \in IIB.E\_Structure(E_{pq})$, $A''_m \in IIB.E\_Structure(E_{qj})$
such that $\langle A''_l, A''_m, f \rangle \in IIB.M.SD$ **and** $f > th_{us}$ **do begin**
    $IIB.A\_Add(A''_{lm}, E_{pq})$;
    $IIB.A\_Characterize(A''_l, A''_m, A''_{lm})$;
    $IIB.A\_Delete(A''_l)$;
    $IIB.A\_Delete(A''_m)$;
    $IIB.M.SoM := IIB.M.SoM \cup \{\langle A''_l, A''_m, A''_{lm}, AMerge \rangle\}$;
    $IIB.M.SoV := IIB.M.SoV \cup \{D\_AMerge(A''_l, A''_m, A''_{lm})\}$
**end**
**end**

## 6.6 Scheme Abstraction

The procedure *Abstract_Scheme* takes in input a support Intensional Information Base $IIB$, a cluster $Cl$ (whose C-scheme must be abstracted), a boolean variable *AbstractYes* and a Data Repository $DR$. It abstracts the C-scheme of the cluster $Cl$, i.e., puts together scheme objects into homogeneous groups and, for each group, substitutes all objects of the group with one object representing all of them. In order to carry out its task, the procedure considers four possible situations that could lead to an abstraction, namely:

– A cyclic relationship $R$ exists linking the entity $E$ twice (e.g., a relationship *Parent* and the entity *Person*);
– Two relationships $R_u$ and $R_v$ link the same pair of entities $(E', E'')$;
– An *is-a* relationship $R$ exists from an entity $E_p$ to an entity $E_q$;
– Two entities $E_p$ and $E_q$ are linked by a relationship $R$, different from the *is-a* and both $E_p$ and $E_q$ and $R$ can be represented by a unique concept.

Note that while the first situation always leads to an abstraction, in the last three cases the possibility to abstract objects depends on their contexts.

For this reason we need an Abstraction Dictionary $AD$ consisting of three components:

– $AD.Rel$, storing triplets of the form $\lfloor R_u, R_v, f \rfloor$, where $R_u$ and $R_v$ are two relationships linking the same pair of entities $(E', E'')$ and $f$ is a fuzzy coefficient, in the real interval $[0, 1]$, denoting the plausibility of abstracting $R_u$ and $R_v$ into a unique relationship $R_{uv}$.
– $AD.Isa$, storing triplets of the form $\lfloor E_p, E_q, f \rfloor$, where $E_p$ is an entity linked by an *is-a* relationship to $E_q$ and $f$ is a fuzzy coefficient, in the real interval $[0, 1]$, representing the plausibility that $E_p$ can be abstracted into $E_q$.
– $AD.Ent$, storing triplets of the form $\lfloor E_p, E_q, f \rfloor$, where $E_p$ is an entity linked by a relationship $R$, different from *is-a*, to $E_q$ and $f$ is a fuzzy coefficient, in the real interval $[0, 1]$, representing the plausibility that $E_p$, $R$ and $E_q$ can be abstracted into $E_{pq}$.

The abstraction of more objects into a unique one representing them is carried out as follows: *(i)* $AD.Rel$, $AD.Isa$ and $AD.Ent$ are constructed; *(ii)* dictionaries are examined and the abstraction is performed taking into consideration their contents. As for this last operation, four possible situations must be considered:

– A cyclic relationship $R$ is always abstracted into the corresponding entity $E$.
– For each triplet $\lfloor R_u, R_v, f \rfloor \in AD.Rel$ such that $f$ is greater than a certain threshold, $R_u$ and $R_v$ must be abstracted into a relationship $R_{uv}$; $R_v$ links the same pair of entities $(E', E'')$ which was previously linked by both $R_u$ and $R_v$; all attributes relative to $R_u$ and $R_v$ are inherited by $R_{uv}$.
– For each triplet $\lfloor E_p, E_q, f \rfloor \in AD.Isa$ such that $f$ is greater than a certain threshold, $E_p$ must be abstracted into $E_q$; all relationships and attributes relative to $E_p$ are inherited by $E_q$.
– For each triplet $\lfloor F_p, E_q, f \rfloor \in AD.Ent$ such that $f$ is greater than a certain given threshold, both $E_p$, $E_q$ and the relationship $R$ between them must be abstracted into an entity $E_{pq}$; all attributes and relationships of $E_p$, $E_q$ and $R$ are inherited by $E_{pq}$.

The abstraction procedure is given next:

---

**Procedure** *Abstract_Scheme*($IIB$: a support Intensional Information Base; **var** $Cl$: a cluster identifier; *AbstractYes*: boolean: **var** $DR$: a Data Repository);
**const**
    $th_{Rel} = 0.55$; $th_{Isa} = 0.43$; $th_{Ent} = 0.6$;
**var**
    $AD$: an Abstraction Dictionary;
    $CRS$: a set of cyclic relationships;
    $R$: a set of relationships;
    $E_{pq}$: an entity;

**begin**
    $CRS := IIB.S\_Cyclic(DR.IdToCluster(Cl).C\text{-}Scheme)$;
    $Compute\_AD.Rel(DR.IdToCluster(Cl).C\text{-}scheme, IIB, AD)$;
    $Compute\_AD.Isa(DR.IdToCluster(Cl).C\text{-}scheme, IIB, AD)$;
    $Compute\_AD.Ent(DR.IdToCluster(Cl).C\text{-}scheme, IIB, AD)$;
    $AbstractYes := (CRS \neq \emptyset)\textbf{or}(AD.Rel \neq \emptyset)\textbf{or}(AD.Isa \neq \emptyset)$
                                  $\textbf{or}(AD.Ent \neq \emptyset)$;
    **for each** $R_u \in CRS$ **do**
        $Abstract\_CR(R_u, IIB)$;
    **for each** $\lfloor R_u, R_v, f \rfloor \in AD.Rel$ **such that** $f > th_{Rel}$ **do**
        $Abstract\_Rel(R_u, R_v, R_{uv}, IIB)$;
    **for each** $\lfloor E_p, E_q, f \rfloor \in AD.Isa$ **such that** $f > th_{Isa}$ **do**
        $Abstract\_Isa(E_p, E_q, IIB)$;
    **for each** $\lfloor E_p, E_q, f \rfloor \in AD.Ent$ **such that** $f > th_{Ent}$ **do**
        $Abstract\_Ent(E_p, E_q, E_{pq}, IIB)$
**end**

---

Procedure $IdToCluster$ takes in input a cluster identifier and yields in output the corresponding cluster. Procedures $Compute\_AD.Rel$, $Compute\_AD.Isa$ and $Compute\_AD.Ent$ construct the Abstraction Dictionary; procedures $Abstract\_CR$,
$Abstract\_Rel$, $Abstract\_Isa$ and $Abstract\_Ent$ manage the four abstraction cases. All these procedures are described in more detail in the following sections.

### 6.6.1 Procedure Compute_AD.Rel

The procedure $Compute\_AD.Rel$ takes in input a scheme $AS$, an Intensional Information Base $IIB$ and an Abstraction Dictionary $AD$ and adds suitable tuples to $AD.Rel$. In particular, it first searches for pairs of relationships $(R_u, R_v)$ such that, for each pair, both $R_u$ and $R_v$ link the same pair of entities $(E', E'')$; then it associates to each pair $(R_u, R_v)$ a coefficient $f_{R_u R_v}$ expressing the plausibility that $R_u$ and $R_v$ must be abstracted into a unique relationship $R_{uv}$. Now, if we set $A_u = IIB.R\_Int\_Structure(R_u)$ and $A_v = IIB.R\_Int\_Structure(R_v)$ (i.e., $A_u$ and $A_v$ represent the set of attributes of $R_u$ and $R_v$, resp.), we are able to define the abstraction coefficient associated to $R_u$ and $R_v$, as follows:

$$f_{R_u R_v} = Matching(A_u, A_v, Mat(IIB.M.SD, A_u, A_v), \omega_R)$$

where functions $Matching$ and $Mat$ have been defined in Section 6.4 and $\omega_R$ is a constant experimentally set to 2.

    The procedure is defined as follows:

---

**Procedure** $Compute\_AD.Rel(AS$: a scheme; $IIB$: a support Intensional Information Base; **var** $AD$: an Abstraction Dictionary);
**const**
    $\omega_R = 2$;
**begin**
    **for each** pair $(R_u, R_v)$ such that $R_u, R_v \in AS$ **and**

$IIB.R\_Ent\_Structure(R_u) = IIB.R\_Ent\_Structure(R_v)$ **do begin**
    $A_u := IIB.R\_Int\_Structure(R_u);$
    $A_v := IIB.R\_Int\_Structure(R_v);$
    $f_{R_u R_v} := Matching(A_u, A_v, Mat(IIB.M.SD, A_u, A_v), \omega_R);$
    $AD.Rel := AD.Rel \cup \{\lfloor R_u, R_v, f_{R_u R_v} \rfloor\}$
   **end**
**end**

### 6.6.2 Procedure Compute_AD.Isa

This procedure takes in input a scheme $AS$, a support Intensional Information Base $IIB$ and an Abstraction Dictionary $AD$ and adds suitable tuples to $AD.Isa$. In particular it searches for pairs of entities ($E_p$, $E_q$) such that an *is-a* relationship exists from $E_p$ to $E_q$ and, for each of these pairs, defines a coefficient $f_{E_p E_q}$ expressing the plausibility of abstracting $E_p$ into $E_q$.

In order to define a formula for $f_{E_p E_q}$, we note that the bigger the number of relationships and intrascheme hyponyms[5] associated to $E_p$ is, the more the difficulty to abstract $E_p$ will be. Therefore $f_{E_p E_q}$ is defined as follows:

$$f_{E_p E_q} = \frac{1}{1 + \alpha N_{Rel}^{E_p} + \beta N_{Hyp}^{E_p}}$$

where $\alpha$ and $\beta$ are suitable coefficients, $N_{Rel}^{E_p}$ represents the number of relationships relative to $E_p$ and $N_{Hyp}^{E_p}$ indicates the number of intrascheme hyponyms of $E_p$. The procedure is encoded as follows:

**Procedure** *Compute_AD.Isa*($AS$: a scheme; $IIB$: a support Intensional Information Base; **var** $AD$: an Abstraction Dictionary);
**const**
    $\alpha = 0.33;\ \beta = 0.5;$
**var**
    $A$: a set of attributes;
    $N_{Rel}$, $N_{Hyp}$: integer;
    $R'_{E_p}$, $R''_{E_p}$, $R_{Isa}$: a set of relationships;
    $f$: a set of reals;
**begin**
    $R_{Isa} := IIB.S\_Isa(AS);$
    **for each** $R_i \in R_{Isa}$ **do begin**
        $(E_{pi}, E_{qi}) = R\_Isa\_Structure(R_i);$
        $R'_{E_{pi}} := IIB.E\_NonIsa\_Context(E_{pi});$
        $N_{Rel} := |R'_{E_{pi}}|;$
        $R''_{E_{pi}} := IIB.E\_Isa\_Context(E_{pi});$
        $N_{Hyp} := |R''_{E_{pi}}| - 1;$
        $f_{E_{pi} E_{qi}} = \frac{1}{1 + \alpha N_{Rel} + \beta N_{Hyp}};$
        $AD.Isa := AD.Isa \cup \{\lfloor E_{pi}, E_{qi}, f_{E_{pi} E_{qi}} \rfloor\}$

---

[5] Remember that if $E'$ is an intrascheme hyponym of $E''$, an *is-a* relationship exists from $E'$ to $E''$.

        **end**
    **end**

Note that an entity $E_{pi}$ can be hyponym of only one entity; consequently, if $IIB.E\_Isa\_Context(E_{pi})$ returns more than one *is-a* relationships, $E_{pi}$ will participate to all of them in the role of hypernym, except for the one linking it to $E_{qi}$.

### 6.6.3 Procedure Compute_AD.Ent

This procedure takes in input a scheme $AS$, a support Intensional Information Base $IIB$ and an Abstraction Dictionary $AD$ and adds suitable tuples to $AD.Ent$. In particular, it searches for pairs of entities $(E_p, E_q)$ such that a relationship $R$ different from *is-a* exists linking $E_p$ and $E_q$ and associates to each of these pairs a coefficient $f_{E_p E_q}$, expressing the plausibility of abstracting $E_p$, $R$ and $E_q$ into $E_{pq}$.

In order to determine if $E_p$, $R$ and $E_q$ can be abstracted into $E_{pq}$, we first define the plausibility coefficient $D_{E_p}$ (resp., $D_{E_q}$) representing the plausibility that $E_p$ (resp., $E_q$) can be abstracted; this depends on the number of its relationships, of its intrascheme hyponyms and the possible existence of an intrascheme hypernym. In particular, the higher the number of relationships and intrascheme hyponyms associated to $E_p$ (resp., $E_q$) is, the more difficult is to abstract $E_p$ (resp., $E_q$). Also, the existence of an interscheme hypernym for $E_p$ (resp., $E_q$) causes a greater difficulty to abstract $E_p$ (resp., $E_q$) into an entity different from its hypernym. The formula relative to the coefficient $D_E$ is as follows:

$$D_E = \frac{1}{1 + \alpha N_{Rel}^E + \beta N_{Hyp}^E};$$

After that $D_{E_p}$ and $D_{E_q}$ have been determined, we can compute $f_{E_p E_q}$ as follows:

$$f_{E_p E_q} = \frac{max(D_{E_p}, D_{E_q})}{D_{E_p} + D_{E_q}}$$

The procedure is, therefore, encoded in the following way:

---

**Procedure** *Compute_AD.Ent(AS*: a scheme; *IIB*: a support Intensional Information Base; **var** *AD*: an Abstraction Dictionary);
**const**
    $\alpha = 0.5$; $\beta = 0.33$;
**var**
    $A$: a set of attributes;
    $N_{Rel}$, $N_{Hyp}$: integer;
    $R'_E$, $R''_E$, $R$: a set of relationships;
    $D$: a set of reals;
    $f$: a set of reals;
**begin**
    $R := IIB.S\_Rel(AS)$;
    **for each** $R_i \in R$ **do begin**

$$(E_{pi}, E_{qi}) = R\_Ent\_Structure(R_i);$$
$$R'_E := IIB.E\_NonIsa\_Context(E_{pi});$$
$$N_{Rel} := |R'_E|;$$
$$R''_E := IIB.E\_Isa\_Context(E_{pi});$$
$$N_{Hyp} := |R''_E|;$$
$$D_{E_{pi}} = \frac{1}{1 + \alpha N_{Rel} + \beta N_{Hyp}};$$
$$R'_E := IIB.E\_NonIsa\_Context(E_{qi});$$
$$N_{Rel} := |R'_E|;$$
$$R''_E := IIB.E\_Isa\_Context(E_{qi});$$
$$N_{Hyp} := |R''_E|;$$
$$D_{E_{qi}} = \frac{1}{1 + \alpha N_{Rel} + \beta N_{Hyp}};$$
$$f_{E_{pi}E_{qi}} = \frac{max(D_{E_{pi}}, D_{E_{qi}})}{D_{E_{pi}} + D_{E_{qi}}};$$
$$AD.Ent := AD.Ent \cup \{\lfloor E_{pi}, E_{qi}, f_{E_{pi}E_{qi}} \rfloor\}$$
    **end**
**end**

### 6.6.4 Procedure Abstract_CR

The procedure *Abstract_CR* takes in input a cyclic relationship $R$ and an Intensional Information Base $IIB$ and abstracts $R$ into the corresponding entity $E$.

First it determines the entity $E$ relative to $R$, then it transfers all attributes (including foreign keys) from $R$ to $E$; finally it deletes $R$ from the metascheme and updates $IIB.M.SoM$ and $IIB.M.SoV$ accordingly. The procedure is realized as follows:

**Procedure** *Abstract_CR*(**var** $R_u$: a relationship; **var** $IIB$: an Intensional Information Base);
**var**
    $E$: a set of entities;
**begin**
    $E := IIB.R\_Ent\_Structure(R_u);$
    Let $E'$ be the only entity of $E$;
    $IIB.RE\_Transfer\_Att(R_u, E');$
    $IIB.RE\_Assign\_ForeignKey(R_u, E');$
    $IIB.RDelete(R_u);$
    $IIB.M.SoM := IIB.M.SoM \cup \{\langle R_u, -, E', CRDelToE \rangle\};$
    $IIB.M.SoV := IIB.M.SoV \cup \{D\_CRDelToE(R_u, E')\}$
**end**

### 6.6.5 Procedure Abstract_Rel

This procedure takes in input three relationships $R_u$, $R_v$ and $R_{uv}$ and an Intensional Information Base $IIB$. The procedure abstracts $R_u$ and $R_v$ into $R_{uv}$.

The abstraction of $R_u$ and $R_v$ into $R_{uv}$ consists of merging $R_u$ and $R_v$ into $R_{uv}$; therefore $R_{uv}$ is added to the same scheme which $R_u$ and $R_v$ belong to, attributes of $R_u$ and $R_v$ are transferred to $R_{uv}$ and $R_u$ and $R_v$ are deleted. Since an attribute of $R_u$ could be synonym of an attribute of $R_v$, $R_{uv}$ could inherit pairs of synonym attributes. If this happens, for each of such pairs $(A_l, A_m)$, $A_l$ and $A_m$ must be merged into a unique attribute. The merging is carried out by adding a new attribute $A_{lm}$ to $R_{uv}$, by characterizing it and by deleting both $A_l$ and $A_m$. The procedure is as follows:

---

**Procedure** *Abstract_Rel*(**var** $R_u, R_v, R_{uv}$: a relationship; **var** $IIB$: a support Intensional Information Base);
**const**
    $th_{us} = 0.75$;
**var**
    $A$: a set of attributes;
    $S$: a scheme;
**begin**
    $S := Detect\_Scheme(R_u)$;
    $IIB.R\_Add(S, R_{uv})$;
    $IIB.R\_Characterize(R_u, R_v, R_{uv})$;
    $IIB.R\_Transfer\_Att(R_u, R_{uv})$;
    $IIB.R\_Transfer\_Att(R_v, R_{uv})$;
    $IIB.R\_Transfer\_Ent(R_u, R_{uv})$;
    $IIB.R\_Delete(R_u)$;
    $IIB.R\_Delete(R_v)$;
    $IIB.M.SoM := IIB.M.SoM \cup \{\langle R_u, R_v, R_{uv}, RMerge \rangle \}$;
    $IIB.M.SoV := IIB.M.SoV \cup \{D\_EMerge(R_u, R_v, R_{uv})\}$;
    **for each** $A_l, A_m \in IIB.R\_Int\_Structure(R_{uv})$ **such that**
    $\langle A_l, A_m, f \rangle \in IIB.M.SD$ **and** $f > th_{us}$ **do begin**
        $IIB.A\_Add(A_{lm}, R_{uv})$;
        $IIB.A\_Characterize(A_l, A_m, A_{lm})$;
        $IIB.A\_Delete(A_l)$;
        $IIB.A\_Delete(A_m)$;
        $IIB.M.SoM := IIB.M.SoM \cup \{\langle A_l, A_m, A_{lm}, AMerge \rangle \}$;
        $IIB.M.SoV := IIB.M.SoV \cup \{D\_AMerge(A_l, A_m, A_{lm})\}$
    **end**
**end**

---

### 6.6.6 Procedure Abstract_Isa

This procedure takes in input two entities $E_p$ and $E_q$ and a support Intensional Information Base $IIB$ and abstracts $E_p$ into $E_q$. First, $E_p$ is merged into $E_q$; as a consequence, the *is-a* relationship from $E_p$ to $E_q$ becomes a cyclic relationship of $E_q$ and can be abstracted into $E_q$. The procedure is as follows:

---

**Procedure** *Abstract_Isa*(**var** $E_p, E_q$: an entity; **var** $IIB$: a support Intensional Information Base);
**var**
    $E$: a set of entities;
    $R_{E_p E_q}$: a relationship;
**begin**

$R_{E_p E_q} = IIB.EE\_Detect\_Isa(E_p, E_q);$
$IIB.E\_Characterize(E_p, E_q, E_q);$
$IIB.E\_Transfer\_Att(E_p, E_q);$
$IIB.E\_Transfer\_Rel(E_p, E_q);$
$IIB.E\_Delete(E_p);$
$IIB.M.SoM := IIB.M.SoM \cup \{\langle E_p, E_q, E_q, EMerge\rangle\};$
$IIB.M.SoV := IIB.M.SoV \cup \{D\_EMerge(E_p, E_q, E_q)\};$
$Abstract\_CR(R_{E_p E_q}, IIB)$
**end**

### 6.6.7 Procedure Abstract_Ent

This procedure takes in input three entities $E_p$, $E_q$ and $E_{pq}$ and a support Intensional Information Base $IIB$ and abstracts $E_p$ and $E_q$ into $E_{pq}$.

At first $E_p$ and $E_q$ are merged into an entity $E_{pq}$; as a consequence the relationships between $E_p$ and $E_q$ become cyclic relationships of $E_{pq}$ and can be merged into $E_{pq}$. The procedure is realized as follows:

**Procedure** *Abstract_Ent*(**var** $E_p, E_q, E_{pq}$: an entity; **var** $IIB$: an Intensional Information Base);
**var**
    $R$: a set of relationships;
    $S$: a scheme;
**begin**
    $R := IIB.EE\_Detect\_NonIsa(E_p, E_q);$
    $S := Detect\_Scheme(E_p);$
    $E\_Merge(S, E_p, E_q, E_{pq}, IIB);$
    **for each** $R_u \in R$ **do**
        $Abstract\_CR(R_u, IIB)$
**end**

# 6.7 The "Template" Language for Defining $IIB.M.SoV$

Views of $IIB.M.SoV$ are defined by a "template" language, independent from conceptual and logic scheme models, whose basic operators are parametric procedures that, once instantiated and translated into procedures valid for the DBMS storing data which they operate upon, compute derived data instances from input data instances. The task of each view consists in taking in input instances of some objects and returning instances of new objects whose structure has been derived in the previous phases. In the following, we illustrate the behaviour of these parametric procedures, one per section.

### 6.7.1 Merging Entities

The procedure *D_EMerge* yields instances of an entity $E_{pq}$ (obtained from merging of entities $E_p$ and $E_q$) from corresponding instances of $E_p$ and $E_q$.

In order to obtain the instances of $E_{pq}$, the analogous, in the E/R model, of the relational operator *Full Outer Join* must be executed on $E_p$ and $E_q$. The attributes associated to the *Full Outer Join* operation are those constituting the set of synonym attributes of $E_p$ and $E_q$; they can be derived by examining the $IIB.M.SoM$. The procedure is, therefore, as follows:

---

**Procedure** $D\_EMerge(E_p, E_q$: an entity; **var** $E_{pq}$: an entity);
**begin**
      $E_{pq}.Data := E_p\ FullOuterJoin\ E_q$
**end**

---

Here $E_{pq}.Data$ indicates the instances of $E_{pq}$.

### 6.7.2 Merging Attributes

The procedure $D\_AMerge$ is activated for deriving instances of an attribute $A_{lm}$, obtained by merging the attributes $A_l$ and $A_m$, from the instances of $A_l$ and $A_m$. If the domain of $A_{lm}$ has been obtained from the domains of $A_l$ or $A_m$, the corresponding instances are taken as the instances of $A_{lm}$; otherwise a suitable translation is necessary; the task to choose the attribute $A_l$ or $A_m$ which the translation must be executed from and the definition of the translation itself is left to the human expert.

### 6.7.3 Merging Relationships

The procedure $D\_RMerge$ derives instances of a relationship $R_{uv}$ (obtained by merging the relationships $R_u$ and $R_v$) from instances of $R_u$ and $R_v$. Remember that $R_u$, $R_v$ and $R_{uv}$ link the same pairs of entities.

The procedure determines the pair of entities linked by $R_u$ and $R_v$; let this be $(E', E'')$. Then it carries out the *Full Outer Join* between $R_u$ and $R_v$ (the attributes associated to the *Full Outer Join* operation are those constituting the set of synonym attributes of $R_u$ and $R_v$) and joins the obtained result with $E'$ and $E''$. Finally the overall result must be projected onto the attributes and the foreign keys of $R_{uv}$.

---

**Procedure** $D\_RMerge(R_u, R_v$: a relationship; **var** $R_{uv}$: a relationship);
**var**
    $E$: a set of entities;
**begin**
    $E := IIB.R\_Ent\_Structure(R_u)$;
    Let $E = \{E', E''\}$;
    $J_1 := R_u\ FullOuterJoin\ R_v$;
    $J_2 := E'\ Join\ J_1\ Join\ E''$;
    $PJ_1 = Project(J_2, IIB.R\_Int\_Structure(R_{uv}) \cup$
                                                  $IIB.R\_ForeignKey(R_{uv}))$
**end**

---

Operators *Join* and *Project* are the analogous, in the $E/R$ model, of the relational operators $\bowtie$ and $\pi$.

### 6.7.4 Creation of an is-a Relationship

The procedure $D\_IsaCreate$ takes in input two entities $E_p$ and $E_q$ and an *is-a* relationship $R$ from $E_p$ to $E_q$ and obtains instances of $R$ from instances of $E_p$ and of $E_q$. To this purpose the *Join* between $E_p$ and $E_q$ must be executed and the result must be projected onto the foreign key of $R$.

```
Procedure D_IsaCreate(Ep, Eq: an entity; var R: a relationship);
begin
        R.Data = Project(Ep Join Eq, IIB.R_ForeignKey(R))
end
```

### 6.7.5 Modification of an is-a Relationship

The procedure $D\_IsaModify$ takes in input two entities $E_q$ and $E_t$ and an *is-a* relationship $R'$ such that the hypernym of $R'$ has changed from $E_q$ to $E_t$; it assumes the existence of another *is-a* relationship $R''$ from $E_t$ to $E_q$. It derives instances of the "new" $R'$ from instances of the "old" $R'$ and of $R''$. In order to obtain them, a join is executed between the "old" $R'$ and $R''$ and the obtained result is projected into the foreign key of the "new" $R'$. The procedure is implemented as follows:

```
Procedure D_IsaModify(var R': an is-a relationship; Eq, Et: an entity );
var
        OR', R'': an is-a relationship;
begin
        OR' := IIB.Old(R');
        R'' := IIB.EE_Detect_Isa(Et, Eq);
        R'.Data := Project(OR' Join R'', IIB.R_ForeignKey(R'));
end
```

### 6.7.6 Abstracting a Cyclic Relationship into the Corresponding Entity

The procedure $D\_CRDelToE$ is associated to the abstraction of the cyclic relationship $R$ into the corresponding entity $E$. In particular, instances of $E$ are obtained from instances of both the "old" $E$ and $R$; in particular instances of the "new" $E$ are obtained by executing a *Full Outer Join* between the "old" $E$ and $R$. The procedure is as follows:

```
Procedure D_CRDelToE(R: a relationship; var E: an entity);
var
        OE: an entity;
begin
        OE := IIB.Old(E);
        E.Data := Project(OE FullOuterJoin R, IIB.E_Structure(E))
end
```

# 7. Construction
# of a Cooperative Information System

*In this chapter we describe a mediator-based architecture for a Cooperative Information System which is specifically conceived for realizing very large systems. The proposed architecture adopts a data repository as the core structure to guarantee a friendly access to available data. The plan of the chapter is as follows: in the first section we state the problem. The general characteristics of the approach are illustrated in the second section whereas the third one describes the general architecture of the CIS. The fourth section is devoted to describe functionalities supported in a CIS complying with the proposed architecture whereas the following two sections present the general structure of the mediator and of the wrappers. Finally, in the last section, we illustrate the Web user interface.*

*All material presented in this chapter has been derived from [38, 40, 39].*

## 7.1 Introduction

The issue of integrating geographically spread, heterogeneous databases has been dealt with since early seventies and has now received a renewed interest because of the recent technological development of networks and of the availability of numerous data sources.

Multidatabase systems can be considered as the first attempt to realize the integration of existing databases [20]. They achieved connection between DBMS by adopting a strong integration approach. Due to this choice, multidatabase systems had necessarily to rely upon a complex and sophisticated software support for communication and information exchange. Besides the implementation difficulties caused by this complexity, these systems were also characterized by important organizational problems in their management, mainly determined by the loss of autonomy for pre-existing databases.

Federated databases [66, 111, 115, 119, 126] have been proposed more recently to overcome these limits. Federation requires a much looser integration amongst sites so that the autonomy of local databases is mostly preserved. Indeed, in this context, the integration step consists in designing interfaces as software layers upon existing DBMS to coordinate and integrate underlying databases without modifying either their structure or their internal behaviour. Therefore, in this case, the integration software is simpler for it

D. Ursino: Extr. and Expl. of Intensional Knowledge ..., LNCS 2282, pp. 143–159, 2002.
© Springer-Verlag Berlin Heidelberg 2002

basically provides support for information exchange and information sharing amongst sites; also the organization is simpler since the autonomy of local systems is preserved. From a functional standpoint, such a structure can be looked at as consisting of information providers supplying their information and information users exploiting them, where each local database site can either act as a provider, or as a user or both.

Even if traditional federated DBMS constitutes an important step forward w.r.t. multidatabase systems, they still have an important drawback in that information flow is not really coordinated, thus possibly causing "dispersion" of information. Such a negative characteristic is negligible for relatively small systems, but becomes relevant when the amount of managed information is large. Unfortunately, especially when geographically dispersed information sources are to be integrated, the latter is the most probable case.

Therefore, the most relevant problem of federated systems towards the satisfactory exploitation of pre-existing information sources seems to be the absence of a sw/hw entity providing the needed information flow coordination amongst provider and user sites. Such an entity would, for instance, give users the opportunity to single out only those data necessary to their information needs, decide access rights to information and, more generally, choose all the presentation details relative to information supplied by Provider Sites. This entity can be thus looked at as an *information mediator* [120, 126] between information sources and information users.

Mediator-based Cooperative Information Systems are two-level structures, consisting of a wrapping layer and a mediation one. *Wrappers* translate local languages, models and concepts of the data sources into the global language, model and concepts shared by some or all sources [120, 126]. *Mediators* take in input information from one or more components below them, and supply as the output either information for the components above them or for external users of the system. Data are not necessarily localized at the mediator. Often the mediator stores just views of real data. These views can be queried by components above them (including system users): it is then up to the mediator retrieving data needed for constructing query answers from the actual data sources. A typical mediator-based architecture is shown in Figure 7.1.

In the last years, some mediator-based systems have been designed and realized. For example, the *Information Manifold* [65], developed at the AT&T Laboratories and *TSIMMIS* [42], designed at Stanford University, are examples of realization of mediator capabilities in integrated information systems.

TSIMMIS [42] is based on a *Query Centric* model, i.e., mediated scheme relations are defined as views over the source relations. The mediator describes information contained in the various sources using a global scheme (so there is only one abstraction level); the global scheme is queried by the user in order to access information. In this system data models of the differ-

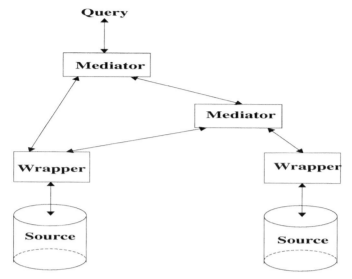

**Fig. 7.1.** Architecture of a mediator-based system

ent local databases are translated into a unique one; the global data model is powerful enough to manage various information representations.

Information Manifold [65] is based on a *Source Centric* model, i.e., for the purpose of integration, the source relations are defined as views over mediated scheme relations. Therefore the global scheme is a collection of virtual classes and relations against which the user poses queries.

In both systems the global scheme specifies the mapping between virtual and real relations; in both of them querying takes place at the level of the global scheme and the mediator has the responsibility of constructing sub-queries which are dispatched to local wrappers and whose results are collected and merged to form the answer to the user query.

Despite its certain merits, the standard mediator-based architecture illustrated above could be difficult to realize when the number of involved databases is very large (in the order of hundreds). Indeed, we argue, there are two main problems to be dealt with:

– The adoption of a "flat" global scheme seems not to be adequate to guarantee a reasonably structured and abstract description of available data. Indeed, it can be anticipated that in situations where hundreds of database schemes are to be integrated, the number and the complexity of relationships holding among involved database objects would be overwhelming. This situation would immediately cause a substantial difficulty for a user to retrieve the information he/she needs.
– The management of querying processes, which could potentially access hundreds of databases for each single user request, may become quite hard a task to be autonomously carried out by the system.

The architecture proposed here, which was explicitly designed with the purpose of supporting such very large integrated access systems, is intended to solve these problems. In order to achieve appropriate support to accessing many data sources (which is the fundamental purpose of our system), it adopts a structured and complex global scheme in the place of an ordinary "flat" global scheme. On the other hand, it lights the burden lying on the mediator modules, by letting the user to perform the selection of local data sources of interest in a friendly, guided manner.

Thus, from the user perspective, querying consists of two distinct phases. In the former one, the user is guided by the system in "navigating" the structured global scheme in order to select a (set of) database(s). In the latter one, the user submits his/her query on the selected data source using either a QBE-like query interface or a query formulation wizard and gets corresponding answers.

More in particular, in our architecture, the global scheme of mediator-based systems is substituted by a data repository, which stores several (partial or total) global views over available data, at different abstraction levels. It should be clear enough that a data repository stores the necessary information for helping the user in locating and retrieving the information of interest, even if he/she has only a partial and abstract knowledge of the data available in the system.

## 7.2 General Characteristics of the Proposed Architecture

The structure of a CIS agreeing with the proposed architecture, as embedded in the general framework of mediator-based integration systems, can therefore be looked at as shown in Figure 7.2.

A CIS agreeing with the proposed architecture is a two-tier distributed system that includes *Provider Sites* and one *Distributor Site*. As explained in more details in the sequel, the Distributor Site stores the data repository and acts as the data mediator of the system, whereas Provider Sites act as wrappers.

The proposed CIS is an Internet-based system allowing for the integrated access to geographically dispersed databases. A Web interface exploits the information encoded in the data repository description for helping the user of the integrated system in locating a local database of interest and in formulating queries on it. Querying is carried out by either a simple QBE-LIKE graphical format or a query formulation wizard; the system also provides for the needed translation from the formulated query into the local system query language.

Main functionalities provided by the proposed CIS are listed below:

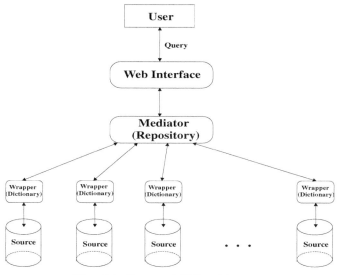

**Fig. 7.2.** Proposed CIS architecture

- dynamic construction of HTML and JavaScript pages for the visualization of repository schemes (including local database schemes of information Provider Sites);
- repository navigation for accessing underlying databases according to user's information needs;
- WWW graphical query formulation support through either a QBE-like interface or a query formulation wizard;
- management of user query submission and query result reception to/from remote Provider Sites (where the databases of interest are physically located);
- dynamic construction of HTML and JavaScript pages for the visualization of user query results.

The proposed CIS matches the application requirements in that:

- it adopts a structured global scheme with several abstraction levels and an interactive navigation strategy through the mediator scheme; as a consequence the user can focus only on the data of interest and, therefore, he/she can retrieve information he/she needs without being puzzled by the presence of large amounts of uninteresting data;
- the querying process becomes very simple since the user queries the databases containing the information of interest and the system limits itself to considering only the data necessary for the answer.

We note that other systems exist having similar purposes as the proposed CIS [66, 120, 123, 126], but they are neither based on a mediator scheme, nor explicitly designed to integrate a large number of local databases. An interesting example is the system Mosaic [123]. This system (and its descendants) hide from the user the specific protocols associated with contacting each information source. However the user needs to know about an information source in order to access it. The architectures presented in [66, 120, 126] are based on semantically rich data models for representing semantic connections between distributed data but they focus on integrating relatively small number of databases.

## 7.3 Structure of the Proposed CIS

The proposed CIS includes two kinds of sites, called the *Provider Site* and the *Distributor Site*, respectively.

The Distributor Site stores the data repository and acts as a data mediator in our system. It receives user information requests and process them, supplying results in the appropriate form back to the user. Note that, in our system, users are only allowed to perform data querying: both data updating and scheme updating are forbidden to them.

The behavior of the system, as illustrated in the context diagram of Figure 7.3, is the following. The user wishing to formulate a query activates a connection to the Distributor Site through a WWW browser. The Distributor Site manages both submission of the query to the Provider Site where the database that was selected by the user is located, and corresponding answer collection and displaying.

If the time slot necessary to obtain an answer from the Provider Site exceeds a given time-out, an off-line answer management process is activated at the Distributor Site and the user is notified disconnection due to time-out. The activated process asynchronously collects all the query results relative to timed-out connections.

The user is also allowed to formulate off-line queries, and to require the Distributor Site to submit them. In general the Distributor Site submits queries to the appropriate Provider Site Manager, which translates the query into the local DBMS language and executes it. The constructed answer is collected by the Provider Site Manager, and sent to the Distributor Site manager which, in turn, displays it to the user. Usually, the user obtains the answer to a submitted query on-line. However if the asynchronous communication mechanism is to be used, the Distributor Site manager stores query results so as to be available to the user to have them displayed during following sessions.

The system also allows to program predefined "parameterized" queries, corresponding to most common requests made by users and which users "complete" by specifying input parameters.

As far as the CIS user interface is concerned, we have already mentioned that it runs within any WWW browser. The connection is established towards

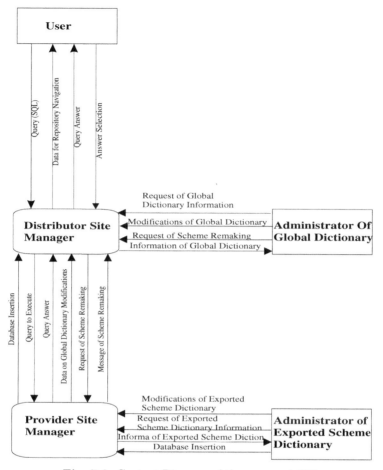

**Fig. 7.3.** Context Diagram of the proposed CIS

the Distributor Site and is, as already noted, generally synchronous in that the user remains connected to the system through the WWW browser until to he/she decides to disconnect the session, or a disconnection due to time-out is forced.

Let us now give some remarks on updates. We have already pointed out that users are not allowed to carry out updating neither on data nor on schemes. However, such updating can take place at the level of local databases. In particular, we have to consider two different cases as far as the modification of local database schemes is concerned. If the modifications carried out locally do not induce changes in the repository structure, then the involved Provider Site Manager automatically sends all data necessary to the modification of the global dictionary to the Distributor Site Manager. Vice versa, when the system is faced with a major modification, such as the insertion of a new database, which can change the repository structure, the intervention of the administrator of the global dictionary is required. Indeed, first of all, a notification message is automatically sent to the Distributor Site; then the new database is inserted and the administrator of the global dictionary is required to brought about appropriate modifications to the data repository. The administrator of the global dictionary accesses the repository through the Distributor Site and requires the information needed for activating the procedures concerning its modification.

A similar process is executed by the administrator of exported scheme dictionary to manage local database schemes which are globally visible in the system.

## 7.4 CIS Functionalities

As pointed out above, the proposed CIS uses the data repository as a tool for navigating the scheme hierarchy represented therein to facilitate user selection and access to underlying databases. Once the user has singled out his/her database of interest, the system helps him/her to query this database, through either a WWW QBE-like graphical query interface or a query formulation wizard.

In more details, our system allows a user, say $U$, to navigate through the data repository according to four different methods:

- *direct access*: in this case clusters grouping local databases which $U$ is allowed to access are visualized. A graphical interface allows $U$ to choose the cluster of interest. As a consequence, the system presents a list of databases associated to the selected clusters that can be queried.
- *hierarchical access*: in this case $U$ navigates the data repository through schemes. In any moment, the system maintains a "current scheme" and displays the list of its subschemes among which the user selects the "new" current scheme. Initially, the current scheme is the *First Level scheme* (see Figure 7.4).
- *access based on sources*: in this case $U$ singles out a source of interest amongst data sources recognized in the system. Once this choice has been made, the system displays the list of databases associated to the selected source.
- *object-guided access*: this is the most important navigation method in that it exploits the repository as a guide for searching the database of interest. This type of access is typically exploited by users who have a just general knowledge about the information of interest but do not know the details of the information structure and localization. At first the system displays objects belonging to the most abstract scheme within the repository. Among the displayed objects, the user then selects that object $O$ which is most closely related to his/her information need. As a consequence, the system

will display objects, belonging to the next level schemes of the repository, from which $O$ has been derived through integration and abstraction steps. The process is iterated by selecting a further object and displaying the associated set of objects in the next level.

As an example, consider the ICGO repository; its first, second and third level abstract schemes are illustrated in Figures 7.4, 7.5 and 7.6. At the beginning the objects *Good, Document, Subject, Office, Territorial References, Event* and *Public Services* are displayed. Suppose the user chooses the entity Subject. The system will therefore display the set of objects $S$ of the

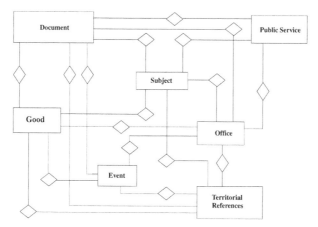

**Fig. 7.4.** First Level Abstract Scheme of the ICGO repository

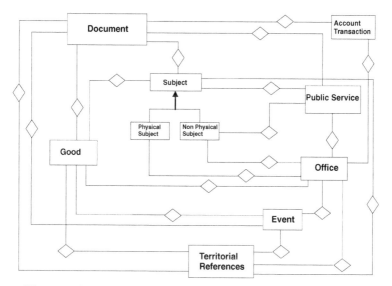

**Fig. 7.5.** Second Level Abstract Scheme of the ICGO repository

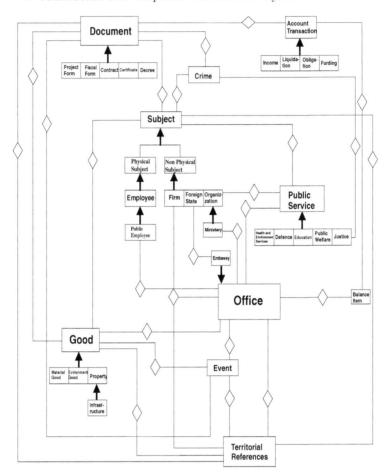

**Fig. 7.6.** Third Level Abstract Scheme of the ICGO repository

second level abstract scheme such that *Subject* has been obtained by abstracting/integrating over *S*; these are *Subject*, *Physical Subject* and *Non Physical Subject*. Suppose the user chooses *Non Physical Subject*: the system displays the objects of the next lower level from which *Non Physical Subject* has been derived through integration and abstraction steps; these objects are *Non Physical Subject*, *Foreign State*, *Firm*, *Organization* and *Ministry*. The process is further iterated and terminates when the level of database schemes is reached, where the user can submit the query of interest.

## 7.5 Structure of the Mediator

In our architecture, mediation functionalities are carried out by the Distributor Site; its purpose is that of providing location transparency on databases managed by various Provider Sites. It carries out two fundamental tasks:

− it manages user access rights to information stored in local databases;
− it reconstructs information supplied by information providers in suitable aggregated structures within the data repository which are used, as previously described, to help the user in accessing the appropriate information sources.

The metascheme which forms the core of the Distributor Site is a global dictionary in which all repository information are stored together with information about user access rights and actual data sources. The global dictionary is shown in Figure 7.7.

Attributes and entities shown in the scheme of Figure 7.7 are reported in Table 7.1 and their meaning is obvious. When the key of an entity consists just of one attribute, this is underlined; as for the other entities, the complete list of the attributes that constitutes the keys is given right after the table.

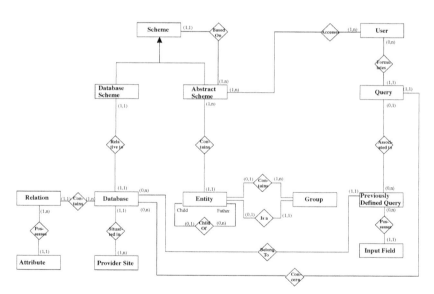

**Fig. 7.7.** Distributor Site Metascheme

A brief description of catalogue content is given next. A scheme can be an abstract scheme or a database one. The entity *database scheme* serves the purpose of describing database schemes, while the entity *abstract scheme* describes repository schemes. In the entity "abstract scheme" the attribute

**Table 7.1.** Attributes of entities of the Global Dictionary Scheme

| | name | description | abstract | | host |
|---|---|---|---|---|---|
| scheme | name | description | abstract | | |
| abstract_scheme | level | | | | |
| database_scheme | source | | | | |
| entity | Id | name | | | |
| group | | | | | |
| provider_site | Id | name | description | e-mail | host |
| database | Id | name | description | last_modif. | |
| relation | Id | name | priority | | |
| attribute | name (1) | type | key | | |
| query | name (3) | description | submiss._date. | arrived_answer. | |
| predefined_query | name (2) | description | priority | | |
| input_fields | name (4) | type | description | | |
| user | login | description | priority | | |

(a) The key of the entity "attribute" consists in the attributes *Id* of "Relation" and *name*.
(b) The key of the entity "predefined query" consists in the attributes *Id* of "Database" and *name*.
(c) The key of the entity "query" consists in the attributes *login* of "User" and *name*.

(d) The key of the entity "input_fields" consists in the attributes *Id* of "Database", *name* of "process" and *name*.

*level* assumes a value equal to the distance of the abstract scheme from the root node of the repository. The only exception is constituted by clusters. To recognize clusters we have decided to use a conventional negative value. Remember that clusters are those structures to which databases are directly associated and have been obtained from their schemes through a one-step integration-abstraction process. An abstract scheme contains one or more entities while an entity occurs just in one abstract scheme. A unique database scheme is associated to each database and vice versa.

An *entity* can be a child of one entity and it can be a father of more than one entity (denoting a generalization process). On the other hand, an entity can be contained in a *group* and a group can contain one or more entities (denoting an abstraction process). The group, in turn, can be represented by only one entity, at the next upper abstraction level.

A database is associated to only one *Provider Site* whereas one of these sites can possess one or more databases.

The *user* can submit queries to databases. This entity has a *priority* field: user can submit predefined queries and access relations with a priority less or equal than his/her own priority. User can access one or more abstract schemes and an abstract scheme can be accessed by one or more users.

The portion of the scheme corresponding to the entities *database*, *relation* and *attribute* has an obvious meaning and therefore is not further illustrated.

The architecture of the Distributor Site is shown in Figure 7.8.

The *Navigation Manager* realizes user navigation through the data repository.

The *Query Manager* is activated when the user formulates a query. The module realizes both a QBE interface and a query formulation wizard. Information necessary to support query formulation is, of course, retrieved from the Global Dictionary.

The *TCP/IP Client* serves the purpose of activating a TCP/IP connection to the Server located at the Provider Site for submitting queries.

The *Dispatcher of Arriving Messages* is a module implementing a daemon that awakes with periodic cadence to verify if new messages have been stored in the mailbox. New messages are examined and the opportune manager is activated depending on their content.

The *Answer Manager* and the *Answer Interface* are activated when the user wishes to have the results of previously submitted query displayed.

Finally the *Manager of Global Dictionary Modifications* and the *Repository Manager* are modules devoted to the management of the data repository.

## 7.6 Structure of the Wrappers

Wrapper functionalities are carried out by the Provider Site. In particular it has to manage the set of databases associated to it in order to make their manipulation uniform, independently on languages and data models they support. Moreover, it communicates with the Distributor Site, accept query requests as the input and constructs query answers as the output. The architecture of the Provider Site is shown in Figure 7.9. The Provider Site consists of a number of software modules, whose functionalities are briefly described in the following.

The *Dispatcher of Arriving Messages* implements a daemon that checks the mailbox for the presence of new messages, examines newly received messages and activates the appropriate management modules.

The *TCP/IP Server* implements a server daemon process which waits for the activation of a connection requested by client processes located at the Distributor Site.

The *Query Manager* takes the query as the input and send it to the DBMS Interface by preliminarily verifying its syntactic correctness. When the corresponding answer is received, the Query Manager restructures it in suitable form and sends it to the TCP/IP Server or to the Distributor Site Manager, depending on the type of connection which was established.

The *DBMS Interface* translates queries submitted by users into the language supported by its corresponding DBMS and submits it to the DBMS itself. Thus, the overall query translation takes place in two steps. First, queries are translated into SQL at the Distributor Site. Second, SQL queries are translated into local languages by DBMS interfaces at the Provider Sites. Obviously, one DBMS interface will be needed for each DBMS to be accessed. In the present release of the system, the only interfaces we actually implemented allow access to Postgres databases. Moreover, the DBMS interface is responsible for sending query answers to the Query Manager.

Finally the *Scheme Loader* and the *Dictionary Manager* are modules devoted to the management of Exported Scheme Dictionary.

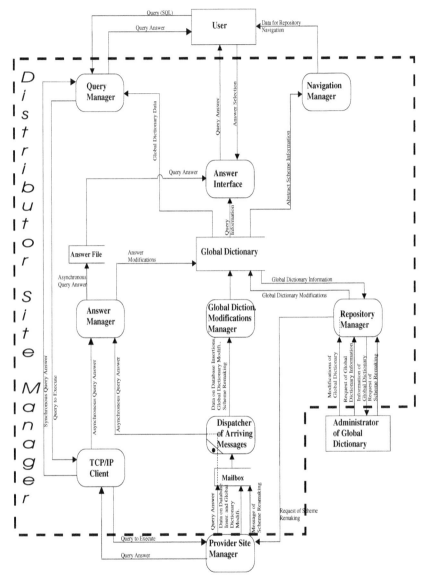

**Fig. 7.8.** Architecture of the Distributor Site

## 7.7 The Web User Interface

The interface of the proposed CIS exploits dynamic construction of HTML and JavaScript pages to supply services to the user. At present, the interface is in Italian, even if an English version will be linked soon. Main page sections

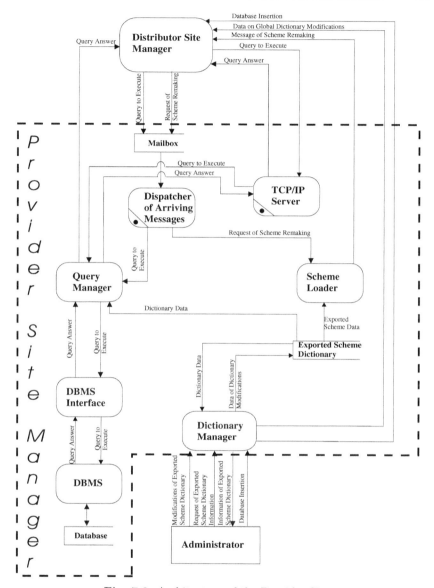

**Fig. 7.9.** Architecture of the Provider Site

included in the Web interface and their hierarchical structure are depicted in Figure 7.10.

The system includes an on-line help and a glossary to assist the user. After logging in, the user can choose among two pages which activate the sections for the visualization of off-line constructed query results and for repository navigation, respectively.

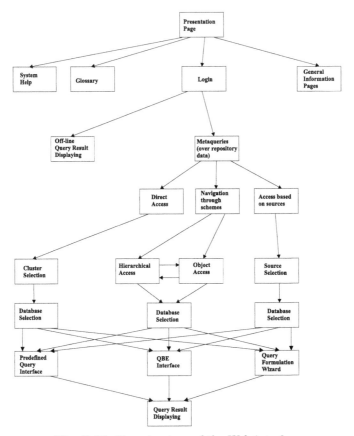

**Fig. 7.10.** Tree structure of the Web interface

The former section includes a number of HTML and JavaScript pages by which the user can select one or more query results of interest and display them. We note that also result tuples displaying is embedded within an HTML and JavaScript dynamic page.

The latter section allows the user to select a navigation method amongst the four available ones. Depending on this choice, several other pages are accessed which guide the user within the metadata towards eventually selecting the database of interest. A further section of the interface consequently accessed allows the user either to formulate a new query through a QBE-like query interface or to construct a query by a query formulation wizard or to request the execution of a predefined query. The Web interface includes also several other pages which supply further minor information services to the user.

Our system is accessible at the address:

http://isi-cnr.deis.unical.it:1080/~ netrdist

by typing the string "ursino" as the login specification. Note that, for security reasons, no "real" IGCO database has been linked to the system, whereas a couple of example databases can be freely accessed.

# 8. Construction of a Data Warehouse

*This chapter is devoted to illustrate a new three level Data Warehouse architecture whose core is constituted by a data repository and which is particularly suited when the operational schemes of the Data Warehouse to be constructed are numerous and complex. The plan of the chapter is as follows: in the first section we define the Data Warehouses and compare three Data Warehouse architecture types. The general characteristics of the Data Warehouse architecture we propose are illustrated in the second section whereas the third one presents the corresponding technical details and pinpoints the differences between classical three level architectures and the one we are proposing in this chapter. Finally a method for automatically synthesizing a Data Warehouse based on the proposed architecture is described in the fourth section.*

*The material presented in this chapter can be found in [86, 84].*

## 8.1 Introduction

Data warehousing is recognized as a key technology for the exploitation of massive amounts of data nowadays available electronically to many organizations, and recent analyses confirm its role as one of the most pervasive technologies in modern database applications. Such increasing success, also determined by the availability of efficient hw/sw support technologies, is due to the fact that data warehousing allows to look at organizational data at the right level of abstraction and aggregation, whereby providing a convenient support to decision making within complex organizations.

Intuitively, a Data Warehouse is a repository of data and related information whose purpose is to allow the extraction, the reconciliation and the re-organization of data stored in traditional operational databases. Data warehousing usually requires the materialization of data stored in operational databases. Moreover, data re-organization almost always includes time-stamping operational data (or aggregates thereof) to obtain historic series, which are then analyzed for decision making [34, 125]. Data Warehouses are query-oriented systems (as opposed to operational, transaction-oriented databases), where updating only takes place as a massive, relatively rare and off-line process by which operational data are migrated into the Data Warehouse.

D. Ursino: Extr. and Expl. of Intensional Knowledge ..., LNCS 2282, pp. 161–169, 2002.
© Springer-Verlag Berlin Heidelberg 2002

A Data Warehouse is obtained by defining its architecture and mappings by which source data are extracted, filtered, integrated and stored into the defined structure. Populating the Data Warehouse by new source data takes place according to a pace decided as part of the design process [125].

In the literature, various *conceptual architectures* have been proposed for Data Warehouses. They can be classified into three groups, depending on the number of levels they are characterized by.

In a *one-level architecture* [55] each piece of data is stored once and only once: a "middleware" level operates as an interface between users and operational databases. Therefore, there is no materialized Data Warehouse but, rather, it is "simulated" using views (virtual Data Warehouse). This kind of architecture allows for a rather quick development of a Data Warehouse with reduced costs. However, it induces the need of planning activities (such as data source identification, data transformation and so on) to be carried out for each query[1], the lack of data historicizing and an unpredictable access time for the end user.

On the contrary, *two-level architectures* [44, 55, 81, 125] are based on the idea of separating source data from derived ones. In such architectures, the "first" level contains source data whereas derived data are stored in the "second" level. Derived data can be either a simple copy of source data or obtained from them by some abstraction/aggregation process. Two-level architectures are the most common ones. They are convenient especially when operational sources are basically homogeneous but have an important disadvantage in that significant data duplication is usually implied. Indeed, since each decision support application has its own derived data, there is no possibility of storing information in common among several decision support applications in a unique place. Therefore, one copy of these common derived data exists for each decision support application exploiting them.

*Three-level architectures* [84, 53] are obtained by considering that the derivation of data for decision support is performed in two phases: *(i)* the reconciliation of operational data belonging to different sources; *(ii)* the derivation of decision support data from reconciled ones. In this sense, three-level architectures are designed to store operational, reconciled and derived data, resp. The classical three-level architecture of a Data Warehouse is represented in Figure 8.1.

In this model, the first level stores operational data, the second one stores reconciled data, whereas the latter one stores support decision data [84, 53]. Therefore, a three-level Data Warehouse can be represented by a 4-tuple

$$DW = \langle OS, BDW, BIWS, M \rangle$$

where *(i)* $OS$ indicates the *Operational Systems* that manage data, schemes, and applications relative to operational data; *(ii)* $BDW$ denotes the *Business Data Warehouse* that has in charge data, schemes and applications rel-

---

[1] And, unfortunately, these are the most expensive steps.

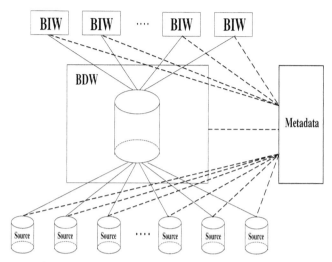

**Fig. 8.1.** A classical three level architecture for the Data Warehouse

ative to reconciled data; *(iii) BIWS* represents the *Business Information Warehouses*, or data marts, that manage data, schemes and applications for decision support, and *(iv) M* indicates the *metadata*, providing information about sources, schemes and interactions among the three levels of the Data Warehouse.

The reconciliation level represents a common view of data available in the whole organization. Reconciling activities eliminate inconsistencies and irregularities of operational data and integrate them in a rational way. Once reconciled data have been constructed, decision support data can be derived from them rather than from operational data.

The presence of a reconciled data level has several important advantages, summarized below:

- the cost paid for obtaining derived data is smaller in three level architectures than in other models, because reconciliation operations are performed once and for all at the beginning and must not be repeated for each derived data set;
- the presence of reconciled data can help in the re-engineering of operational applications: for instance, it may happen that some information, such as historic data, have been stored in operational data simply because the organization had no other place for storing them; the presence of a reconciled data level allows to transfer these data from the operational level to the reconciliation one, thus simplifying the operational systems;
- some decision support information may exist that cannot be extracted in a simple manner from operational data each time they are needed (for example because the extraction is expensive or because transactions in the operational systems must be suspended for carrying it out); in a two

level architecture these information must be stored with each derived data set that uses it, simply because there is no other place where it can be stored, whereby inducing a significant amount of data replication; in a three level architecture storing these information is done once and for all in the reconciled data level.

Apparently, the main drawback of three-level architectures is, again, data replication in the reconciled level. However, introducing the third level does not actually increase significantly needed storing resources, since *(i)* the reconciled data level stores only one copy of each information, *(ii)* the additional space needed to store data at the reconciled level is balanced considering that space is spared in storing common data and difficult-to-derive data once and for all in the reconciled level (instead of duplicating them within the derived data workspace associated to each application using them).

However, in spite of its advantages, classical three-level Data Warehouse architectures show important limitations within application environments (like those typical of Central Public Administrations) comprising lots of complex heterogeneous operational source systems. In such cases, the flat global scheme used within the reconciled level, and obtained by integrating schemes of operational databases, presumably encodes an enormous number and variety of objects, and becomes far too complex to be effectively used. As a result, the derivation of decision support information from this level becomes too complex a task. The application context just described has not a mere speculative relevance, since this is precisely the situation one encounters nowadays in many organizations. We point out that the problem here is due to data source complexity and heterogeneity and not to the Data Warehouse architecture itself; indeed, analogous difficulties arise also with one- and two-level architectures.

## 8.2 General Characteristics of the Proposed Architecture

A first purpose of our approach is to provide an alternative three-level Data Warehouse architecture overcoming the above mentioned limitation. In our approach, we do not directly integrate operational schemes to construct a global flat scheme. Rather, we first collect subsets of operational schemes into homogeneous clusters and construct a Data Repository which is used as the core of the reconciled data level. In other words the reconciled data are stored at various abstraction levels into a data repository. By adopting such a data repository as the global scheme of the reconciled level, we obtain a DW architecture as represented in Figure 8.2.

In all Data Warehouse architectures presented in the literature, metadata, which are fundamental both for the efficient derivation of data and for their appropriate exploitation in decision making, are derived and updated

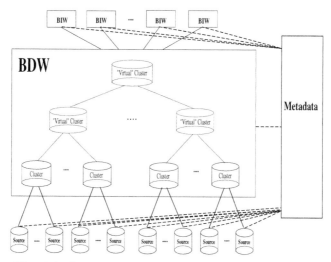

**Fig. 8.2.** Our proposal of three level architecture for DW

separately from operational, reconciled and derived data; therefore, they are often not well related to corresponding schemes (e.g., they can be out of date). A data repository does not only collect database schemes but can also store metadata they are related to; therefore, in our approach, metadata are obtained during the derivation of reconciled data; each time the data repository (and consequently the reconciled data level) is updated also the corresponding metadata are updated. This marks a further advantage of our architecture over classical one in its capability to maintain the consistency among reconciled data, metadata and derived data.

When the number of involved data sources is large, manual methodologies for Data Warehouse design are difficult to be applied. This is due to the presence of presumably hundreds of objects (entities, relationships, attributes) belonging to involved database schemes to be analyzed for the Data Warehouse design purposes. Our approach for the construction of a Data Warehouse tackles this difficulty in that it is semi-automatic and this requires a limited contribution of human experts.

## 8.3 Technical Details

In our approach, the $BDW$ can be thought of as being a triplet

$$BDW = \langle Rep, Map, SoV \rangle$$

As pointed out in Section 6.1, the repository $BDW.Rep$ consists of a hierarchy of clusters. Each cluster represents a group of homogeneous schemes and is, in its turn, represented by a scheme (hereafter called *C-scheme*[2]). The cluster hierarchy consists of several levels so that each cluster belongs to one level; clusters of level $n$ are obtained grouping some C-schemes of level $n-1$; clusters of level 0 are obtained grouping operational schemes. Therefore each cluster $Cl$ is characterized by: *(i)* its identifier C-Id; *(ii)* its C-scheme; *(iii)* the group of identifiers of clusters whose C-schemes originated the C-scheme of $Cl$ (hereafter called O-identifiers) and *(iv)* a level index. Given a cluster $Cl$, we define O-schemes all schemes associated to O-identifiers of $Cl$. Clusters are classified as basic and derived. A *basic cluster* has level 0 and its O-schemes are operational ones; a *derived cluster* is a cluster obtained grouping C-schemes representing other clusters.

More formally the *BDW.Rep* can be represented as:

$$BDW.Rep = \{c \mid c \text{ has the form } \langle C\text{-}Id, C\text{-}scheme, O\text{-}Identifiers, lev \rangle$$
$$\text{and } c \text{ is a cluster}\}$$

As illustrated in Chapter 6, the *Set of Mappings BDW.Map* can be looked at as to store the way a scheme object has been obtained from other objects through integration/abstraction steps. *BDW.Map* includes an entry for each new object obtained along the Data Warehouse construction; it is used to define views belonging to *BDW.SoV*. Thus, a mapping can be assumed to consist of a set of tuples, each of which must have one of the forms described in Section 6.2.1.

The Set of Views *BDW.SoV*, already introduced in Section 6.2.1, stores a view for each new object obtained along the *BDW* construction (and, therefore, a view for each *BDW.Map* entry). Views allow to obtain instances of an object from istances of objects it derives from.

Among data represented in the data repository, generally only those pertaining clusters at level 0 are materialized. In particular, we assume that all of them, as a whole, form the *data component* of the *BDW*. Data relative to more abstract levels of the repository can be easily obtained from them by defining suitable virtual views. Clearly, some or all clusters of some level $i > 0$ can be materialized if this is necessary and if enough memory is available. Views can be either *materialized*, if they take in input operational data and return the materialized data of the repository, or *virtual*, if they take in input materialized or virtual reconciled data of a level $i \geq 0$ and deliver reconciled data of the level $i + 1$.

Views are defined by a meta-language, independent from conceptual and logical scheme models, whose basic operators are parametric procedures that, once instantiated, compute derived data instances from input data instances; the possible forms of these parametric procedures are illustrated in Section 6.2.1. Each basic operation of our meta-language can be easily translated in an operation valid for the DBMS storing data a certain view operates upon. In particular, all virtual views operate on materialized data of the *BDW*;

---

[2] As for other schemes, also C-schemes are characterized by unique identifiers.

these are stored, presumably, in relational databases. Therefore operations of the meta-language must be generally translated in relational operations, when these views are implemented. Materialized views, instead, must obtain materialized $BDW$ data from operational ones; these can be stored in legacy systems, flat files, hierarchical or relational databases and so on; operations of the meta-language must be translated into operations of these systems.

In order to pinpoint the differences between classical three level architectures and the one we are proposing here, the following observations can be drawn:

1. A classical three-level architecture is a particular case of the one proposed here, since it corresponds to a case where source operational databases are all grouped into one cluster and no abstraction is carried out over the associated C-scheme.

2. The architecture we propose here is naturally conducive to an incremental Data Warehouse construction. Moreover, differently from classical three-level architectures, adding, removing or modifying a source operational database scheme causes only the schemes of the clusters involving this database to be updated (at most one scheme per level), rather than causing the modification of the entire reconciled global scheme.

3. In a classical three-level architecture designed over a large number of source databases, presumably hundreds of objects are represented in the global scheme; this makes it very difficult to analyze for the designing purposes. In particular, the global scheme can be seen as partitioned into subschemes loosely related to each other, whereas each subscheme contains objects tightly related to each other. Therefore, while it is easy to figure out a semantics of each subscheme, it is quite hard to assign a semantics to the global scheme as a whole. Such difficulty does not characterize our architecture where a database cluster would correspond to each of these subschemes and, therefore, would have been associated to a precise semantics.

4. In our architecture, $BIW$ (i.e., data mart) design is presumably simpler than with classical architectures, since each data mart will insist over a bunch of data sources spanned by a subtree of our core data repository rooted at some C-scheme of level $k$, for some $k$; therefore, the designer will be allowed to focus over a restricted subset of data objects looked at the appropriate abstraction level.

5. In our approach metadata are derived (resp., updated) during the derivation (resp., updating) of reconciled data (see above); consequently the proposed approach automatically maintains the consistency among reconciled data, metadata and derived data.

6. In our architecture, reconciled data are (virtually) represented at various abstraction levels within the core data repository. Note that maintaining several abstraction levels does not cause significant problems; indeed:

- required memory resources are limited since, generally, only reconciled data at the lowest abstraction level are materialized, whereas other abstraction level data are stored as views that are executed on demand;
- required time resources needed to retrieve data by executing views are moderate because *(a)* they are executed on a unique, centralized DBMS (i.e., that storing the materialized data of the reconciled level and, in general, the $BDW$); *(b)* they typically involve a restricted data set (i.e., that corresponding to the cluster the view is defined upon); *(c)* since they are defined when the $BDW$ is constructed, indexing can be designed in order to quickly access needed data .

It follows from these observations that, by paying a limited price in terms of required space and computation time, we obtain an architecture that retains all worths of classical three-level architectures but overcomes some of their limitations in the presence of a large number of data sources. Note, by the way, that in such application contexts, problems analogous to those described for classical three-level architectures characterize also one- and two- level architectures.

## 8.4 Automatic Synthesis of a Data Warehouse

In this section, we present an algorithm for obtaining, in a fairly automatic manner, a Data Warehouse designed over a set of source operational databases.

The proposed algorithm for Data Warehouse design takes in input a list of database schemes $S$, a Synonymy Dictionary $SD$, an Homonymy Dictionary $HD$, an Hyponymy Dictionary $HyD$ and an Overlapping Dictionary $OD$; the structure and the semantics of these dictionaries have been described in Section 6.2.1. The algorithm yields in output a Data Warehouse $DW$. It can be encoded as follows:

---

**Algorithm for a Data Warehouse design**
*Input:* a list of database schemes $S = S_1, \ldots, S_n$; a Synonymy Dictionary $SD$; an Homonymy Dictionary $HD$; an Hyponymy Dictionary $HyD$; an Overlapping Dictionary $OD$;
*Output:* a Data Warehouse $DW$;
**var**
    $BDW$: a Business Data Warehouse;
    $BIWS$: a set of Business Information Warehouses;
    $M$: a set of metadata;
**begin**
    $Derive\_BDW(S, SD, HD, HyD, OD, BDW)$;
    $Derive\_BIWS(SD, HD, HyD, OD, BDW, BIWS)$;
    $Derive\_Metadata(S, SD, HD, HyD, OD, BDW, BIWS, M)$;
    **return** $DW = S \uplus BDW \uplus BIWS \uplus M$
**end**

---

Here, the expression $DW = S \uplus BDW \uplus BIWS \uplus M$ indicates that $DW$ is constituted by the four components $S$, $BDW$, $BIWS$ and $M$.

The procedure $Derive\_BDW$ takes in input a list $S$ of database schemes, a Synonymy Dictionary $SD$, an Homonymy Dictionary $HD$, an Hyponymy Dictionary $HyD$ and an Overlapping Dictionary $OD$; it yields in output a $BDW$. Since the $BDW$ is mainly composed by a Data Repository constructed on the operational databases, the algorithm for deriving a $BDW$ is analogous to the algorithm for constructing a Data Repository illustrated in Section 6.3.

The procedure $Derive\_BIWS$ derives the data marts of the repository; since the data marts' front-end are largely application dependent we do not consider them into details. The procedure first determines which set of data and which abstraction level is the most appropriate to feed a certain data mart application. Data marts can then be obtained from selected data sets using the techniques presented in [44].

The procedure $Derive\_Metadata$ takes in input metadata derived during the $BDW$ construction, derives other necessary warehouse metadata and stores all metadata in a suitable form.

In our approach, human intervention may be required in some phases. Moreover, it is in any case needed that a human expert validates the results produced by intermediate steps.

# Part III

# System Description and Experimentations

This part is devoted to describing a system which implements both the approaches to property extraction described in Part I and the methodologies for constructing a Cooperative Information System or a Data Warehouse illustrated in Part II; in addition this part illustrates some of the experiments we have conducted on Italian Central Governmental Office databases. In more detail the plan of this part is the following: Chapter 9 describes our system called DIKE (Database Intensional Knowledge Extractor). Chapter 10 describes the experiments we have carried out on ICGO databases concerning the derivation of synonymies, homonymies, type conflicts and object cluster similarities whereas the experiments relative to the extraction of hyponymies are illustrated in Chapter 11. Chapter 12 describes the experiments related to the derivation of assertions between knowledge patterns. The experiments regarding the semi-automatic construction of a data repository are illustrated in Chapter 13. Finally Chapter 14 describes an example of the exploitation of the Cooperative Information System constructed for ICGO databases.

# 9. The System D.I.K.E.

*This chapter's purpose is to describe DIKE, the system implementing our algorithms for deriving intensional knowledge and for constructing a Data Repository, a Cooperative Information System and a Data Warehouse. The plan of the chapter is as follows: the first section summarizes the overall approach we proposed and implemented in DIKE. The second section presents the context diagram of DIKE; the description of DIKE modules is carried out in the third section whereas in the last one we describe a "trip" through the system.*

*The material presented in this chapter can be found in [121, 94, 93, 99, 102].*

## 9.1 Introduction

The methodologies for deriving and exploiting intensional knowledge from a set of heterogeneous databases presented in the previous chapters have been implemented in a system called DIKE (Database Intensional Knowledge Extractor). The overall approach implemented in DIKE consists of the following steps:

- The enrichment of scheme description, obtained by (semi-automatically) extracting intensional knowledge; this task is carried out into three sub-steps:
  - the derivation of simple interscheme properties relating pairs of scheme objects;
  - the derivation of similarities between subschemes;
  - the derivation of assertions involving complex patterns, relating intensionally defined objects.
- The exploitation of derived interscheme properties for obtaining, in a semi-automatic fashion, an integrated and abstracted representation of available data, encoded in a *Data Repository*; we recall that a Data Repository organizes the description of involved databases at various levels of abstractions (see Chapter 6); the construction of a specific Data Repository is a complex task [39, 9]; however, its availability is beneficial, expecially in the large application contexts we are focusing on, since it provides an effective

D. Ursino: Extr. and Expl. of Intensional Knowledge ..., LNCS 2282, pp. 175–187, 2002.

scheme description framework for designing new application layers on the top of pre-existing databases.
- The exploitation of the repository (and of the properties encoded therein) and derived in previous steps to support the designer in realizing mediator-based Cooperative Information Systems or Data Warehouses over available data.

We have tested DIKE against several real example cases. Interestingly, we had the chance to apply our techniques on the set of ICGO databases. With the support of DIKE, we have extracted intensional knowledge from the schemes, we have constructed a Data Repository and we have exploited the Data Repository thus obtained for constructing a CIS; we are also planning the construction of a Data Warehouse. The overall results we have obtained have been finally compared with those achieved manually by AIPA, obtaining satisfactory results. In the following chapters we illustrate some of the experiments we have carried out on ICGO databases.

## 9.2 Context Diagram of DIKE

Four main components can be recognized in our system, namely, one module for extracting intensional knowledge, the second one for constructing the Data Repository, the third one for exploiting the Data Repository in order to obtain a Cooperative Information System and the fourth one for constructing a Data Warehouse. System behaviour is described in the diagram of Figure 9.1.

A user activates the *User Interface (UI)* for specifying information about involved schemes and lexical properties. The information are stored into the *First Level Metascheme*. Scheme information are graphically specified by the user, who draws the E/R diagrams of the database schemes, which are then converted to an appropriate internal format to be stored in the First Level Metascheme. Lexical information are specified with the support of suitable forms. The User Interface can be exploited the other way round, to display both scheme and lexical information whenever necessary.

The user activates the *Intensional Knowledge Extractor (IKE)* through the *UI* for deriving interscheme properties about input schemes. In order to carry out its task, this module takes information about involved schemes, lexical properties and (possibly) previously derived interscheme properties from the First Level Metascheme. Derived interscheme properties are stored into the First Level Metascheme in their turn. Information about derived interscheme properties may be presented to the user either for the validation purposes or in response to an explicit user request.

After that interscheme properties have been extracted, the user can activate the *Data Repository Constructor (DRC)* through the *UI*. The Data Repository is obtained by constructing new schemes through integration and

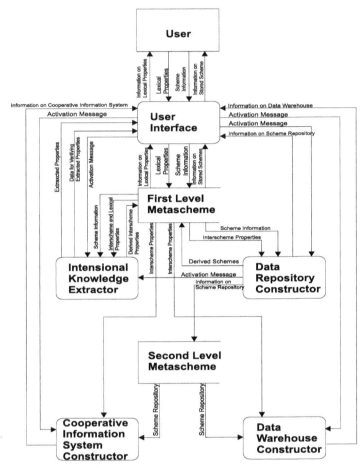

**Fig. 9.1.** Context Diagram of DIKE

abstraction steps. These are stored in the First Level Metascheme. The construction proceeds hierarchically and interscheme properties holding among newly constructed schemes must be derived: this is obtained by activating the *IKE* over the new schemes. All information pertaining the Data Repository, including also the Set of Mappings and the Set of Views (see Section 6.1) which denote correspondences among objects belonging to different Data Repository levels, are stored in the *Second Level Metascheme* and are presented to the user.

Finally, the user can activate the *Cooperative Information System Constructor* (*CISC*) and/or the *Data Warehouse Constructor* (*DWC*) through the *UI*. These take interscheme properties from the First Level Metascheme and both the Data Repository and the Set of Mappings and the Set of Views, from the Second Level Metascheme, and carry out all operations for synthesizing a Cooperative Information System or a Data Warehouse structure. As usual, results are displayed to the user.

## 9.3 Description of DIKE Modules

In this section we provide a more detailed description of the modules constituting DIKE. All modules of DIKE and information exchanged among them are illustrated in Figure 9.2.

### 9.3.1 Intensional Knowledge Extractor (IKE)

The $IKE$ derives intensional knowledge between objects belonging to different database schemes. In particular the $IKE$ can activate the following four modules:

- **Extractor of Object Synonymies-Homonymies and Type Conflicts (OSTCE)**
  This module derives both synonymies and homonymies and type conflicts; in particular, it handles the interaction between similarity property and type conflict derivation, on the one hand, and type conflict resolution, on the other hand (see Chapter 2). Recall that the resolution of a type conflict may cause some type conflicts to become synonymies and vice versa; the $OSTCE$ takes care of this interaction by activating an iterative computation. During one iteration, it calls the modules:
  - **Similarity Property Extractor (SPE)**; this takes in input *(i)* some lexical synonymy properties, *(ii)* the information about schemes and *(iii)* previously derived interscheme properties (if any) stored in the First Level Metascheme. The $SPE$ yields in output similarities among entities and relationships. All details about the derivation of object similarities can be found in Section 2.4.2.
  - **Type Conflict Extractor (TCE)**; it detects type conflicts existing in the schemes. The $TCE$ computes five kinds of type conflicts: *(i)* conflicts between entities and relationships, *(ii)* conflicts between an entity attribute and an entity, *(iii)* conflicts between a relationship attribute and an entity, *(iv)* conflicts between an entity attribute and a relationship, and *(v)* conflicts between a relationship attribute and a relationship. Detected type conflicts are validated by the user and valid ones are finally solved within schemes. The algorithm for deriving type conflicts is described into details in Section 2.4.2.

  The $OSTCE$ terminates its computation when, during one iteration, no type conflict is detected. The validation of similarity properties is carried out when the $OSTCE$ terminates, whereas type conflicts are validated at the end of each type conflict detection steps, in order for the subsequent

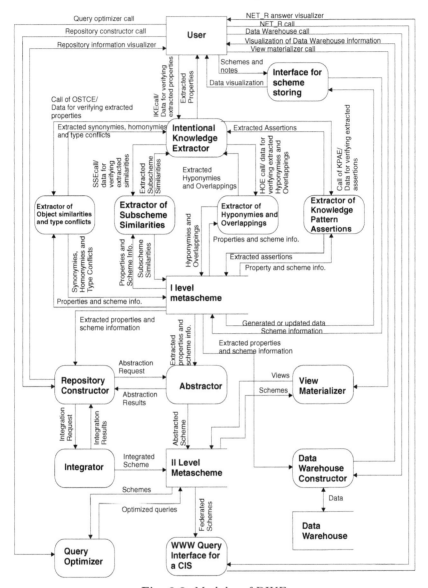

**Fig. 9.2.** Modules of DIKE

type conflict resolution step to be correctly carried out. From extracted similarity properties the $OSTCE$ derives synonymies, i.e., similarities with a coefficient greater than a certain threshold, and homonymies, i.e., similarities between objects having the same name and a similarity coefficient lesser than a certain threshold. All details about the algorithms implemented by the $OSTCE$ can be found in Chapter 2.

– **Extractor of Subscheme Similarities (SSE)**
  The $SSE$ takes in input properties derived by the $OSTCE$ and singles out similarities between two different groups of connected objects (subschemes) within two schemes.
– **Extractor of Hyponymies and Overlappings (HOE)**
  The $HOE$ derives hyponymies and overlappings between objects belonging to different schemes. The derivation of these properties is carried out by two modules:
  – **Basic Hyponymy and Overlapping Extractor (BHOE)**; it derives basic hyponymies and overlappings which are valid in a particular scenario. For the complete description of the underlying algorithms see Section 4.2.2.
  – **General Hyponymy Extractor (GHE)**; it takes in input a set of schemes, a Synonymy Dictionary and a Hyponymy Dictionary containing basic properties derived by the $BHOE$ and returns an enriched Hyponymy Dictionary; the $GHE$ does not derive any new overlapping property. The complete description of the algorithms implemented by the $GHE$ can be found in Section 4.3.1.
– **Knowledge Pattern Assertion Extractor (KPAE)**
  The $KPAE$ takes in input properties derived by both the $OSTCE$ and the $HOE$ and derives assertions between knowledge patterns. For reasoning about properties of knowledge patterns, a Description Logics (DL) variant, called $DL_P$, is used; this is described in details in Section 5.2. The $KPAE$ proceeds in three main phases:
  – *Phase 1*, in which an Inclusion Dictionary is constructed.
  – *Phase 2*, in which, for each database, the most interesting classes, i.e., those which semantically best characterize it, are determined.
  – *Phase 3*, in which assertions involving interesting classes, as identified in the Phase 2, are extracted.

  All details about the algorithms implemented in the $KPAE$ can be found in Chapter 5.

### 9.3.2 Data Repository Constructor (DRC)

The $DRC$ generates a Data Repository that is a hierarchical structured global scheme allowing to look at the overall cooperative system as organized in various abstraction levels (see Section 6.1). The $DRC$ first groups database schemes into clusters. Then, databases belonging to each cluster are integrated into a scheme which is abstracted into a higher level scheme representing the cluster. This process is iterated over (higher level) schemes thus produced, to yield further higher level schemes. The process terminates when a sufficiently abstract scheme set (usually consisting of one single scheme) is obtained. Repository construction is not completely automatic: in some cases the system asks the user to provide some additional information or to supply some design decisions. In order to construct the Data Repository, the $DRC$ must activate the following modules:

- **Scheme Integrator (SI)**
  This module is activated by the $DRC$ whenever a group of schemes must be integrated into a global one. The algorithms implemented by the $SI$ is described in Section 6.5.
- **Scheme Abstractor (SA)**
  This module is activated by the $DRC$ for producing the abstracted scheme associated to each global scheme obtained by the $SI$. The algorithms underlying the $SA$ are described in Section 6.6.

The $DRC$ yields in output also some information structures for supporting both the CIS Constructor and the DW Constructor. Support information structures for the construction of CIS and DW are strictly connected with transformations carried out during the integration and abstraction steps. These structures consist of *(i)* a *Set of Mappings* describing the way an object belonging to output schemes has been obtained from one or more objects belonging to input schemes, *(ii)* a *Set of Views* allowing to obtain instances of objects of the output schemes from instances at the input scheme level.

The algorithms for the construction of a Data Repository are illustrated in all details in Chapter 6.

### 9.3.3 Cooperative Information System Constructor (CISC)

This module realizes a Cooperative Information System by exploiting interscheme properties, knowledge patterns and the Data Repository. In our CIS architecture, the Data Repository is used as the core structure of an Internet-based mediator for integrating geographically dispersed databases. A WWW interface exploits the information encoded in the Data Repository to help the user of the integrated system in locating a local database of interest and in formulating queries on it. Querying is carried out by either a simple QBE-like graphical format or a graphical query formulation wizard: the system provides for the needed translation from the graphically-formulated query to the local system query language.

This approach has been realized into a special module, called $Net\_R$. The module includes two kinds of sites: provider and distributor. The *provider sites* contain the data sources to be queried: they may be heterogeneous both in the data model and in the query language they support. The *distributor site* stores the Data Repository and acts as a (form of) mediator [39, 126].

The algorithm implemented in the $CISC$ is described in Chapter 7.

### 9.3.4 Data Warehouse Constructor (DWC)

This module takes in input the Data Repository and the interscheme properties, and synthesizes a Data Warehouse structure. The DW structure is realized according to a three level architecture, where the Data Repository is used as the structure realizing the reconcilied data level. The proposed DW architecture consists of four components, namely *(i)* data sources, storing operational data, *(ii)* the Business Data Warehouse (BDW), storing reconciled data, *(iii)* Business Information Warehouses (BIW) or data marts, storing derived data, and *(iv)* metadata.

Different from classical three-level architectures, in our case the BDW is not based on a flat scheme obtained by the integration of all involved schemes, but uses three structures, namely *(i)* the Data Repository, *(ii)* the Set of Mappings, *(iii)* the Set of Views. Note that a Data Repository does not only collect database schemes, but can also store metadata they are related to; consequently, in our approach, metadata, obtained during the derivation of reconciled data, are kept within the Data Repository.

Details about the algorithms implemented in the *DWC* can be found in Chapter 8.

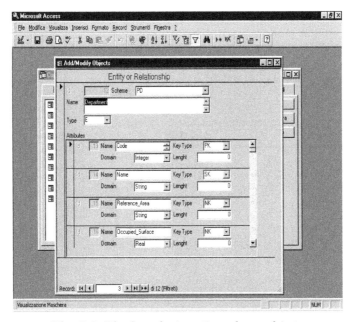

**Fig. 9.3.** The form for inserting scheme objects

## 9.4 A Trip throughout DIKE

DIKE has been realized under Windows95/98 using Visual Basic and Microsoft Access. Here we describe a brief trip through the system prototype.

At the beginning the user can insert scheme names, scheme groups, object belonging to schemes, object relationships and lexical synonymies in the metascheme. These insertions are carried out through suitable forms. As an example, Figure 9.3 shows the form for the insertion of scheme objects.

After that, the user can choose the databases of interest: indeed DIKE was designed in such a way that it can be applied to several database sets; a metascheme instance is then associated to each of these sets and, consequently, the choice of a given set of databases is carried out by choosing the corresponding metascheme instance. Figure 9.4 illustrates how the selection of the metascheme instance can be done.

Each metascheme instance can store several databases; however a user could be interested in analyzing only a subset of all databases stored in the selected metascheme instance. Therefore, for each metascheme instance (and, consequently, for each set of schemes), the user can define some groups of schemes, each containing a subset of schemes. A scheme can belong to more groups. Figure 9.5 shows how the group of interest can be selected.

After that the metascheme instance has been selected, the system allows to choose the desired computation among the following possibilities: *(i)* computation of object synonymies and type conflicts; *(ii)* computation of object

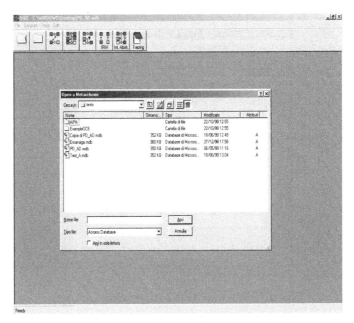

**Fig. 9.4.** The form for selecting the metascheme instance

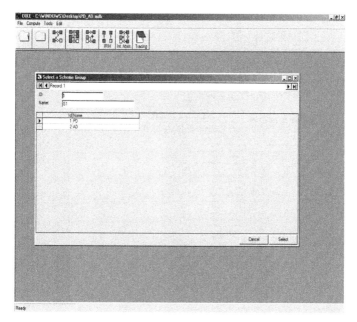

**Fig. 9.5.** The form for selecting the database group of interest

cluster similarities; *(iii)* computation of hyponymies and overlappings; *(iv)* computation of assertions between knowledge patterns; *(v)* both *(i)* and *(ii)* and *(iii)* and *(iv)*.

Suppose the user chooses the option *(i)*. In this case, DIKE computes first the object similarities and displays them to the user. Figure 9.6 illustrates the form visualizing them.

After that, the system shows all derived type conflicts; in particular the corresponding form is subdivided into three windows; the first one shows the threshold; the second one presents all type conflicts judged interesting whereas all type conflicts considered not interesting are shown in the third window. The user can discard some type conflicts judged interesting by the system, as well as he can force the system to consider significant some discarded type conflicts. Figure 9.7 shows the corresponding form.

The last two forms described above are visualized for each iteration of the external fixpoint (see Section 2.3). When the computation terminates, the obtained synonymies are presented to the user by exploiting a form similar to that described in Figure 9.7. Also in this case the user can modify system choices in a way analogous to that described for type conflicts.

If the user chooses to compute object cluster similarities, the system derives them and displays obtained properties using a form similar to that we have described for type conflicts (see Figure 9.8).

After that interscheme properties have been extracted, they are exploited for constructing the Data Repository. The module for deriving the Data

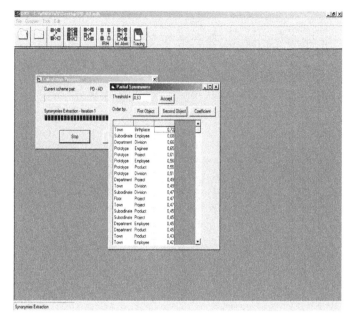

**Fig. 9.6.** The form for visualizing synonymies between entities

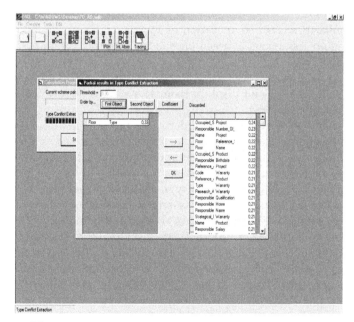

**Fig. 9.7.** The form for visualizing derived type conflicts

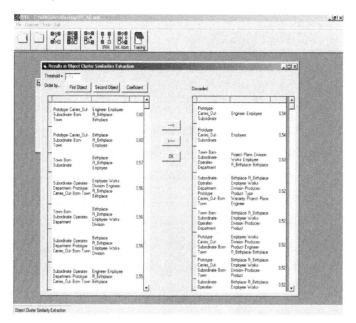

**Fig. 9.8.** The form for visualizing derived object cluster similarities

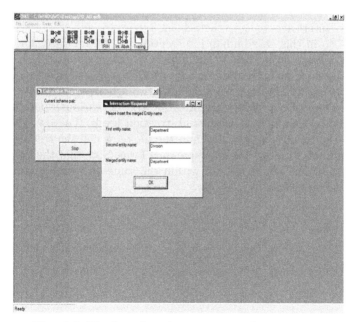

**Fig. 9.9.** The form for selecting a merged entity name

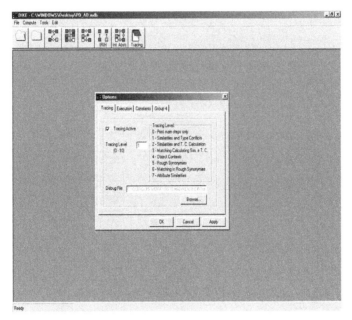

**Fig. 9.10.** The form for setting tracing options

Repository interleaves calls to the Scheme Integrator and to the Scheme Abstactor. Also in this case human intervention can be required, for example, when interscheme properties do not suffice to take integration decisions. Figure 9.9 shows, for instance, the form by which the user is asked to select the name of the entity obtained from merging two synonym entities.

The system also provides facilities for tracing various operations. The tracing can be executed at various abstraction levels. The user can choose both the desired abstraction level and the file on which the tracing must be stored. Figure 9.10 shows the corresponding form. Note that the examination of the tracing can be carried out within the same operational environment used for the other tasks.

# 10. Experiments on the Derivation of Similarities and Type Conflicts

*This chapter is the first one devoted to describe experiments we have carried out on ICGO databases to verify the validity of our techniques. It has a twofold purpose: on the one hand, it presents the databases we have used, on the other hand, it describes the experiments carried out on those databases. More in particular, in the first section we describe the ICGO databases and the ICGO Data Repository whereas the second section is devoted to describe six groups of databases which the experiments described in this thesis have been executed on. In the last six sections, we describe the extraction of synonymies, homonymies, type conflicts and object cluster similarities from the six groups of databases under consideration.*

*The material presented in this chapter is taken from [92, 122, 87, 90, 117, 118].*

## 10.1 The Italian Central Governmental Office Databases

The most important series of experiments which we have conducted for testing our algorithms have been carried out on Italian Central Governmental Office (ICGO) databases. In Chapter 1, we have seen that a study developed at the "Italian Information System Authority for Public Administration" (AIPA) brought to the identification, classification and representation of about 300 main databases owned by various Central Offices [7]. The presence of such a big number of databases makes it necessary the reorganization of information by exploiting integrated ad structural models in such a way that the involved information become comprehensible and can be exploited more easily.

In addition, some of the ICGO databases (e.g., those owned by central tax administration offices) have a relevant size. Finally, they are based on a variety of data models and systems, and almost no integration form whatsoever existed among them.

All these observations led to the necessity of constructing a Data Repository for ICGO databases. The ICGO Data Repository has the tree structure shown in Figure 10.1. In order to obtain it, the pre-existing databases have

D. Ursino: Extr. and Expl. of Intensional Knowledge ..., LNCS 2282, pp. 189–214, 2002.
© Springer-Verlag Berlin Heidelberg 2002

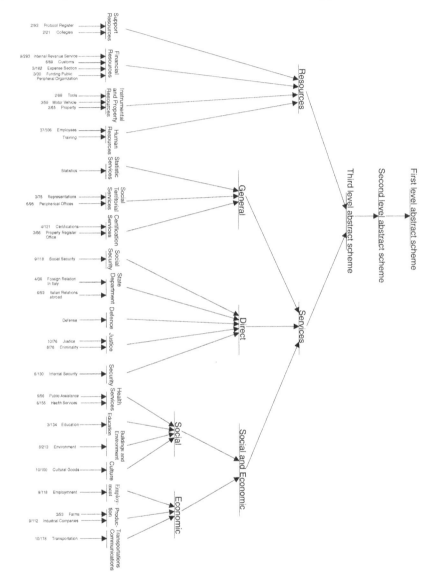

**Fig. 10.1.** The ICGO Data Repository

been grouped into 30 clusters; each cluster encloses semantically homogeneous databases. Upper levels of the tree have been obtained by carrying out integration-abstraction phases to schemes of lower levels. Each node within the tree structure represents a portion of the integrated system of the ICGO at a certain abstraction level.

## 10.2 The Six Groups of Databases under Consideration

We have conducted several experiments on ICGO databases by applying each of our algorithms to numerous databases of the repository itself. In the following sections and in the next chapters we describe some of these experiments; in particular we consider six groups of databases and we describe the results obtained from applying our algorithms to each of these groups.

### 10.2.1 Group A

This group consists of three databases belonging to the cluster "Internal Revenue Service". Involved databases are "Anagrafe Tributaria" (Tax Collection Database – TCD), "Base Dati del Registro" (Registry Database – RD) and "Base dati Ipotecaria" (Mortgage Estate Database – MED). Databases are illustrated in Figures 10.2, 10.3 and 10.4. For the sake of simplicity scheme attributes are not shown.

### 10.2.2 Group B

This group consists of two databases belonging to the cluster "Justice". Involved databases are "Database Automazione Civile" (Civil Suit Database – CSD) and "Database Automazione Penale" (Criminal Case Database – CCD). Databases are illustrated in Figures 10.5 and 10.6. For the sake of simplicity scheme attributes are not shown.

### 10.2.3 Group C

This group consists of three databases belonging to the cluster "Employment". In more details, involved databases are "Fondo Sociale Europeo" (European Social Fund – ESF), "Progetti di Interesse Comunitario" (European Union Projects – EUP) and "Sistema Informativo Sorveglianza Valutazione" (Monitoring and Evaluation Information System - MEIS). Databases are illustrated in Figures 10.7, 10.8 and 10.9.
Attributes belonging to the objects of the database "European Social Fund" are[1]:

- **Judicial Person**: (*Code*, Address, Branch Number, Current Account Number);
- **Ministry**: (*Judicial Person Code*, Address, Branch Number, Current Account Number);
- **District**: (*Judicial Person Code*, Address, Branch Number);
- **Other Body Corporate**: (*Judicial Person Code*, Address, Branch Number);

---

[1] We denote key attributes using italics.

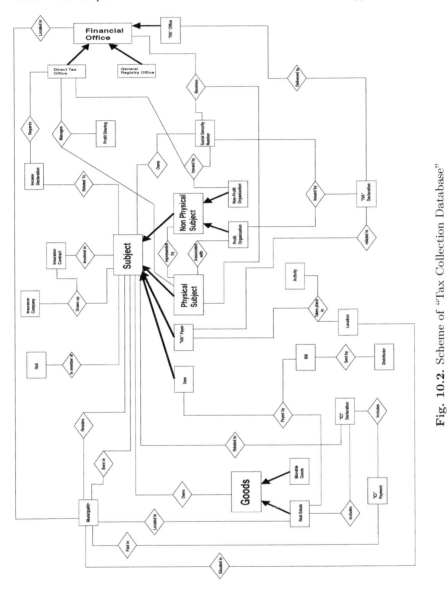

**Fig. 10.2.** Scheme of "Tax Collection Database"

- **Operative Program**: (*Dossier Number*, Economic Field, Regulation, Starting Date, Ending Date, Country, ESF Contribution, Country Share, Description);
- **Project**: (*Year, Code*, Economic Field, Type, Country, Starting Date, Ending Date, ESF Contribution, Country Share, Description);
- **Payment**: (*Number*, Amount, Date, Year, Payment Type).

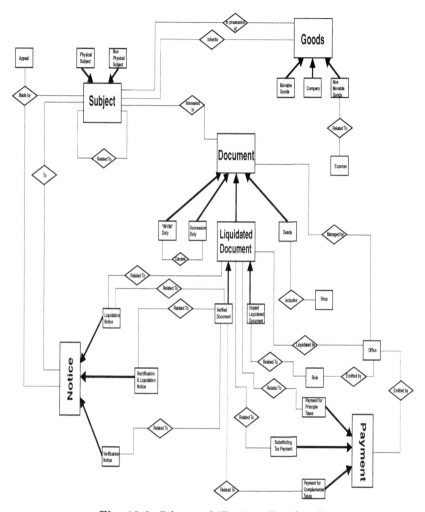

**Fig. 10.3.** Scheme of "Registry Database"

Attributes associated with the objects of the database "European Union Projects" are:

- **Project**: (*Dossier Number*, District Code, Type, ESF Contribution, Country Share, Public Funds, Private Funds, User Number, Decree Number, Decree Date, District Priority, Duration, Score, Country, Operative Program Code, Economic Field);
- **Partner**: (*Partner Code*, Address, City, Nationality);
- **Payment**: (*Number*, Year, Date, Amount, Item, Bank, Residual Asset, Movement Type, Payment Type);

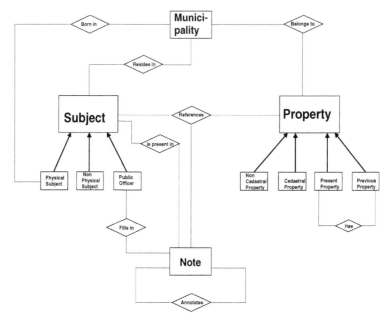

**Fig. 10.4.** Scheme of "Mortgage Estate Database"

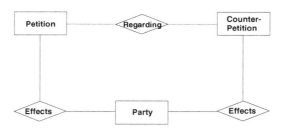

**Fig. 10.5.** Scheme of "Civil Suit Database"

- **Promoter**: (*Promoter Code*, Social Security Number, Juridical Nature, Address, City, Zip Code, Description);
- **Institute**: (*Code*).

Attributes relative to the objects belonging to the database "Monitoring and Evaluation Information System" are:

- **Operative Program**: (*Dossier Number*, Economic Field, Regulation, Starting Date, Ending Date, ESF Contribution, Country Share, Description);
- **Project**: (*Year, Code*, Type, Country, Economic Field, ESF Contribution, Country Share);
- **Payment**: (*Number*, Amount, Date, Year, Payment Type);

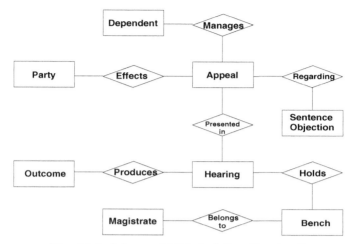

**Fig. 10.6.** Scheme of "Criminal Case Database"

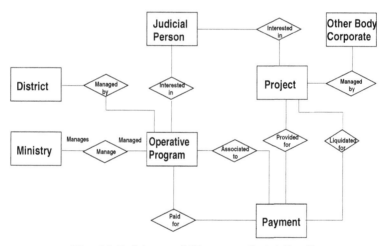

**Fig. 10.7.** Scheme of "European Social Fund"

– **Judicial Person**: (*Code*, Branch Number, Address, Current Account Number);
– **District**: (*District Code*).

### 10.2.4 Group D

This group consists of two databases belonging to the cluster "Property Register Office". The databases here are "Catasto Terreni" (Land Property Register – LPR) and "Catasto Urbano" (Urban Property Register – UPR). Databases are illustrated in Figures 10.10 and 10.11 (scheme attributes are not shown).

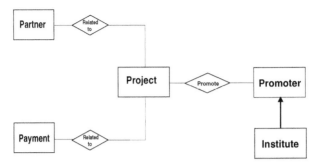

**Fig. 10.8.** Scheme of "European Union Projects"

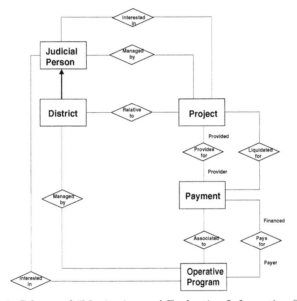

**Fig. 10.9.** Scheme of "Monitoring and Evaluation Information System"

### 10.2.5 Group E

This group consists of four databases belonging to the cluster "Resources". Involved databases are "Risorse di Supporto" (Support Resources – SR), "Risorse Finanziarie" (Financial Resources – FR), "Risorse Strumentali ed Immobiliari" (Instrumental and Property Resources – IPR) and "Risorse Umane" (Human Resources – HR). Databases are illustrated in Figures 10.12, 10.13, 10.14 and 10.15. For the sake of simplicity scheme attributes are not shown.

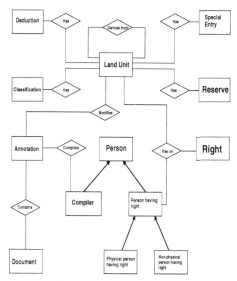

**Fig. 10.10.** Scheme of "Land Property Register"

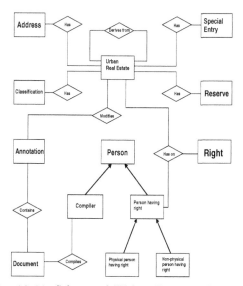

**Fig. 10.11.** Scheme of "Urban Property Register"

### 10.2.6 Group F

This group consists of five databases belonging to the cluster "Industrial Companies". In more details, involved databases are "Banca Dati Legge 185 - Credito Agevolato per piccole e medie imprese" (Database of Facilitated Credit for small and medium firms – FCD), "Banca Dati Legge 317 - Contributo a Fondo Perduto per piccole e medie imprese" (Database of Sunk

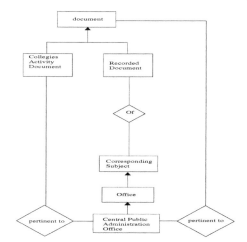

**Fig. 10.12.** Scheme of "Support Resources"

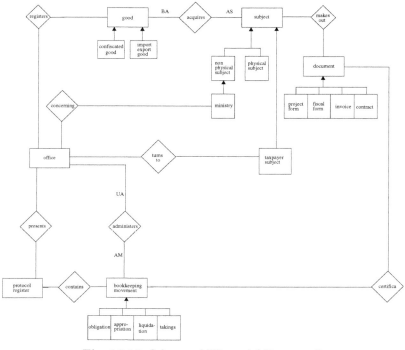

**Fig. 10.13.** Scheme of "Financial Resources"

Contributions for small and medium firms – SCD), "Banca Dati Legge 46 - Richieste di imprese per contributi" (Database of Firm Requests for Contributions - FRCD), "Banca Dati Obiettivi CEE - Contributi Unione Europea per Piccole e Medie Imprese" (Database of European Union Contributions

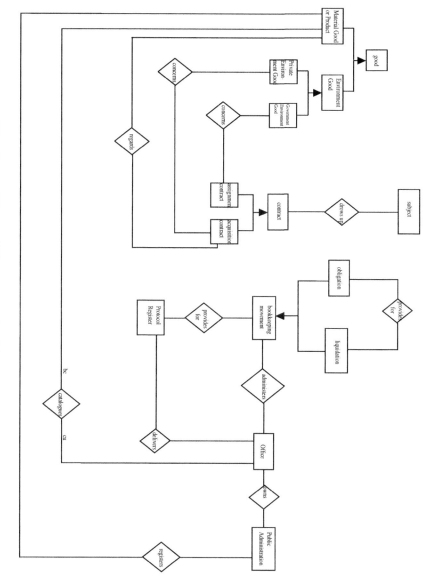

**Fig. 10.14.** Scheme of "Instrumental and Property Resources"

for small and medium firms – EUCD), "Albo delle Imprese" (Firm Database
– FD) . Databases are illustrated in Figures 10.16, 10.17, 10.18, 10.19 and
10.20.
Attributes belonging to the objects of the database $FCD$ are:

– **Firm**: (Trade Name, Code, Fiscal Code, Dependent Number);
– **Factory**: (Municipality, Province, Region);

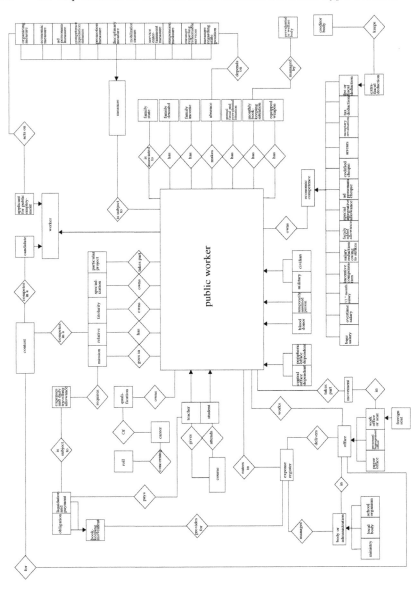

**Fig. 10.15.** Scheme of "Human Resources"

- **Producing Activity**: (Code, Description, Economic Field);
- **Contribution**: (Answer Date, Outcome);
- **Machine**: (Code, Description);
- **Credit Institute**: (Code)

Attributes associated to the objects of the database $SCD$ are:

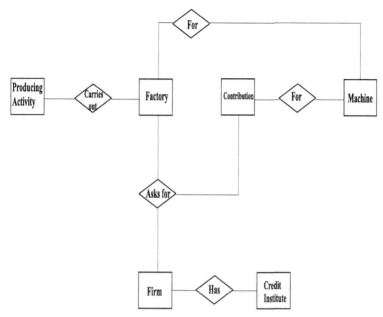

**Fig. 10.16.** Scheme of "Database of Facilitated Credit for small and medium firms"

- **Factory**: (Municipality, Province, Region);
- **Producing Activity**: (Code, Description, Economic Field);
- **Contribution**: (Answer Date, Firm's Bank, Outcome);
- **Machine**: (Code, Description, Invoice Numbers for its purchase, Order Date);
- **Credit Institute**: (Code);
- **Firm**: (Fiscal Code, Dependent Number, Medium/Small, Code, Board of Directors, Trade Name);
- **Artisan**: (Code)

Attributes relative to the objects belonging to the database $FRCD$ are:

- **Economic Account**: (Year, Burden of Taxation, Turnover, Costs, Output Value);
- **Firm**: (Code for Chamber of Commerce, Fiscal Code, Dependent Number, Category, Trade Name);
- **Factory**: (Municipality, Province, Region);
- **Program**: (Duration, Request Date, Characteristics, Resolution, Investment, Start Date, End Date, Involved Dependents);
- **Work Progress**: (Work Code, Work Description, Start Date);
- **Refund**: (Interest, Date, Receipt, Instalment);
- **Granting**: (Money, Order Decree);
- **Funds**: (Contract Number, Date)

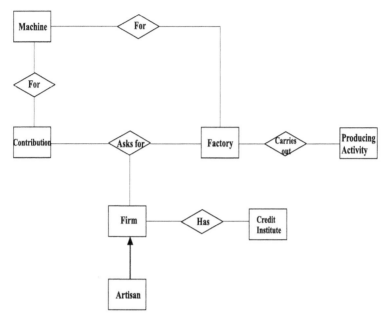

**Fig. 10.17.** Scheme of "Database of Sunk Contributions for small and medium firms"

Attributes belonging to the objects of the database $EUCD$ are:

- **Firm**: (Dependent Number, Code, Fiscal Code, Trade Name);
- **Factory**: (Municipality, Province, Region);
- **Producing Activity**: (Code, Description, Economic Field);
- **Program**: (Description, Duration);
- **Sunk Contribution**: (Contribution Grant Decree, Liquidation Decree);
- **Category**: (Category Type)

Attributes associated to the objects of the database $FD$ are:

- **Company**: (Matriculation Number, "Antimafia" Certificate, Head-Offices, Trade Name, Fiscal Data, Registry-Office information, Enrollment);
- **Technical Manager**: (Surname, Name, Company Matriculation Number, Historical Register, Personal Data);
- **Legal Representative**: (Hystorical Register, Company Matriculation Number, Surname, Name, Personal Data);
- **Historical Register**: (Company Matriculation Number, Company Information, Variation Date, Operator Code);
- **Class**: (Class Code, Amount)

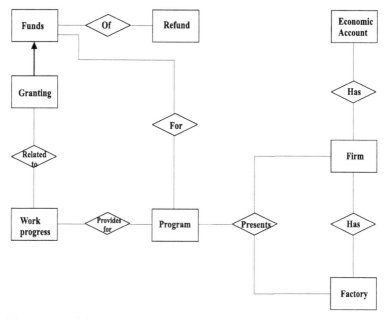

**Fig. 10.18.** Scheme of "Database of Firm Requests for Contributions"

## 10.3 Group A – Similarity and Type Conflict Extraction

### 10.3.1 Properties Holding between the Objects of TCD and of RD

In this section we describe the results we have obtained by applying to databases $TCD$ and $RD$ the algorithms for deriving synonymies, homonymies and type conflicts described in Chapter 2, as well as the algorithms for detecting object cluster similarities illustrated in Chapter 3. Resulting properties are illustrated in the following.

**Interesting Synonymies.** In this case $th_{syn}$ is 0.54. Interesting synonymies between objects belonging to $TCD$ and $RD$ are shown in Table 10.1[2].

**Interesting Homonymies.** The homonymy threshold is $th_{hom} = 0.25$; no homonymy is detected.

**Interesting Type Conflicts.** In this case the algorithm does not detect any interesting type conflict.

---

[2] In this table and in the following ones, column name *First object* (resp., *Second object*) must read *Object of the first scheme* (resp., *Object of the second scheme*). Similarly for table column name *First* (resp., *Second*) *object cluster*.

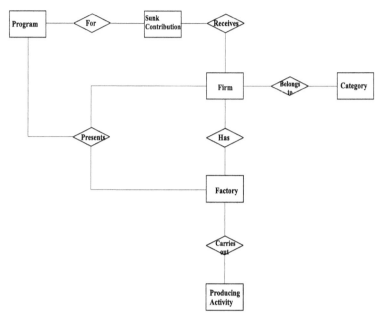

**Fig. 10.19.** Scheme of "Database of European Union Contributions for small and medium firms"

**Table 10.1.** Interesting synonymies between objects belonging to $TCD$ and $RD$

| First Object | Second Object | Value |
|---|---|---|
| Movable Goods | Movable Goods | 0.73 |
| Real Estate | Non Movable Goods | 0.69 |
| Goods | Goods | 0.60 |
| Distributor | Company | 0.59 |
| Distributor | Movable Goods | 0.59 |
| Movable Goods | Company | 0.58 |
| Subject | Subject | 0.58 |

**Interesting Object Cluster Similarities.** In this case $th_{oc}$ is 0.54. Six interesting object cluster similarities, among those having a plausibility coefficient greater than the threshold, are shown in Table 10.2. The complete list of derived object cluster similarities for the test case at hand can be found at the address:

http://wwwinfo.deis.unical.it/~ursino/tests.html

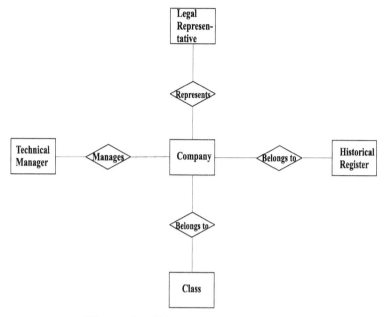

**Fig. 10.20.** Scheme of "Firm Database"

## 10.3.2 Properties Holding between the Objects of RD and MED

**Interesting Synonymies.** In this case $th_{syn}$ is 0.50. Interesting synonymies between objects belonging to $RD$ and $MED$ are shown in Table 10.3.
Note that the algorithm does not consider acceptable the similarity for pairs (*Physical Subject*, *Physical Subject*). Actually, for this pair, the contexts, and in general the meanings, of involved entities are neither similar enough for them to be recognized as synonyms, nor sufficiently different for them to be classified as homonyms[3].

**Interesting Homonymies.** The homonymy threshold is $th_{hom} = 0.15$; no homonymy is found.

**Interesting Type Conflicts.** In this case the algorithm does not detect any interesting type conflict.

**Interesting Object Cluster Similarities.** In this case $th_{oc}$ is 0.50. Interesting similarities between object clusters belonging to $RD$ and $MED$ are illustrated in Table 10.4.

---

[3] As a matter of fact, in Section 11.1.1, we show that an overlapping property exists between these two entities.

**Table 10.2.** Interesting similarities between object clusters belonging to $TCD$ and $RD$

| First object cluster | Second object cluster | Value |
|---|---|---|
| Goods ↔ Movable Goods ↔ ↔ Real Estate | Goods ↔ Movable Goods ↔ ↔ Non Movable Goods | 0.77 |
| Subject ↔ Owns ↔ ↔ Goods | Goods ↔ In possession of ↔ ↔ Subject | 0.70 |
| Subject ↔ Physical Subject ↔ ↔ Non Physical Subject ↔ ↔ Owns ↔ Goods ↔ ↔ Movable Goods ↔ Real Estate | Goods ↔ Movable Goods ↔ ↔ Non Movable Goods ↔ ↔ Company ↔ ↔ In possession of ↔ ↔ Subject ↔ Subject ↔ ↔ Subject ↔ ↔ Non Physical Subject | 0.69 |
| Bill ↔ Payed by ↔ ↔ Real Estate | Expense ↔ Related To ↔ ↔ Non Movable Goods | 0.68 |
| Subject ↔ Physical Subject ↔ ↔ Non Physical Subject ↔ ↔ Profit Organization ↔ ↔ Non Profit Organization | Subject ↔ Physical Subject ↔ ↔ Non Physical Subject | 0.59 |
| Subject ↔ User ↔ "Iva" Payer ↔ ↔ Physical Subject ↔ ↔ Non Physical Subject ↔ ↔ Profit Organization ↔ ↔ Non Profit Organization | Subject ↔ Related To ↔ ↔ Physical Subject ↔ ↔ Non Physical Subject | 0.55 |

**Table 10.3.** Interesting synonymies between objects belonging to $RD$ and $MED$

| First Object | Second Object | Value |
|---|---|---|
| Non-physical Subject | Non-physical Subject | 0.53 |
| Subject | Subject | 0.52 |

**Table 10.4.** Interesting similarities between object clusters belonging to $RD$ and $MED$

| First object cluster | Second object cluster | Value |
|---|---|---|
| Subject ↔ Physical Subject ↔ ↔ Non Physical Subject | Subject ↔ Physical Subject ↔ ↔ Non Physical Subject | 0.66 |
| Goods ↔ In possession of ↔ ↔ Subject ↔ ↔ Physical Subject ↔ ↔ Non Physical Subject ↔ | Property ↔ References ↔ ↔ Subject ↔ ↔ Physical Subject ↔ ↔ Non Physical Subject ↔ ↔ Public Officer | 0.55 |

## 10.4 Group B – Similarity and Type Conflict Extraction

### 10.4.1 Interesting Synonymies

In this case $th_{syn}$ is 0.51. Interesting synonymies between objects belonging to databases of Group B are shown in Table 10.5.

**Table 10.5.** Interesting synonymies between objects belonging to $CSD$ and $CCD$

| First Object | Second Object | Value |
|---|---|---|
| Counter-Petition | Sentence Objection | 0.65 |
| Petition | Sentence Objection | 0.64 |
| Counter-Petition | Appeal | 0.62 |
| Petition | Appeal | 0.61 |
| Counter-Petition | Bench | 0.59 |
| Counter-Petition | Outcome | 0.59 |
| Petition | Bench | 0.56 |
| Petition | Outcome | 0.56 |

### 10.4.2 Interesting Homonymies

The homonymy threshold is $th_{hom} = 0.31$ and an homonymy is detected between *Party* and *Party* (see Table 10.6).

**Table 10.6.** Interesting homonymies between objects belonging to $CSD$ and $CCD$

| First Object | Second Object | Value |
|---|---|---|
| Party | Party | 0.74 |

### 10.4.3 Interesting Type Conflicts

No interesting type conflicts are detected.

### 10.4.4 Interesting Object Cluster Similarities

In this case $th_{oc}$ is 0.50. Interesting similarities between object clusters belonging to databases of Group B are shown in Table 10.7. Note that both derived object cluster similarities are meaningful.

**Table 10.7.** Interesting similarities between object clusters belonging to $CSD$ and $CCD$

| First object cluster | Second object cluster | Value |
|---|---|---|
| Counter-Petition ↔ <br> ↔ Regarding ↔ <br> ↔ Petition | Sentence Objection ↔ <br> ↔ Regarding ↔ <br> ↔ Appeal | 0.71 |
| Counter-Petition ↔ Regarding ↔ Petition | Sentence Objection | 0.60 |

## 10.5 Group C – Similarity and Type Conflict Extraction

### 10.5.1 Interesting Synonymies

Interesting synonymies between objects belonging to databases of Group C are shown in Table 10.8[4].

**Table 10.8.** Interesting synonymies between objects belonging to $ESF$, $EUP$ and $MEIS$

| First Object | Second Object | |
|---|---|---|
| Payment$_{[ESF]}$ | Payment$_{[EUP]}$ | 0.78 |
| Other Body Corporate$_{[ESF]}$ | Partner$_{[EUP]}$ | 0.71 |
| Project$_{[ESF]}$ | Project$_{[EUP]}$ | 0.70 |
| Judicial Person$_{[ESF]}$ | Promoter$_{[EUP]}$ | 0.65 |
| Payment$_{[ESF]}$ | Payment$_{[MEIS]}$ | 0.95 |
| Operative Program$_{[ESF]}$ | Operative Program$_{[MEIS]}$ | 0.93 |
| Judicial Person$_{[ESF]}$ | Judicial Person$_{[MEIS]}$ | 0.88 |
| Project$_{[ESF]}$ | Project$_{[MEIS]}$ | 0.84 |
| Payment$_{[EUP]}$ | Payment$_{[MEIS]}$ | 0.79 |
| Project$_{[EUP]}$ | Project$_{[MEIS]}$ | 0.72 |
| Promoter$_{[EUP]}$ | Judicial Person$_{[MEIS]}$ | 0.65 |

### 10.5.2 Interesting Homonymies

The only interesting homonymy between objects belonging to databases of Group C is shown in Table 10.9.

---

[4] In this table $O_{[S]}$ indicates the object $O$ of the scheme $S$.

**Table 10.9.** Interesting homonymies between objects belonging to $ESF$, $EUP$ and $MEIS$

| First Object | Second Object | |
|---|---|---|
| District$_{[EUP]}$ | District$_{[MEIS]}$ | 0.7 |

### 10.5.3 Interesting Type Conflicts

No type conflicts are detected in these schemes.

### 10.5.4 Object Cluster Similarities

Some of the most interesting similarities between object clusters belonging to databases of Group C are shown in Table 10.10[5].

## 10.6 Group D – Similarity and Type Conflict Extraction

### 10.6.1 Interesting Synonymies

In this case $th_{syn}$ is 0.68. Interesting synonymies between objects belonging to databases of Group D are presented in Table 10.11.

### 10.6.2 Interesting Homonymies

The homonymy threshold is $th_{hom} = 0.28$; no homonymy is found.

### 10.6.3 Interesting Type Conflicts

In this case the algorithm does not detect any interesting type conflict.

### 10.6.4 Interesting Object Cluster Similarities

In this case $th_{oc}$ is 0.61. Six interesting object cluster similarities, among those having a plausibility coefficient greater than $th_{oc}$, are shown in Table 10.12. The complete list of derived object cluster similarities for this test case can be found at the address:

http://wwwinfo.deis.unical.it/~ursino/tests.html.

---

[5] In this table $\langle C \rangle_{[S]}$ indicates the cluster $C$ of the scheme $S$.

**Table 10.10.** Interesting similarities between object clusters belonging to $ESF$, $EUP$ and $MED$

| First object cluster | Second object cluster | |
|---|---|---|
| ⟨ Payment ↔ Provided For ↔ ↔ Project ⟩$_{[ESF]}$ | ⟨ Payment ↔ Related To ↔ ↔ Project ⟩$_{[EUP]}$ | 0.76 |
| ⟨ Payment ↔ Provided For ↔ ↔ Project ↔ Managed By ↔ ↔ Other Body Corporate ⟩$_{[ESF]}$ | ⟨ Payment ↔ Related To ↔ ↔ Project ↔ Related To ↔ ↔ Partner ⟩$_{[EUP]}$ | 0.74 |
| ⟨ Project ↔ Interested In ↔ ↔ Judicial Person ↔ Payment ↔ ↔ Provided For ⟩$_{[ESF]}$ | ⟨ Payment ↔ Related To ↔ ↔ Project ↔ Related To ↔ ↔ Partner ⟩$_{[EUP]}$ | 0.73 |
| ⟨ Payment ↔ Paid For ↔ ↔ Operative Program ⟩$_{[ESF]}$ | ⟨ Payment ↔ Related To ↔ ↔ Project ⟩$_{[EUP]}$ | 0.71 |
| ⟨ Project ↔ Managed By ↔ ↔ Other Body Corporate ⟩$_{[ESF]}$ | ⟨ Partner ↔ Related To ↔ ↔ Project ⟩$_{[EUP]}$ | 0.71 |
| ⟨ Payment ↔ ↔ Associated To ↔ ↔ Operative Program ⟩$_{[ESF]}$ | ⟨ Payment ↔ ↔ Associated To ↔ ↔ Operative Program ⟩$_{[MEIS]}$ | 0.91 |
| ⟨ Payment ↔ Provided For ↔ ↔ Project ⟩$_{[ESF]}$ | ⟨ Payment ↔ Associated To ↔ ↔ Operative Program ⟩$_{[MEIS]}$ | 0.87 |
| ⟨ Payment ↔ Associated To ↔ ↔ Operative Program ↔ ↔ Provided For ↔ ↔ Project ⟩$_{[ESF]}$ | ⟨ Payment ↔ Associated To ↔ ↔ Operative Program ↔ ↔ Provides For ↔ ↔ Project ⟩$_{[MEIS]}$ | 0.82 |
| ⟨ Payment ↔ Associated To ↔ ↔ Operative Program ↔ ↔ Interested In ↔ ↔ Judicial Person ⟩$_{[ESF]}$ | ⟨ Payment ↔ Associated To ↔ ↔ Operative Program ↔ ↔ Judicial Person ↔ ↔ Interested In ⟩$_{[MEIS]}$ | 0.81 |
| ⟨ Payment ↔ Associated To ↔ ↔ Operative Program ↔ ↔ Interested In ↔ ↔ Judicial Person ↔ ↔ Provided For ↔ ↔ Project ⟩$_{[ESF]}$ | ⟨ Project ↔ Interested In ↔ ↔ Judicial Person ↔ ↔ Payment ↔ ↔ Provides For ⟩$_{[MEIS]}$ | 0.79 |
| ⟨ Project ↔ Interested In ↔ ↔ Judicial Person ↔ ↔ Interested In ↔ ↔ Operative Program ↔ ↔ Payment ↔ ↔ Provided For ⟩$_{[ESF]}$ | ⟨ Payment ↔ Associated To ↔ ↔ Operative Program ↔ ↔ Judicial Person ↔ ↔ Interested In ↔ ↔ Project ↔ ↔ Provides For ⟩$_{[MEIS]}$ | 0.79 |
| ⟨ Payment ↔ Related To ↔ ↔ Project ⟩$_{[EUP]}$ | ⟨ Payment ↔ Provides For ↔ ↔ Project ⟩$_{[MEIS]}$ | 0.78 |
| ⟨ Payment ↔ Related To ↔ ↔ Project ⟩$_{[EUP]}$ | ⟨ Payment ↔ Associated To ↔ ↔ Operative Program ⟩$_{[MEIS]}$ | 0.70 |

**Table 10.11.** Interesting synonymies between objects belonging to $LPR$ and $UPR$

| First Object | Second Object | Value |
|---|---|---|
| Compiler | Compiler | 0.91 |
| Physical person having right | Physical person having right | 0.91 |
| Person having right | Person having right | 0.84 |
| Person | Person | 0.83 |
| Person | Person having right | 0.81 |
| Document | Document | 0.79 |
| Non-physical person having right | Non-physical person having right | 0.79 |
| Person having right | Person | 0.78 |
| Compiler | Non-physical person having right | 0.75 |
| Right | Right | 0.74 |
| Non-physical person having right | Compiler | 0.73 |
| Person having right | Physical person having right | 0.72 |
| Reserve | Reserve | 0.70 |
| Special Entry | Special Entry | 0.70 |
| Classification | Classification | 0.70 |
| Physical person having right | Person having right | 0.69 |
| Land Unit | Urban Real Estate | 0.69 |

**Table 10.12.** Interesting similarities between object clusters belonging to $LPR$ and $UPR$

| First object cluster | Second object cluster | Value |
|---|---|---|
| Non-physical person having right ↔ ↔ Person having right ↔ ↔ Physical person having right | Non-physical person having right ↔ ↔ Person having right ↔ ↔ Physical person having right | 0.87 |
| Compiler ↔ Person ↔ ↔ Person having right ↔ ↔ Physical person having right | Compiler ↔ Person ↔ ↔ Person having right ↔ ↔ Physical person having right | 0.87 |
| Physical person having right ↔ ↔ Person having right ↔ ↔ Person ↔ Compiler ↔ ↔ Non-physical person having right | Physical person having right ↔ ↔ Person having right ↔ ↔ Person ↔ Compiler ↔ ↔ Non-physical person having right | 0.83 |
| Person ↔ Compiler ↔ ↔ Compiles ↔ Annotation ↔ ↔ Contains ↔ Document | Person ↔ Compiler ↔ ↔ Compiles ↔ Document ↔ ↔ Contains ↔ Annotation | 0.77 |
| Person ↔ Compiler ↔ ↔ Compiles ↔ Annotation ↔ ↔ Contains ↔ Document ↔ ↔ Person having right | Annotation ↔ Contains ↔ ↔ Document ↔ ↔ Person having right ↔ ↔ Person ↔ Compiler ↔ ↔ Compiles | 0.77 |
| Person ↔ Compiler ↔ ↔ Compiles ↔ Annotation ↔ ↔ Contains ↔ Document ↔ ↔ Physical person having right ↔ ↔ Person having right | Annotation ↔ Contains ↔ ↔ Document ↔ ↔ Physical person having right ↔ ↔ Person having right ↔ ↔ Person ↔ Compiler ↔ ↔ Compiles | 0.77 |

## 10.7 Group E – Similarity and Type Conflict Extraction

### 10.7.1 Interesting Synonymies

Interesting synonymies between objects belonging to databases of Group E are presented in Table 10.13[6].

**Table 10.13.** Interesting synonymies between objects belonging to $SR$, $FR$, $IPR$ and $HR$

| First Object | Second Object | |
|---|---|---|
| Office$_{[SR]}$ | Office$_{[FR]}$ | 0.78 |
| Subject$_{[SR]}$ | CorrespondingSubject$_{[FR]}$ | 0.71 |
| Presents$_{[FR]}$ | Delivers$_{[IPR]}$ | 0.94 |
| Administers$_{[FR]}$ | Administers$_{[IPR]}$ | 0.91 |
| ProtocolRegister$_{[FR]}$ | ExpenseRegister$_{[IPR]}$ | 0.89 |
| Subject$_{[FR]}$ | Subject$_{[IPR]}$ | 0.87 |
| Contains$_{[FR]}$ | ProvidesFor$_{[IPR]}$ | 0.84 |
| Registers$_{[FR]}$ | Catalogues$_{[IPR]}$ | 0.77 |
| MaterialGoodOrProduct$_{[FR]}$ | ConfiscatedGood$_{[IPR]}$ | 0.54 |
| MakesOut$_{[FR]}$ | DrawsUp$_{[IPR]}$ | 0.53 |
| EnvironmentGood$_{[FR]}$ | ConfiscatedGood$_{[IPR]}$ | 0.46 |
| EnvironmentGood$_{[FR]}$ | ImportExportGood$_{[IPR]}$ | 0.46 |
| Office$_{[FR]}$ | Office$_{[HR]}$ | 0.95 |
| BookKeepingMovement$_{[FR]}$ | BookKeepingMovement$_{[HR]}$ | 0.80 |
| Office$_{[IPR]}$ | Office$_{[HR]}$ | 0.95 |
| Owns$_{[IPR]}$ | In$_{[HR]}$ | 0.92 |
| PublicAdministration$_{[IPR]}$ | CreditorBody$_{[HR]}$ | 0.90 |
| Delivers$_{[IPR]}$ | Delivers$_{[HR]}$ | 0.74 |
| ProvidesFor$_{[IPR]}$ | ProvidesFor$_{[HR]}$ | 0.66 |

## 10.8 Group F – Similarity and Type Conflict Extraction

### 10.8.1 Interesting Synonymies

Interesting synonymies between objects belonging to databases of Group F are shown in Table 10.14[7].

---

[6] As usual, in this table, $O_{[S]}$ indicates the object $O$ of the scheme $S$.
[7] As usual, in this table, $O_{[S]}$ indicates the object $O$ of the scheme $S$.

**Table 10.14.** Interesting synonymies between objects belonging to $FCD$, $SCD$, $FRCD$, $EUCD$ and $FD$

| First Object | Second Object | |
|---|---|---|
| Producing Activity$_{[FCD]}$ | Producing Activity$_{[SCD]}$ | 0.98 |
| Factory$_{[FCD]}$ | Factory$_{[SCD]}$ | 0.94 |
| Contribution$_{[FCD]}$ | Contribution$_{[SCD]}$ | 0.90 |
| Machine$_{[FCD]}$ | Machine$_{[SCD]}$ | 0.87 |
| Firm$_{[FCD]}$ | Firm$_{[SCD]}$ | 0.85 |
| Credit Institute$_{[FCD]}$ | Credit Institute$_{[SCD]}$ | 0.80 |
| Factory$_{[FCD]}$ | Factory$_{[FRCD]}$ | 0.80 |
| Firm$_{[FCD]}$ | Firm$_{[FRCD]}$ | 0.72 |
| Producing Activity$_{[FCD]}$ | Producing Activity$_{[EUCD]}$ | 0.94 |
| Factory$_{[FCD]}$ | Factory$_{[EUCD]}$ | 0.93 |
| Firm$_{[FCD]}$ | Firm$_{[EUCD]}$ | 0.86 |
| Firm$_{[FCD]}$ | Company$_{[FD]}$ | 0.54 |
| Factory$_{[SCD]}$ | Factory$_{[FRCD]}$ | 0.78 |
| Firm$_{[SCD]}$ | Firm$_{[FRCD]}$ | 0.66 |
| Producing Activity$_{[SCD]}$ | Producing Activity$_{[EUCD]}$ | 0.92 |
| Factory$_{[SCD]}$ | Factory$_{[EUCD]}$ | 0.90 |
| Firm$_{[SCD]}$ | Firm$_{[EUCD]}$ | 0.76 |
| Firm$_{[SCD]}$ | Company$_{[FD]}$ | 0.52 |
| Factory$_{[FRCD]}$ | Factory$_{[EUCD]}$ | 0.80 |
| Firm$_{[FRCD]}$ | Firm$_{[EUCD]}$ | 0.67 |
| Program$_{[FRCD]}$ | Program$_{[EUCD]}$ | 0.59 |
| Firm$_{[FRCD]}$ | Company$_{[FD]}$ | 0.47 |
| Firm$_{[EUCD]}$ | Company$_{[FD]}$ | 0.54 |

### 10.8.2 Interesting Homonymies

No homonymies have been found between objects belonging to databases of Group F.

### 10.8.3 Interesting Type Conflicts

The application of the algorithm for detecting type conflicts derives the presence of a type conflict between the attribute *Category* of the entity *Firm* in the database $FRCD$ and the entity *Category* of the database $EUCD$.

### 10.8.4 Interesting Object Cluster Similarities

Some of the most interesting similarities between object clusters belonging to databases of Group F are presented in Table 10.15 [8].

**Table 10.15.** Interesting similarities between object clusters belonging to $FCD$, $SCD$, $FRCD$, $EUCD$ and $FD$

| First object cluster | Second object cluster | |
|---|---|---|
| ⟨ Producing Activity ↔ ↔ Carries Out ↔ ↔ Factory ⟩$_{[FCD]}$ | ⟨ Producing Activity ↔ ↔ Carries Out ↔ ↔ Factory ⟩$_{[SCD]}$ | 0.93 |
| ⟨ Contribution ↔ Asks For ↔ ↔ Factory ↔ ↔ Carries Out ↔ ↔ Producing Activity ⟩$_{[FCD]}$ | ⟨ Contribution ↔ Asks For ↔ ↔ Factory ↔ ↔ Carries Out ↔ ↔ Producing Activity ⟩$_{[SCD]}$ | 0.89 |
| ⟨ Machine ↔ For ↔ ↔ Factory ↔ ↔ Carries Out ↔ ↔ Producing Activity ⟩$_{[FCD]}$ | ⟨ Machine ↔ For ↔ ↔ Factory ↔ ↔ Carries Out ↔ ↔ Producing Activity ⟩$_{[SCD]}$ | 0.87 |
| ⟨ Contribution ↔ Asks For ↔ ↔ Factory ⟩$_{[FCD]}$ | ⟨ Contribution ↔ Asks For ↔ ↔ Factory ⟩$_{[SCD]}$ | 0.86 |
| ⟨ Factory ↔ Asks For ↔ ↔ Firm ⟩$_{[FCD]}$ | ⟨ Factory ↔ Has ↔ ↔ Firm ⟩$_{[FRCD]}$ | 0.80 |
| ⟨ Producing Activity ↔ ↔ Carries Out ↔ ↔ Factory ⟩$_{[FCD]}$ | ⟨ Producing Activity ↔ ↔ Carries Out ↔ ↔ Factory ⟩$_{[EUCD]}$ | 0.90 |
| ⟨ Producing Activity ↔ ↔ Carries Out ↔ ⟨ Factory ↔ Asks For ↔ ↔ Firm ⟩$_{[FCD]}$ | ⟨ Producing Activity ↔ ↔ Carries Out ↔ ⟨ Factory ↔ Has ↔ ↔ Firm ⟩$_{[EUCD]}$ | 0.85 |
| ⟨ Factory ↔ Asks For ↔ ↔ Firm ⟩$_{[FCD]}$ | ⟨ Factory ↔ Has ↔ ↔ Firm ⟩$_{[EUCD]}$ | 0.84 |
| ⟨ Firm ↔ Asks For ↔ ↔ Factory ⟩$_{[SCD]}$ | ⟨ Factory ↔ Has ↔ ↔ Firm ⟩$_{[FRCD]}$ | 0.66 |
| ⟨ Producing Activity ↔ ↔ Carries Out ↔ ↔ Factory ⟩$_{[SCD]}$ | ⟨ Producing Activity ↔ ↔ Carries Out ↔ ↔ Factory ⟩$_{[EUCD]}$ | 0.88 |
| ⟨ Factory ↔ Has ↔ ↔ Firm ⟩$_{[FRCD]}$ | ⟨ Factory ↔ Has ↔ ↔ Firm ⟩$_{[EUCD]}$ | 0.76 |

---

[8] As usual, in this table, $\langle C \rangle_{[S]}$ indicates the cluster $C$ of the scheme $S$.

# 11. Experiments on the Extraction of Hyponymies

*This chapter describes some experiments we have carried out on ICGO databases for deriving hyponymies, overlappings and all other properties described in Chapter 4. In particular we consider the databases belonging to Group A.*

*The material presented in this chapter is taken from [95, 97, 88].*

## 11.1 Group A: Hyponymy and Overlapping Extraction

In this section we present experiments we have carried out for deriving hyponymies, overlappings and the other properties we have described in Chapter 4. In particular we consider databases of Group A described in Section 10.2.1. In the following we analyze database pairs, one pair per section.

### 11.1.1 Properties Holding between Objects of RD and of MED

By running the synonymy derivation algorithm presented in Chapter 2, we obtain a synonymy between *Subject* of *RD* and *Subject* of *MED* with plausibility coefficient equal to 0.52 (see Section 10.3.2). Therefore, intrascheme hyponyms to be considered are: {*Physical Subject, Non Physical Subject*} of *RD* and {*Physical Subject, Non Physical Subject, Public Officer*} of *MED*.

As far as the database *RD* is concerned, the attributes of intrascheme hyponyms and hypernyms into consideration are[1]:

- **Subject**: (*Social Security Number*);
- **Physical Subject**: (General Information, First Name, Last Name, Address);
- **Non Physical Subject**: (Typology, Location, Denomination).

Analogously, as for *MED*, the attributes of intrascheme hyponyms and hypernyms to be considered are:

---

[1] We indicate key attributes in italics.

D. Ursino: Extr. and Expl. of Intensional Knowledge ..., LNCS 2282, pp. 215–219, 2002.
© Springer-Verlag Berlin Heidelberg 2002

– **Subject**: (*Social Security Number*, Bank Account);
– **Physical Subject**: (First Name, Last Name, Sex, BirthDate, Residence, Match-Code);
– **Non Physical Subject**: (Denomination, Location);
– **Public Officer**: (Last Name/Denomination, Title, Office).

In the following we consider in detail some of the most interesting pairs (the first entity of the pair belongs to $RD$, the second to $MED$):

– **Non Physical Subject - Non Physical Subject**. The application of the synonymy derivation algorithm presented in Chapter 2 detects that *Non Physical Subject* of $RD$ and *Non Physical Subject* of $MED$ are synonyms with coefficient 0.53 (see Section 10.3.2); therefore the tuple

$$\langle Non\ Physical\ Subject, Non\ Physical\ Subject, 0.53 \rangle$$

is inserted into $IHSD$.
– **Non Physical Subject - Physical Subject**. The synonymy coefficient derived for these two entities is 0.08; therefore the corresponding pair is not added to $IHSD$; as a consequence
$[Non\ Physical\ Subject,\ Physical\ Subject] \in CandH$.
The computation of $\delta_\sigma(Non\ Physical\ Subject, Physical\ Subject)$ returns a value lesser than $th_l$; therefore $[Non\ Physical\ Subject,\ Physical\ Subject] \notin PotH$. As a consequence, the tuple

$$\langle\langle Non\ Physical\ Subject, Non\ Physical\ Subject, 0.92 \rangle\rangle$$

is inserted into $IHHD$.
– **Physical Subject - Physical Subject**. The application of the algorithm for detecting synonymies presented in Chapter 2 does not detect a synonymy between *Physical Subject* of $RD$ and *Physical Subject* of $MED$; therefore a tuple

$$\langle Physical\ Subject, Physical\ Subject, f \rangle$$

does not belong to $IHSD$. Then, it is checked if the two objects are completely distinct. We have:
$A' = \{\langle First\ Name, First\ Name, 1\rangle, \langle Last\ Name, Last\ Name, 1\rangle,$
$$\langle Address, Residence, 0.8\rangle\}$$

$\frac{\overline{\phi}(A')}{|A'|} = 0.93$; therefore, the function $\delta_\sigma$ returns: $\left(1 - \frac{1}{2} \times 2 \times \frac{4}{10}\right) \times 0.93 = 0.56 > th_l$ and we can conclude that the two entities are not completely distinct. In addition, none of them is an hyponym of the other; hence, we must verify if they are partially overlapped. Since
$\delta_\nu(Physical\ Subject, Physical\ Subject) = 0.56 > th_d$, the tuple

$$\|Physical\ Subject, Physical\ Subject, 0.56\|$$

is inserted into $IHOD$; the overlapping attributes of *Physical Subject* of *RD* are *First Name, Last Name, Address* whereas those of *Physical Subject* of *MED* are *First Name, Last Name, Residence*.

Table 11.1 summarizes derived interscheme relationships between intrascheme hyponyms; each row of the table is associated with a candidate intrascheme hyponym of scheme *RD*, each column corresponds to a candidate intrascheme hyponym of scheme *MED*; each element indicates the dictionary which the corresponding pair belongs to.

**Table 11.1.** Relationships between intrascheme hyponyms of *Subject* of *RD* and *Subject* of *MED*

|  | *Physical Subject* | *Non Physical Subject* | *Public Officer* |
|---|---|---|---|
| *Physical Subject* | *IHOD* | *IHDD* | *IHDD* |
| *Non Physical Subject* | *IHDD* | *IHSD* | *IHDD* |

As an example of the application of the algorithm for deriving further hyponymies (presented in Section 4.3.1) we note that the existence of the properties

$$\langle Subject_{[RD]}, Subject_{[MED]}, 0.52\rangle \text{ and}$$
$$\lceil Public\ Officer_{[MED]}, Subject_{[MED]}, 1\rceil$$

allows to obtain

$$\lceil Public\ Officer_{[MED]}, Subject_{[RD]}, \tau_2(0.52, 1) = 0.52\rceil$$

## 11.1.2 Properties between RD and TCD

The application of the algorithm for detecting synonymies presented in Chapter 2 derives the presence of a synonymy between *Goods* of *RD* and *Goods* of *TCD* with plausibility coefficient 0.60, and between *Subject* of *RD* and *Subject* of *TCD* with plausibility coefficient 0.58 (see Section 10.3.1).

Candidate intrascheme hyponyms belonging to *RD* are {*Movable Goods, Non Movable Goods, Company*}, relative to the interscheme hypernymy *Goods*, and {*Physical Subject, Non Physical Subject*}, relative to the intrascheme hypernym *Subject*.

Analogously, candidate intrascheme hyponyms of the database *TCD* are {*Movable Goods, Real Estate*}, associated to the intrascheme hypernym *Goods*, and {*Physical Subject, Non Physical Subject, "IVA" Payer, User*} associated to the intrascheme hypernym *Subject*.

As for the database *RD*, the attributes of *Subject, Physical Subject, Non Physical Subject* have been listed in the previous section. As for the other intrascheme hyponyms and hypernyms, we have:

- **Goods**: (*Code*, Original Value, Final Value);
- **Movable Goods**: (*Code*, Description);
- **Non Movable Goods**: (*Code*, Classification, Address, Superficial Data, Income, Cadastral References);
- **Company**: (*Code*, Location, Value).

As for the database $TCD$, the attributes of intrascheme hyponyms and hypernyms into consideration are:

- **Goods**: (*Code*);
- **Movable Goods**: (*Code*, Technical Characteristics);
- **Real Estate**: (Address, Classification, Cadastral Reference, Income, Denomination);
- **Subject**: (*Social Security Number*);
- **Physical Subject**: (First Name, Last Name);
- **Non Physical Subject**: (Legal Status, Denomination);
- **"IVA" Payer**: (Payment Number);
- **User**: (*Code*).

Table 11.2 summarizes relationships derived by applying our techniques to pairs of intrascheme hyponyms corresponding to *Goods* of $RD$ and *Goods* of $TCD$ (rows are associated to intrascheme hyponyms of $RD$ and columns to intrascheme hyponyms of $TCD$).

**Table 11.2.** Relationships between intrascheme hyponyms of *Goods* of $RD$ and *Goods* of $TCD$

|  | Movable Goods | Real Estate |
|---|---|---|
| Movable Goods | IHSD | IHDD |
| Non Movable Goods | IHDD | IHSD |
| Company | IHDD | IHDD |

Furthermore, Table 11.3 presents derived relationships between pairs of intrascheme hyponyms corresponding to *Subject* of $RD$ and *Subject* of $TCD$ (rows are associated to intrascheme hyponyms of $RD$ and columns to intrascheme hyponyms of $TCD$).

As far as an example of the application of the algorithm for deriving further hyponymies is concerned, we note that the existence of the properties

$$\langle Goods_{[RD]}, Goods_{[TCD]}, 0.60 \rangle \text{ and } \lceil Company_{[RD]}, Goods_{[RD]}, 1 \rceil$$

allows to obtain

$$\lceil Company_{[RD]}, Goods_{[TCD]}, \tau_2(1, 0.60) = 0.60 \rceil$$

**Table 11.3.** Relationships between intrascheme hyponyms of *Subject* of $RD$ and *Subject* of $TCD$

|  | Physical Subject | Non Physical Subject | "IVA" Payer | User |
|---|---|---|---|---|
| Physical Subject | $IHHD^a$ | $IHDD$ | $IHDD$ | $IHDD$ |
| Non Physical Subject | $IHDD$ | $IHHD^b$ | $IHDD$ | $IHDD$ |

[a] In particular, *Physical Subject* of $RD$ is an hyponym of *Physical Subject* of $TCD$

[b] In particular, *Non Physical Subject* of $RD$ is an hyponym of *Non Physical Subject* of $TCD$ (in order to clarify this result, it is necessary pointing out that we have supposed that the attribute *Typology* of the entity *Non Physical Subject* of $RD$ has a high similarity with the attribute *Legal Status* of the entity *Non Physical Subject* of $TCD$).

### 11.1.3 Properties between MED and TCD

Consider the databases $MED$ and $TCD$; by applying the algorithm for detecting synonymies, shown in Chapter 2, we derive that the intrascheme hypernyms *Subject* of $MED$ and *Subject* of $TCD$ are in their turn synonyms. Intrascheme hyponyms of *Subject* of $MED$ and *Subject* of $TCD$ and associated attributes have been listed above. Table 11.4 represents relationships derived by applying our algorithm for them.

**Table 11.4.** Relationships between intrascheme hyponyms of *Subject* of $MED$ and *Subject* of $TCD$

|  | Physical Subject | Non Physical Subject | "IVA" Payer | User |
|---|---|---|---|---|
| Physical Subject | $IHHD^a$ | $IHDD$ | $IHDD$ | $IHDD$ |
| Non Physical Subject | $IHDD$ | $IHOD$ | $IHDD$ | $IHDD$ |
| Public Officer | $IHDD$ | $IHHD$ | $IHDD$ | $IHDD$ |

[a] In particular, *Physical Subject* of $MED$ is an hyponym of *Physical Subject* of $TCD$

# 12. Experiments on the Extraction of Assertions between Knowledge Patterns

*This chapter is devoted to describe experiments we have carried out on ICGO databases for deriving assertions between knowledge patterns. In particular we derive assertions involving objects belonging to databases of Group E (see Chapter 10).*

*The material presented in this chapter has been derived from [16, 17, 18, 96, 19].*

## 12.1 Group E – Extraction of Assertions between Knowledge Patterns

In this section we describe the application of the algorithms for extracting assertions between knowledge patterns (described in Chapter 5) to ICGO databases belonging to Group E defined in Chapter 10.

The algorithm for deriving assertions between knowledge patterns takes in input the set of synonymies and the set of hyponymies holding between objects belonging to involved schemes. As for databases of Group E, the set of synonymies is illustrated in Section 10.7. As pointed out in Chapter 5, the technique is composed of three phases.

The first phase constructs the *Inclusion Dictionary*; as for databases belonging to Group E assume the tuples of Table 12.1 have been derived.

The $KPAD$ is initially populated with all the tuples already stored in the Inclusion Dictionary.

The second phase of the technique is devoted to single out the most interesting classes and to construct some basic assertions which are inserted in the $KPAD$. As for schemes into considerations basic assertions are:

$\lfloor \forall Acquires[AS].BA : Good_{[FR]}, Subject_{[FR]}, 0.41 \rfloor$
$\lfloor \exists Administers[AM].UA : Office_{[FR]}, BookKeepingMovement_{[FR]}, 0.92 \rfloor$

The third phase of our approach derives complex assertions between knowledge patterns. By applying rules described in Section 5.5 we derive the following assertions:

D. Ursino: Extr. and Expl. of Intensional Knowledge ..., LNCS 2282, pp. 221–223, 2002.
© Springer-Verlag Berlin Heidelberg 2002

**Table 12.1.** Inclusion properties between objects belonging to databases of Group E

| First Object | Second Object | |
|---|---|---|
| BookKeepingMovement$_{[FR]}$ | BookKeepingMovement$_{[IPR]}$ | 0.95 |
| ImportExportGood$_{[FR]}$ | MaterialGoodOrProduct$_{[IPR]}$ | 0.40 |
| Liquidation$_{[FR]}$ | Liquidation$_{[IPR]}$ | 0.12 |
| Obligation$_{[FR]}$ | Obligation$_{[IPR]}$ | 0.10 |
| MaterialGoodOrProduct$_{[IPR]}$ | Good$_{[FR]}$ | 0.40 |
| Contract$_{[IPR]}$ | Document$_{[FR]}$ | 0.12 |
| ExpenseRegister$_{[HR]}$ | ProtocolRegister$_{[FR]}$ | 0.53 |
| PublicWorker$_{[HR]}$ | PhysicalSubject$_{[FR]}$ | 0.35 |
| ExpenseRegister$_{[HR]}$ | ProtocolRegister$_{[IPR]}$ | 0.47 |
| PhysicalSubject$_{[FR]}$ | Subject$_{[SR]}$ | 0.70 |
| ImportExportGood$_{[FR]}$ | Good$_{[SR]}$ | 0.64 |
| Invoice$_{[FR]}$ | RecordedDocument$_{[SR]}$ | 0.35 |
| FiscalForm$_{[FR]}$ | RecordedDocument$_{[SR]}$ | 0.30 |
| Obligation$_{[FR]}$ | BookKeepingMovement$_{[FR]}$ | 0.30 |
| Project$_{[FR]}$ | RecordedDocument$_{[SR]}$ | 0.20 |
| Liquidation$_{[FR]}$ | BookKeepingMovement$_{[FR]}$ | 0.20 |
| Contract$_{[FR]}$ | RecordedDocument$_{[SR]}$ | 0.15 |
| Contract$_{[FR]}$ | Document$_{[FR]}$ | 0.12 |
| ConfiscatedGood$_{[FR]}$ | Good$_{[SR]}$ | 0.50 |
| Liquidation$_{[IPR]}$ | BookKeepingMovement$_{[IPR]}$ | 0.62 |
| Obligation$_{[IPR]}$ | BookKeepingMovement$_{[IPR]}$ | 0.28 |

$\lfloor \exists Registers[CU].BC : ImportExportGood_{[FR]}, Office_{[IPR]},$
$$1 - \left((1 - 0.96) \times \left(\tfrac{1}{0.4}\right)^2\right) = 0.75\rfloor$$

$\lfloor \exists Registers[CU].BC : Good_{[FR]}, Office_{[IPR]},$
$$1 - \left((1 - 0.75) \times (0.64)^2\right) = 0.89\rfloor$$

$\lfloor ConfiscatedGood_{[FR]} \sqcap MaterialGoodOrProduct_{[IPR]}, Good_{[FR]}, 0.2 \rfloor$

$\lfloor ConfiscatedGood_{[FR]} \sqcup MaterialGoodOrProduct_{[IPR]}, Good_{[FR]}, 0.7 \rfloor$

$\lfloor Good_{[FR]} \sqcap \neg ConfiscatedGood_{[FR]}, Good_{[FR]}, 0.5 \rfloor$

$\lfloor \forall Acquires[AS].BA : MaterialGoodOrProduct_{[IPR]} \sqcap ConfiscatedGood_{[FR]},$
$$Subject_{[FR]}, 0.41 \times (0.2)^2 = 0.02 \rfloor$$

$\lfloor \forall Acquires[AS].BA : Good_{[FR]} \sqcap \neg ConfiscatedGood_{[FR]}, Subject_{[FR]},$
$$0.41 \times (0.5)^2 = 0.103 \rfloor$$

$\lfloor \forall Acquires[AS].BA : Good_{[FR]}, PhysicalSubject_{[FR]}, 0.28 \rfloor$

$\lfloor \forall Acquires[AS].BA : Good_{[FR]}, PublicWorker_{[HR]}, 0.10 \rfloor$

$\lfloor \exists Administers[AM].UA : Office_{[FR]}, BookKeepingMovement_{[IPR]},$
$$1 - (1 - 0.92) \times (0.95)^2 = 0.93 \rfloor$$

$\lfloor \exists Administers[AM].UA : Office_{[FR]}, Liquidation_{[IPR]},$
$$1 - (1 - 0.93) \times \left(\tfrac{1}{0.62}\right)^2 = 0.818 \rfloor$$

$\lfloor Liquidation_{[IPR]}, BookKeepingMovement_{[FR]}, 0.63 \rfloor$

$$\lfloor Obligation_{[IPR]}, BookKeepingMovement_{[FR]}, 0.27 \rfloor$$

For instance,

$$\lfloor ConfiscatedGood_{[FR]} \sqcap MaterialGoodOrProduct_{[IPR]}, Good_{[FR]}, 0.2 \rfloor$$

indicates that the proportion of *goods* in $FR$, which are also *confiscated goods* in $FR$ and *material goods or products* in $IPR$, is 0.2. Similarly,

$$\lfloor \exists Administers[AM].UA : Office_{[FR]}, BookKeepingMovement_{[IPR]}, 0.93 \rfloor$$

indicates that the proportion of *bookkeeping movements* in $IPR$, which are also *bookkeeping movements* administered by at least an office in $FR$, is 0.93.

# 13. Experiments on the Construction of a Data Repository

*This chapter aims at presenting some experiments we have carried out on ICGO databases for the semi-automatic construction of a data repository. In particular we illustrate the experiments we have carried out on ICGO databases by applying the Integration and the Abstraction Algorithms to databases belonging to groups A, B, C, D and F defined in Chapter 10.*

*The material presented in this chapter has been derived from [28, 95, 91, 97, 85, 83].*

## 13.1 Group A – Integration of Schemes and Abstraction of the Global Scheme

In this section we apply the integration and the abstraction algorithms to schemes of Group A defined in Chapter 10.

### 13.1.1 Integration Algorithm

The Integration Algorithm takes in input interscheme properties and exploits them in order to decide which objects of the involved schemes must be considered coincident, hyponym, overlapping or distinct in the global scheme. When a transformation is carried out, the Integration Algorithm must add the corresponding tuples to the Set of Mappings and to the Set of Views.

Interscheme properties necessary for the Integration Algorithm are synonymies and homonymies, illustrated in Section 10.3, as well as hyponymies and overlappings, presented in Chapter 11.

From these interscheme properties the Integration Algorithm can take the following decisions (hereafter we indicate the Global Integrated Scheme as *A-GIS*):

- *Movable Goods*$_{[TCD]}$ and *Movable Goods*$_{[RD]}$ are merged into *Movable Goods*$_{[A-GIS]}$;
- *Real Estate*$_{[TCD]}$ and *Non Movable Goods*$_{[RD]}$ are merged into *Real Estate*$_{[A-GIS]}$;
- *Goods*$_{[TCD]}$ and *Goods*$_{[RD]}$ are merged into *Goods*$_{[A-GIS]}$;
- *Distributor*$_{[TCD]}$ and *Company*$_{[RD]}$ are merged into *Company*$_{[A-GIS]}$;

D. Ursino: Extr. and Expl. of Intensional Knowledge ..., LNCS 2282, pp. 225–241, 2002.
© Springer-Verlag Berlin Heidelberg 2002

– *Non Physical Subject$_{[RD]}$* and *Non Physical Subject$_{[MED]}$* are merged into *Non Physical Subject$_{[A-GIS]}$*;

– *Subject$_{[RD]}$* and *Subject$_{[MED]}$* are merged into *Subject$_{[A-GIS]}$*;

– *Subject$_{[TCD]}$* and *Subject$_{[MED]}$* are merged into *Subject$_{[A-GIS]}$*;

– *Physical Subject$_{[RD]}$* (which is linked by an *is-a* relationship *R_Isa$_{[RD]}$* to *Subject$_{[RD]}$*) is an hyponym of *Physical Subject$_{[TCD]}$*; in the global scheme *Physical Subject$_{[RD]}$* is represented by *Registry Physical Subject$_{[A-GIS]}$* whereas *Physical Subject$_{[TCD]}$* is represented by *Physical Subject$_{[A-GIS]}$*;

– *Non Physical Subject$_{[RD]}$* (which is linked by an *is-a* relationship *R'_Isa$_{[RD]}$* to *Subject$_{[RD]}$*) is an hyponym of *Non Physical Subject$_{[TCD]}$*; in the global scheme *Non Physical Subject$_{[RD]}$* is represented by *Registry Non Physical Subject$_{[A-GIS]}$* whereas *Non Physical Subject$_{[TCD]}$* is represented by *Non Physical Subject$_{[A-GIS]}$*;

– *Physical Subject$_{[RD]}$* and *Physical Subject$_{[MED]}$* are linked by an overlapping property; their overlapping attributes are inherited by *Physical Subject$_{[A-GIS]}$*. In the global scheme there are the two entities *Registry Physical Subject$_{[A-GIS]}$* and *MED Physical Subject$_{[A-GIS]}$* owning non overlapping attributes of *Physical Subject$_{[RD]}$* and *Physical Subject$_{[MED]}$*, resp.

Some tuples which are added to the Set of Mappings are the following:

⟨*Movable Goods$_{[TCD]}$, Movable Goods$_{[RD]}$, Movable Goods$_{[A-GIS]}$, EMerge*⟩
⟨*Real Estate$_{[TCD]}$, Non Movable Goods$_{[RD]}$, Real Estate$_{[A-GIS]}$, EMerge*⟩
⟨*R_Isa$_{[RD]}$, Subject$_{[RD]}$, Physical Subject$_{[A-GIS]}$, IsaModify*⟩
⟨*R'_Isa$_{[RD]}$, Subject$_{[RD]}$, Non Physical Subject$_{[A-GIS]}$, IsaModify*⟩

The merge of entities *Real Estate$_{[TCD]}$* and *Non Movable Goods$_{[RD]}$* leads to the insertion of the following tuples into *KB.M.SoM*[1]:

⟨*Classification, Classification, Classification, AMerge*⟩
⟨*Address, Address, Address, AMerge*⟩
⟨*Cadastral Reference, Cadastral References, Cadastral Reference, AMerge*⟩
⟨*Income, Income, Income, AMerge*⟩

Correspondingly some instances which are added to the Set of Views are:

*D_EMerge(Movable Goods$_{[TCD]}$, Movable Goods$_{[RD]}$, Movable Goods$_{[A-GIS]}$)*
*D_EMerge(Real Estate$_{[TCD]}$, Non Movable Goods$_{[RD]}$, Real Estate$_{[A-GIS]}$)*
*D_IsaModify(R_Isa$_{[RD]}$, Subject$_{[RD]}$, Physical Subject$_{[A-GIS]}$)*
*D_IsaModify(R'_Isa$_{[RD]}$, Subject$_{[RD]}$, Non Physical Subject$_{[A-GIS]}$)*
*D_AMerge(Classification, Classification, Classification)*

The Global Integrated Scheme, obtained by carrying out all transformations described above, is represented in Figure 13.1.

---

[1] In the following tuples the first attribute is relative to *Real Estate$_{[TCD]}$*, the second attribute belongs to *Non Movable Goods$_{[RD]}$* whereas the third attribute is relative to *Real Estate$_{[A-GIS]}$*.

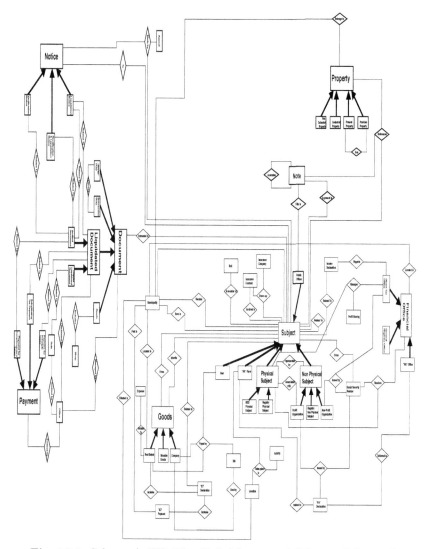

**Fig. 13.1.** Scheme A-GIS: The Global Integrated Scheme of Group A

## 13.1.2 Abstraction Algorithm

The algorithm for scheme abstraction takes in input the scheme *A-GIS* and abstracts it. The Abstraction Algorithm constructs the Abstraction Dictionary and exploits it for deciding which objects of the Global Scheme must be abstracted.

In particular some of the decisions taken by the Abstraction Algorithm are the following (hereafter we indicate the Global Abstracted Scheme as *A-GAS*):

– The cyclic relationship *Related To* of *Subject* is abstracted into *Subject*;
– The cyclic relationship *Annotates* of *Note* is abstracted into *Note*;
– The entity *User* and the corresponding *is-a* relationship $R\_Isa_{[User]}$ are abstracted into the entity *Subject*;
– The entity *Liquidation Notice* and the corresponding *is-a* relationship $R\_Isa_{[Liq]}$ are abstracted into the entity *Notice*;
– The entity *Roll* and the relationship *Is Member Of* are abstracted into the entity *Subject*;
– The entity *Expense* and the relationship *Related To* are abstracted into the entity *Real Estate*

Some of the tuples added to the Set of Mappings are:

$\langle Related\ To, -, Subject, CRDelToE \rangle$
$\langle Annotates, -, Note, CRDelToE \rangle$
$\langle User, Subject, Subject, EMerge \rangle$
$\langle R\_Isa_{[User]}, -, Subject, CRDelToE \rangle$
$\langle Liquidation\ Notice, Notice, Notice, EMerge \rangle$
$\langle R\_Isa_{[Liq]}, -, Notice, CRDelToE \rangle$
$\langle Roll, Subject, Subject, EMerge \rangle$
$\langle Is\ Member\ Of, -, Subject, CRDelToE \rangle$
$\langle Expense, Real\ Estate, Real\ Estate, EMerge \rangle$
$\langle Related\ To, -, Real\ Estate, CRDelToE \rangle$

The corresponding instances added to the Set of Views are:

$D\_CRDelToE(Related\ To, Subject)$
$D\_CRDelToE(Annotates, Note)$
$D\_EMerge(User, Subject, Subject)$
$D\_CRDelToE(R\_Isa_{[User]}, Subject)$
$D\_EMerge(Liquidation\ Notice, Notice, Notice)$
$D\_CRDelToE(R\_Isa_{[Liq]}, Notice)$
$D\_EMerge(Roll, Subject, Subject)$
$D\_CRDelToE(Is\ Member\ Of, Subject)$
$D\_EMerge(Expense, Real\ Estate, Real\ Estate)$
$D\_CRDelToE(Related\ To, Real\ Estate)$

The Global Abstracted Scheme obtained by the Abstraction Algorithm is illustrated in Figure 13.2.

## 13.2 Group B – Integration of Schemes and Abstraction of the Global Scheme

In this section we apply the integration and the abstraction algorithms to schemes of Group B defined in Chapter 10.

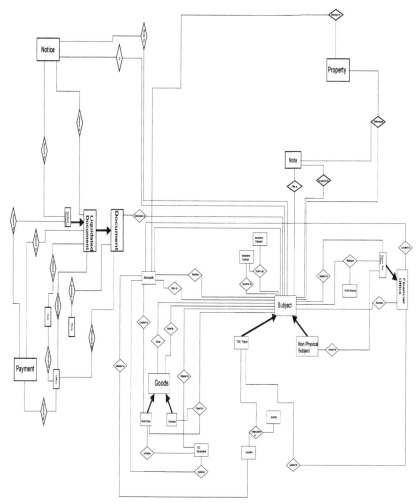

**Fig. 13.2.** Scheme A-GAS: The Global Abstracted Scheme of Group A

## 13.2.1 Integration Algorithm

The interscheme properties necessary for the Integration Algorithm are synonymies and homonymies illustrated in Section 10.4. The involved schemes do not have intrascheme hyponyms; therefore hyponymies and overlappings do not play any role in this integration case.

From the interscheme properties illustrated in Section 10.4, the Integration Algorithm can take the following decisions (hereafter we indicate the constructed Global Integrated Scheme as $B\text{-}GIS$):

- $Counter\text{-}Petition_{[CSD]}$ and $Sentence\ Objection_{[CCD]}$ are merged into $Sentence\ Objection_{[B-GIS]}$;

– $Petition_{[CSD]}$ and $Appeal_{[CCD]}$ are merged into $Appeal_{[B-GIS]}$;
– $Party_{[CSD]}$ and $Party_{[CCD]}$ must be considered two distinct entities;

Some tuples which are added to the Set of Mappings are the following:

$\langle Counter\text{-}Petition[CSD], Sentence\ Objection_{[CCD]},$
$\qquad\qquad\qquad\qquad Sentence\ Objection_{[B-GIS]}, EMerge \rangle$
$\langle Petition_{[CSD]}, Appeal_{[CCD]}, Appeal_{[B-GIS]}, EMerge \rangle$

Correspondingly some instances which are added to the Set of Views are:

$D\_EMerge(Counter\text{-}Petition_{[CSD]}, Sentence\ Objection_{[CCD]},$
$\qquad\qquad\qquad\qquad Sentence\ Objection_{[B-GIS]})$
$D\_EMerge(Petition_{[CSD]}, Appeal_{[CCD]}, Appeal_{[B-GIS]})$

The Global Integrated Scheme, obtained by executing all transformations described above, is represented in Figure 13.3.

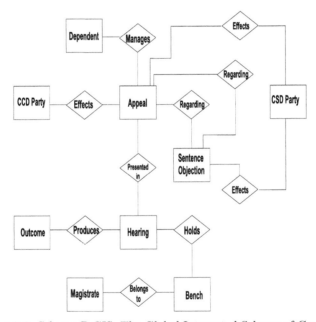

**Fig. 13.3.** Scheme B-GIS: The Global Integrated Scheme of Group B

## 13.2.2 Abstraction Algorithm

The Algorithm for Scheme Abstraction takes in input the scheme $B\text{-}GIS$ and abstracts it. As far as the databases of Group B are concerned, some of the decisions taken by the Abstraction Algorithm are the following (hereafter we indicate the Global Abstracted Scheme as $B\text{-}GAS$):

- Relationships *Regarding* and *Regarding* between *Appeal* and *Sentence Objection* are merged into a unique relationship *Regarding*;
- The entity *Dependent* and the relationship *Manages* are abstracted into the entity *Appeal*;
- The entity *CSD-Party* and the relationship *Effects* are abstracted into the entity *Sentence Objection*

Some of the tuples added to the Set of Mappings are:

$\langle Regarding, Regarding, Regarding, RMerge \rangle$
$\langle Dependent, Appeal, Appeal, EMerge \rangle$
$\langle Manages, -, Appeal, CRDelToE \rangle$
$\langle CSD\text{-}Party, Sentence\ Objection, Sentence\ Objection, EMerge \rangle$
$\langle Effects, -, Sentence\ Objection, CRDelToE \rangle$

The corresponding instances added to the Set of Views are:

$D\_RMerge(Regarding, Regarding, Regarding)$
$D\_EMerge(Dependent, Appeal, Appeal)$
$D\_CRDelToE(Manages, Appeal)$
$D\_EMerge(CSD\text{-}Party, Sentence\ Objection, Sentence\ Objection)$
$D\_CRDelToE(Effects, Sentence\ Objection)$

The Global Abstracted Scheme obtained by the Abstraction Algorithm is illustrated in Figure 13.4.

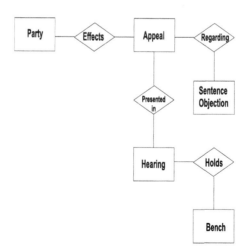

**Fig. 13.4.** Scheme B-GAS: The Global Abstracted Scheme of Group B

## 13.3 Group C – Integration of Schemes and Abstraction of the Global Scheme

In this section we apply the integration and the abstraction algorithms to schemes of Group C defined in Chapter 10.

### 13.3.1 Integration Algorithm

The interscheme properties necessary for the Integration Algorithm are synonymies, homonymies, hyponymies and overlappings. As for synonymies and homonymies the properties we have discovered for this group of schemes are shown in Section 10.5; as far as hyponymies and overlappings are concerned no interesting properties have been found by the corresponding algorithms.

Taking into account these interscheme properties, the Integration Algorithm can take the following decisions (hereafter we indicate the Global Integrated Scheme as *C-GIS*):

– *Payment*$_{[ESF]}$ and *Payment*$_{[EUP]}$ are merged into the entity *Payment*$_{[C-GIS]}$;
– *Other Body Corporate*$_{[ESF]}$ and *Partner*$_{[EUP]}$ are merged into the entity *Partner*$_{[C-GIS]}$;
– *Project*$_{[ESF]}$ and *Project*$_{[EUP]}$ are merged into the entity *Project*$_{[C-GIS]}$;
– *Judicial Person*$_{[ESF]}$ and *Promoter*$_{[EUP]}$ are merged into the entity *Promoter*$_{[C-GIS]}$;
– *Payment*$_{[ESF]}$ and *Payment*$_{[MEIS]}$ are merged into the entity *Payment*$_{[C-GIS]}$;
– *Operative Program*$_{[ESF]}$ and *Operative Program*$_{[MEIS]}$ are merged into the entity *Operative Program*$_{[C-GIS]}$;
– *Judicial Person*$_{[ESF]}$ and *Judicial Person*$_{[MEIS]}$ are merged into the entity *Judicial Person*$_{[C-GIS]}$;
– *Project*$_{[ESF]}$ and *Project*$_{[MEIS]}$ are merged into the entity *Project*$_{[C-GIS]}$;
– *Payment*$_{[EUP]}$ and *Payment*$_{[MEIS]}$ are merged into the entity *Payment*$_{[C-GIS]}$;
– *Project*$_{[EUP]}$ and *Project*$_{[MEIS]}$ are merged into the entity *Project*$_{[C-GIS]}$;
– *Promoter*$_{[EUP]}$ and *Judicial Person*$_{[MEIS]}$ are merged into the entity *Judicial Person*$_{[C-GIS]}$;

Some of the tuples added to the Set of Mappings are the following:

$\langle Payment_{[ESF]}, Payment_{[EUP]}, Payment_{[C-GIS]}, EMerge \rangle$
$\langle Other\ Body\ Corporate_{[ESF]}, Partner_{[EUP]}, Partner_{[C-GIS]}, EMerge \rangle$
$\langle Judicial\ Person_{[ESF]}, Promoter_{[EUP]}, Promoter_{[C-GIS]}, EMerge \rangle$

The merge of entities *Payment*$_{[ESF]}$ and *Payment*$_{[EUP]}$ leads to the insertion of the following tuples in the Set of Mappings:

⟨*Number, Number, Number, AMerge*⟩
⟨*Amount, Amount, Amount, AMerge*⟩
⟨*Date, Date, Date, AMerge*⟩
⟨*Year, Year, Year, AMerge*⟩
⟨*Payment Type, Payment Type, Payment Type, AMerge*⟩

Views added to the Set of Views corresponding to some of the tuples inserted in the Set of Mappings are:

*D_EMerge(Payment[ESF], Payment[EUP], Payment[C−GIS])*
*D_EMerge(Other Body Corporate[ESF], Partner[EUP], Partner[C−GIS])*
*D_EMerge(Judicial Person[ESF], Promoter[EUP], Promoter[C−GIS])*
*D_AMerge(Number, Number, Number)*

The Global Integrated Scheme, obtained by executing all transformations described above, is represented in Figure 13.5.

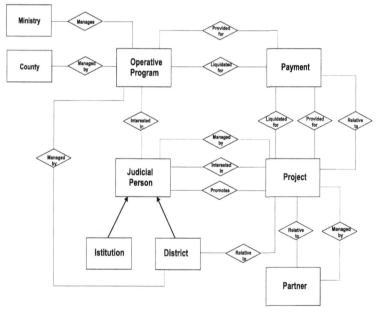

**Fig. 13.5.** Scheme C-GIS:The Global Integrated Scheme of Group C

### 13.3.2 Abstraction Algorithm

The Algorithm for Scheme Abstraction takes in input the scheme *C-GIS* and abstracts it. As far as databases of the Group C are concerned, some of the decisions taken by the Abstraction Algorithm are the following (hereafter we indicate the Global Abstracted Scheme as *C-GAS*):

- The relationships *Liquidated For* and *Provided For* between *Payment* and *Project* are merged into a unique relationship *Provided For*;
- The entity *Institution* and the corresponding *is-a* relationship *R_Isa* are abstracted into the entity *Judicial Person*;
- The entity *Ministry* and the relationship *Manages* are abstracted into the entity *Operative Program*

Tuples corresponding to the transformations outlined above and added to the Set of Mappings are:

⟨*Liquidated For, Provided For, Provided For, RMerge*⟩
⟨*Institution, Judicial Person, Judicial Person, EMerge*⟩
⟨*R_Isa, −, Judicial Person, CRDelToE*⟩
⟨*Ministry, Operative Program, Operative Program, EMerge*⟩
⟨*Manages, −, Operative Program, CRDelToE*⟩

The corresponding instances added to the Set of Views are:

*D_RMerge(Liquidated For, Provided For, Provided For)*
*D_EMerge(Institution, Judicial Person, Judicial Person)*
*D_CRDelToE(R_Isa, Judicial Person)*
*D_EMerge(Ministry, Operative Program, Operative Program)*
*D_CRDelToE(Manages, Operative Program)*

The Global Abstracted Scheme obtained by the Abstraction Algorithm is illustrated in Figure 13.6.

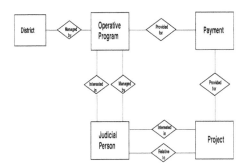

**Fig. 13.6.** Scheme C-GAS: The Global Abstracted Scheme of Group C

## 13.4 Group D – Integration of Schemes and Abstraction of the Global Scheme

In this section we apply the integration and the abstraction algorithms to schemes of Group D defined in Chapter 10.

### 13.4.1 Integration Algorithm

The interscheme properties necessary for the Integration Algorithm are synonymies, homonymies, hyponymies and overlappings. As for synonymies and homonymies, the properties we have discovered for this group of schemes are shown in Section 10.6; as far as hyponymies and overlappings are concerned, no interesting properties have been found by the corresponding algorithms.

Taking into account these interscheme properties, the Integration Algorithm can take the following decisions (hereafter we indicate the Global Integrated Scheme as $D$-$GIS$):

- $Right_{[LPR]}$ and $Right_{[UPR]}$ are merged into the entity $Right_{[D-GIS]}$;
- $Reserve_{[LPR]}$ and $Reserve_{[UPR]}$ are merged into the entity
  $Reserve_{[D-GIS]}$;
- $Classification_{[LPR]}$ and $Classification_{[UPR]}$ are merged into the entity
  $Classification_{[D-GIS]}$;
- $Document_{[LPR]}$ and $Document_{[UPR]}$ are merged into the entity
  $Document_{[D-GIS]}$;
- $Person_{[LPR]}$ and $Person_{[UPR]}$ are merged into the entity $Person_{[D-GIS]}$;
- $Person\ having\ right_{[LPR]}$ and $Person\ having\ right_{[UPR]}$ are merged into the
  entity $Person\ having\ right_{[D-GIS]}$;
- $Physical\ Person\ having\ right_{[LPR]}$ and $Physical\ Person\ having\ right_{[UPR]}$
  are merged into the entity $Physical\ Person\ having\ right_{[D-GIS]}$;
- $Non\ physical\ person\ having\ right_{[LPR]}$ and
  $Non\ physical\ person\ having\ right_{[UPR]}$ are merged into the entity
  $Non\ physical\ person\ having\ right_{[D-GIS]}$;
- $Compiler_{[LPR]}$ and $Compiler_{[UPR]}$ are merged into the entity
  $Compiler_{[D-GIS]}$;
- $Special\ Entry_{[LPR]}$ and $Special\ Entry_{[UPR]}$ are merged into the entity $Special\ Entry_{[D-GIS]}$;
- $Land\ Unit_{[LPR]}$ and $Urban\ Real\ Estate_{[UPR]}$ are merged into the entity
  $Register\ Unit_{[D-GIS]}$;

Some tuples which are added to the Set of Mappings are the following:

$\langle Right_{[LPR]}, Right_{[UPR]}, Right_{[D-GIS]}, EMerge \rangle$
$\langle Land\ Unit_{[LPR]}, Urban\ Real\ Estate_{[UPR]}, Register\ Unit_{[D-GIS]}, EMerge \rangle$

The corresponding instances which are added to the Set of Views are:

$D\_EMerge(Right_{[LPR]}, Right_{[UPR]}, Right_{[D-GIS]})$
$D\_EMerge(Land\ Unit_{[LPR]}, Urban\ Real\ Estate_{[UPR]}, Register\ Unit_{[D-GIS]})$

The Global Integrated Scheme, obtained by executing all transformations described above, is represented in Figure 13.7.

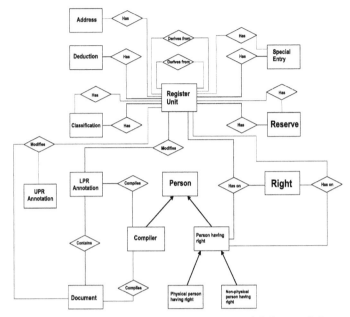

**Fig. 13.7.** Scheme D-GIS: The Global Integrated Scheme of Group D

## 13.4.2 Abstraction Algorithm

The Algorithm for Scheme Abstraction takes in input the scheme $D$-$GIS$ and abstracts it. As far as the databases of the Group D are concerned, some of the decisions taken by the Abstraction Algorithm are the following (hereafter we indicate the Global Abstracted Scheme as $D$-$GAS$):

- The relationships $Has$ and $Has$ between $Classification$ and $Register\ Unit$ are merged into a unique relationship $Has$;
- The cyclic relationship $Derives\ From$ of the entity $Register\ Unit$ is abstracted into $Register\ Unit$;
- The entity $Special\ Entry$ and the relationship $Has$ are abstracted into the entity $Register\ Unit$

Tuples corresponding to the transformations outlined above and added to the Set of Mappings are:

$\langle Has, Has, Has, RMerge \rangle$
$\langle Derives\ From, -, Register\ Unit, CRDelToE \rangle$
$\langle Special\ Entry, Register\ Unit, Register\ Unit, EMerge \rangle$
$\langle Has, -, Register\ Unit, CRDelToE \rangle$

The corresponding instances added to the Set of Views are:

$D\_RMerge(Has, Has, Has)$
$D\_CRDelToE(Derives\ From, Register\ Unit)$
$D\_EMerge(Special\ Entry, Register\ Unit, Register\ Unit)$
$D\_CRDelToE(Has, Register\ Unit)$

The Global Abstracted Scheme obtained by the Abstraction Algorithm is illustrated in Figure 13.8.

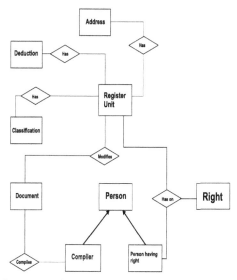

**Fig. 13.8.** Scheme D-GAS: The Global Abstracted Scheme of Group D

## 13.5 Group F – Integration of Schemes and Abstraction of the Global Scheme

In this section we apply the integration and the abstraction algorithms to schemes of Group F defined in Chapter 10.

### 13.5.1 Integration Algorithm

The interscheme properties necessary for the Integration Algorithm are synonymies, homonymies, hyponymies and overlappings. As for synonymies and homonymies the properties we have discovered for this group of schemes are shown in Section 10.8; as far as hyponymies and overlappings are concerned no interesting properties have been found by the corresponding algorithms.

Taking into account these interscheme properties, the Integration Algorithm can take the following decisions (hereafter we indicate the Global Integrated Scheme as $F\text{-}GIS$):

- $Firm_{[FCD]}$ and $Firm_{[SCD]}$ are merged into the entity $Firm_{[F-GIS]}$;
- $Factory_{[FCD]}$ and $Factory_{[SCD]}$ are merged into the entity $Factory_{[F-GIS]}$;
- $Producing\ Activity_{[FCD]}$ and $Producing\ Activity_{[SCD]}$ are merged into the entity $Producing\ Activity_{[F-GIS]}$;
- $Contribution_{[FCD]}$ and $Contribution_{[SCD]}$ are merged into the entity $Contribution_{[F-GIS]}$;
- $Machine_{[FCD]}$ and $Machine_{[SCD]}$ are merged into the entity $Machine_{[F-GIS]}$;
- $Credit\ Institute_{[FCD]}$ and $Credit\ Institute_{[SCD]}$ are merged into the entity $Credit\ Institute_{[F-GIS]}$;
- $Firm_{[FCD]}$ and $Firm_{[FRCD]}$ are merged into the entity $Firm_{[F-GIS]}$;
- $Factory_{[FCD]}$ and $Factory_{[FRCD]}$ are merged into the entity $Factory_{[F-GIS]}$;
- $Firm_{[FCD]}$ and $Firm_{[EUCD]}$ are merged into the entity $Firm_{[F-GIS]}$;
- $Factory_{[FCD]}$ and $Factory_{[EUCD]}$ are merged into the entity $Factory_{[F-GIS]}$;
- $Producing\ Activity_{[FCD]}$ and $Producing\ Activity_{[EUCD]}$ are merged into the entity $Producing\ Activity_{[F-GIS]}$;
- $Firm_{[FCD]}$ and $Company_{[FD]}$ are merged into the entity $Firm_{[F-GIS]}$;
- $Program_{[FRCD]}$ and $Program_{[EUCD]}$ are merged into the entity $Program_{[F-GIS]}$;
- $Factory_{[SCD]}$ and $Factory_{[FRCD]}$ are merged into the entity $Factory_{[F-GIS]}$;
- $Firm_{[SCD]}$ and $Firm_{[FRCD]}$ are merged into the entity $Firm_{[F-GIS]}$;
- $Producing\ Activity_{[SCD]}$ and $Producing\ Activity_{[EUCD]}$ are merged into the entity $Producing\ Activity_{[F-GIS]}$;
- $Factory_{[SCD]}$ and $Factory_{[EUCD]}$ are merged into the entity $Factory_{[F-GIS]}$;
- $Firm_{[SCD]}$ and $Firm_{[EUCD]}$ are merged into the entity $Firm_{[F-GIS]}$;
- $Firm_{[SCD]}$ and $Company_{[FD]}$ are merged into the entity $Firm_{[F-GIS]}$;
- $Factory_{[FRCD]}$ and $Factory_{[EUCD]}$ are merged into the entity $Factory_{[F-GIS]}$;
- $Firm_{[FRCD]}$ and $Firm_{[EUCD]}$ are merged into the entity $Firm_{[F-GIS]}$;
- $Firm_{[FRCD]}$ and $Company_{[FD]}$ are merged into the entity $Firm_{[F-GIS]}$;
- $Firm_{[EUCD]}$ and $Company_{[FD]}$ are merged into the entity $Firm_{[F-GIS]}$

Some of the tuples added to the Set of Mappings are the following:

$\langle Firm_{[FCD]}, Firm_{[SCD]}, Firm_{[F-GIS]}, EMerge\rangle$
$\langle Factory_{[FCD]}, Factory_{[FRCD]}, Factory_{[F-GIS]}, EMerge\rangle$
$\langle Producing\ Activity_{[FCD]}, Producing\ Activity_{[EUCD]},$
$\qquad\qquad\qquad\qquad Producing\ Activity_{[F-GIS]}, EMerge\rangle$
$\langle Program_{[FRCD]}, Program_{[EUCD]}, Program_{[F-GIS]}, EMerge\rangle$

The merge of entities $Firm_{[FCD]}$ and $Firm_{[SCD]}$ lead to the insertion of the following tuples in the Set of Mappings:

⟨*Trade Name, Trade Name, Trade Name, AMerge*⟩
⟨*Code, Code, Code, AMerge*⟩
⟨*Fiscal Code, Fiscal Code, Fiscal Code, AMerge*⟩
⟨*Dependent Number, Dependent Number, Dependent Number, AMerge*⟩

Views added to the Set of Views corresponding to some of the tuples inserted in the Set of Mappings are:

$D\_EMerge(Firm_{[FCD]}, Firm_{[SCD]}, Firm_{[F-GIS]})$
$D\_EMerge(Factory_{[FCD]}, Factory_{[FRCD]}, Factory_{[F-GIS]})$
$D\_EMerge(Producing\ Activity_{[FCD]}, Producing\ Activity_{[EUCD]},$
$\qquad\qquad\qquad\qquad\qquad\qquad\qquad Producing\ Activity_{[F-GIS]})$
$D\_EMerge(Program_{[FRCD]}, Program_{[EUCD]}, Program_{[F-GIS]})$
$D\_AMerge(Trade\ Name, Trade\ Name, Trade\ Name)$

The Global Integrated Scheme, obtained by executing all transformations described above, is represented in Figure 13.9.

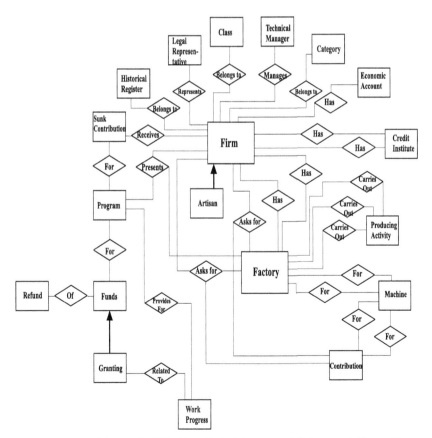

**Fig. 13.9.** Scheme F-GIS: The Global Integrated Scheme of Group F

### 13.5.2 Abstraction Algorithm

The Algorithm for Scheme Abstraction takes in input the scheme *F-GIS* and abstracts it. As far as the databases of Group F are concerned, some of the decisions taken by the Abstraction Algorithm are the following (hereafter we indicate the Global Abstracted Scheme as *F-GAS*):

- The relationships *Carries Out* and *Carries Out* between *Factory* and *Producing Activity* are merged into a unique relationship *Carries Out*;
- The entity *Artisan* and the corresponding *is-a* relationship *R_Isa* are abstracted into the entity *Firm*;
- The entity *Producing Activity* and the relationship *Carries Out* are abstracted into the entity *Factory*

Tuples corresponding to the transformations outlined above and added to the Set of Mappings are:

⟨*Carries Out, Carries Out, Carries Out, RMerge*⟩
⟨*Artisan, Firm, Firm, EMerge*⟩

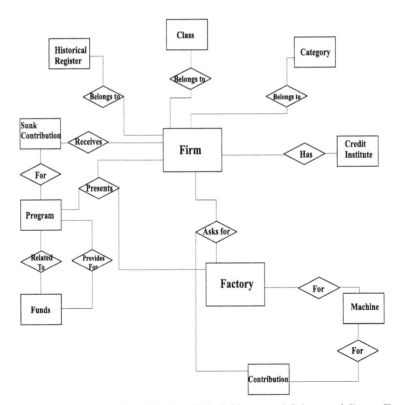

**Fig. 13.10.** Scheme F-GAS: The Global Abstracted Scheme of Group F

$\langle R\_Isa, -, Firm, CRDelToE \rangle$
$\langle Producing\ Activity, Factory, Factory, EMerge \rangle$
$\langle Carries\ Out, -, Factory, CRDelToE \rangle$

The corresponding instances in the Set of Views are:

$D\_RMerge(Carries\ Out, Carries\ Out, Carries\ Out)$
$D\_EMerge(Artisan, Firm, Firm)$
$D\_CRDelToE(R\_Isa, Firm)$
$D\_EMerge(Producing\ Activity, Factory, Factory)$
$D\_CRDelToE(Carries\ Out, Factory)$

The Global Abstracted Scheme obtained by the Abstraction Algorithm is illustrated in Figure 13.10.

# 14. Using the CIS Relative to ICGO Databases

*In this chapter we describe the behaviour of the Cooperative Information System we have constructed for ICGO. The chapter is to be intended as a user guide for the constructed CIS; in particular we show all methods the user has for determining the database of interest, all possibilities provided by the system for constructing a query and for reading corresponding results. Finally, we illustrate some utilities provided by the system, such as an on-line help and a glossary.*

*All material presented in this chapter has been derived from [38, 40, 39].*

## 14.1 General Options of the ICGO CIS

The Cooperative Information System we have constructed for Italian Central Governmental Office databases is called *Net_R*. *Net_R* can be accessed by any browser supporting JavaScript at the address:

http://isi-cnr.deis.unical.it:1080/~netrdist

Presently the forms of the system are in italian.

The system home page is shown in Figure 14.1. In the figure there are two frames. The first one contains some buttons, one for each program option: *(i) Naviga* (Navigate), *(ii) Home, (iii) Help, (iv) Glossario* (Glossary), *(v) About, (vi) Autori* (Authors), *(vii)* DEIS, *(viii)* AIPA. In addition the home page has two fields showing the date and the current time. The second frame presents *Net_R* and its icon.

Options *Help* and *Glossary* are two on line services of *Net_R*. Options *AIPA* and *DEIS* are two links to the web pages of AIPA (Autorità per l'Informatica nella Pubblica Amministrazione - Italian Information System Authority for Public Administration) and DEIS (Dipartimento di Elettronica, Informatica e Sistemistica). Option *Autori* visualizes some information about the authors of *Net_R*; option *About* provides information on *Net_R* whereas option *Home* allows to return to Home Page. The document selected by each of these options will be visualized in the other frame.

Option *Naviga* allows to exploit the ICGO Cooperative Information System; the first step of the navigation consists of the specification of the login

D. Ursino: Extr. and Expl. of Intensional Knowledge ..., LNCS 2282, pp. 243–250, 2002.
© Springer-Verlag Berlin Heidelberg 2002

**Fig. 14.1.** The Home Page of Net_R

(see Figure 14.2); the corresponding form has the three buttons *Submit*, allowing to submit the request, *Reset*, allowing to reset it, and *Back* for returning to the previous page.

If the login is valid the user enters the system. First, a main section is displayed showing two options, namely Repository Querying and Deferred Answer Visualization, whose functionalities are described in the following sections.

## 14.2 Repository Querying

ICGO database querying can be carried out by three different methods: *(i) Accesso Diretto* (Direct Access), *(ii) Navigazione attraverso gli schemi* (Access based on schemes) e *(iii) Navigazione attraverso le fonti di provenienza* (Access based on sources) (see Figure 14.3).

### 14.2.1 Direct Access

If the user selects the Direct Access, the system directly shows basic clusters of the repository; clusters are visualized through suitable icons (see Figure 14.4).

The selection of a cluster allows to access the databases belonging to it. The interface relative to the definition of a query or of a process (predefined query - see below) is shown in Figure 14.7.

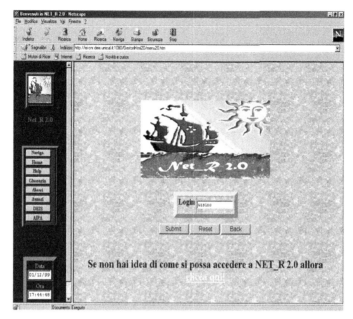

**Fig. 14.2.** The Login Page

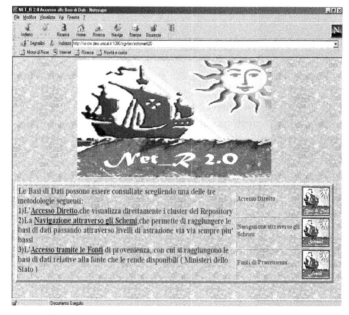

**Fig. 14.3.** Methods for ICGO database querying

**Fig. 14.4.** The form for Direct Access

## 14.2.2 Access Based on Schemes

If a user chooses the access based on schemes the form in Figure 14.5 is shown.

If the user pushes the button *Salpa dal I livello* (Go to the First Level Abstract Scheme), the system shows a web page representing the most abstract scheme of the repository with all its objects and a link to the next abstraction level (see Figure 14.6).

Two kinds of accesses are possible from this form: *(i)* access based on scheme hierarchy or *(ii)* access based on objects. If the user chooses the option *(i)* the system visualizes a document analogous to that shown above which presents the entities belonging to the selected scheme and all schemes belonging to the next lower abstraction level. If the user chooses the option *(ii)* then he/she selects an entity and the system shows all schemes belonging to the next lower level but, for each of these schemes, it shows only entities which the selected entity has been derived from by integration and abstraction steps.

The process is iterated until to the user reaches a basic cluster; at this point the system shows all databases belonging to this cluster and the user chooses the database of interest. After that, the user can define a query through the interface shown in Figure 14.7.

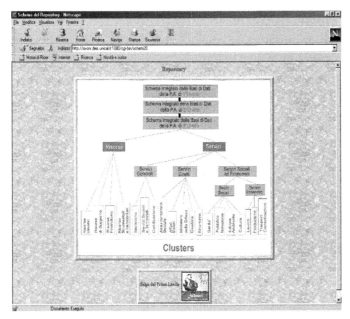

**Fig. 14.5.** The form for the access based on schemes

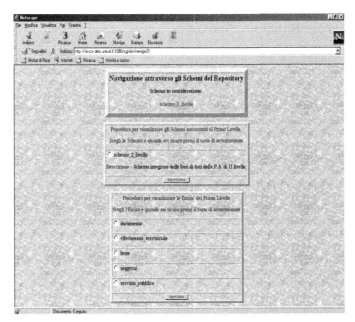

**Fig. 14.6.** Objects of a scheme and schemes of the lower abstraction level

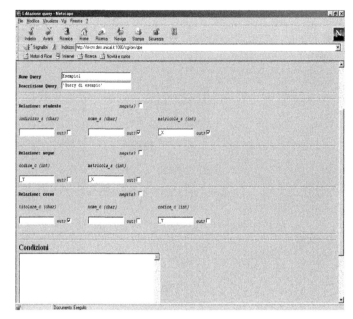

**Fig. 14.7.** The QBE-like editor for constructing a query

### 14.2.3 Access Based on Sources

If a user chooses the access based on sources, the system shows a form analogous to that illustrated in Figure 14.4. In more detail, the system shows the icons relative to the available database sources and, if a user selects one of them, the system displays all databases the sources provide. Then, the user can formulate a query by exploiting the interface shown in Figure 14.7.

### 14.2.4 Query Formulation

After that the user has selected the database of interest, the system asks if he/she wants to submit a query or a process. A query can be submitted using a QBE-like query language or a graphical query formulation wizard; a process is a parametric predefined query.

**Process Submission.** If a user chooses to submit a process the system visualizes the processes available on the selected database; the user then chooses the process of interest and the system asks the user to supply parameter values. After that, the form is submitted and the corresponding answer is constructed by the server. If the connection to the server breaks down, the system sends a suitable message to the user, who can examine the answer afterwards by opening a session of Deferred Answer Visualization.

**Submission of a Query by a QBE-Like Interface.** If a user chooses to submit a query through the QBE-like interface, the system activates a QBE-like editor (Figure 14.7).

First the editor shows relations belonging to the selected databases and asks the user to select all relations necessary for query formulation; for each relation, if necessary, two or more instances can be selected. After the user has been selected the relations of interest, the system shows the form of Figure 14.7.

In order to formulate the query, the user must fill a number of fields: first the user must insert the name and the description of the query; the name must identify the query in the corresponding database. The button *Negata?*(Negative?), associated to each relation, is used for implementing the "NOT EXISTS" operator. The button *Out*, associated to each attribute, allows the user to indicate that values of the corresponding attribute must be visualized in the answer. Beside the attributes, a part *Condizioni* (Conditions) is present for inserting all complicated conditions which cannot be expressed graphically.

After a query has been submitted the system provides for the answer; if the connection to server breaks down the system sends a suitable message to the user which can see the answer by opening a session of Deferred Answer Visualization.

**Submission of a Query by a Graphical Wizard.** The system provides also a wizard which guides the user to graphically formulate a query; this wizard consists of a set of forms, which, in the whole, lead to the construction of a query having the following format:

> SELECT [DISTINCT] ⟨ table name ⟩ .⟨ attribute name ⟩ { [, ⟨ table name ⟩ .⟨ attribute name ⟩ ] } FROM ⟨ table name ⟩ { [, ⟨ table name ⟩ ] } [WHERE ⟨ table name ⟩ .⟨ attribute name ⟩ OP ⟨ value ⟩ | ⟨ table name ⟩ .⟨ attribute name ⟩ { [AND | OR ⟨ table name ⟩ .⟨ attribute name ⟩ OP ⟨ value ⟩ | ⟨ table name ⟩ .⟨ attribute name ⟩ ] } [ORDER BY ⟨ attribute name ⟩ [USING ⟨ | ⟩ ] {, ⟨ attribute name ⟩ [USING⟨ | ⟩ ] }]

In particular there is a form for each subpart of the query: the first one implements the subpart "FROM", the second one implements the subpart "SELECT", the third one implements the subpart "DISTINCT" and the fourth one implements the subpart "ORDER BY". Finally two other forms allow to define the subpart "WHERE" of the clause. After that the query has been submitted, the system computes it and yields in output one answer; connection break-downs are handled as explained above.

## 14.3 Deferred Answer Visualization

As previously pointed out, it can happen that, after that a query or a process has been submitted and before the corresponding answer has been visualized to the user, the connection between the client and the server can break down or the time necessary for producing the answer is greater than a predefined interval. In this case the user can read the answer by activating a session and by choosing the option for the Deferred Answer Visualization.

The Deferred Answer Visualization has a form consisting of two frames. The first one has three buttons: *(i) Back*, allowing to return to the previous page, *(ii) Processi* (Processes) and *(iii)* Queries, allowing to visualize the answers of processes and queries previously submitted.

If a user pushes the button *Queries* the system visualizes a table containing the queries he defined having a deferred answer. Each query has a name, a description, a date of composition and the name of the database which it corresponds to. If the user selects one of these queries the system visualizes all tuples of the answer and a button *Ok* allowing to eliminate the answer from the archive.

Analogously, if a user chooses the button *Processi*, the system visualizes a table containing the processes he defined. Each process has a name, a description, the date of construction and the name of the corresponding database. If a user chooses one of these processes, the system shows all tuples of the corresponding answer and a button *Ok* allowing to eliminate the answer from the archive.

Part IV

**Final Issues**

This part is devoted to point out some final remarks about the argument of this thesis. In particular in Chapter 15 we have a look at the future research issues whereas in Chapter 16 we draw our conclusions. In addition, in this part, we include a bibliography indicating both the papers presented in the literature which are related to arguments treated by us and our contributions. Finally in the Appendix we describe in all detail the E/R model and the theory of type conflict resolution in E/R schemes.

# 15. A Look at the Future

*In this chapter we have a look at future developments of our research. In particular we show that our methodologies seem to be well suited for the integration of semi-structured information sources. In order to show this, we first describe a general framework allowing to handle this problem suitably; then we introduce the Object Exchange Model which was designed for representing semi-structured data. In the third section we give an overview of the first step of the presented approach, devoted to the construction of a graph-based structure for measuring the semantic closeness of objects belonging to different semi-structured information sources; finally, in the fourth section, we show some examples.*

*The material presented in this chapter can be found in [116].*

## 15.1 Introduction

Till now we have described an approach to the semi-automatic construction of a CIS or a DW involving a large number of heterogeneous databases; these can be considered structured information sources. In the last years, a remarkable increase in the number of information sources available over the internet took place. In many cases, these rich information sources are semi-structured (this is the case for most web sites). It is, therefore, interesting to design techniques allowing for an integrated exploitation of these information sources, while maintaining their operational autonomy.

It appears, therefore, natural to look at a possible evolution of the proposed approach in such a way that it allows the integration of numerous structured and semi-structured heterogeneous information sources by guaranteeing both the transparency of data and the operational autonomy of sites.

With regard to this, we argue that basic ideas underlying the techniques presented here (extracting interscheme properties, using them for describing information sources, exploiting thus obtained descriptions to synthesize an integrated query layer) can be applied also to these new integration problems.

Obviously, the necessity arises of re-defining the graph-based structures and the algorithms we have described in this thesis. In particular the *SD-Graph* (designed for measuring the semantic similarity of objects belonging

D. Ursino: Extr. and Expl. of Intensional Knowledge . . . , LNCS 2282, pp. 255–265, 2002.
© Springer-Verlag Berlin Heidelberg 2002

to structured information sources) must be re-defined in such a way that it can represent also semantic distances of objects belonging to semi-structured information sources (generally represented by models based on graphs such as the Object Exchange Model). In addition intra/interscheme properties must be possibly modified by adding new kinds of properties and by removing other ones in order to make them significant to describe relative semantics of semi-structured data sources. Finally, extraction, integration and abstraction algorithms must be modified to make them work properly on semi-structured information.

In this chapter we show a first step of this future work, i.e., we illustrate how a graph-based structure, called *SDR-Network*, can be derived for measuring the semantic distance between objects of semi-structured information sources. It will appear, from the definitions, that SD-Graphs are particular cases of SDR-Networks. More details about this part can be found in [116].

## 15.2 The Object Exchange Model

The Object Exchange Model (hereafter OEM) [1, 2, 23, 80, 103] is one of the most common models used for representing semi-structured data. Data described in a semi-structured information source are associated to objects in the OEM. Each object has a unique *object identifier (oid)* whose value belongs to the type oid.

There are two kinds of possible objects, namely Atomic Objects and Complex Objects. Concepts associated to *Atomic Objects* are described by a single value, taken from one of the disjoint basic atomic types, e.g., integer, real, string, gif, html, audio, java, etc. All non-atomic objects are *Complex Objects*; they are specified by a set of object references. Each object reference has the form *(label, oid)*, in which *label* describes the reference and *oid* specifies the referred object. The domain of the labels is the atomic type string.

A representation in the OEM basically consists of a labeled rooted graph. Each node of this graph represents an (atomic or complex) object; each arc is associated to a reference; in particular, an arc from a node $N_S$ to a node $N_T$ having a label $l$ represents the reference $(l, N_T)$ specifying $N_S$.

An *OEM-Graph* can be represented as:

$$\langle N_A^{OEM}(S) \cup N_C^{OEM}(S), A^{OEM}(S) \rangle$$

where $N_A^{OEM}(S)$ is the set of atomic nodes, $N_C^{OEM}(S)$ denotes the set of complex nodes and $A^{OEM}(S)$ indicates the set of arcs.

An example of an OEM-Graph is illustrated in Figure 15.1. Note that leaf nodes correspond to atomic objects whereas complex objects are represented by the other nodes.

## 15.3 The Conceptual Model and the Related Metrics

The construction of a *conceptual model* and of a *related metrics* for measuring semantic distances and relevances of object classes belonging to an information source is much more difficult in the semi-structured than in the structured case. As a matter of fact, the difficulties are both syntactic and semantic.

In particular, *syntactic difficulties* are due to the fact that structured information sources can be represented by the E/R model; this is simple, complete and commonly accepted. Vice versa models for representing semi-structured data are more complex and various [1, 2, 12, 23, 78, 79, 80, 103]; as an example, the OEM is based on concepts as graphs, nodes, labels, arcs; these concepts are different from those characterizing the E/R model. In addition the OEM represents instances, i.e. extensional data, whereas the E/R model represents object classes, i.e. intensional data. Since the metrics is referred to object classes, the corresponding conceptual model we propose must consider intensional data and the necessity arises to derive object classes associated to instances represented in the OEM.

*Semantic difficulties* arise since, in semi-structured information sources, the various objects of the same class can be described by different properties. In other words, a property can be present in some objects of a class whereas can be absent from other ones. As a consequence we have the need to take into account how often a property participates in the definition of the objects of a class.

### 15.3.1 The SDR-Network

In this section we formally introduce the *SDR-Network Net(S)* associated to a semi-structured information source $S$.

Given a source $S$ the associated *SDR-Network Net(S)* is:

$$Net(S) = \langle N^{SDR}(S), A^{SDR}(S) \rangle$$

where $N^{SDR}(S)$ represents a set of nodes and $A^{SDR}(S)$ denotes a set of arcs. In more detail, each node is characterized by a name; each arc can be represented by a triplet $\langle x, y, l_{xy} \rangle$, where $x$ is the source, $y$ is the target and $l_{xy}$ is a label associated to the arc. $l_{xy}$ can be represented, in its turn, as a pair $[d_{xy}, r_{xy}]$, where both $d_{xy}$ and $r_{xy}$ belong to the real interval $[0, 1]$. We call $d_{xy}$ the *semantic distance coefficient*; it indicates the capability of the concept associated to $y$ to characterize the concept associated to $x$. We call $r_{xy}$ the *semantic relevance coefficient*; it denotes the participation degree of the concept expressed by $y$ in the definition of the concept associated to $x$; the precise semantics of these coefficients and their derivation are described in Section 15.3.1.

Before illustrating how a SDR-Network can be constructed from a corresponding OEM-Graph, it is worth pointing out that, in an OEM-Graph, nodes represent objects whereas, in a SDR-Network, nodes are associated to classes of objects. Therefore, from now on, we use the term *object* to indicate the object associated to an OEM node whereas we use the term *class* to indicate the class of objects represented by a SDR-Network node.

The process of constructing a SDR-Network from the corresponding OEM-Graph consists of four phases: *(i)* pre-processing: it basically creates a modified OEM-Graph where a unique name is associated to each node; *(ii)* definition of the SDR-Network nodes; *(iii)* definition of the SDR-Network arcs; *(iv)* definition of labels associated to SDR-Network arcs. In the following subsections we describe these phases in more detail; two examples of the construction of the SDR-Network associated to an OEM-Graph are also given.

**The Pre-processing Phase.** The pre-processing phase is intended to obtain a modified OEM-Graph in which each node has an associated name.

Generally, the name associated to each node is inherited from the label of the arc which the considered node is target of. However two particular cases must be considered:

1. If an atomic node $t$ exists being the target of more than one arc, the pre-processing phase creates a new target node $t_i$ for each arc $a_i$ incident onto $t$; the name of $t_i$ is inherited from the label of $a_i$.
2. If a complex node $t$ exists being the target of more than one arc and some of these have different labels, the necessity arises to determine what are the significant roles associated to $t$; this task is carried out with the support of human experts, which must decide if either the involved labels have the same meaning or one has a more specific meaning than the other or they have different meanings. In the first case only one node is maintained and the user must choose the label which best characterizes it; in the second and in the third case the user must choose if either the node must be duplicated (in which case names associated to obtained nodes are inherited from the corresponding labels) or if only one node must be maintained (in which case the user must choose, as the name of the node, the label which best characterizes it).

In the following we assume that, when referring to an OEM-Graph, we intend the OEM-Graph modified by the pre-processing phase.

**Definition of the SDR-Network Nodes.** The set $N^{SDR}(S)$ of nodes in the SDR-Network is actually composed by the union of two sets of nodes:

$$N^{SDR}(S) = N_C^{SDR}(S) \cup N_A^{SDR}(S)$$

$N_C^{SDR}(S)$ is the set of nodes in the SDR-Network derived from complex nodes in the OEM-Graph. In particular, for each set of complex nodes in the OEM-Graph having the same name $M$, a node of $N_C^{SDR}(S)$ is associated to them whose name is $M$. Nodes belonging to $N_C^{SDR}(S)$ constitute the set of *complex nodes* of $Net(S)$.

$N_A^{SDR}(S)$ is the set of nodes in the SDR-Network derived from atomic nodes in the OEM-Graph. In particular, for each set of atomic nodes in the OEM-Graph such that they have the same name $M$ and there does not exist a complex node in the OEM-Graph whose name is $M$, a node of $N_A^{SDR}(S)$, named $M$, is associated to them. Nodes belonging to $N_A^{SDR}(S)$ form the set of *atomic nodes* of $Net(S)$.

**Definition of the SDR-Network Arcs.** Before introducing rules for obtaining SDR-Network arcs from the corresponding OEM-Graph, the following definitions are needed.

**Definition 15.3.1.** An *OEM-arc* is an arc in an OEM-Graph. It can be represented by a triplet $\langle S, T, L \rangle$, where $S$ is the source node, $T$ is the target node and $L$ is the corresponding label. A *SDR-arc* is an arc in a SDR-Network. It can be represented by a triplet $\langle S, T, L \rangle$, where $S$ is the source node, $T$ is the target node and $L$ is the corresponding label. □

**Definition 15.3.2.** Let $G_{OEM}$ be an OEM-Graph and $Net_{SDR}$ be the corresponding SDR-Network. Let $N_G$ be a node of $G_{OEM}$. The *SDR-Corr-Node* of $N_G$ is the node $N_N$ of $Net_{SDR}$ corresponding to $N_G$. The *OEM-Corr-NodeSet* of $N_N$ is the set of nodes of $G_{OEM}$ which $N_N$ is derived from. □

A function $SDR\text{-}Corr\text{-}Node(N_G)$ is defined, which takes in input a node $N_G$ of an OEM-Graph and yields in output the SDR-Corr-Node $N_N$ of $N_G$. A function $OEM\text{-}Corr\text{-}NodeSet(N_N)$ is defined, which takes in input a node $N_N$ of a SDR-Network and returns the OEM-Corr-NodeSet $NS_G$ of $N_N$.

We are now able to define the rules for obtaining arcs of a SDR-Network from the corresponding OEM-Graph. In particular, all the OEM-arcs $\langle S_i, T_i, L \rangle$ such that, for each $i$, the SDR-Corr-Node of $S_i$ is a unique node $N_S$ and the SDR-Corr-Node of $T_i$ is a unique node $N_T$, are represented by an arc from $N_S$ to $N_T$. Note that an OEM-arc $\langle S, T, L \rangle$ such that the SDR-Corr-Node of $S$ is equal to the SDR-Corr-Node of $T$ produces a cyclic arc in the SDR-Network.

**Definition of Labels Associated to Arcs of the SDR-Network.** Let $Net_{SDR}$ be a SDR-Network and let $\langle S, T, L \rangle$ be one of its SDR-arcs. We have seen that the label $L$ can be represented by a pair of values $[d_{ST}, r_{ST}]$, where $d_{ST}$ is the semantic distance coefficient and $r_{ST}$ is the semantic relevance coefficient.

In order to compute $d_{ST}$ and $r_{ST}$ from the nodes, the arcs and the labels associated to the corresponding OEM-Graph, we must first define the following sets of nodes: *(i)* $NS_S$ denotes the OEM-Corr-NodeSet of $S$; *(ii)* $NS_T$ indicates the OEM-Corr-NodeSet of $T$; *(iii)* $RNS_{S,T}$ represents the set of nodes $n_i$ such that, for each $i$, $n_i \in NS_S$ and there exists at least one node $q \in NS_T$ such that an OEM-arc $\langle n_i, q, l_{n_i q} \rangle$ is present in the corresponding OEM-Graph.

We are now able to formally define $d_{ST}$ and $r_{ST}$. In particular, as for the *semantic distance coefficient*, we have:

$$d_{ST} = \frac{\sum_{n_i \in RNS_{S,T}} \gamma(n_i, T)}{|RNS_{S,T}|}, \qquad \text{where}$$

$$\gamma(n_i, T) = \begin{cases} 0 & \text{if } \exists \langle n_i, p, l_{n_i p} \rangle \text{ such that } p \in NS_T, p \text{ is an atomic} \\ & \text{node and } \nexists \langle n_i, q, l_{n_i q} \rangle \text{ such that } q \in NS_T, q \neq p \\ 0.5 & \text{if } \exists \langle n_i, p, l_{n_i p} \rangle \text{ and } \exists \langle n_i, q, l_{n_i q} \rangle \text{ such that} \\ & p, q \in NS_T, p \neq q \text{ and } p, q \text{ are atomic nodes and} \\ & \nexists \langle n_i, r, l_{n_i r} \rangle \text{ such that } r \in NS_T, \text{ r is a complex} \\ & \text{node} \\ 1 & \text{if } \exists \langle n_i, p, l_{n_i p} \rangle \text{ such that } p \in NS_T \text{ and } p \text{ is a} \\ & \text{complex node} \end{cases}$$

The reasoning underlying the definition of $d_{ST}$ is as follows: an atomic OEM-node defines directly the concept associated to the corresponding atomic object; a complex OEM-node defines the concept associated to the corresponding object by means of the set of its references. Thus, given an OEM-node $N_O$ (belonging to $RNS_{S,T}$), an atomic OEM-node $N'_O$ (belonging to $NS_T$ and connected to $N_O$) is semantically closer to $N_O$ than a complex OEM-node $N''_O$ (belonging to $NS_T$ and connected to $N_O$) because it does not need the support of further nodes for defining a property of $N_O$. Moreover, if two or more atomic OEM-nodes with the same name are linked to the same OEM-node $N_O$, we can conclude that one of them alone is not enough to completely specify a given property of $N_O$ whereas they, as a whole, do specify this property. In this case the semantic distance between each of these atomic nodes and $N_O$ is intermediate w.r.t. the distances defined above.

As far as the *semantic relevance coefficient* is concerned, we have:

$$r_{ST} = \frac{|RNS_{S,T}|}{|NS_S|}$$

This formula directly derives from the definition of the semantic relevance of $T$ w.r.t. $S$ as the participation degree of the concept associated to $T$ in defining the concept associated to $S$.

**Examples.** Consider the OEM-Graph shown in Figure 15.1, relative to a Cardiology Division of an hospital, and the corresponding SDR-Network shown in Figure 15.2 (example taken from [14]).

The following considerations can be drawn:

– All nodes of the OEM-Graph having an incident arc with label *Patient* are represented, in the corresponding SDR-Network, by a unique node having

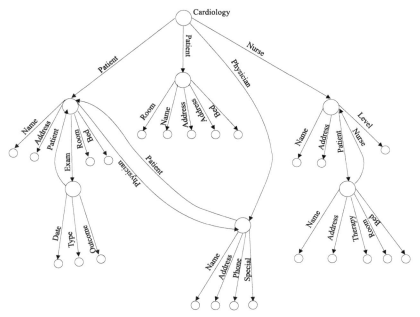

**Fig. 15.1.** The OEM-Graph of a Cardiology Division of a hospital

name *Patient*. The same reasoning has been applied for obtaining both nodes *Physician*, *Exam* and *Nurse* of the SDR-Network as well as those nodes of the SDR-Network derived from atomic nodes of the OEM-Graph.
- The SDR-arc between nodes *Patient* and *Physician* corresponds to all OEM-arcs $\langle S_i, T_i, L \rangle$ such that, for each $i$, the SDR-Corr-Node of $S_i$ is the node *Patient* and the SDR-Corr-Node of $T_i$ is the node *Physician*. In the same way all the other SDR-arcs are obtained.
- $d_{Patient,Physician}$ is 1 since *(i)* $NS_{Patient}$ is composed by three nodes, *(ii)* $NS_{Physician}$ is composed by one node, *(iii)* $RNS_{Patient,Physician}$ is composed by the unique node $n_p$ of $NS_{Patient}$ linked by an arc to the unique node belonging to $NS_{Physician}$, *(iv)* the value of $\gamma(n_p, Physician)$ is 1 since the node belonging to $NS_{Physician}$ is complex. All the other semantic distance coefficients are obtained in the same way.
- For the computation of $r_{Patient,Physician}$ we observe that $|RNS_{Patient,Physician}| = 1$, $|NS_{Patient}| = 3$, therefore $r_{Patient,Physician} = 0.33$. $r_{Physician,Patient} = 1$ because $|RNS_{Physician,Patient}| = 1$ and $|NS_{Physician}| = 1$. It is worth pointing out that $r_{Patient,Physician} \neq r_{Physician,Patient}$. An analogous reasoning allows to obtain all the other semantic relevance coefficients.

As a further example of the construction of the SDR-Network from an OEM-Graph consider the OEM-Graph shown in Figure 15.3, relative to a

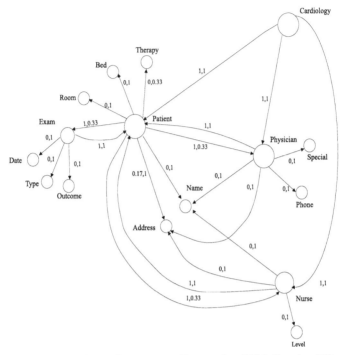

**Fig. 15.2.** The SDR-Network corresponding to the OEM-Graph of Figure 15.1

Restaurant Guide (this example has been derived from [1, 2]), and the corresponding SDR-Network depicted in Figure 15.4.

The following considerations can be drawn:

- In the OEM-Graph there are two arcs having the same label *Price* being incident on the same target atomic node; in this case, during the pre-processing phase, the target node is duplicated and both nodes have name *Price*.
- In the OEM-Graph there are some nodes which are the target nodes of arcs having both *Restaurant* and *Nearby* as labels. In this case, during the pre-processing phase, the intervention of a human expert is required; this determines that the two labels have different meanings; however he judges that there is no necessity to duplicate the corresponding nodes since *Nearby* represents a relationship between two objects and not a concept of its own. Therefore the name *Restaurant* is associated to these nodes.
- After the pre-processing phase, in the OEM-Graph, there is a set of atomic nodes such that *(i)* they have the same name *Address* and *(ii)* in the OEM-Graph a complex node $N_C$ *exists* whose name is *Address*. In this situation, in the SDR-Network, all these atomic nodes are represented by *SDR-Corr-Node*($N_C$).

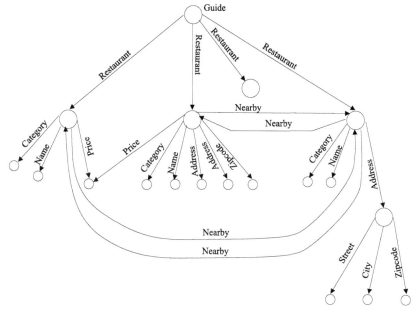

**Fig. 15.3.** The OEM-Graph of a Restaurant Guide

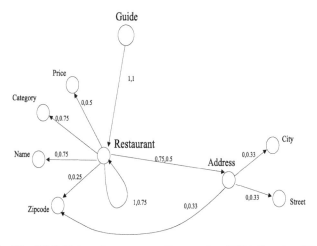

**Fig. 15.4.** The SDR-Network corresponding to the OEM-Graph of Figure 15.2

### 15.3.2 Definition of the Metrics

We are now in the position of establishing our metrics for measuring the semantic distance and the semantic relevance between two classes $C$ and $C'$ within an Information Source $S$. Before describing our metrics we must introduce the following support functions:

– $ClassOf(N) \rightarrow C$, which takes in input a node $N$ of the *SDR-Network* $Net(S)$ associated to an information source $S$ and yields in output the class $C$ of $S$ corresponding to $N$;
– $NodeOf(C) \rightarrow N$, which takes in input a class $C$ of an information source $S$ and yields in output the node $N$ of the associated *SDR-Network* $Net(S)$ corresponding to $C$.

Now, consider the following definitions:

**Definition 15.3.3.** Define the *Path Semantic Distance* of a path $P$ in $Net(S)$ (denoted by $PSD_P$) as the sum of the semantic distance coefficients associated to the arcs constituting the path. Define the *Path Semantic Relevance* of a path $P$ in $Net(S)$ (denoted by $PSR_P$) as the product of the semantic relevance coefficients associated to the arcs constituting the path. □

**Definition 15.3.4.** The *D_Shortest_Path* between two nodes $N$ and $N'$ in $Net(S)$ (denoted by $\lfloor N, N' \rfloor$) is the path having the minimum Path Semantic Distance among the paths connecting $N$ and $N'$. If more than one path exists having the same minimum Path Semantic Distance, one of those having the maximum Path Semantic Relevance is chosen. Define the *CD_Shortest_Path* (Conditional D_Shortest_Path) between two nodes $N$ and $N'$ in $Net(S)$ and including an arc $A$ (denoted by $\lfloor N, N' \rfloor_A$) as the path having the minimum Path Semantic Distance among those connecting $N$ and $N'$ and including $A$. If more than one path exists having the same minimum Path Semantic Distance, one of those having the maximum Path Semantic Relevance is chosen. □

**Definition 15.3.5.** Define a *D_Path$_n$* as a path $P$ in $Net(S)$ such that $n \leq PSD_P < n + 1$. □

**Definition 15.3.6.** Define the *i_th neighborhood* of a class $x$ as:

$$nbh(x, i) = \{A | A \in A^{SDR}(S), A = \langle z, y, l_{zy} \rangle,$$
$$\lfloor NodeOf(x), y \rfloor_A \text{ is a } D\_Path_i, NodeOf(x) \neq y,$$
$$(\forall j < i)(A \notin nbh(x, j))\} \quad i \geq 0$$

□

Thus, an arc $\langle z, y, l_{zy} \rangle$ belongs to $nbh(x, i)$ if it does not belong to any neighborhood lesser than $i$ and there exists a CD_Shortest_Path from $NodeOf(x)$ to $y$ including $\langle z, y, l_{zy} \rangle$ which is a $D\_Path_i$. Note that the possibility exists that $NodeOf(x) = z$.

**Proposition 15.3.1.** *Let $x$ be a class. Then, for each $i > 0$, $nbh(x, i) = \emptyset$ implies that $((\forall j > i)(nbh(x, j) = \emptyset))$.*

*Proof. Immediate from the definitions of neighborhood and of D_Path$_i$ and by noting that the semantic distance coefficient associated to an arc is lesser than or equal to 1.*

**Proposition 15.3.2.** *Let $x$ be a class and let $\bar{i} > 0$ be the maximum integer such that $nbh(x, \bar{i}) \neq \emptyset$; then $\bigcup_{0 \leq j \leq (k-1)} nbh(x, j) \subset \bigcup_{0 \leq j \leq k} nbh(x, j)$ for each $k$ such that $0 < k \leq \bar{i}$.*

*Proof. Immediate from Proposition 15.3.1 and by noting that an arc belongs to $nbh(x, i)$ only if it does not belong to $nbh(x, j)$ for all $j < i$.*

**Example.** Consider the node *Exam* of the *SDR-Network* shown in Figure 15.2[1]. We have that:

$$nbh(Exam, 0) = \{\langle Exam, Date, [0, 1]\rangle, \langle Exam, Type, [0, 1]\rangle,$$
$$\langle Exam, Outcome, [0, 1]\rangle\}$$

Indeed the first arc belongs to $nbh(Exam, 0)$ because $\lfloor Exam, Date \rfloor_{\langle Exam, Date, [0,1]\rangle}$ is a $D\_Path_0$ and $Exam \neq Date$. An analogous reasoning can be done for the other two arcs.

$$nbh(Exam, 1) = \{\langle Exam, Patient, [1, 1]\rangle, \langle Patient, Therapy, [0, 0.33]\rangle,$$
$$\langle Patient, Bed, [0, 1]\rangle, \langle Patient, Room, [0, 1]\rangle,$$
$$\langle Patient, Address, [0.17, 1]\rangle, \langle Patient, Name, [0, 1]\rangle\}$$

Indeed the arc $A = \langle Patient, Therapy, [0, 0.33]\rangle$ belongs to $nbh(Exam, 1)$ because $\lfloor Exam, Therapy \rfloor_A$ is a $D\_Path_1$, $Exam \neq Therapy$ and $A$ does not belong to $nbh(Exam, 0)$. The other arcs of $nbh(Exam, 1)$ are obtained by an analogous reasoning. Finally the other non-empty neighborhoods of *Exam* are:

$$nbh(Exam, 2) = \{\langle Patient, Physician, [1, 0.33]\rangle, \langle Physician, Special, [0, 1]\rangle,$$
$$\langle Physician, Phone, [0, 1]\rangle, \langle Physician, Name, [0, 1]\rangle,$$
$$\langle Physician, Address, [0, 1]\rangle, \langle Patient, Nurse, [1, 0.33]\rangle,$$
$$\langle Nurse, Level, [0, 1]\rangle, \langle Nurse, Name, [0, 1]\rangle,$$
$$\langle Nurse, Address, [0, 1]\rangle\}$$

$$nbh(Exam, 3) = \{\langle Physician, Patient, [1, 1]\rangle, \langle Nurse, Patient, [1, 1]\rangle\}$$

---

[1] As stated above, there is a complete correspondence between a class of an information source $S$ and a node of $Net(S)$; therefore, in order to simplify the notation, we use the same name (e.g., *Exam*) for indicating the class and the SDR-Network node corresponding to this class.

# 16. Conclusions

In this thesis we have presented a novel approach for managing great amounts of data distributed on heterogeneous data management systems. We have illustrated how traditional approaches to data management are not adequate in this context; moreover we have shown how Cooperative Information Systems and Data Warehouses are able to allow for users to query pre-existing autonomous data sources in a way that guarantees model, language and location transparency.

We have then proposed our approach consisting in three steps, namely:

- the enrichment of scheme description, obtained by the semi-automatic extraction of intensional knowledge from schemes;
- the exploitation of derived interscheme properties for obtaining, in a semi-automatic fashion, an integrated and abstracted representation of available data, encoded in a data repository;
- the exploitation of the repository (and of properties therein encoded), derived in previous steps, to support the designer in realizing either a mediator-based Cooperative Information System or a Data Warehouse over available data.

We have also shown the application of our techniques to the Italian Central Governmental Office (ICGO) databases. These consist of about 300 databases many of which having a relevant size; databases into consideration are owned by various central offices and are based on a variety of data models and systems. We have illustrated that results obtained by applying our approach to this example case are very encouraging.

Finally we have taken a look at the future and we have illustrated how our approach can be extended for allowing the integration of numerous structured and semi-structured heterogeneous information sources by guaranteeing the transparency of data and the operational autonomy of sites.

D. Ursino: Extr. and Expl. of Intensional Knowledge . . . , LNCS 2282, p. 267, 2002.

# References

1. S. Abiteboul. Querying semi-structured data. In *Proc. of International Conference on Database Theory (ICDT'97)*, pages 1–18, Delphi, Greece, 1997. Lecture Notes in Computer Science, Springer-Verlag.
2. S. Abiteboul, D. Quass, J. McHugh, J. Widom, and J.L. Wiener. The lorel query language for semistructured data. *International Journal on Digital Libraries*, 1(1):68–88, 1997.
3. R. Agrawal, T. Imielinski, and A. Swami. Database mining: A performance perspective. *IEEE Transactions on Software Engineering*, 5(6):914–925, 1993.
4. Y. Arens and C. A. Knoblock: C. Y. Chee, C. Hsu. Retrieving and integrating data from multiple information sources. *International Journal of Cooperative Information Systems*, 2(2):127–158, 1993.
5. R. Barquin and S. Edelstein. *Planning and Designing the Data Warehouse.* Prentice Hall, Englewood Cliffs, USA, 1996.
6. C. Batini, S. Castano, V. De Antonellis, M.G. Fugini, and B. Pernici. Analysis of an inventory of information systems in the public administration. *Requirement Engineering Journal*, 1(1):47–62, 1996.
7. C. Batini, S. Castano, M.G. Fugini, P. Naggar, M. Pellizzoni, and B. Pernici. Tecniche per l'analisi di descrizioni di processi nella pubblica amministrazione. In *Atti del Congresso Annuale dell'AICA (AICA'95)*, pages 247–258, Cagliari, Italy, 1995. (In Italian).
8. C. Batini, S. Ceri, and S.B. Navathe. *Conceptual Database Design.* The Benjamin/Cummings Publishing Company, 1992.
9. C. Batini and M. Lenzerini. A methodology for data schema integration in the entity relationship model. *IEEE Transactions on Software Engineering*, 10(6):650–664, 1984.
10. C. Batini, M. Lenzerini, and S.B. Navathe. A comparative analysis of methodologies for database scheme integration. *ACM Computing Surveys*, 15(4):323–364, 1986.
11. C. Beeri, A. Levy, and M.C. Rousset. Rewriting queries using views in description logics. In *Proc. of Symposium on Principles of Database Systems (PODS'97)*, pages 99–108, Tucson, Arizona, USA, 1997. ACM Press.
12. C. Beeri and T. Milo. Schemas for integration and translation of structured and semi-structured data. In *Proc. of International Conference on Database Theory (ICDT'99)*, pages 296–313, Jerusalem, Israel, 1999. Lecture Notes in Computer Science, Springer Verlag.
13. D. Beneventano, S. Bergamaschi, C. Sartori, and M. Vincini. ODB-Tools: A description logics based tool for schema validation and semantic query optimization in object oriented databases. In *Proc. of Advances in Artificial Intelligence, 5th Congress of the Italian Association for Artificial Intelligence (AI\*IA'97)*, pages 435–438, Roma, Italy, 1997. Lecture Notes in Computer Science, Springer Verlag.

14. S. Bergamaschi, S. Castano, and M. Vincini. Semantic integration of semistructured and structured data sources. *SIGMOD Record*, 28(1):54–59, 1999.

15. P.A. Bernstein and E. Rahm. Data warehouse scenarios for model management. In *Proc. of International Conference on Conceptual Modeling (ER'00)*, pages 1–15, Salt Lake City, Utah, USA, 2000. Lecture Notes in Computer Science, Springer Verlag.

16. A. Bonifati, L. Palopoli, D. Saccà, and D. Ursino. Discovering description logic assertions from database schemes. In *Proc. of International Workshop on Description Logics (DL '97)*, pages 144–148, Gif sur Yvette, France, 1997.

17. A. Bonifati, L. Palopoli, D. Saccà, and D. Ursino. Automatic extraction of database scheme semantic properties using knowledge discovery techniques. In *Proc. of International Workshop on Issues and Applications of Database Technology (IADT '98)*, pages 392–399, Berlin, Germany, 1998. Society for Design and Process Science (SDPS).

18. A. Bonifati, L. Palopoli, D. Saccà, and D. Ursino. Utilizzo della logica descrittiva per l'estrazione di proprietà terminologiche e strutturali complesse. In *Atti del Congresso su Sistemi Evoluti per Basi di Dati (SEBD'98)*, pages 71–86, Ancona, Italy, 1998.

19. A. Bonifati, L. Palopoli, D. Saccà, and D. Ursino. Automatic extraction of database scheme semantic properties using knowledge discovery techniques. *Journal of Integrated Design and Process Science*, 3(1):55–78, 1999.

20. Y. Breitbart. Multidatabase interoperability. *ACM SIGMOD RECORD*, 19(3):53–60, 1990.

21. M.W. Bright, A.R. Hurson, and S. Pakzad. Automated resolution of semantic heterogeneity in multidatabases. *ACM Transactions on Database Systems*, 19(2):212–253, 1994.

22. P. Buitelaar and R. P. Van De Riet. The use of a lexicon to interpret er-diagrams: A like project. In *Proc. of International Conference on the Entity-Relationship Approach, (ER'92)*, pages 162–177, Karlsruhe, Germany, 1992. Lecture Notes in Computer Science, Springer Verlag.

23. P. Buneman. Semistructured data. In *Proc. of Symposium on Principles of Database Systems, (PODS'97)*, pages 117–121, Tucson, Arizona, USA, 1997. ACM Press.

24. D. Calvanese, G. De Giacomo, and M. Lenzerini. On the decidability of query containment under constraints. In *Proc. of Symposium on Principles of Database Systems (PODS'98)*, pages 149–158, Seattle, Washington, USA, 1998. ACM Press.

25. D. Calvanese, G. De Giacomo, and M. Lenzerini. Modeling and querying semi-structured data. *Networking and Information Systems Journal*, 2(2):253–273, 1999.

26. D. Calvanese, G. De Giacomo, M. Lenzerini, D. Nardi, and R. Rosati. Description logic framework for information integration. In *Proc. of International Conference on Principles of Knowledge Representation and Reasoning (KR'98)*, pages 2–13, Trento, Italy, 1998. Morgan Kaufman.

27. D. Calvanese, G. De Giacomo, M. Lenzerini, D. Nardi, and R. Rosati. Source integration in data warehousing. In *Proc. of Workshop on Data Warehouse Design and OLAP Technology*, pages 192–197, Wien, Austria, 1998. IEEE Computer Society.

28. M. La Camera, L. Palopoli, D. Saccà, and D. Ursino. Knowledge discovery su schemi per l'integrazione di sistemi di basi di dati. In *Atti del Congresso sui Sistemi Evoluti per Basi di Dati (SEBD'97)*, pages 166–190, Verona, Italy, 1997.

29. S. Castano and V. De Antonellis. Reference conceptual architecture for re-engineering information systems. *International Journal of Cooperative Information Systems*, 4(2):213–235, 1995.

30. S. Castano and V. De Antonellis. Semantic dictionary design for database interoperability. In *Proc. of International Conference on Data Engineering (ICDE'97)*, pages 43–54, Birmingham, United Kingdom, 1997. IEEE Computer Society.

31. S. Castano, V. De Antonellis, M.G. Fugini, and B. Pernici. Conceptual schema analysis: Techniques and applications. *Technical Report, Politecnico di Milano*, pages 95–160, 1995.

32. T. Catarci and M. Lenzerini. Representing and using interschema knowledge in cooperative information systems. *Journal of Intelligent and Cooperative Information Systems*, 2(4):375–398, 1993.

33. S. Ceri and G. Pelagatti. *Distributed Databases, Principles & Systems*. McGraw Hill, New York, USA, 1985.

34. S. Chaudhuri and U. Dayal. An overview of data warehousing and OLAP technology. *ACM SIGMOD RECORD*, 26(1):65–74, 1997.

35. S. Chaudhuri, R. Krishnamurthy, S. Potamianos, and K. Shim. Optimizing queries with materialized views. In *Proc. of International Conference on Data Engineering (ICDE'95)*, pages 190–200, Taipei, Taiwan, 1995. IEEE Computer Society.

36. P.P. Chen. The entity-relationship model - towards a unified view of data. *ACM Transactions on Database Systems*, 1(1):9–36, 1976.

37. P. Fankhauser, M. Kracker, and E.J. Neuhold. Semantic vs. structural resemblance of classes. *ACM SIGMOD RECORD*, 20(4):59–63, 1991.

38. S. Flesca, L. Palopoli, D. Saccà, and D. Ursino. NET_R: un sistema per l'interfacciamento su internet, tramite WWW, del repository della pubblica amministrazione. In *Atti del Congresso nazionale dell' AICA (AICA '97)*, pages 49–70, Milano, Italy, 1997.

39. S. Flesca, L. Palopoli, D. Saccà, and D. Ursino. An architecture for accessing a large number of autonomous, heterogeneous databases. *Networking and Information Systems Journal*, 1(4-5):495–518, 1998.

40. S. Flesca, L. Palopoli, D. Saccà, and D. Ursino. Using a data repository as a mediator for constructing federated information systems. In *Proc. of International Workshop on Innovative Internet Information Systems (IIIS '98)*, pages 189–204, Pisa, Italy, 1998.

41. Z. Galil. Efficient algorithms for finding maximum matching in graphs. *ACM Computing Surveys*, 18:23–38, 1986.

42. H. Garcia-Molina, Y. Papakonstantinou, D. Quass, A. Rajaraman, Y. Sagiv, J. Ullman, V. Vassalos, and J. Widom. The TSIMMIS approach to mediation: Data models and languages. *Journal of Intelligent Information Systems*, 8:117–132, 1997.

43. R. Goldman and J. Widom. Dataguides: Enabling query formulation and optimization in semistructured databases. In *Proc. of Very Large Data Bases (VLDB'97)*, pages 436–445, Athens, Greece, 1997. Morgan Kaufman.

44. M. Golfarelli, D. Maio, and S. Rizzi. Conceptual design of data warehouses from E/R schemes. In *Proc. of the Hawaii International Conference on System Sciences*, Kona, Hawaii, USA, 1998.

45. W. Gotthard, P.C. Lockemann, and A. Neufeld. System-guided view integration for object-oriented databases. *IEEE Transactions on Knowledge and Data Engineering*, 4(1):1–22, 1992.

46. R.V. Guha. *Contexts: A Formalization and Some Applications*. PhD Thesis, Stanford University, 1991.

47. A. Gupta, I.S. Mumick, and K.A. Ross. Adapting materialized views after redefinitions. In *Proc. of International Conference on Management of Data (SIGMOD'95)*, pages 211–222, San Jose, California, USA, 1995. ACM Press.

48. L. M. Haas, R. J. Miller, B. Niswonger, M. T. Roth, P. M. Schwarz, and E. L. Wimmers. Transforming heterogeneous data with database middleware: Beyond integration. *IEEE Data Engineering Bulletin*, 22(1):31–36, 1999.

49. J. Hammer and D. McLeod. An approach to resolving semantic heterogenity in a federation of autonomous, heterogeneous database systems. *Journal of Intelligent and Cooperative Information Systems*, 2(1):51–83, 1993.

50. E.H. Hanson. A performance analysis of view materialization strategies. In *Proc. of International Conference on Management of Data (SIGMOD'87)*, pages 440–453, San Francisco, California, USA, 1987. ACM Press.

51. S. Hayne and S. Ram. Multi-user view integration system (muvis): An expert system for view integration. In *Proc. of International Conference on Data Engineering (ICDE'90)*, pages 402–409, Los Angeles, California, USA, 1990. IEEE Computer Society.

52. G.B. Ianni, L. Palopoli, D. Ursino, and D. Vasile. Un tool di ausilio alla progettazione di data warehouse. In *Atti del Congresso nazionale dell'AICA (AICA'99)*, pages 118–131, Padova, Italy, 1999.

53. IBM. *Information Warehouse Architecture I*. IBM Corporation, 1993.

54. T. Imielinski and H. Mannila. A database perspective on knowledge discovery. *Communications of the ACM*, 39(11):58–64, 1996.

55. W.H. Inmon. What is a data warehouse? *Prism Tech. Topic*, 1(1), 1997.

56. A.K. Jain and R.C. Dubes. *Algorithms for Clustering Data*. Prentice Hall, Englewood Cliffs, 1988.

57. P. Johannesson. Using conceptual graph theory to support schema integration. In *Proc. of International Conference on the Entity-Relationship Approach (ER'93)*, pages 283–296, Arlington, Texas, USA, 1993. Lecture Notes in Computer Science, Springer-Verlag.

58. R. J. Bayardo Jr., B. Bohrer, R. S. Brice, A. Cichocki, J. Fowler, A. Helal, V. Kashyap, T. Ksiezyk, G. Martin, M. H. Nodine, M. Rashid, M. Rusinkiewicz, R. Shea, C. Unnikrishnan, A. Unruh, and D. Woelk. Infosleuth: Semantic integration of information in open and dynamic environments. In *Proc. of International Conference on Management of Data (SIGMOD'97)*, pages 195–206, Tucson, Arizona, USA, 1997. ACM Press.

59. V. Kashyap and A. P. Sheth. Semantic and schematic similarities between database objects: A context-based approach. *Very Large Data Base Journal*, 5(4):276–304, 1996.

60. L. Kaufman and P.J. Rousseeuw. *Findings Groups in Data: an Introduction to Cluster Analysis*. John Wiley & Sons, New York, 1990.

61. A.M. Keller and J. Basu. A predicate-based caching scheme for client-server database architecture. In *Proc. of Third International Conference on Parallel and Distributed Information Systems (PDIS'94)*, pages 229–238, Austin, Texas, USA, 1994. IEEE Computer Society.

62. D. Koller, A. Levy, and A. Pfeffer. P-CLASSIC: A tractable probabilistic description logic. In *Proc. of National Conference on Artificial Intelligence (AAAI'97)*, pages 390–397, Providence, Rhode Island, USA, 1997. AAAI Press / The MIT Press.

63. R. Krishnamurthy, W. Litwin, and W. Kent. Language features for interoperability of databases with schematic discrepancies. In *Proc. of ACM SIGMOD International Conference on Management of Data (SIGMOD'91)*, pages 40–49, Denver, Colorado, USA, 1991. ACM Press.

64. J.A. Larson, S.B. Navathe, and R. Elmastri. A theory of attribute equivalence in databases with application to schema integration. *IEEE Transactions on Software Engineering*, 15(4):449–463, 1989.

65. A. Levy, A. Rajaraman, and J. Ordille. Querying heterogeneous information sources using source descriptions. In *Proc. of International Conference on Very Large Data Bases (VLDB'96)*, pages 251–262, Bombay, India, 1996. Morgan Kaufmann.

66. W. Litwin, L. Mark, and N. Roussopolus. Interoperability of multiple autonomous databases. *ACM Computer Surveys*, 22(3):267–292, 1990.

67. H. Mannila and K.J. Raiha. *The design of relational databases*. Addison Wesley Publishing Company, Reading, Massachusetts, USA, 1991.

68. M.V. Mannino and W. Effelsberg. Matching techniques in global schema design. In *Proc. of International Conference on Data Engineering (ICDE'84)*, pages 418–425, Los Angeles, California, USA, 1984. IEEE Computer Society.

69. C.J. Matheus, P.K. Chan, and G. Piatetsky-Shapiro. Systems for knowledge discovery in databases. *IEEE Transactions on Knowledge and Data Engineering*, 5(6):903–913, 1993.

70. E. Mena, A. Illarramendi, V. Kashyap, and A. P. Sheth. Observer: An approach for query processing in global information systems based on interoperation across pre-existing ontologies. *Distributed and Parallel Databases*, 8(2):223–271, 2000.

71. E. Metais, Z. Kedad, I. Comyn-Wattiau, and M. Bouzeghoub. Using linguistic knowledge in view integration: Toward a third generation of tools. *Data & Knowledge Engineering*, 23(1):59–78, 1997.

72. E. Metais, J.N. Meunier, and G. Levreau. Database schema design: A perspective from natural language techniques to validation and view integration. In *Proc. of International Conference on Conceptual Modeling (ER'93)*, pages 190–205, Dallas (Texas), USA, 1993. Lecture Notes in Computer Science, Springer-Verlag.

73. A.G. Miller. WordNet: A lexical database for english. *Communications of the ACM*, 38(11):39–41, 1995.

74. T. Milo and S. Zohar. Using schema matching to simplify heterogenous data translations. In *Proc. of Conference on Very Large Data Bases (VLDB'98)*, pages 122–133, New York City, USA, 1998. Morgan Kaufmann.

75. I. Mirbel. Semantic integration of conceptual schemes. In *Proc. of International Workshop on Applications of Natural Language to Data Bases (NLDB'95)*, Versailles, France, 1995. AFCET.

76. P. Mitra, G. Wiederhold, and J. Jannink. Semi-automatic integration of knowledge sources. In *Proc. of Fusion'99*, Sunnyvale, California, USA, 1999.

77. S.B. Navathe, R. Elmasri, and J.A. Larson. Integrating user views in database design. *IEEE Computer*, 19(1):50–62, 1986.

78. S. Nestorov, S. Abiteboul, and R. Motwani. Inferring structure in semistructured data. *SIGMOD Record*, 26(4):39–43, 1997.

79. S. Nestorov, S. Abiteboul, and R. Motwani. Extracting schema from semistructured data. In *Proc. of International Conference on Management of Data (SIGMOD'98)*, pages 295–306, Seattle, Washington, USA, 1998. ACM Press.

80. S. Nestorov, J.D. Ullman, J.L. Wiener, and S.S. Chawathe. Representative objects: Concise representations of semistructured, hierarchial data. In *Proc. of International Conference on Data Engineering (ICDE'97)*, pages 79–90, Birmingham, United Kingdom, 1997. IEEE Computer Society.

81. K. Orr. Understanding data warehousing. *American Programmer*, 8(5):2–7, 1995.

82. A.M. Ouksel and C.F. Naiman. Coordinating context building in heterogeneous information systems. *Journal of Intelligent Information Systems*, 3(2):151–183, 1994.

83. L. Palopoli, L. Pontieri, G. Terracina, and D. Ursino. Intensional and extensional integration and abstraction of heterogeneous databases. *Data & Knowledge Engineering*, 35(3):201–237, 2000.

84. L. Palopoli, L. Pontieri, G. Terracina, and D. Ursino. Semi-automatic construction of a data warehouse from numerous large databases. In *Proc. of International Conference on Re-Technologies for Information Systems (ReTIS'00)*, pages 55–75, Zurich, Switzerland, 2000. Osterreichische Computer Gesellschaft 2000.

85. L. Palopoli, L. Pontieri, and D. Ursino. Automatic and semantic techniques for scheme integration and scheme abstraction. In *Proc. of International Conference on Database and Expert Systems Applications (DEXA'99)*, pages 511–520, Firenze, Italy, 1999. Lecture Notes in Computer Science, Springer-Verlag.

86. L. Palopoli, L. Pontieri, and D. Ursino. Progettazione semi-automatica di data warehouse di grandi dimensioni. In *Atti del Congresso su Sistemi Evoluti per Basi di Dati (SEBD'99)*, pages 3–17, Como, Italy, 1999.

87. L. Palopoli, D. Saccà, G. Terracina, and D. Ursino. A unified graph-based framework for deriving nominal interscheme properties, type conflicts and object cluster similarities. In *Proc. of Fourth IFCIS Conference on Cooperative Information Systems (CoopIS'99)*, pages 34–45, Edinburgh, United Kingdom, 1999. IEEE Computer Society.

88. L. Palopoli, D. Saccà, G. Terracina, and D. Ursino. Semi-automatic extraction of hyponymies and overlappings from heterogeneous database schemes. In *Proc. of International Conference on Database and Expert Systems Applications (DEXA 2000)*, pages 614–623, Greenwich (England), United Kingdom, 2000. Lecture Notes in Computer Science, Springer-Verlag.

89. L. Palopoli, D. Saccà, G. Terracina, and D. Ursino. Una metodologia per l'estrazione e l'utilizzo di conoscenza intensionale da sorgenti informative eterogenee. *AI*IA Notizie*, 13(2):53–67, 2000.

90. L. Palopoli, D. Saccà, G. Terracina, and D. Ursino. Uniform techniques for deriving similarities of objects and subschemes in heterogeneous databases. *IEEE Transaction on Knowledge and Data Engineering*, Di prossima pubblicazione.

91. L. Palopoli, D. Saccà, and D. Ursino. Automatic derivation of terminological properties from database schemes. In *Proc. of International Conference on Database and Expert Systems Application (DEXA '98)*, pages 90–99, Vienna, Austria, 1998. Lecture Notes in Computer Science, Springer-Verlag.

92. L. Palopoli, D. Saccà, and D. Ursino. An automatic technique for detecting type conflicts in database schemes. In *Proc. of ACM Conference on Information and Knowledge Management (CIKM'98)*, pages 306–313, Bethesda, Maryland, USA, 1998. ACM Press.

93. L. Palopoli, D. Saccà, and D. Ursino. D.I.K.E.: un sistema per l'estrazione, la rappresentazione e l'utilizzo di conoscenza interschema su basi di dati eterogenee. In *Atti del sesto convegno della Associazione Italiana per l'Intelligenza Artificiale (AIIA'98)*, pages 67–71, Padova, Italy, 1998.

94. L. Palopoli, D. Saccà, and D. Ursino. A novel approach to cooperative information system construction and management. In *Proc. of Workshop on Intelligent Information Integration*, pages 109–126, Brighton, United Kingdom, 1998.

95. L. Palopoli, D. Saccà, and D. Ursino. Semi-automatic, semantic discovery of properties from database schemes. In *Proc. of International Database En-*

*gineering and Applications Symposium (IDEAS '98)*, pages 244–253, Cardiff (Wales), UK, 1998. IEEE Computer Society.

96. L. Palopoli, D. Saccà, and D. Ursino. DL$_P$: a description logic for extracting and managing complex terminological and structural properties from database schemes. *Information Systems*, 24(5):403–425, 1999.

97. L. Palopoli, D. Saccà, and D. Ursino. Semi-automatic techniques for deriving interscheme properties from database schemes. *Data & Knowledge Engineering*, 30(4):239–273, 1999.

98. L. Palopoli, D. Saccà, and D. Ursino. Estrazione semi-automatica e semantica di proprietà terminologiche e strutturali tra oggetti di schemi di basi di dati federate. *Rivista di Informatica*, 30(1):29–55, 2000.

99. L. Palopoli, G. Terracina, and D. Ursino. Experiences with using dike, a system for supporting cooperative information system and data warehouse design. *Sottomesso per la pubblicazione su Rivista Internazionale*.

100. L. Palopoli, G. Terracina, and D. Ursino. Approcci e strumenti semi-automatici per il re-engineering di basi di dati eterogenee. In *Atti del Congresso nazionale dell'AICA (AICA'99)*, pages 151–168, Padova, Italy, 1999.

101. L. Palopoli, G. Terracina, and D. Ursino. Derivazione di iponimie/iperonimie tra entità appartenenti a basi di dati eterogenee. In *Atti del Congresso su Sistemi Evoluti per Basi di Dati (SEBD 2000)*, pages 357–370, L'Aquila, Italy, 2000.

102. L. Palopoli, G. Terracina, and D. Ursino. The system dike: Towards the semi-automatic synthesis of cooperative information systems and data warehouses. In *Proc. of Challenges of Symposium on Advances in Databases and Information Systems (ADBIS-DASFAA 2000)*, pages 108–117, Prague, Czech Republic, 2000. Matfyzpress.

103. Y. Papakonstantinou, H. Garcia-Molina, and J. Widom. Object exchange across heterogeneous information sources. In *Proc. of International Conference on Data Engineering (ICDE'95)*, pages 251–260, Taipei, Taiwan, 1995. IEEE Computer Society.

104. M.P. Papazoglou, S.C. Laufmann, and T.K. Sellis. An organizational framework for cooperative information systems. *Journal of Intelligent and Cooperative Information Systems*, 1(1), 1992.

105. C. Pizzuti, G. Spezzano, and D. Ursino. A cellular genetic algorithm for satisfiability problems. In *Proc. of International Symposium on Advances in Intelligent Systems*, pages 408–413, Reggio Calabria, Italy, 1997. IOS Press.

106. E. Rahm and P.A. Bernstein. On mathing schemas automatically. In *Technical Report MSR-TR-2001-17*, http://www.research.microsoft.com/scripts/pubs/view.asp?TR_ID=MSR-TR-2001-17, 2001.

107. S.D. Richardson, W.B. Dolan, and L. Vanderwende. Mindnet: acquiring and structuring semantic information from text. In *Proc. of International Conference on Computational Linguistics (COLING-ACL'98)*, pages 1098–1102, Montreal, Quebec, Canada, 1998. Morgan Kaufmann.

108. N. Rishe, J. Yuan, R. Athauda, S-C. Chen, X. Lu, X. Ma, A. Vaschillo, A. Shaposhnikov, and D. Vasilevsky. Semantic access: Semantic interface for querying databases. In *Proc. of International Conference on Very Large Data Bases (VLDB 2000)*, pages 591–594, Il Cairo, Egypt, 2000. Morgan Kaufmann.

109. M.T. Roth and P.M. Schwarz. Don't scrap it, wrap it! a wrapper architecture for legacy data sources. In *Proc. of International Conference on Very Large Data Bases (VLDB 1997)*, pages 266–275, Athens, Greece, 1997. Morgan Kaufmann.

110. E. Sciore, M. Siegel, and A. Rosenthal. Using semantic values to facilitate interoperability among heterogeneous information systems. *ACM Transactions on Database Systems*, 19(2):254–290, 1994.

111. A.P. Sheth and J.A. Larson. Federated database system for managing distributed heterogeneous and autonomous databases. *ACM Computer Surveys*, 22(3):183–236, 1990.

112. A.P. Sheth, J.A. Larson, A. Cornelio, and S.B. Navathe. A tool for integrating conceptual schemata and user views. In *Proc. of International Conference on Data Engineering (ICDE'88)*, pages 176–183, Los Angeles, California, USA, 1988. IEEE Computer Society.

113. A. Silberschatz, H.F. Korth, and S. Sudarshan. *Database System Concepts*. McGraw-Hill, New York, 1997.

114. S. Spaccapietra and C. Parent. View integration: A step forward in solving structural conflicts. *IEEE Transactions on Knowledge and Data Engineering*, 6(2):258–274, 1994.

115. S.Y.W. Su, H. Lam, T. Yu, J.A. Arroyo-Figueroa, Z. Yang, and S. Lee. NCL: a common language for achieving rule-based interoperability among heterogeneous systems. *Journal of Intelligent Information Systems*, 6(2-3):171–198, 1996.

116. G. Terracina and D. Ursino. Deriving synonymies and homonymies of object classes in semi-structured information sources. In *Proc. of International Conference on Management of Data (COMAD 2000)*, pages 21–32, Pune, India, 2000. McGraw Hill.

117. G. Terracina and D. Ursino. A study on the interaction between interscheme property extraction and type conflict resolution. In *Proc. of International Database Engineering and Applications Symposium (IDEAS '00)*, pages 25–36, Yokohama, Japan, 2000. IEEE Computer Society.

118. G. Terracina and D. Ursino. A uniform approach for deriving type conflicts and object cluster similarities from database schemes. *Information Systems*, 25(8):527–552, 2001.

119. G. Thomas, G.R. Thompson, C.W. Chung, E. Barkmeyer, F. Carter, M. Templeton, S. Fox, and B. Hartman. Heterogenous distributed database systems for production use. *ACM Computer Surveys*, 22(3):236–266, 1990.

120. J.D. Ullman. Information integration using logical views. In *Proc. of International Conference on Database Theory (ICDT'97)*, pages 19–40, Delphi, Greece, 1997. Lecture Notes in Computer Science, Springer-Verlag.

121. D. Ursino. Cooperative information systems: property extraction, global scheme synthesis and www access. In *Proc. of Conference on Advanced Information Systems Engineering - Doctoral Consortium (CAiSE '98 - DC)*, Pisa, Italy, 1998. Eidgenossische Technische Hochschule.

122. D. Ursino. Deriving type conflicts and object cluster similarities in database schemes by an automatic and semantic approach. In *Proc. of Symposium on Advances in Databases and Information Systems (ADBIS'99)*, pages 46–60, Maribor, Slovenia, 1999. Lecture Notes in Computer Science, Springer-Verlag.

123. R.J. Vetter, C.G. Spell, and C.R.Ward. Mosaic and the world wide web. *IEEE Computer*, 27(10):49–57, 1994.

124. J.A. Wald and P.G. Sorenson. Explaining ambiguity in a formal query language. *ACM Transaction on Database Systems*, 15(2):125–161, 1990.

125. J. Widom. Research problems in data warehousing. In *Proc. of International Conference on Information and Knowledge Management (CIKM'95)*, pages 25–30, Baltimore, Maryland, USA, 1995. ACM Press.

126. G. Wiederhold. Mediators in the architecture of future information systems. *IEEE Computer*, 25(3):38–49, 1992.

127. W.A. Woods and J.G. Schmolze. The KL-ONE family. *Computer & Mathematics with Applications*, 23(2–5):133–177, 1991.
128. C.T. Yu and C.C. Chang. Distributed query processing. *ACM Computer Surveys*, 16(4):400–430, 1984.

# A. Appendix

*In this chapter we describe the entity-relationship model and the theory of type conflict resolution in E/R schemes. The first of these arguments is interesting for all chapters of the thesis since we assume that all schemes are represented by the E/R model. The second argument we treat here is important for the comprehension of the methodology for the resolution of type conflicts we have described in Section 2.3.2.*

## A.1 Entity-Relationship Schemes

A data model allows to describe the structure of data used in an information source. It provides a notation for describing stored data as well as their interrelationships. The entity-relationship model belongs to the category of conceptual data models and describes the semantics of data by classifying the application domain into entities and relationships among entities.

In particular, *entities* represent concepts that exist independently of other concepts, whereas *relationships* denote semantic connections between two or more entities. Entities and relationships denote, at the intentional level, set of instances, that is, concrete objects with a corresponding structure. Entities and relationships are jointly called *ER-objects*. ER-objects have *attributes* describing their properties. Each attribute is associated with a domain representing the set of possible values that the attribute can assume. A *database* scheme may contain many entities with the same structure (that is, with the same set of attributes) but their names are unique within the scheme. Vice versa, attribute and relationship names need not to be unique. Attributes and ER-objects are generically called *objects* [8, 67].

Entities taking part into a relationship $R$ are said to be the *participants* in $R$. Since an entity may participate into a relationship more than once, the necessity arises to associate a *role* to various participants. In a relationship, the name of roles must be unique and distinct from the name of involved objects.

For each entity, there is a set of attributes that uniquely identifies its instances; these form the *key* of the entity. Generally, attributes forming the key of an entity belong to the entity itself (in this case they are called *internal keys*). Sometimes, the attributes of the key may belong to a different

D. Ursino: Extr. and Expl. of Intensional Knowledge ..., LNCS 2282, pp. 279–283, 2002.

entity linked through a relationship to the entity into consideration. These attributes are in this case said to form a *foreign key*. An entity can have several *candidate* (alternative) keys. One of the keys is designated as the *primary* key. For each relationship $R$, we say that the keys of the entities participating therein form its *foreign key*.

Some rules can be stated which define the possible ways according to which entities can take part in a relationship. *Cardinality constraints* are represented by pairs of numbers $(C_{min}, C_{max})$, where $0 \leq C_{min} \leq C_{max}$ with $C_{max} > 0$, for each entity taking part in a relationship. A cardinality constraint tells that each instance of the entity must take part in at least $C_{min}$ and in at most $C_{max}$ instances of the relationship.

A particular type of relationship is the *is-a relationship*. This is not named, and no attribute is associated with it. In $E$ *is-a* $E'$, $E$ is called the *child*, whereas $E'$ is called the *parent*. The child entity has some attributes on its own. In addition, it also inherits, as its attributes, the attributes of the parent. The parent's key is a candidate key for the corresponding child.

An entity-relationship scheme is usually represented in graphical form, called *entity-relationship diagram*, or E/R diagram, for short. Figure A.1 shows how the various elements of the E/R model are expressed in E/R diagrams.

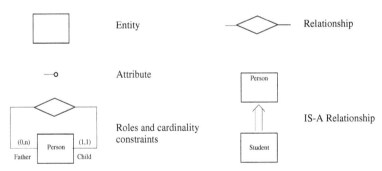

**Fig. A.1.** The entity-relationship diagram

## A.2 Type Conflict Resolution

This section is devoted to describe the theory concerning the resolution of type conflicts in E/R diagrams. We recall that, in E/R diagrams, the type of an object $O$ denotes if $O$ is an entity, a relationship or an attribute; as a consequence, a type conflict holds between two objects belonging to two different schemes if they represent the same concept, yet having different types.

Once detected, a type conflict can be solved by applying methods as those illustrated in [9]. These methods basically consist in transforming one of the objects involved in a type conflict to assume the type of the other one. Generally two kinds of transformations have been proposed in the literature for solving type conflicts [9], namely *(i)* transformations which are always applicable, even if they may sometimes fail to produce optimal transformed schemes, and *(ii)* transformation which always produce optimal transformed schemes even if they are applicable only in some particular cases. Since our approach is semi-automatic we have taken into consideration only transformations which are always applicable.

In the following sections we describe always applicable transformations which can be carried out for solving type conflicts when schemes are represented by E/R diagrams; these transformations constitute the theoretical basis for the corresponding ones we have proposed in Section 2.3.2 for solving type conflicts in SD-Graphs.

### A.2.1 Resolution of an Entity–Relationship Conflict

A type conflict involving an entity and a relationship is solved by transforming the relationship into an entity. Assume that the relationship $R$ to be transformed is linked to entities $E_1, \ldots, E_m$. Then, the relationship $R$ is transformed into a new entity (with the same name $R$) connected with each entity $E_i$ through $m$ new relationships (see Figure A.2). The minimum and the maximum cardinality associated with the new entity participating into each of the $m$ new relationships are both equal to 1. Minimum and maximum cardinalities associated with the entities $E_i$ participating into the new $m$ relationships are inherited from the original relationship. The new entity $R$ inherits all the attributes of the original relationship plus its foreign keys.

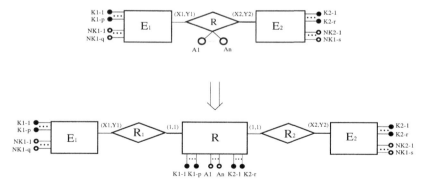

**Fig. A.2.** Transforming a relationship into an entity

## A.2.2 Resolution of an Entity Attribute–Entity Conflict

This type conflict is solved by transforming the involved attribute $A$ into a new entity $A$. Assume $A$ belongs to an entity $E$. Then the new entity $A$ resulting from the transformation is connected to $E$ through a new relationship $R$ (see Figure A.3). The new entity $A$ has associated a key attribute $A_I$, with the same value set as the original attribute. The minimum and the maximum cardinality associated with $E$ participating into $R$ are both equal to 1. The minimum cardinality for $A$ participating into $R$ is 1, whereas the maximum cardinality is 1 if and only if the original attribute $A$ was a key for $E$, $n$ otherwise.

If the attribute $A$ was (part of) the key for $E$, the key of the new entity $A$ will be (part of) the key for $E$ as a foreign key.

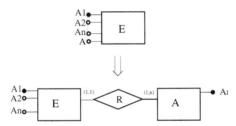

**Fig. A.3.** Transforming an entity attribute into an entity

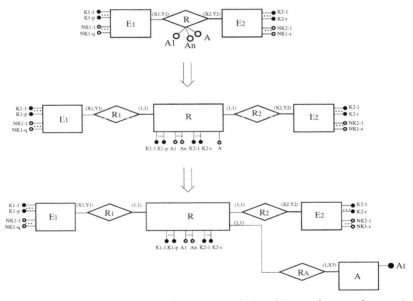

**Fig. A.4.** Resolution of a conflict between a relationship attribute and an entity

### A.2.3 Resolution of a Relationship Attribute–Entity Conflict

To solve this type conflict, we transform the involved attribute into an entity. This is done in two steps (see Figure A.4):

– transforming the relationship relative to the involved attribute into an entity using the technique described in Section A.2.1 above; by doing so, the conflict becomes one involving an entity attribute and an entity;
– solving the new conflict by applying the technique illustrated in Section A.2.2 above.

### A.2.4 Resolution of an Entity Attribute (resp., a Relationship Attribute)–Relationship Conflict

This type conflict is solved by transforming the involved relationship into an entity as described in Section A.2.1 (see Figure A.2); therefore the original conflict becomes a conflict between an entity attribute (resp., a relationship attribute) and an entity and can be solved by applying the technique described in Section A.2.2 (resp., Section A.2.3).

# Index

Administration Department Database, 50, 101

CandH, 77
CandS, 76
Complexity
– data repository construction, 124
– homonymy derivation, 54–59
– object cluster similarity derivation, 67–69
– synonymy derivation, 54–59
– type conflict derivation, 54–59
Context
– of a relationship, 116
– of an attribute, 116
– of an entity, 116
Context Diagram, 149
Cooperative Information System, 12, 143–159
– mediator, 13, 144
– query centric, 13, 144
– source centric, 14, 145
– wrapper, 13, 144

Data Repository, 113, 175
– c-id, 114
– c-scheme, 114
– construction, 122–124
– O-identifier, 114
– O-scheme, 114
Data Warehouse, 14, 161–169
– BDW, 162
– – C-id, 166
– – C-scheme, 166
– – O-identifier, 166
– – O-scheme, 166
– BDW.Map, 166
– BDW.Rep, 166
– BDW.SoV, 166
– BIW, 163
– one-level architecture, 14, 162
– three-level architecture, 15, 162

– two-level architecture, 14, 162
Dictionary
– Abstraction (AD), 134
– Homonymy (HD), 27, 34
– Inclusion (ID), 92–93
– Inclusion Dictionary (ID), 88
– Knowledge Pattern Assertion (KPAD), 88, 92, 94
– Lexical Synonymy Property (LSPD), 3
– – sensitivity analysis, 59–60
– Object Cluster Similarity (OCSD), 65
– of Distinctnesses between Intrascheme Hyponyms (IHDD), 76, 78, 79
– of Hyponymies between Intrascheme Hyponyms (IHHD), 76, 82
– of Overlappings between Intrascheme Hyponyms (IHOD), 76, 79
– of Synonymies between Intrascheme Hyponyms (IHSD), 76
– Starting Synonymy (SSD), 75
– Synonymy (SD), 27, 34
DIKE, 175–187
– basic hyponymy and overlapping extractor, 180
– context diagram, 176, 177
– cooperative information system constructor, 177, 181
– data repository constructor, 176, 180
– data warehouse constructor, 181
– general hyponymy extractor, 180
– hyponymy and overlapping extractor, 180
– intensional knowledge extractor, 176, 178
– knowledge pattern assertion extractor, 180
– object synonymy-homonymy extractor, 178
– scheme abstractor, 181

# Lecture Notes in Computer Science

For information about Vols. 1–2209
please contact your bookseller or Springer-Verlag

Vol. 2248: C. Boyd (Ed.), Advances in Cryptology – ASIACRYPT 2001. Proceedings, 2001. XI, 603 pages. 2001.

Vol. 2249: K. Nagi, Transactional Agents. XVI, 205 pages. 2001.

Vol. 2250: R. Nieuwenhuis, A. Voronkov (Eds.), Logic for Programming, Artificial Intelligence, and Reasoning. Proceedings, 2001. XV, 738 pages. 2001. (Subseries LNAI).

Vol. 2251: Y.Y. Tang, V. Wickerhauser, P.C. Yuen, C.Li (Eds.), Wavelet Analysis and Its Applications. Proceedings, 2001. XIII, 450 pages. 2001.

Vol. 2252: J. Liu, P.C. Yuen, C. Li, J. Ng, T. Ishida (Eds.), Active Media Technology. Proceedings, 2001. XII, 402 pages. 2001.

Vol. 2253: T. Terano, T. Nishida, A. Namatame, S. Tsumoto, Y. Ohsawa, T. Washio (Eds.), New Frontiers in Artificial Intelligence. Proceedings, 2001. XXVII, 553 pages. 2001. (Subseries LNAI).

Vol. 2254: M.R. Little, L. Nigay (Eds.), Engineering for Human-Computer Interaction. Proceedings, 2001. XI, 359 pages. 2001.

Vol. 2255: J. Dean, A. Gravel (Eds.), COTS-Based Software Systems. Proceedings, 2002. XIV, 257 pages. 2002.

Vol. 2256: M. Stumptner, D. Corbett, M. Brooks (Eds.), AI 2001: Advances in Artificial Intelligence. Proceedings, 2001. XII, 666 pages. 2001. (Subseries LNAI).

Vol. 2257: S. Krishnamurthi, C.R. Ramakrishnan (Eds.), Practical Aspects of Declarative Languages. Proceedings, 2002. VIII, 351 pages. 2002.

Vol. 2258: P. Brazdil, A. Jorge (Eds.), Progress in Artificial Intelligence. Proceedings, 2001. XII, 418 pages. 2001. (Subseries LNAI).

Vol. 2259: S. Vaudenay, A.M. Youssef (Eds.), Selected Areas in Cryptography. Proceedings, 2001. XI, 359 pages. 2001.

Vol. 2260: B. Honary (Ed.), Cryptography and Coding. Proceedings, 2001. IX, 416 pages. 2001.

Vol. 2261: F. Naumann, Quality-Driven Query Answering for Integrated Information Systems. X, 166 pages. 2002.

Vol. 2262: P. Müller, Modular Specification and Verification of Object-Oriented Programs. XIV, 292 pages. 2002.

Vol. 2263: T. Clark, J. Warmer (Eds.), Object Modeling with the OCL. VIII, 281 pages. 2002.

Vol. 2264: K. Steinhöfel (Ed.), Stochastic Algorithms: Foundations and Applications. Proceedings, 2001. VIII, 203 pages. 2001.

Vol. 2265: P. Mutzel, M. Jünger, S. Leipert (Eds.), Graph Drawing. Proceedings, 2001. XV, 524 pages. 2002.

Vol. 2266: S. Reich, M.T. Tzagarakis, P.M.E. De Bra (Eds.), Hypermedia: Openness, Structural Awareness, and Adaptivity. Proceedings, 2001. X, 335 pages. 2002.

Vol. 2267: M. Cerioli, G. Reggio (Eds.), Recent Trends in Algebraic Development Techniques. Proceedings, 2001. X, 345 pages. 2001.

Vol. 2268: E.F. Deprettere, J. Teich, S. Vassiliadis (Eds.), Embedded Processor Design Challenges. VIII, 327 pages. 2002.

Vol. 2270: M. Pflanz, On-line Error Detection and Fast Recover Techniques for Dependable Embedded Processors. XII, 126 pages. 2002.

Vol. 2271: B. Preneel (Ed.), Topics in Cryptology – CT-RSA 2002. Proceedings, 2002. X, 311 pages. 2002.

Vol. 2272: D. Bert, J.P. Bowen, M.C. Henson, K. Robinson (Eds.), ZB 2002: Formal Specification and Development in Z and B. Proceedings, 2002. XII, 535 pages. 2002.

Vol. 2273: A.R. Coden, E.W. Brown, S. Srinivasan (Eds.), Information Retrieval Techniques for Speech Applications. XI, 109 pages. 2002.

Vol. 2274: D. Naccache, P. Paillier (Eds.), Public Key Cryptography. Proceedings, 2002. XI, 385 pages. 2002.

Vol. 2275: N.R. Pal, M. Sugeno (Eds.), Advances in Soft Computing – AFSS 2002. Proceedings, 2002. XVI, 536 pages. 2002. (Subseries LNAI).

Vol. 2276: A. Gelbukh (Ed.), Computational Linguistics and Intelligent Text Processing. Proceedings, 2002. XIII, 444 pages. 2002.

Vol. 2277: P. Callaghan, Z. Luo, J. McKinna, R. Pollack (Eds.), Types for Proofs and Programs. Proceedings, 2000. VIII, 243 pages. 2002.

Vol. 2281: S. Arikawa, A. Shinohara (Eds.), Progress in Discovery Science. Proceedings. XIV, 684 pages. 2002. (Subseries LNAI).

Vol. 2282: D. Ursino, Extraction and Exploitation of Intensional Knowledge from Heterogeneous Information Sources. XXVI, 289 pages. 2002.

Vol. 2284: T. Eiter, K.-D. Schewe (Eds.), Foundations of Information and Knowledge Systems. Proceedings, 2002. X, 289 pages. 2002.

Vol. 2285: H. Alt, A. Ferreira (Eds.), STACS 2002. Proceedings, 2002. XIV, 660 pages. 2002.

Vol. 2287: C.S. Jensen, K.G. Jeffery, J. Pokorny, Saltenis, E. Bertino, K. Böhm, M. Jarke (Eds.), Advances in Database Technology – EDBT 2002. Proceedings, 2002. XVI, 776 pages. 2002.

Vol. 2288: K. Kim (Ed.), Information Security and Cryptology – ICISC 2001. Proceedings, 2001. XIII, 457 pages. 2002.

Vol. 2289: C.J. Tomlin, M.R. Greenstreet (Eds.), Hybrid Systems: Computation and Control. Proceedings, 2002. XIII, 480 pages. 2002.

Vol. 2291: F. Crestani, M. Girolami, C.J. van Rijsbergen (Eds.), Advances in Information Retrieval. Proceedings, 2002. XIII, 363 pages. 2002.

Vol. 2292: G.B. Khosrovshahi, A. Shokoufandeh, A. Shokrollahi (Eds.), Theoretical Aspects of Computer Science. IX, 221 pages. 2002.

Vol. 2293: J. Renz, Qualitative Spatial Reasoning with Topological Information. XVI, 207 pages. 2002. (Subseries LNAI).

Vol. 2300: W. Brauer, H. Ehrig, J. Karhumäki, A. Salomaa (Eds.), Formal and Natural Computing. XXXVI, 431 pages. 2002.

Vol. 2314: S.-K. Chang, Z. Chen, S.-Y. Lee (Eds.), Recent Advances in Visual Information Systems. Proceedings, 2002. XI, 323 pages. 2002.